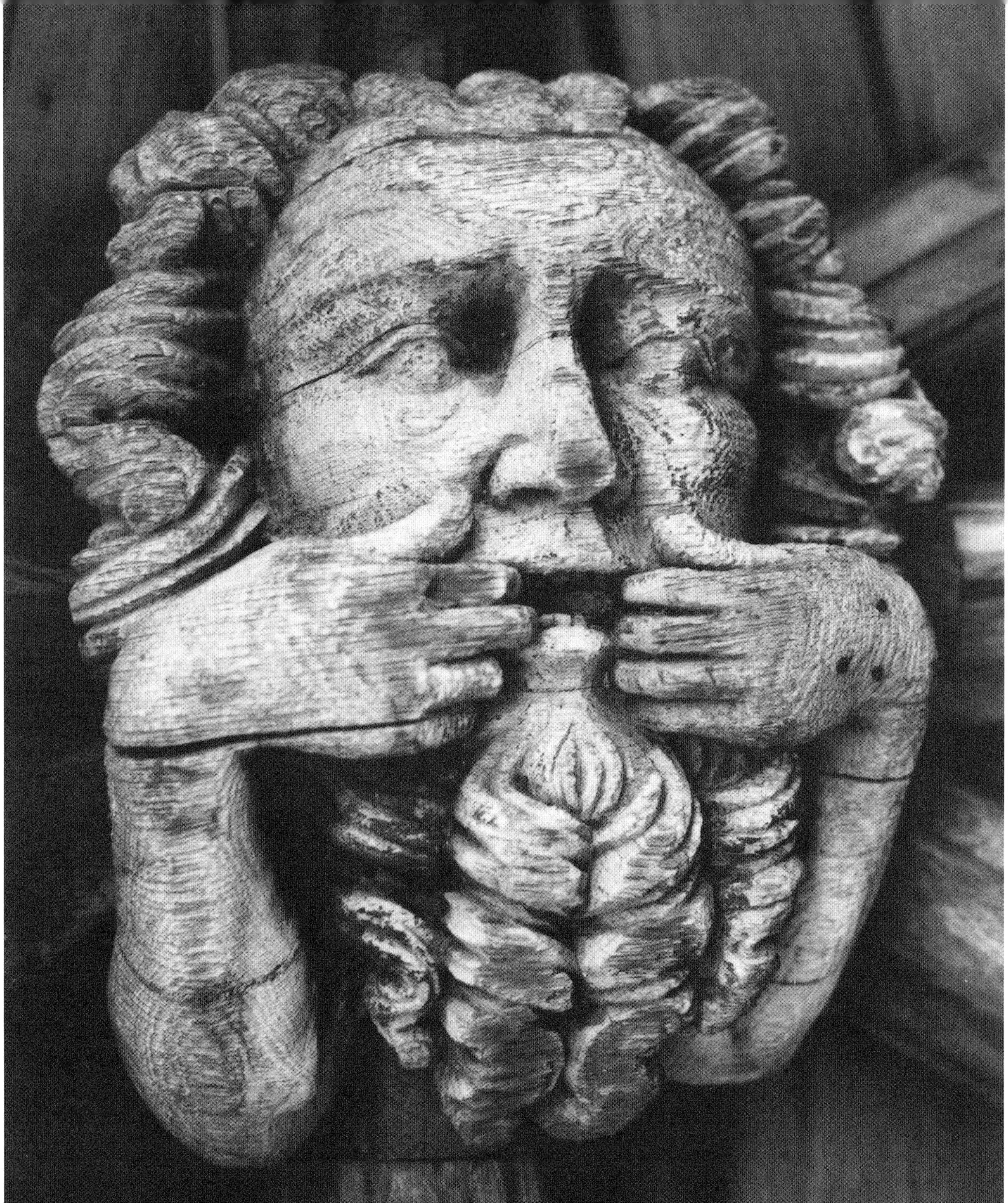

INTERPRETING LINCOLN CATHEDRAL

THE MEDIEVAL IMAGERY

LYNNE BROUGHTON

LINCOLN CATHEDRAL PUBLICATIONS
1996

In memory of my parents
ENID and LESLIE BROUGHTON
and of a beloved friend
CHRIS ASH

nunc illi vivunt in sinu Abraham

Published 1996 by Lincoln Cathedral Publications
Lincoln Cathedral
Lincoln LN2 1PZ

Reprinted 1999

ISBN 1 870561 10 4

Designed by Max Marschner, Ampersand Designs, Lincoln LN5 8PN
Production by Yard Publishing Services, Sudbury CO10 2AG
Printed by G. W. Belton Ltd, Gainsborough DN21 2ED

Cover photograph by David Edwards, David Edwards Photography, Nettleham, Lincoln

Cataloguing-in-Publication Data

A catalogue record for this book is obtainable from the British Library

Contents

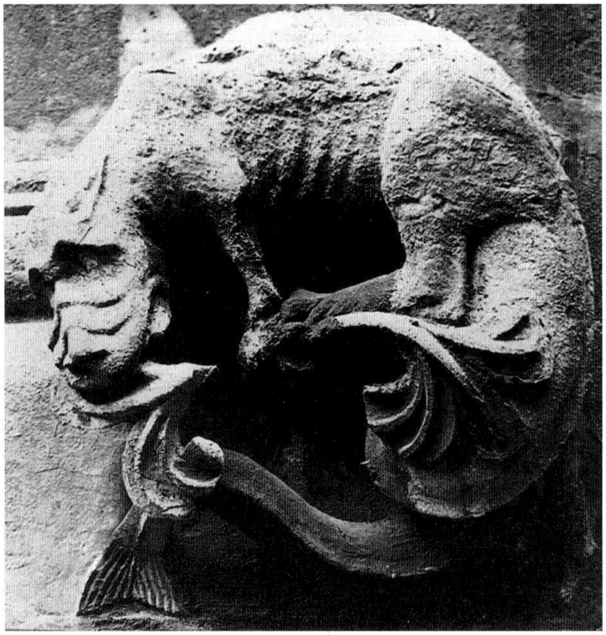

List of illustrations

Acknowledgements for figures

For permission to reproduce photographs, I am grateful to the following: Betty Nye Carpenter (no. 4); Mark Edwards (no. 43); Max Marschner (nos 6, 15, 32, 33, 48–50, 59, 60, 61, 63, 69, 86, 87, 92, 93, 99, 103); A. W. Reynolds (nos 3, 7, 16, 17, 19–31, 44, 46, 47, 52, 62, 65, 68, 82, 96–98, 100, 101); Allan Smith (no. 57); Pauline Ward (nos 9, 64, 70, 76, 87, 88, 104, 106); the Dean and Chapter of Lincoln Cathedral (frontispiece, tailpiece and nos 11, 14, 18, 35, 36, 45, 51, 73, 74, 79, 80, 84, 85, 94, 95); the Courtauld Institute of Art (nos 34, 37, 38, 75, 77, 78, 81, 90).

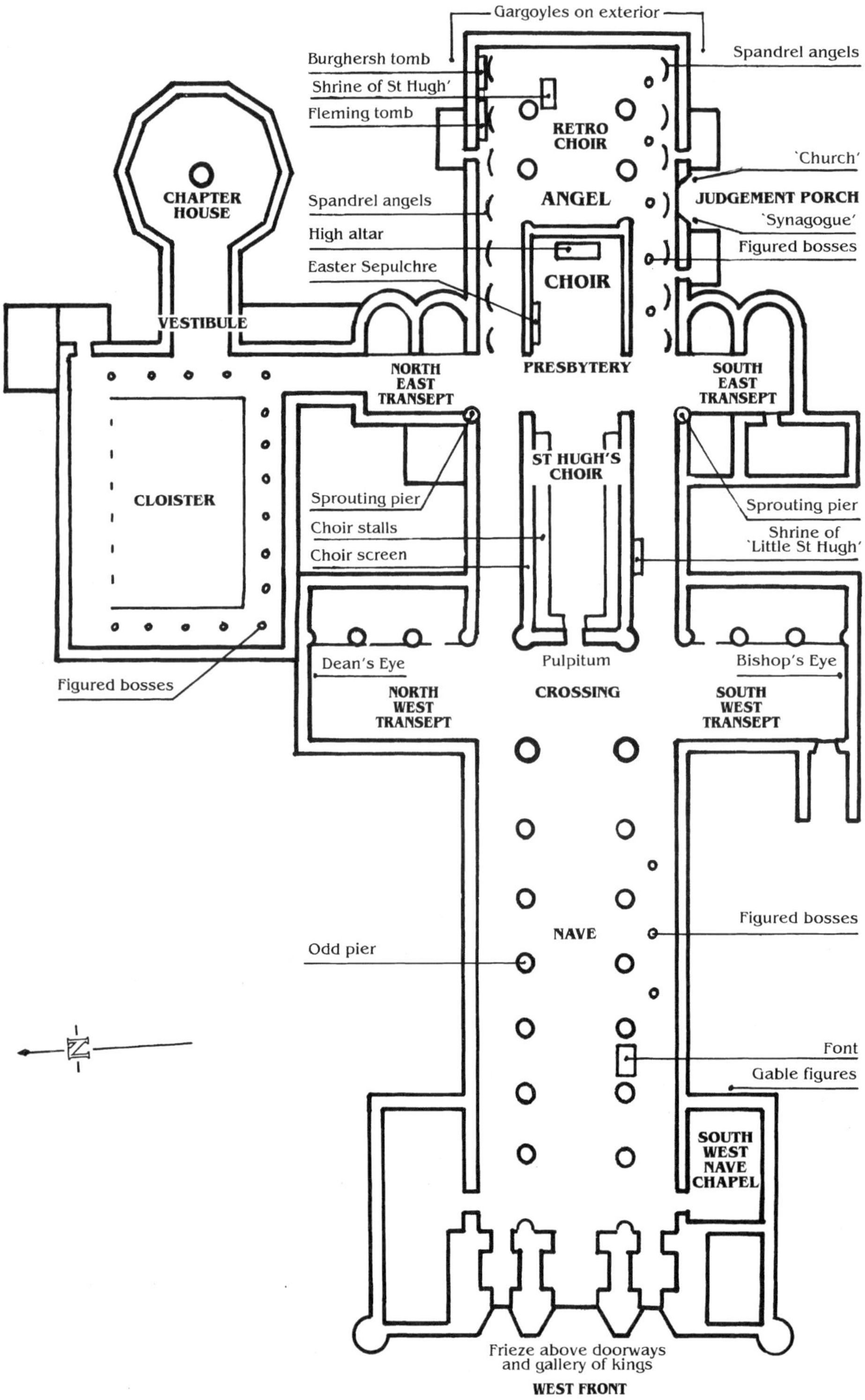

Gargoyles on exterior
Burghersh tomb
Shrine of St Hugh'
Fleming tomb
Spandrel angels
RETRO CHOIR
CHAPTER HOUSE
'Church'
ANGEL
JUDGEMENT PORCH
Spandrel angels
'Synagogue'
High altar
Figured bosses
Easter Sepulchre
CHOIR
VESTIBULE
NORTH EAST TRANSEPT
PRESBYTERY
SOUTH EAST TRANSEPT
ST HUGH'S CHOIR
CLOISTER
Sprouting pier
Sprouting pier
Choir stalls
Shrine of 'Little St Hugh'
Choir screen
Dean's Eye
Pulpitum
Bishop's Eye
Figured bosses
NORTH WEST TRANSEPT
CROSSING
SOUTH WEST TRANSEPT
Figured bosses
NAVE
Odd pier
N
Font
Gable figures
SOUTH WEST NAVE CHAPEL
Frieze above doorways and gallery of kings
WEST FRONT

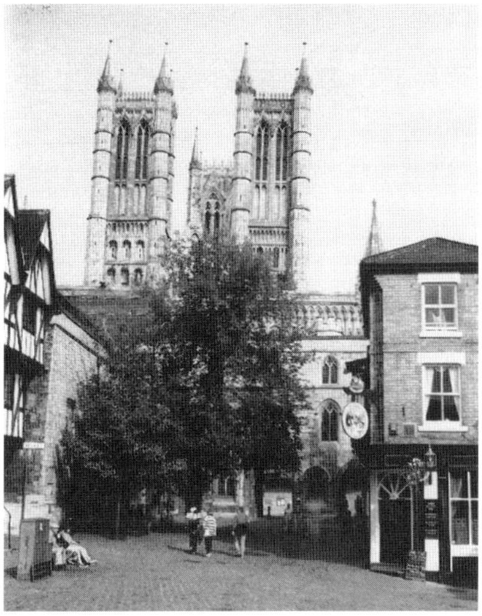

3 West towers seen through Exchequer Gate

Preface

An interpretation of Lincoln Cathedral requires the resources of more than one scholarly discipline. In this book I have ranged over theology, history, art history, literature and music. Since the cathedral was the mother church of the diocese and had a message for everyone, I have attempted to write compactly for a wide audience. This has meant avoiding technical terms as far as possible and explaining arguments and evidence as simply as could be done without falsifying either. At the same time I have tried to base the argument on sound scholarship, using interpretations already in print; in some cases my interpretation has differed from those of other scholars. I have also provided my own interpretations of some of the imagery which has not previously been noticed, the study of the bosses in Exchequer Gate being the major piece of original work. References and arguments are provided in end notes and it is there that I also give the original versions of quotations which appear in the text in modern translations. Non-expert readers who would like to know more about particular topics raised in this book can find pointers to further reading in the Notes and the Bibliography.

The approach taken in this book is synthetic and integrative. I have followed themes through the medieval centuries and, in some cases, up to the present. The advantage of such an approach is that it demonstrates how the major beliefs and practices of Christianity have, although somewhat changed in their modes of expression, formed the basis of the cathedral's message from the time when it was first built to the present. The disadvantage is that it smooths away great differences over time. The twelfth-century cathedral looked very different from that of the fourteenth century; a late fifteenth-century person transposed into the eighteenth-century cathedral would hardly have recognised the building, let alone have thought that the Communion service was similar to the Mass that he or she knew. Both the continuities and the discontinuities need to be acknowledged. But I have found, in talking even to those who have known and loved the cathedral for years, that the building and its decorations are generally perceived in chunks rather than as a whole: the Angel Choir is thirteenth century, the Bishop's Eye is fourteenth century and the Imp is an awkward curiosity that visitors will persist in being interested in. What is lacking is a sense that – and how – it all fits together. This book is an attempt to show the integrity of the building and its message.

I cannot hope to have entirely succeeded in this complex task. Nevertheless I hope that this book will contain matter of interest to scholars and clergy, as well as enhancing the enjoyment of those who visit the cathedral.

Acknowledgements

This book would never have been conceived, let alone written, had I not spent some years teaching in Lincoln Theological College. My interest in medieval architecture could hardly fail to become focused on the cathedral. Its towers were an inspiration in even the most miserable weather as I walked to college for the morning prayer which began each day. Soon I was puzzling over the sculptures, reading what art historians had to say, finding out how much there was to interpret and how little was available to the non-specialist visitor. It is out of my attempts to convey the meaning and excitement of the building to theological students and cathedral guides that this book has arisen.

I am grateful to the Warden, the Revd Dr Bill Jacob, for offering me a Lectureship in the college and encouraging me to take students on guided tours of the cathedral. My colleagues and students challenged and stimulated me to the task of interpretation. Kindly queries in the college corridors as to when the book would be ready kept me going at times when my confidence was fading and it seemed a foolish and impossible undertaking. The final stages of writing were helped along by a term's study leave from the college and by a fortnight's stay at St Deiniol's Library on a Bishop J. R. H. Moorman scholarship. Publication has been aided by a generous grant from the Marc Fitch Fund. I have relied heavily on the superb resources of the Cambridge University Library and on the kindness and efficiency of its research librarians.

The Chancellor of Lincoln Cathedral, the Revd Canon Vernon White, and the Cathedral Librarian, Dr Nicholas Bennett, have been most patient and supportive throughout a longer than expected gestation period.

The illustrations are mostly new photographs, many of them taken under difficult conditions. I am grateful to Mr Mark Edwards, Mr Max Marschner, Mr Anthony Reynolds and Mrs Pauline Ward for many of these. The Courtauld Institute of Art and Mr Michael O'Connor of the cathedral Works Department kindly provided some illustrations from their archives. Mr Allan Smith of the City of Lincoln Archaeology Unit provided the reconstruction drawing of the original state of the south-east transept. Photographs not otherwise credited were taken by me. I am also grateful to Mrs Elizabeth Nurser for her help with the book and to Mr Max Marschner for its layout and design.

As with any work of scholarship, I am deeply indebted for encouragement and assistance in writing this book to more people than I can readily record, but mention must be made here of some. Dr Jan Srzednicki was the kindest of doctoral supervisors and has remained the best of friends. Characteristically, he has unfailingly supported and encouraged my work even in realms of research with which he normally would have little sympathy. Prof. Christopher Brooke has been most generous with advice and encouragement. Bishop David Connor helped me to continue believing that the interpretation of old churches is a worthwhile task. It is a pleasure also to thank those others who read and commented on drafts: the late Prof. Andrew Martindale, Prof. David Ford, Dr Veronica Sekules, Dr Robin Small, the Revd Canon Rex Davis, the Revd Canon Peter Hammond, Sr Jane Mary SPB, Sr Julia Bolton Holloway N,CHF, the Revd Dr Jane Steen, the Revd Dr Alan Doig and the Revd Cathy Collins. Finally my thanks to my husband Nicholas Denyer whose contributions range from giving me some help with the Latin quotations to doing most of the cooking during the last few months of writing. The book's many defects are entirely my own responsibility.

Lynne Broughton, Cambridge, July 1996

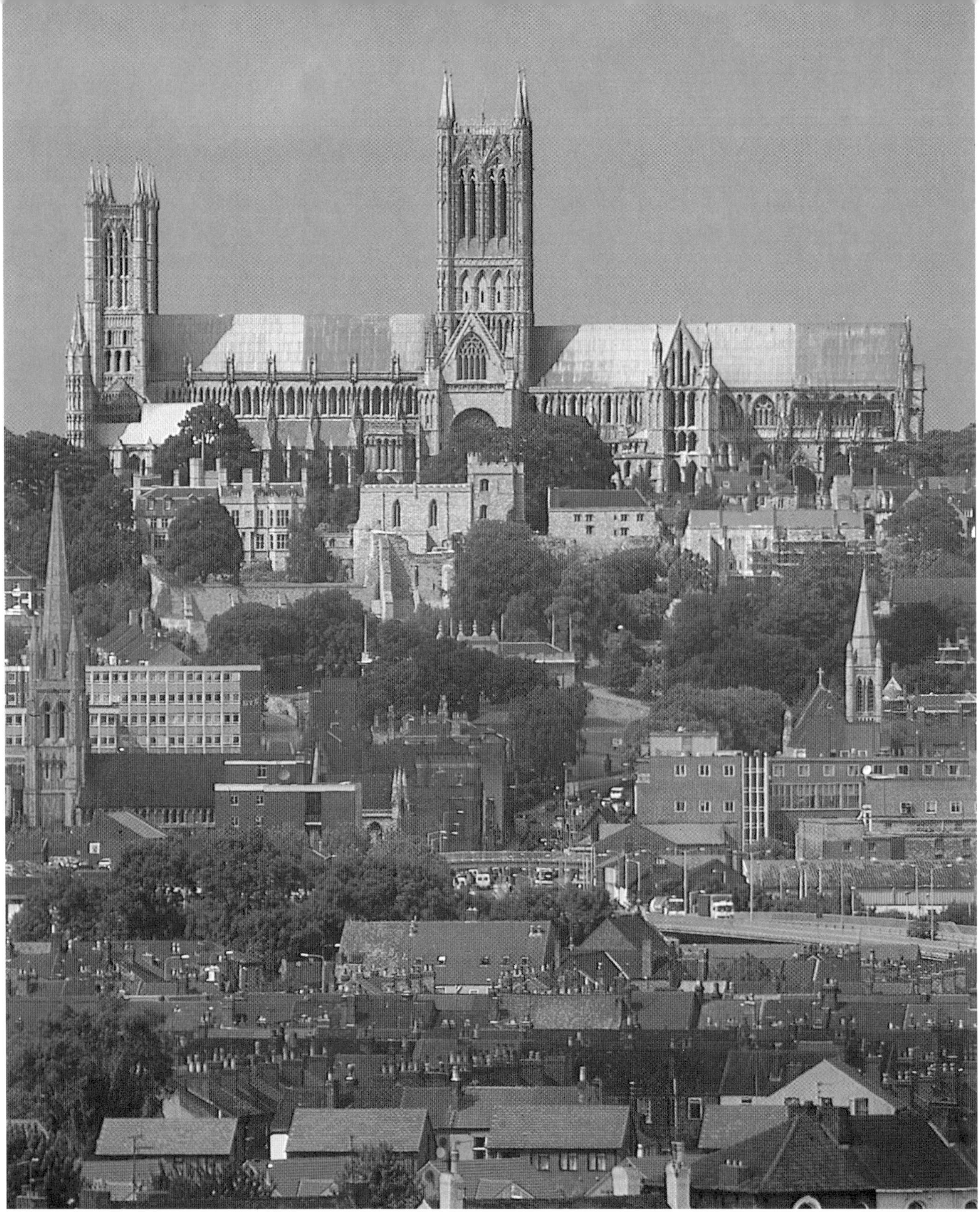

Introduction: Thou hast founded it upon a hill

Lincoln cathedral demands interpretation.[1] Why was it built on the hill, and why so large and elaborate? Are all the attractive carvings simply decorative, or do they have a deeper meaning? Are all the beasts and grotesques, such as the famous Imp, just products of the masons' playful fancy? What sort of people built the cathedral and why? In what follows I shall attempt an answer to these questions, showing that the building does indeed have a meaning which is engraved in its stones and can be recovered.[2]

When the cathedral was built, it was intended to convey a powerful Christian meaning. Its purpose was to remind people of the facts of their faith, and teach them to grasp those facts more securely. But above all it was meant to inspire them with a glimpse of the awesome loveliness of God. A cathedral is a holy place, a place where the veil between the physical and the spiritual worlds is very thin. The building and its surroundings were designed to provide the visitor with an experience of gradual movement from the secular world with all its ills to a participation in the joys of heaven. Those who approach can be led to a sense of the nearness and yet transcendence of God. 'Art like prayer could lead to visions... enlarging the pilgrim's personal sphere and making his life intelligible in the perspective of the divine plan. It could offer an environment neither temporal nor eternal – a half-way house in which ordinary events might be seen anew in the light of eternity.'[3]

As we see it today the cathedral is many-layered. It was worked on, rebuilt and improved over the course of some five centuries, from the late eleventh century to the early sixteenth (though the major rebuilding of the body of the church ended with the completion of the Angel Choir in the late thirteenth century). During those hundreds of years attitudes changed, artistic styles altered, theological ideas developed.[4] Since the end of the 'Middle Ages' further changes have taken place. Two periods of destruction, in the mid sixteenth and mid seventeenth centuries, caused the loss of much of the imagery that was certainly present at the beginning of the sixteenth century. This destruction was followed by other changes, and by attempts to understand and preserve what

opposite
4 Cathedral and city

remained. In this book I shall concentrate on the overall message of the building, as it was gradually developed, as it was available to the late-medieval visitor and as it has survived into the present.

There is little, if any, direct surviving evidence of what was intended by those who built, worked upon, and paid for this building. So in attempting to interpret the imagery at Lincoln it is necessary to make use of indirect evidence. This is of various kinds. Some images, such as the cross of Christ, are so well known and understood that their meaning can be confidently given. Other images are frequently used throughout the medieval period, both visually and in written descriptions, so we can call upon the writings of contemporary people to explain these.

The medieval clergy who commissioned and paid for the building, rebuilding and decoration of the cathedral were steeped in biblical imagery. They knew the psalms by heart (the psalms were chanted in the cathedral every day, as they are still today) and were expected to meditate regularly upon other passages from the Bible. In commissioning the designs for their great building they called upon their knowledge of biblical teaching. The cathedral was to be, not merely a functional space for worship, but an inspiring resource for attracting people to the knowledge and love of God. The Bible, then, is a source of evidence about the meaning of the cathedral.[5]

An important means of communicating the Bible to the people was the liturgy, by which are meant all the formal worship services of the Church. The liturgy consisted of two main parts: the Mass, or eucharistic service; and the services held at regular hours during the day, known as the Office. In addition to these there were the occasional services such as marriage, baptism and the consecration of churches. During each of these services parts of the Bible were read out and these biblical readings were carefully chosen to illuminate the particular occasion. The medieval consecration liturgy is another useful source of evidence for the meaning of the cathedral and its imagery.[6]

Every church, when complete enough to be usable, was set aside for the Christian congregation in this special service of consecration.[7] The form of the service has survived and a study of it allows us an insight into how the cathedral building was understood. The liturgy for the consecration of a church goes back to the tenth century, if not earlier, and changed very little throughout the Middle Ages.[8] We can therefore be sure that it was used for this cathedral and that its images were in the minds of those who commissioned the design.[9]

This liturgy contains repeated references to the church as the City of God, the Heavenly Jerusalem on Mount Zion. There are various readings from the scriptures, including the Old Testament passages about the building and dedication of Solomon's temple (1 Kings 6–8). Those who built this cathedral will have understood themselves to be following the biblical account of God's instructions to Solomon: 'Thou gavest command to build a sanctuary in thy holy mountain ... a copy of the holy tabernacle which thou preparedst aforehand from the beginning.' (Wisdom of Solomon 9:8). King Solomon built a temple in Jerusalem for the worship of the one God. Its dimensions and materials were divinely ordained and when it was finished Solomon dedicated it with a special ceremony. His prayer at the dedication provides an insight into the Jewish understanding of the Temple and also the Christian attitude to church buildings. 'I have surely built thee an house to dwell in, a settled place to abide in for ever... But will God indeed dwell on the earth? Behold, the heaven and heaven of heavens cannot contain thee, how much less this house that I have builded? Yet have thou respect unto the prayer of thy servant... That thine eyes may be open toward this house night and day...' (1 Kings 8:13, 27–29). Rabbinic Judaism taught that God made a heavenly Jerusalem to serve as a counterpart to the earthly city; the two function in sympathy and harmony. So prayers made in Jerusalem are made as if directly towards the Throne of God itself.[10] Christian theologians saw all church buildings as earthly counterparts of the heavenly Jerusalem.[11] Although God cannot be contained in any mere work of human hands, nevertheless human pilgrims will find him especially accessible in these places built for and dedicated to his worship.

The biblical Book of Psalms holds a special place in Jewish and Christian prayer. These songs and poetic meditations have been the basis of corporate and individual prayer from before the time of

Christ.[12] They were greatly loved and warmly recommended to all who wished to progress in the spiritual life. In the mid fourteenth century they were translated into English, with an explanatory commentary, by the Yorkshire hermit Richard Rolle. He wrote of them with affectionate enthusiasm: 'Indeed, this radiant book is a choice song in God's presence, like a lamp brightening our life, health for a sick heart, honey to a bitter soul... In the psalms there is... great beauty of meaning and medicine from the words...'.[13] All these examples represent the public teaching of the Church; and there is ample evidence that then, as now, ordinary people found in their own experience of using the psalms that such descriptions are accurate.

All the early saints of the Church will have known them by heart; Jesus himself prayed in the words of one of them (Ps. 22) as he hung dying on the cross.

The psalms have continued to be central to the Church's liturgy right up to the present. In Lincoln cathedral, as in other great English cathedrals, the canons' stalls are marked with the psalms which each is required to pray daily.[14] Richard Rolle's estimation of the psalms was echoed in the seventeenth century by the Anglican John Donne, preaching in St Paul's London on a text from one of his own psalms (Ps. 63:7); 'The Psalmes are the Manna of the Church. As Manna tasted to every man like that he liked best, so doe the Psalmes minister Instruction, and satisfaction, to every man, in every emergency and occasion.'[15] Extracts from the psalms are used extensively in the Church's liturgy; those in the consecration service refer to the city of Jerusalem and within it the Temple. They include Psalm 24: 'Who shall ascend into the hill of the Lord?...Lift up your heads, O ye gates; and be ye lift up, ye everlasting doors...'; also Psalm 84: 'How amiable are thy tabernacles, O Lord of hosts...'; and Psalm 87: 'His foundation is in the holy mountains. The Lord loveth the gates of Zion...Glorious things are spoken of thee, O city of God...'.[16] So we see that the liturgy strongly suggests this view of the cathedral as the City of God, Zion founded upon a hill.

It is no accident that this building is in such a commanding position on its hill. The position is easily defensible; William the

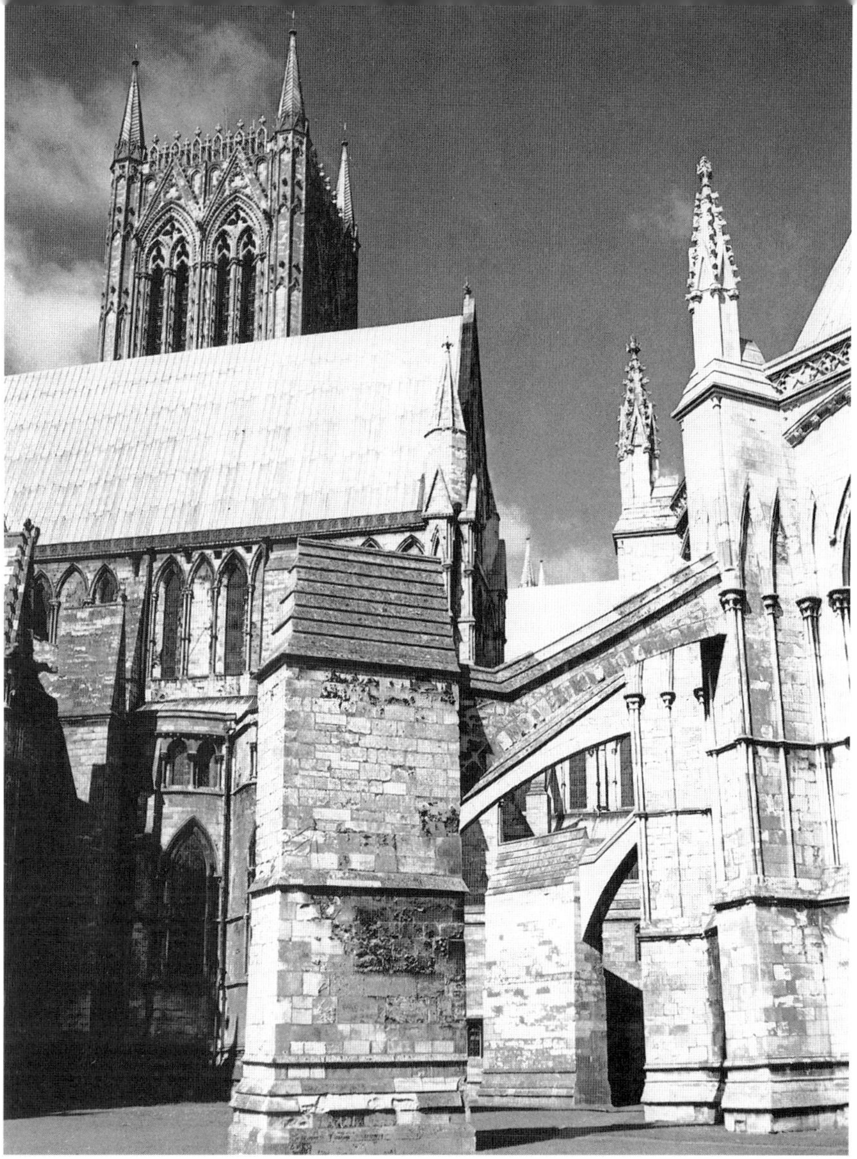

5 Cathedral from north-east

Conqueror found it a good place for a castle, as had the Roman garrison before him. The hill of Zion was also an ancient defensive site and the image of a fortified place went deep into Judaeo-Christian religious thought. This is clear in the psalms and is still evident in Luther's famous hymn: 'A safe stronghold our God is still...'.[17] The need for security is a basic human need: we know ourselves to be vulnerable and requiring protection. The image of a defended place still speaks of safety in a dangerous world and the cathedral stands as a readily understood image of the biblical message that our true safety is in God and our true home heaven. The metaphor of building, which comes from the writings of St Paul, is very powerful, appealing as it does to some of our deepest needs and fears.

From the New Testament the consecration liturgy made use of the book of Revelation, and great prominence is given to the vision of St John; 'And I... saw the holy city, new Jerusalem, coming down from God out of heaven, prepared as a bride adorned for her husband' (21:2). This deepens the meaning of the Old Testament passages; that city which is the focus of the Israelites' worship is also an image of heaven itself. The seventh-century Latin hymn *Urbs beata*, still sung in translation as 'Blessed city, heavenly Salem',[18] belongs in this context. It describes the city of St John's vision, both the Church Triumphant and the church building, splendid and shining at the last day. Each visitor to the cathedral could have an experience analogous to that of St John: it was hoped that those who moved through the building attending to its imagery 'would be raised in spirit to the presence of the triumphant Christ and would enter into conversation with the apostles and prophets as a foretaste of the eternal banquet to be enjoyed by the blessed after the Last Judgement'.[19] The text from Revelation applies, of course, to all medieval churches; it was read not only during the consecration of a church but also repeated in the yearly Mass of the feast of the Dedication.[20] Later in the chapter St John describes the great variety of precious stones out of which the city is built (Revelation 21:10–21) and it may well be that the use of splendid and glittering materials inside the cathedral, and of 'marbles' such as Purbeck to contrast with the main building stones are all meant to contribute to the representation of the Heavenly City.

Also in the consecration liturgy was a reading from a sermon of St Augustine of Hippo in which he, following St Paul (1 Cor. 3:9–11; Eph. 2:20–22),[21] intertwines two meanings of the word 'church': the church as a physical structure built of stone and the church as a group of people, the 'living stones'. The importance of the church building for each individual was brought out by the same St Augustine in his *Confessions*. There he describes the conversion of a prominent pagan teacher who claimed, but was for some time reluctant to admit publicly, that he was a Christian. The Christian friend in whom he confided said: '"I will not believe it, nor will I rank you among Christians, unless I see you in the church of Christ." The other, in banter, replied, "Do walls then make Christians?"'[22] Augustine's implied answer is 'Yes'. The church walls contain, and define, those who belong to the Church. Individuals are only part of the Church when they have been joined with others in the congregation, within the walls of a church. In the twelfth century, Hugh of St Victor[23] explained the consecration ceremony itself in personal terms: '...whatever things be here done visibly, the same doth God work by His invisible power in the soul, which is the true Temple of God: wherein Faith layeth the foundation, Hope raiseth the buildings, and Charity finisheth it.'[24] And Durandus, the late-thirteenth-century bishop of Mende, wrote that 'this festival specially denoteth that eternal dedication, in which that other church, the holy soul, shall be so dedicated and united to God that it shall never be transferred to other uses'.[25]

The analogy has remained fruitful within the life of the Church. In the seventeenth century John Donne could use it thus in a sermon: 'The Holy Ghost seemes to have delighted in the Metaphore of *Building*. I know of no figurative speech so often iterated in the Scriptures, as the name of a *House*; Heaven and Earth are called by that name, and wee, who being upon earth, have our conversation in heaven, are called so too...'[26]

So the overall meaning of the cathedral, with its towers and gates, set upon its hill, is the Heavenly Jerusalem, a vision of the dwelling-place of God himself. Even the ground plan, which is in the shape of a cross, displays its Christian significance and the details of sculpture, glass and (originally, though little of it survives) painting, work together to fill out that significance. It is a place where opposites are united, where God is especially present to those who seek him, where the veil that separates earth and heaven is gossamer-thin.[27] Anyone who catches sight of Lincoln cathedral from a distance when it is glowing in the sunlight or floating upon the mist of the valley below will have little difficulty appreciating this visionary interpretation.

6 Exchequer Gate, west face

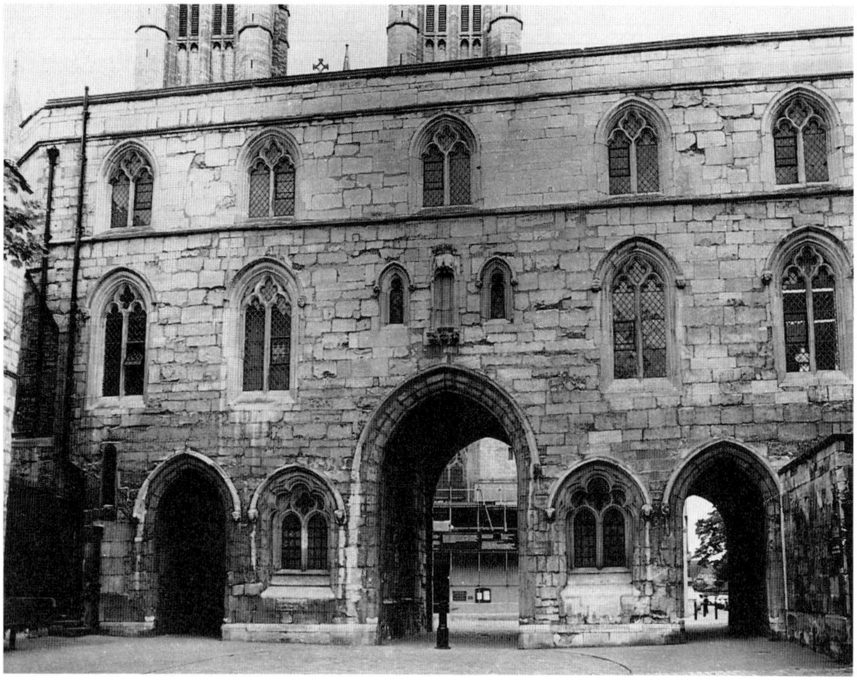

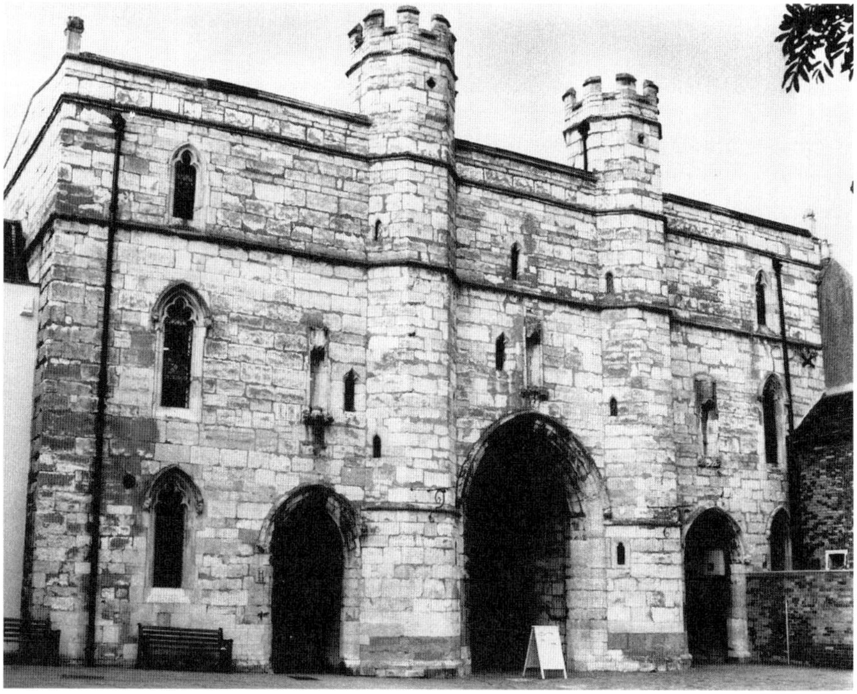

7 Exchequer Gate, east face

Exchequer Gate:
The Lord loveth the Gates of Zion

The psalms refer frequently to the gates of Jerusalem, also known as Zion; Lincoln cathedral likewise was surrounded by a number of gates. Not all of these survive but the elaborate inner west gate, Exchequer Gate remains intact before the main entrance to the cathedral. The gates had a practical purpose, to protect the precinct and its inhabitants. They also had a symbolic function.[28] The city of Jerusalem is surrounded by defensive walls and entered through gates. Heavenly Zion has triple gates facing in the cardinal directions. This earthly counterpart of the heavenly city also has a surrounding wall and gates. A further symbolic meaning is suggested by Pevsner[29] who points out that a monumental triple gateway of this kind calls to mind the ancient form of the triumphal arch. To the Romans this was a celebration and reminder of the exploits of victorious generals; the arch erected in Rome by the first Christian emperor, Constantine, is of this triple form. The form was taken over by the early church and used in various ways to assert the victory of Christ. It is quite likely that the great triple arches of the west front of the cathedral were meant to convey this impression and that the later gate was both a triumphal arch itself and prepared for the greater effect of the cathedral.[30]

Medieval gates have not been studied much; scholars have tended to concentrate on the church building itself, largely ignoring its surrounding structures.[31] Little is known about the functions of gateways to cathedral precincts but some uses can be inferred with confidence. Since the precinct was surrounded by a circuit of walls (much of which still survives) everyone entering or leaving would have to go through a gate. These gates could, of course, be shut in case of danger and were kept closed and guarded at night.[32] During the day the gates would ideally be open to allow all peaceable people access to the church and its services. The larger gates, such as Exchequer Gate, contained rooms for the transaction of business. As with monastery gates (and those of Oxbridge colleges), there will have been a porter in attendance to provide information to visitors and keep an eye on those coming and going. In this case

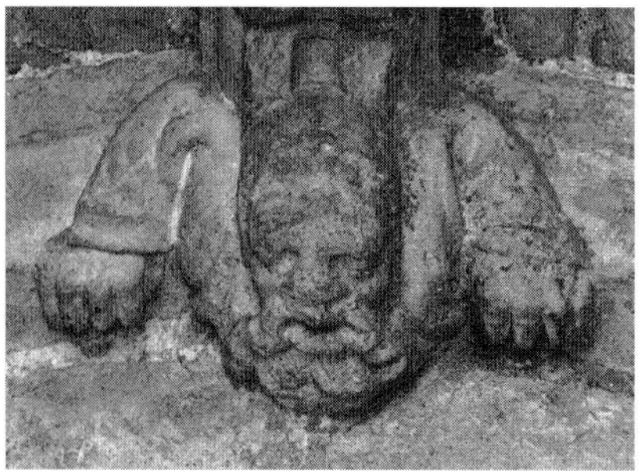

8 Crouching man, Exchequer Gate, north passage

9 *Crucifixion*, Exchequer Gate, north passage
10 Dragons, Exchequer Gate, north passage

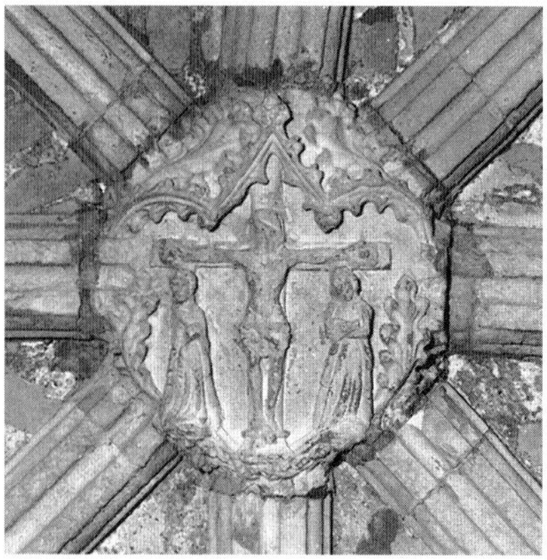

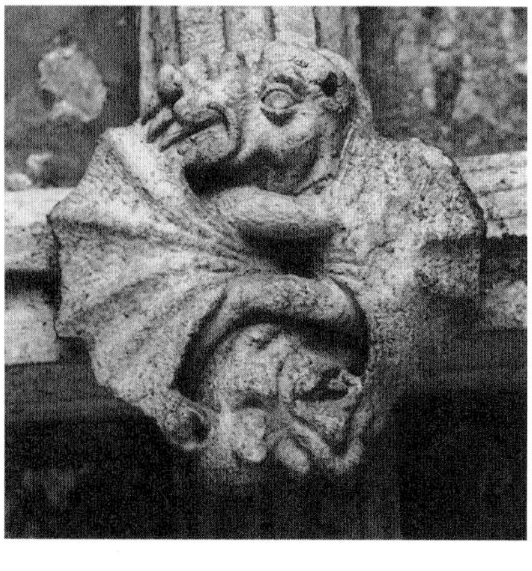

the porter's lodge is known to have been in the south part of the lost outer gate, which originally stood in line with the west end of St Mary Magdalene's church.[33]

Since so many people of all conditions moved through the gates, they were good places to put images with a Christian message. Exchequer Gate contains images, of which some certainly and the others probably have such a significance. Of particular interest are the carved bosses at the junctions of the ribs of the vaults in each passageway. At present these are not easy to read, partly because they are worn and some are damaged, partly because they lack the colouring that would originally have made them more arresting and their details clearer.

The bosses in the central passageway vary in their direction, to suit both those entering and those leaving the precinct. In the other two, pedestrian, entrances there seems to have been a one-way system in operation; the bosses are pointing in opposite directions.

In the north passage the bosses are arranged to be the right way round for those entering the precinct. At the west end is a crouching figure, a man staring intently towards the east as if indicating the way to go and suggesting that there are things worth looking at in that direction. The middle boss is a crucifixion scene: Christ on the cross is flanked by the figures of his mother the Virgin Mary and St John the Evangelist. Its placing here seems to be related to the common tendency in medieval churches to have a crucifix at the entrance to the sanctuary so that one walks beneath it when going into the holy place.[34] The cathedral precinct is holy in comparison with the outside world. This boss is a reminder to those who enter that they are approaching the House of God and that the way to heaven leads beneath the arms of Christ's cross. The message is that of the Gospel of St John: 'Then said Jesus... "I am the door..."' (10:7) That this symbolism was intended is made clear by a number of medieval writers. For instance Durandus, in his *Rationale*, says quite simply: 'The door is Christ'.[35]

The next boss shows two dragons, curled up on themselves, and at the eastern end a devil. The dragon was frequently used as a symbol of Satan,[36] so these should be interpreted as devilish. It is unusual to have the devil to the east since the east is the holier end;

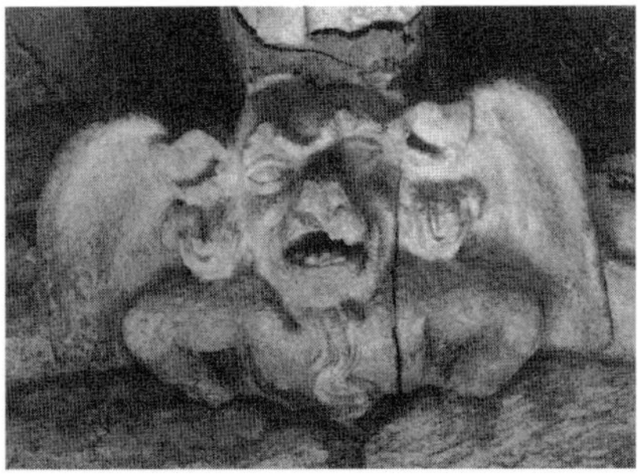

11 Devil, Exchequer Gate, north passage

12 Devilish face in foliage, Exchequer Gate, south passage
13 Sprouting heart, Exchequer Gate, south passage

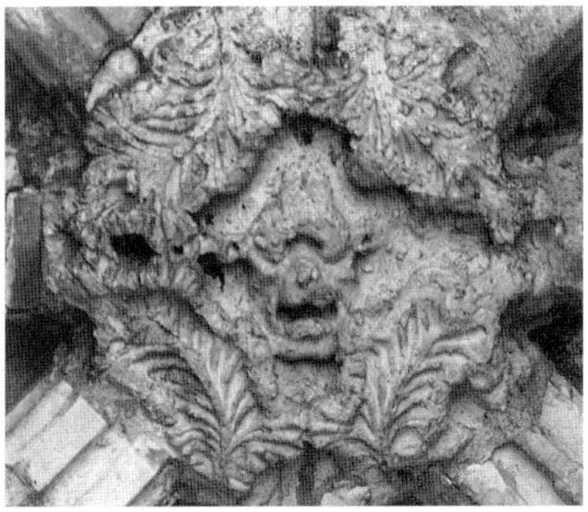

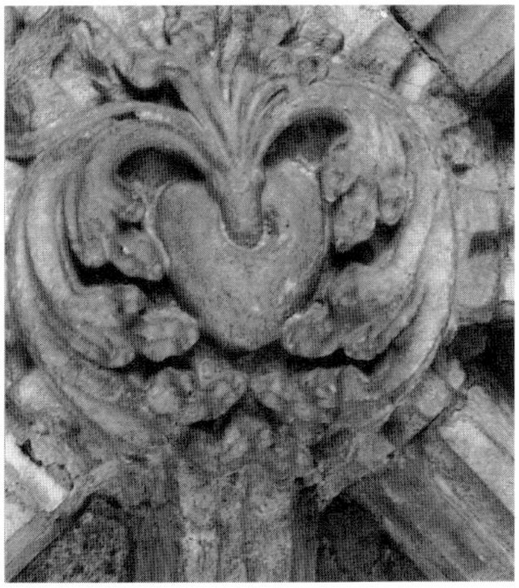

inside churches the altar was almost invariably at the east end. From early times churches were oriented so that the congregation at the morning worship would be facing the rising sun. This was a reminder of the risen Christ, 'Sun of righteousness', an image deeply imbedded in the Church's liturgy and devotion. The image still retains a full charge of devotional meaning in Wesley's much-loved hymn 'Christ, whose glory fills the skies'.[37] But here in Exchequer Gate the symbolism is different; dragons and devil are beneath Christ's feet, an up–down symbolism here takes precedence over that of east and west. As we shall see, a similar alteration of the standard symbolism had to be devised for the Judgement Porch on the south side of the Angel Choir. Christ is often shown trampling on a dragon, in illustration of one of the psalms used at the service of Compline every night: 'the young lion and the dragon shalt thou trample under feet' (Ps. 91:13).[38]

In the southern passageway of Exchequer Gate the bosses all point the other way, and are readable on the way out of the precinct. The two easternmost bosses are diabolical; a grotesque head with bat's wings and a devilish face leering out of foliage. These represent the battle that must be faced and the temptations that must be put behind as one returns to the outer world (again the normal east–west symbolism has been over-ruled, this time by the direction of movement away from the cathedral). The devil, in various forms, is constantly on the attack.

The middle boss shows what is required of the Christian. It shows a heart sprouting foliage. This was a common image, related to what in recent times has been known to Roman Catholics as the Sacred Heart. Nowadays it is shown in flames to symbolise the fiery love with which Christ loves humankind. In the Middle Ages it was rather the fruitfulness of that love which was symbolised by the sprouting of the heart.[39] The heart was seen as the centre of affection and compassion, so this was an image of the Redemption, the suffering and death of Jesus undertaken out of love for sinful humanity. Placed here for those who are leaving the precinct it is also a reminder that their own hearts should, like Christ's, be fertile. Their faith should be made fruitful through good works. As they have received the love of God, so they should pour it out in charity to their fellow creatures. As St Augustine had written in his Commentary on the first Epistle of John: 'God finds the hearts of humankind like a field... There he wants to plant a tree: charity. ... Let each of us test his own action, to see whether it emanates from the vein of charity, whether from the root of love burgeon branches of good works.'[40]

The next boss is of foliage forming a cross. Following that is a castle with three concentric walls in a tight, high design, with a prominent gate, corner towers and cross-shaped loopholes.[41] It becomes visible just as one leaves the cathedral precinct and comes within sight of the actual, secular castle at the other end of Castle Hill.[42] This may well be a deliberate reminder, as suggested by Psalm 31, that God is the true fortress and that all secular power ultimately depends upon him. But this was not its only meaning. The castle was a potent image much used for the purpose of moral instruction.[43] One common interpretation is of the human body as a castle under attack by the forces of evil; if it is guarded by the virtues the soul within will remain safe. This use of the castle image was spelled out in the fifteenth century in the play *The Castle of Perseverance* where the protagonist Mankind is involved in a fight between the virtues and vices. At one point in the play Mankind addresses the audience, telling them to 'withstonde youre temptacioun' and he continues by pointing out that he would be

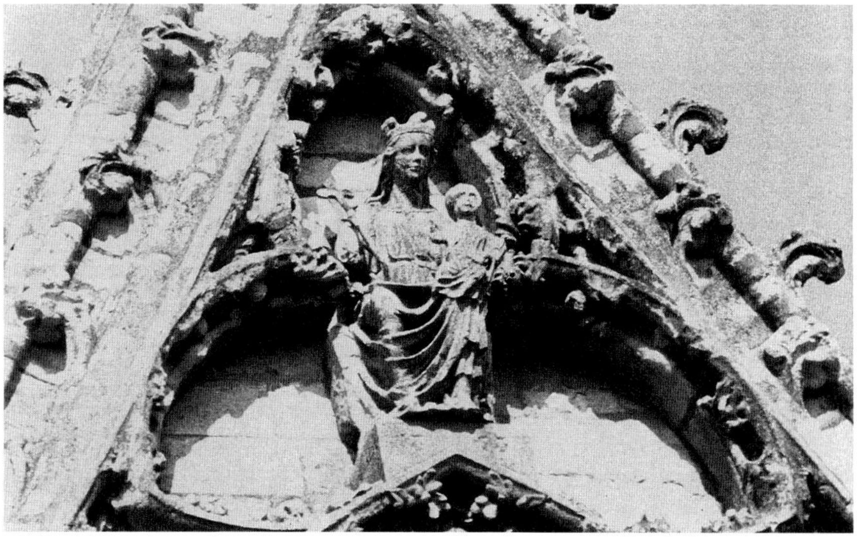

14 Virgin Mary, patroness of the cathedral, East End gable

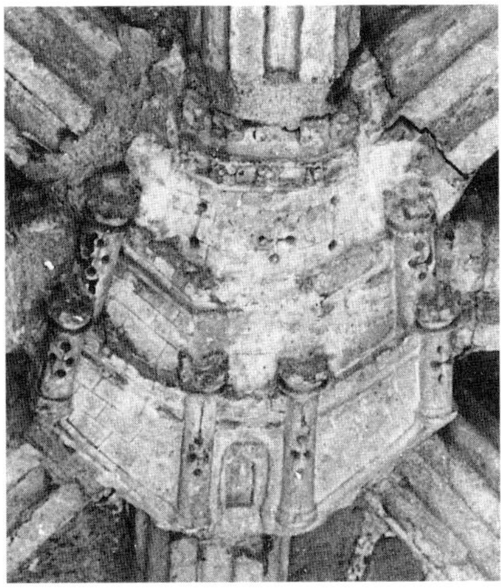

15 Castle, Exchequer Gate, south passage
16 Ihc, the initials of Jesus, Exchequer Gate, central passage
17 Figure on horseback, Exchequer Gate, central passage

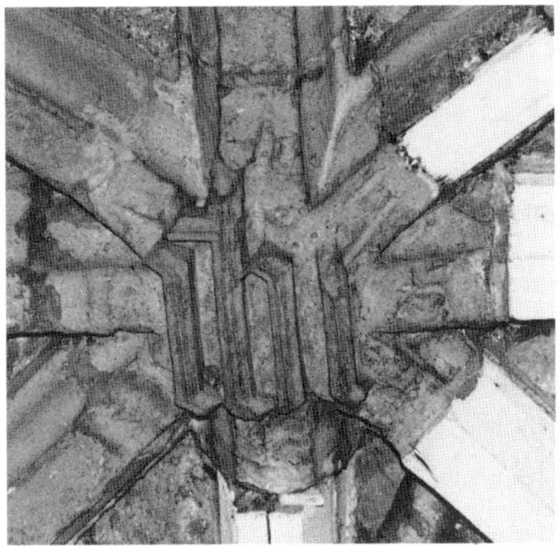

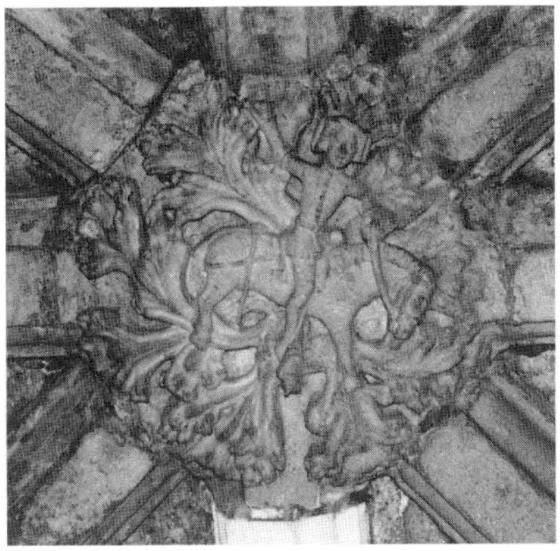

overwhelmed by the vices if he did not have the protection of the castle.[44] The threefold walls of this castle might well refer to the major virtues of faith, hope and love; love grows in the compassionate heart and is shown in practical works of charity.

The image of the castle was also used to refer to the Virgin Mary, to whom Lincoln cathedral is dedicated. The thirteenth-century scholar-bishop of Lincoln Robert Grosseteste[45] wrote a poem, entitled *Le Château d'Amour*, in which the castle is the body of the Virgin.[46] Although this was by no means the first application of the image to Mary, its place in Lincoln and the fact that the cathedral is under her patronage make it seem very likely that this boss of a castle will also have resonated with thoughts of Mary, who guarded her own soul with all the virtues.

The central boss of the eastern bay of the central passageway is finely carved but difficult to read. It seems at first sight to be simply foliage but closer inspection will reveal an enigmatic figure on horseback. To the west of this boss is one carved with *Ihc*, an abbreviation of the name of Jesus. To the east of it is an angel holding a scroll which seems to bear the inscription INRI, which represents the initial letters of the Latin form of the inscription placed by Pilate's order on the cross: 'Jesus of Nazareth, King of the Jews' (*Iesus Nazarenus, Rex Iudaeorum*). Devotion to the Name of Jesus became popular in the fourteenth century, especially under the influence of Richard Rolle.[47] The Name, in biblical as in medieval thought, encapsulated the essence of a person; so the inscriptions of the name and titles of Jesus denote his presence, as does the crucifix in the north passageway. Lay people were recommended to use prayers which focused on the name, as in this little verse: 'O Jesu, for thy holy name;/ Schelde me this day from syn and schame.' This emphasis on the name continued into the seventeenth century when, among others, John Donne preached: 'Carry it always to your heart, always in your hand and so insure that all your affections, all your action, are directed to Jesus.'[48] And George Herbert took up the theme in two poems, *Jesu* ('Jesu is in my heart, his sacred name/ Is deeply carved there') and *Love-joy*.

The message of this central passageway, then, is similar to that of the northern passage: Christ is the door.

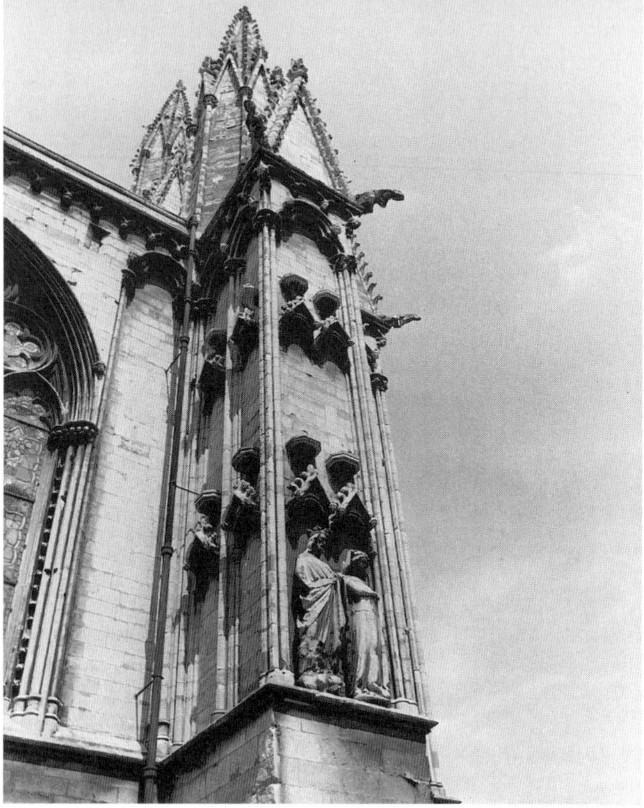

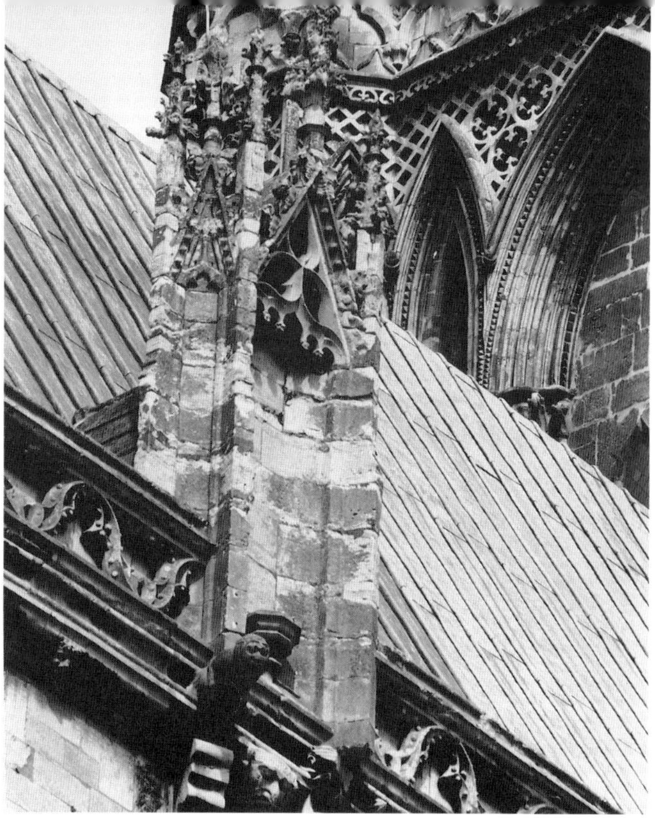

18 Statue niches and gargoyles, Angel Choir exterior
19 Statue niche, nave exterior

Exterior: Go about her walls

Earthly Jerusalem was a place of pilgrimage and so was the medieval cathedral. Pilgrimage was, and still is, a potent religious metaphor. The Christian life as a whole is seen as a pilgrimage, a journey through difficult terrain to attain a better state. People came singly and also in groups and processions. The journey was often long and difficult; on the more arduous journeys some might die before reaching their goal, or reach it but not return home. Some pilgrims were more devout than others but they all travelled in hope and expectation.[49] Chaucer's *Canterbury Tales* give some insight into the varied motivations with which pilgrims then, as now, travelled to holy places.[50] But it must be remembered that Chaucer was satirising those who went travelling more as a holiday than as a true pilgrimage. A later medieval woman, Margery Kempe, was more devout than many of Chaucer's characters and more deeply moved by her experiences of pilgrimage. When she reached Jerusalem and was taken to the places where Christ suffered: 'the aforesaid creature wept and sobbed as plenteously as though she had seen Our Lord with her bodily eye, suffering His Passion at that time. Before her in her soul she saw Him verily by contemplation, and that caused her to have compassion.'[51]

For those who stayed at home an important part of the Church's liturgy was the procession, which was itself a pilgrimage in miniature. On certain days[52] the clergy, and often lay people as well, walked around the cathedral singing psalms and hymns.[53] These processions usually took place inside the cathedral but on special feast days, such as Ascension Day, Pentecost and Corpus Christi, it moved around the outside. The Palm Sunday procession started down in the town and made its way up to the cathedral.[54] Many of the psalms were originally written for Jewish pilgrims going to Jerusalem. 'I had gone with the multitude. I went with them to the house of God, with the voice of joy and praise, with a multitude that kept holyday.' (Ps. 42:4) 'I was glad when they said unto me, Let us go into the house of the Lord.' (Ps. 122:1) As is clear from the New Testament, Christ himself, and the earliest Christians, will also have gone up to Jerusalem to celebrate the special feasts. Jewish males were expected to do this at the feasts of Passover, Pentecost and Tabernacles. The celebration of Tabernacles was rather like that of Palm Sunday. The Christian Easter represents a culmination of the significance of the Jewish Passover. Medieval processions were a continuation of these Jewish and early Christian joyful excursions, generation after generation of pilgrims going to a meeting with God.[55]

20 Pig, symbolising greed

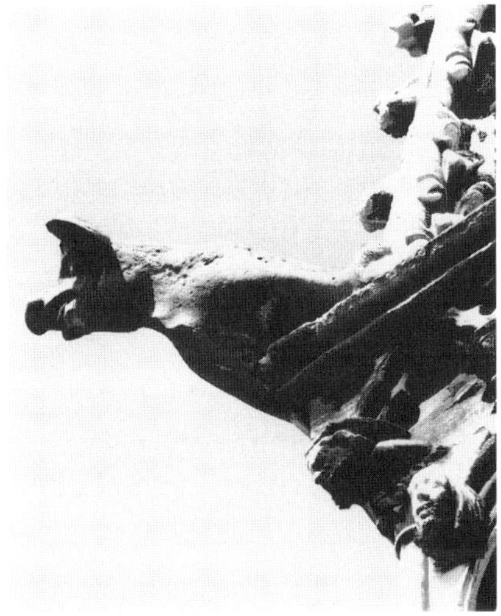

Palm Sunday was a special day, when the procession dramatically re-enacted Christ's entry into Jerusalem shortly before his death.[56] The participants carried branches of palm (in England, where this was not available, willow was often substituted) in emulation of the people who greeted Jesus on his entry into Jerusalem. The Palm Sunday procession drew together all the principal clergy of the city's churches and as many of their parishioners as could come.[57] These processions dramatised the incompleteness of life on earth, for Christians live in two worlds at

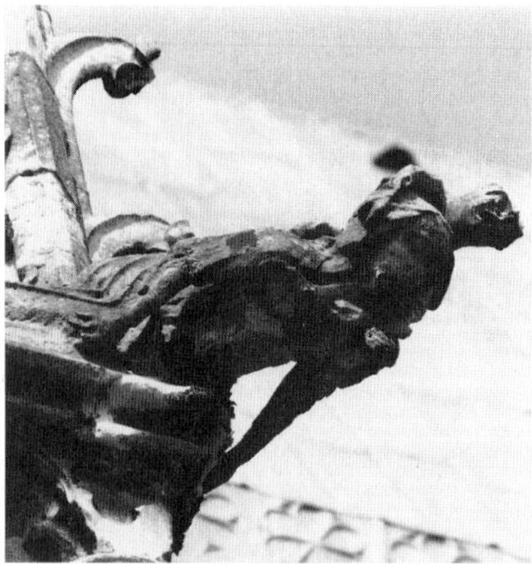

21 Bedevilled man

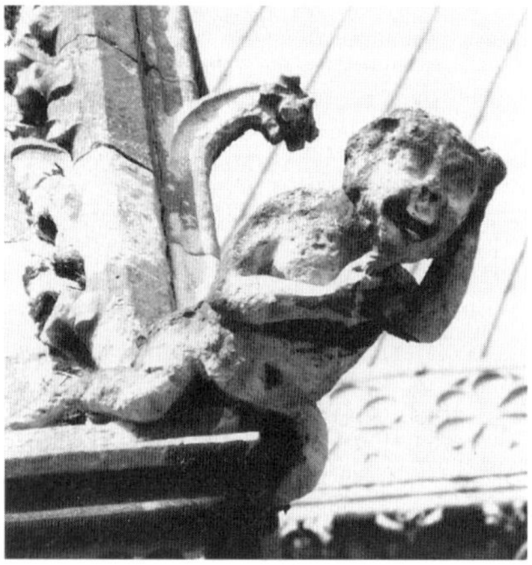

22 Man pulling hair and beard, symbolising Anger, exterior of Angel Choir
23 Drummer, exterior of Angel Choir

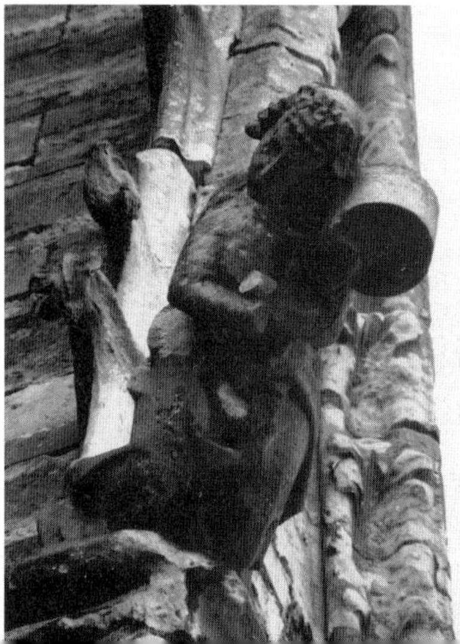

once. They are citizens of this world and also of Heaven. Heaven is both present and yet still to be achieved; it is possible to choose the wrong way and forfeit the promised reward. So the procession brought the members of the community together to express, by their prayers and their movement, the hope that they were indeed travelling towards Heaven.[58]

The Palm Sunday procession was strictly liturgical and took place as part of the worship of that day. Other processions there were which seem to have been associated with secular groups who presented religious plays for the entertainment and instruction of the populace. For example, the Guild of Cordwainers (shoemakers) used annually to process with the St Anne Guild on St Anne's day from the lower town up to the cathedral with a pageant wagon and there put on a play about the Assumption of the Virgin Mary into Heaven.[59] Presumably the heavy wagon went along the less steep road around the hill to approach the cathedral from the east but it is likely that most members will have taken the symbolically apt, steep and narrow way up Steep Hill. Another procession is known, at least during the fifteenth century, to have taken place on the Sunday after the feast of Corpus Christi. This feast celebrated the body of Christ, as given in the Eucharist, and was held in mid-summer. Many cities produced religious plays on or around this feast day and Lincoln was no exception.[60] A Guild of Corpus Christi was founded in Lincoln in 1350. In 1419 the bishop ordered their procession to be started from the suburb of Wigford, perhaps from the church of St Mary at the base of the hill.[61] Thus it will have moved along the High Street and up Steep Hill, probably collecting people from all the parishes en route[62] and gathering them together in their cathedral, 'sewing the whole town together with a processional thread'.[63] There is no definite evidence of a full Corpus Christi Play being presented until 1472, but plays based on the lives of various saints were produced frequently from the late fourteenth century onwards.

As early as the tenth century there is evidence in monastic churches of a beginning of dramatic presentations of the Gospel account of Christ's resurrection, though it is not clear whether lay people would have been present at, or able to understand, these.[64]

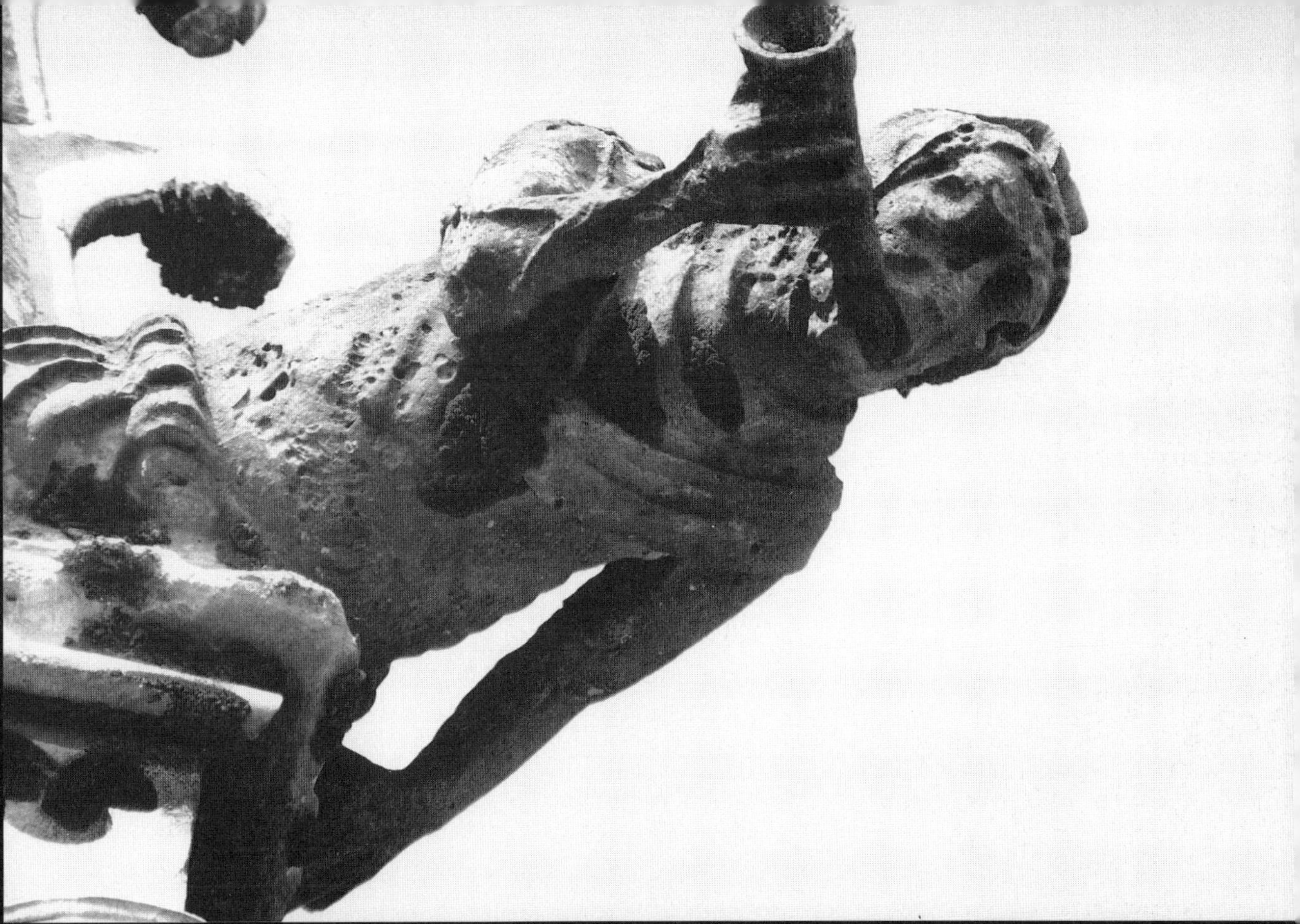

24 Man blowing horn, exterior of Angel Choir
25 Goat, symbol of Lust, exterior of Angel Choir
26 Grotesque, exterior of Angel Choir

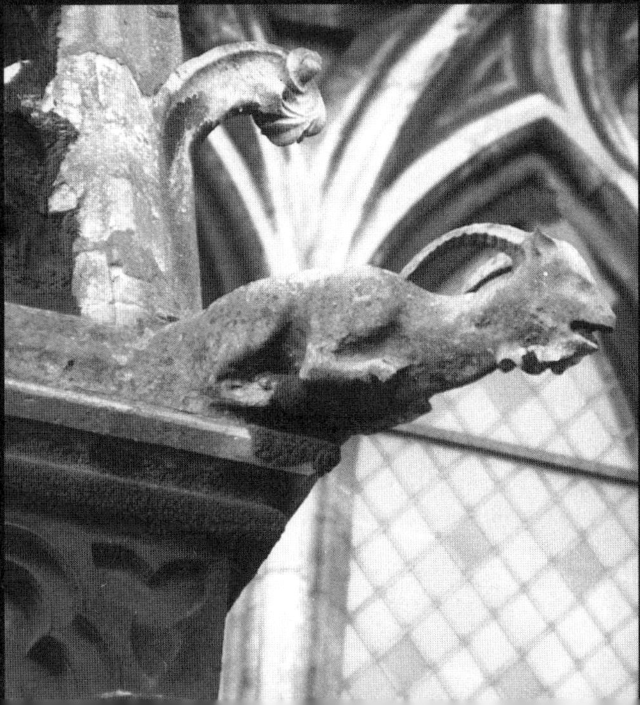

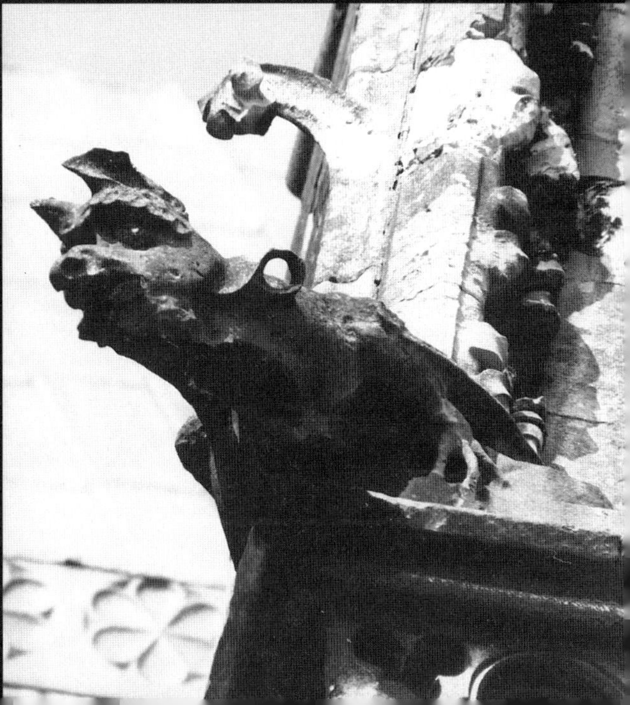

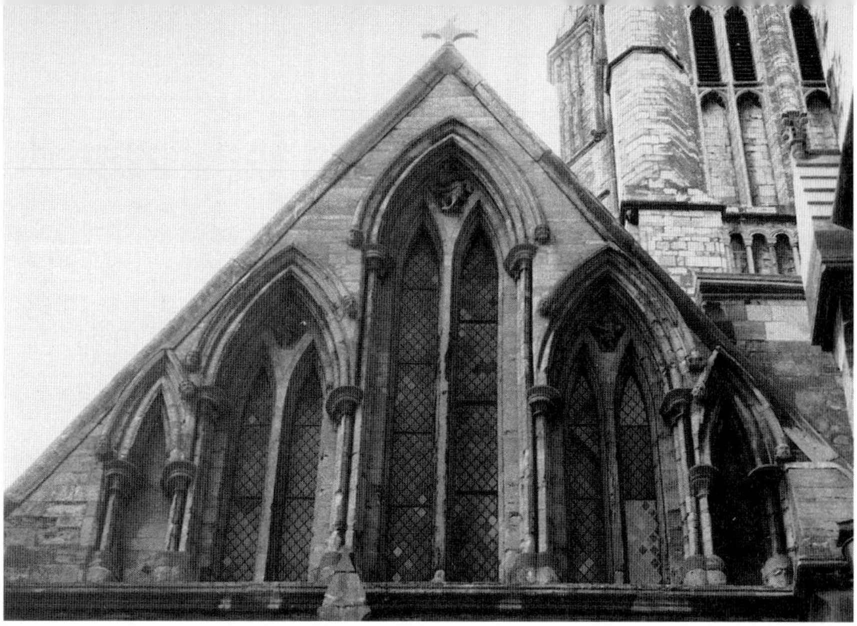

27 East gable of south-west nave chapel (now the bookshop) with three figures in niches; the two outer figures are walking towards the central devil

From the early fourteenth century some dramatic performances were being presented by the clergy and choirboys in the nave of the cathedral itself. On Easter Monday there was a play of the Resurrection of Christ and at Pentecost the descent of the Holy Spirit was symbolised by a dove let down from the vault.[65] At Epiphany, the three Wise Men followed a mobile star along the nave to visit the Christ-child.

Most of the liturgical processions were confined to the cathedral interior, or moved around the outside of the cathedral within the precinct. Even these would have presented a dramatic spectacle for participants and onlookers. The clergy and choir were dressed in silken vestments, their colours chosen to symbolise the particular season of the Church's year; a silver and gold crucifix, candles and incense-burners were carried; the choir sang appropriate chants.[66]

As they followed the processions or simply walked around the outside of the cathedral pilgrims would look up to see symbolic and instructive carvings. Along the exterior of the nave of the cathedral, at roof level, are pinnacles with elaborate niches. These niches are now empty but they originally contained statues of saints such as still survive on the outside of York Minster. They are the heavenly protectors of the faithful people, forerunners who lived in such a way as obviously to merit heaven. Their example was held before the living as a pattern for their own lives.

Around the upper parts of the exterior of the Angel Choir are

opposite

28 Tramp in spandrel of south-west nave chapel
29 Devil
30 Peddler

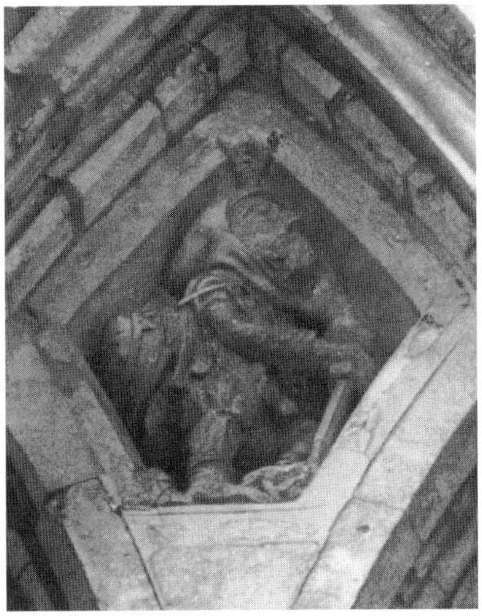

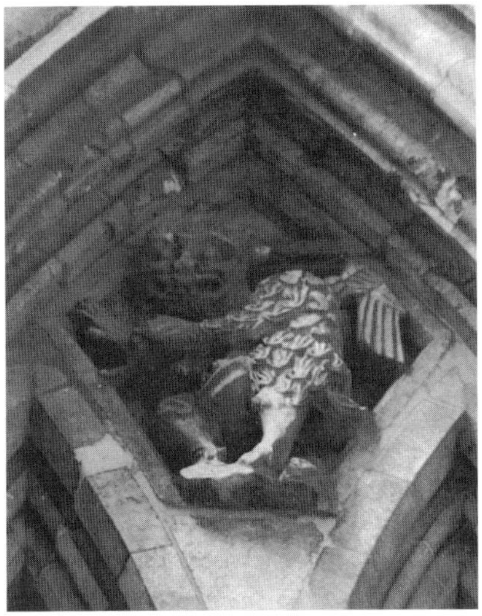

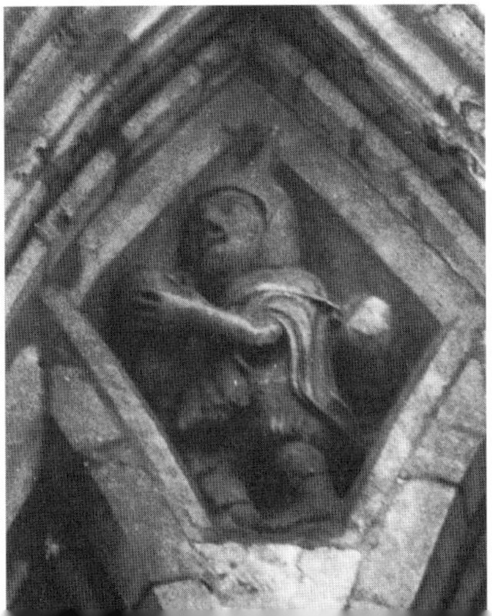

grotesque carvings of the kind generally known as gargoyles; the upper part of the south-west chapel of the nave also has enigmatic figures. Unlike the figures of saints on the nave and lower down on this part of the building, these figures are not set into niches. They lean out and peer at the passer-by; they pull faces and take up contorted poses. Their very outlines, although often amusing, give the impression of blasphemy. It is known that such carvings on some churches represent in detail the sorts of behaviour which should be left outside the church: vices, violence, devilish tricks of all kinds. The church of Heckington, in south Lincolnshire, has a fine series of such carvings including images of Lust and Avarice, Anger and Folly.[67]

The Lincoln carvings have not so far been closely studied or interpreted in detail. However, some of the figures do seem to have such meanings. The east gable of the south-west nave chapel has three figures in the spandrels of the windows. In the centre is a devil. Walking towards him are a peddler and a tramp; they are going his way. On the north side of the Angel Choir is a goat, often used as a symbol of Lust, and a man pulling his hair and beard, a common way of representing Anger. On the south is a pig, a frequent symbol of Greed and a man with a devilish figure on its back, being overcome by the fiend.[68] Also present are musicians, including a bagpiper and a drummer. These raucous instruments were played by wandering jugglers and entertainers who, as providing noisy, bawdy and sometimes criminal entertainments, were considered apt images of sin.[69] Other figures simply pull hideous faces or make rude gestures, symbolising enmity towards the things of God.[70] The distinction between figures in niches and those without is in itself symbolic. The niches signify the mansions of heaven, the orderliness of the divine plan for humanity.[71] Those figures without niches have put themselves outside God's ordinances; they are unprotected and disorderly as is the chaos of Hell. In this way scenes of Heaven and Hell were generally portrayed, with the blessed entering a beautiful building (not unlike a gothic cathedral) and the damned writhing tormentedly in confused heaps.[72]

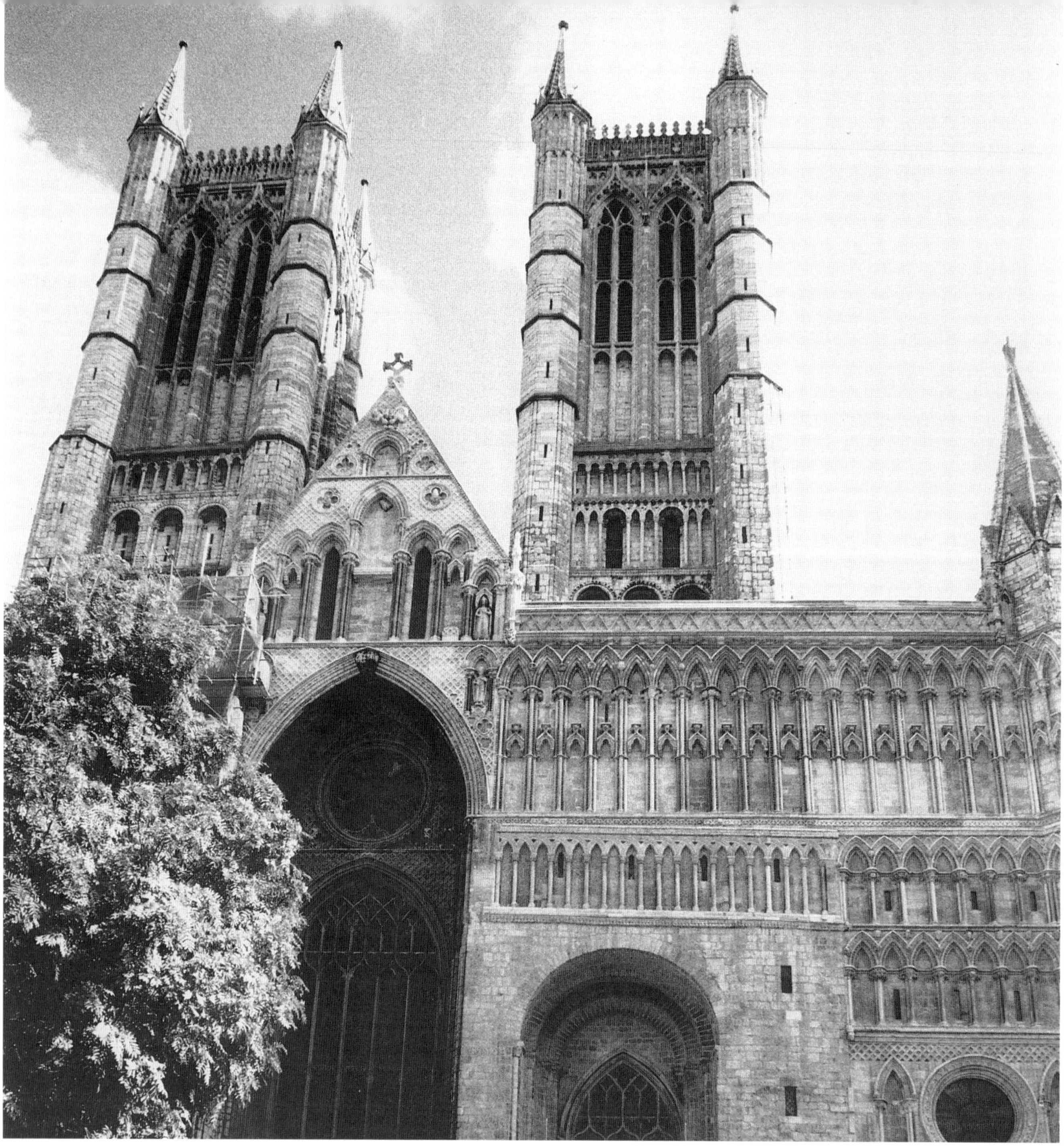

The West Front: Gate of Heaven

Whether one has processed around the cathedral or come directly into the precinct through Exchequer Gate, one enters through the west front of the cathedral where the main doorway is situated.

31 West Front

Here is the great, eleventh-century, triple portal. The doorways were embellished in the mid twelfth century by Bishop Alexander, who also added the Romanesque frieze of sculpted panels. Above, in the fourteenth century, was placed the gallery of kings. The original Norman west front, as reconstructed by Richard Gem,[73] had a strongly military aspect which echoed that of the castle built at the same time. In the immediate wake of the Conquest great churches were being built as much, it seems, to show how firmly the invaders were in control as to give glory to God.[74] 'The new regime... was at first extremely insecure and needed propaganda as well as force to support it. The cathedrals... were a constant reminder of God's blessing on the new rulers.'[75] Lincoln's original west front was the most dramatic example of this alliance between the secular and religious hierarchies.[76] By the mid twelfth century the Church was seeking more independence in order to have a moderating influence on the exercise of power by king and nobility.[77] Bishop Alexander's changes to the west front can readily be understood in this context, as a dilution of its military aspect and the assertion of the primacy of religious faith.[78] In particular, the sculptured frieze and ornate doorways seem to have been added at this time.[79]

On either side of the central doorway are colonnettes, some of which are carved with inhabited scrolls. The greater part of these is modern restoration but the upper part of the right hand column is original and from this it is clear that the restored work is a fairly reliable copy. A thick, fleshy vine twines all around and in its convolutions little naked figures fight their way upwards. At the top a clothed figure, no longer caught in the tendrils, grasps a serpent by the neck in each hand. T. A. Heslop, in a study of contemporary manuscripts, has found evidence of the meaning of such figures.[80] They are caught in the coils of sin, striving up toward the light (of Christ). Such figures are also on the Gloucester Candlestick, where they are literally looking upwards to the pricket where the candle will have been placed.[81] They are naked, as Adam and Eve knew themselves to be after they had disobeyed the commands of God (Genesis 2:15–3:24). About half way up the Lincoln colonnette a centaur with a bow aims his arrow upwards at a man who looks

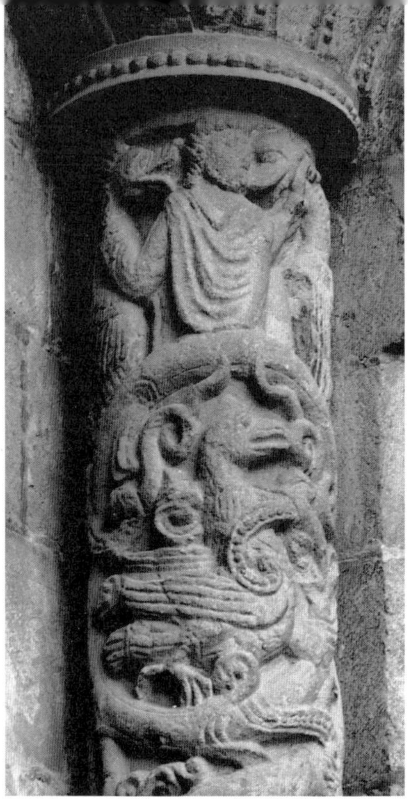

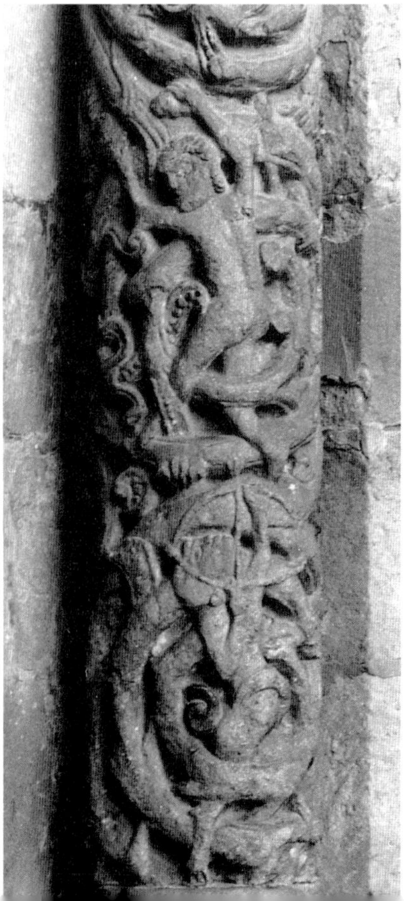

back apprehensively as he tries to scramble higher.[82] This motif is common in manuscripts of the thirteenth century and may well represent the sin of (or temptation to) lust.[83] The figure at the top has escaped and gained control over the forces of evil, represented by the serpents. He is clothed with the righteousness of Christ which ensures victory over evil.

Above the portals is the frieze, also dating from the twelfth century. From the centre running round to the south it portrays episodes from the Old Testament: Adam and Eve, the story of Noah and the Flood, and Daniel in the lions' den. These represent important episodes in the biblical story of how evil came into the world and were also seen as foreshadowing Christ's triumph over evil. From the centre to the north there are scenes portraying God's judgement on the good and the wicked: the parable of Dives and Lazarus, the Elect in Heaven, the souls of the faithful in the Bosom of Abraham, Christ bringing the souls of the righteous out of Hell (known as the Harrowing of Hell).[84] Some of these stories may have been presented as part of the Mystery Play cycle each year; this seems to have been first produced some time in the late fourteenth century.[85]

The Old Testament story of Adam and Eve is a reminder of how sin and evil became a part of human life, through the self-assertion of this first couple and their disobedience to God's laws. Daniel, the good man who was thrown into a pit with lions but survived through the grace of God, shows how the faithful are under God's protection. Although the Daniel panel was not originally designed for this place and interrupts the sequence of the Noah story, its theme fits with that of Noah's Ark. When God sent a great flood upon the world because of the wickedness of its human inhabitants, the good man Noah was instructed to build a large ship in which he and his family were saved. In this biblical story the sea represents chaos and the forces of evil, allowed by God to wipe out the wicked people but not to overcome the good.[86]

These Old Testament stories were considered to have further meaning; they were seen as 'types', foretastes, of the life of Christ and by extension of the lives of all Christians. This way of understanding the Old Testament goes back to the teaching of

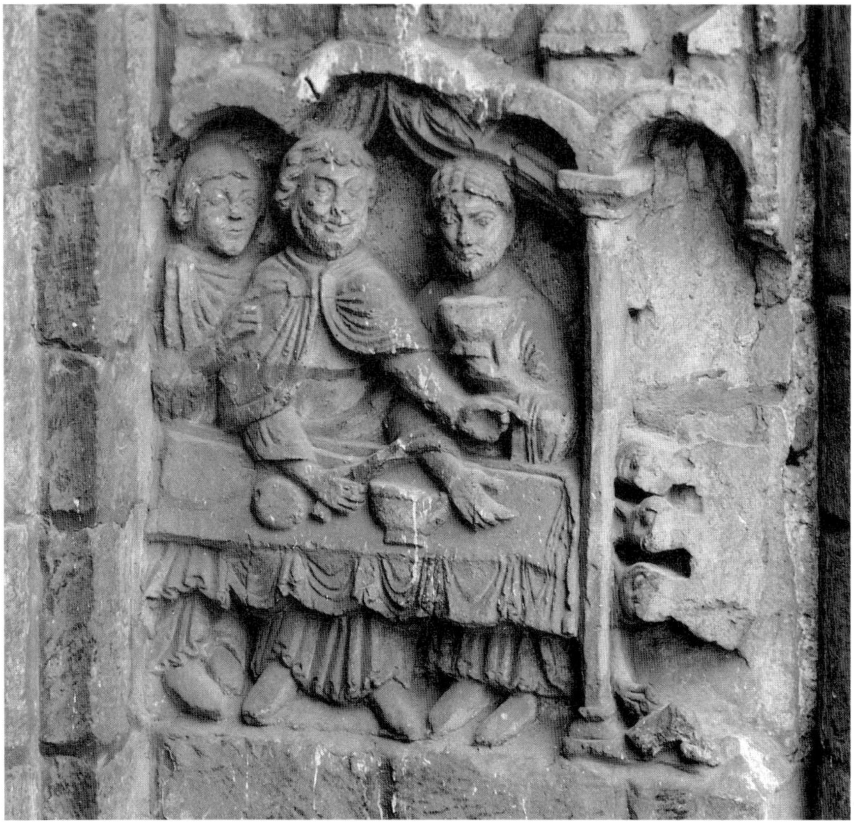

34 *The Feast of Dives*; only the dogs' heads survive from the scene of Lazarus lying outside the house

Christ himself. In the story of the disciples on the road to Emmaus (Lk. 24: 26–7), it is said of Jesus that: 'Beginning at Moses and all the prophets, he expounded unto them in all the scriptures the things concerning himself.'[87]

The New Testament parable of Dives and Lazarus (Luke 16:19–31) tells of Dives, a rich man, and a poor man, Lazarus. Lazarus lay sick and starving outside Dives' house but Dives made no attempt to help. When they both died Lazarus went to Heaven but Dives to Hell. The story is shown in two panels; one shows Dives feasting with his friends while Lazarus lies outside his door with dogs licking his sores. Dives gestures towards Lazarus, indicating that he knows of the need but ignores it. He is damned for deliberate refusal to help, not for an omission caused by ignorance. The second panel is divided horizontally into two sections. Above lies the dead Lazarus, his soul shown as a small figure being lifted up by angels. Below, a very vigorous devil uses a

opposite

32 Colonnette, west doorway
33 Archer aiming at nude; symbol of Lust, colonnette west doorway

35 *The Death of Dives and Lazarus.* Lazarus is lifted up by angels; Dives and his friends are tormented by a devil

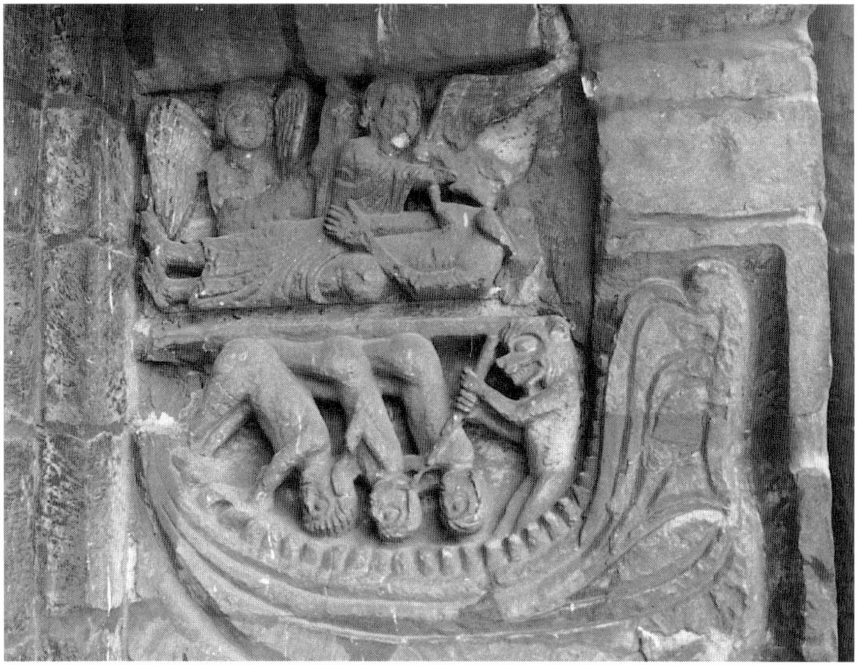

pitchfork to thrust Dives and his friends into a massive gaping Mouth of Hell. The message is clear and seems to have been received, if not always sufficiently acted upon. It has been pointed out in a study of the religion of the gentry in the fifteenth century that, although by no means all rich people behaved compassionately, no one could have failed to get the Church's message that Heaven would only be open to the rich if they came to the aid of the poor.[88]

36 Souls of the righteous in Abraham's bosom

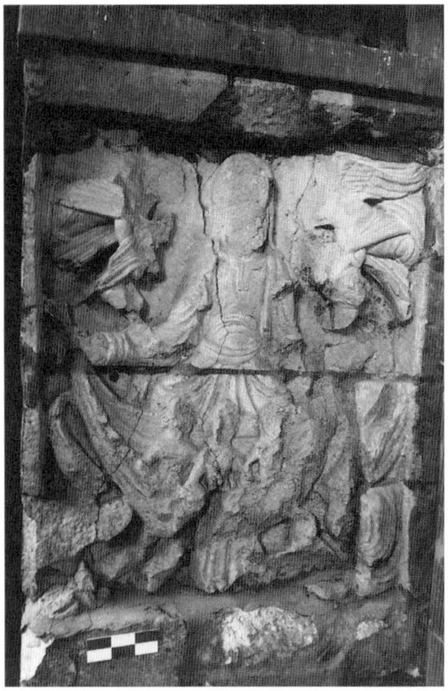

In the Gospel account the angels are said to have taken Lazarus' soul to the bosom of Abraham,[89] shown on panel 6 of the north section of the frieze.[90] This was an attempt to portray visually a metaphor used by early Christian writers as a comforting way of thinking about the state of those who had died. St Augustine, in his *Confessions,* wrote of the death of a close friend: 'And now he lives in the bosom of Abraham. Whatever it is that is signified by "bosom", there lives my Nebridius, my sweet friend...'.[91] The medieval funeral service also took up the metaphor: 'We pray your mercy, almighty and everlasting God... that [your servant] after being placed in the bosom of Abraham the patriarch, may rejoice that he has found a place of light and refreshment...'.[92]

These themes are appropriate for the entrance to the church. They remind all who enter of the precondition for coming into the presence of the divine: the fight against evil and the attempt to pursue the good by faith and by works of mercy. They also show the reward of good behaviour and the penalty for those who collude with evil.

Into the middle of the frieze, at some time in the late fourteenth century, was inserted the gallery of kings.[93] There is no definitive evidence of who these kings are meant to be. They may represent the kings of England.[94] They may be the ancestors of Jesus, the 'House of David', the kings of Israel who foreshadowed the heavenly kingship of Christ. This latter interpretation would fit in with the Romanesque work: both present images from the Old Testament, the precursor of the faith in Christ which is found within the church. They are also the ancestors of Mary, to whom the cathedral is dedicated.[95] It seems likely that their separate niches represent the many mansions of heaven.[96] Some of them have crossed legs, a common medieval sign of power and authority.[97]

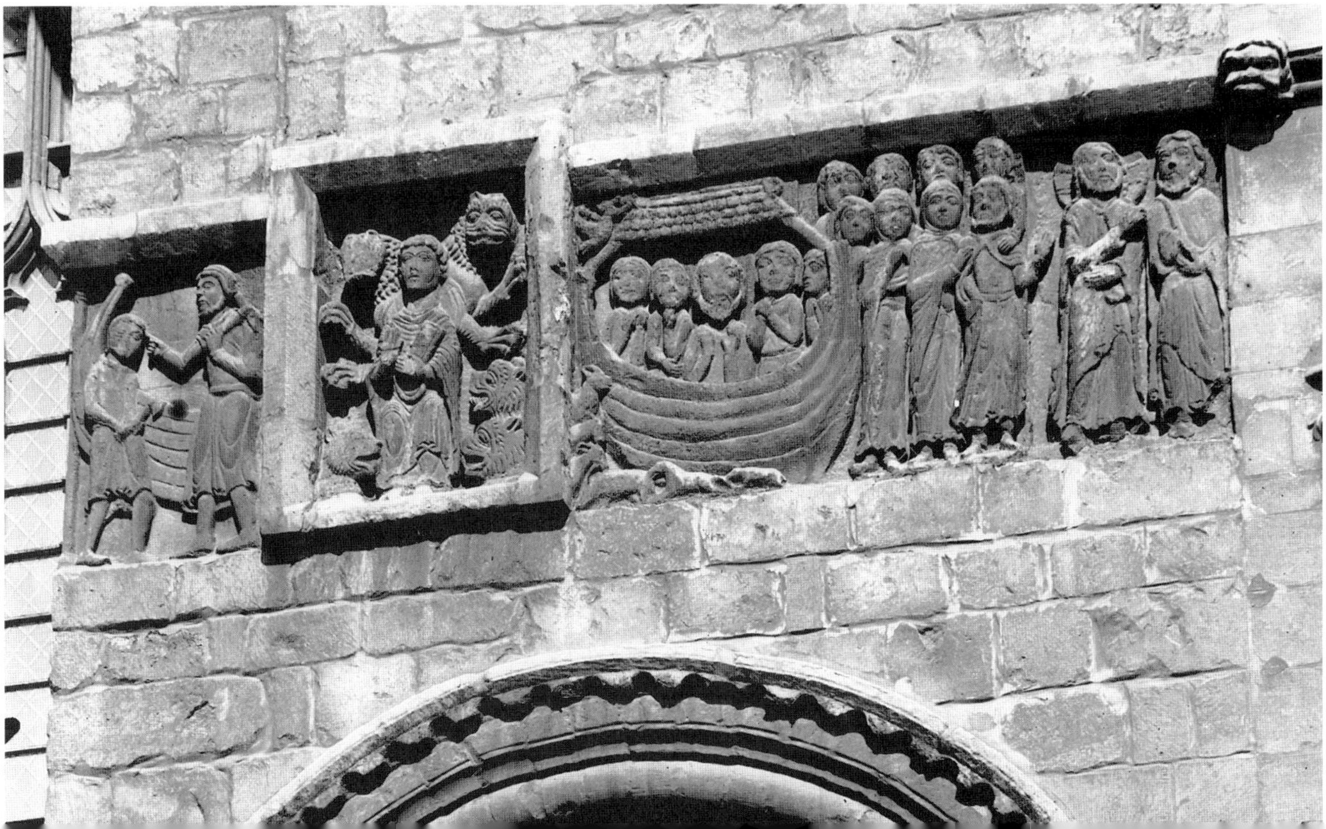

37 The frieze, from left to right: God instructs Noah to build the Ark, Daniel in the Den of Lions, Noah's family in the Ark, Noah's family disembarking, God's Covenant with Noah

A frieze of kings had earlier been inserted into the west front of the cathedral of Notre Dame in Paris. There also it is not certain who they are meant to represent; perhaps the kings of France. But what seems true is that their presence above the entrance to the church would enhance the authority of the earthly rulers as well as carrying a religious significance. So these rows of kings may well refer both to earthly kings and to biblical figures; earthly kingship was a continuation of the kingship of the Old Testament. The kings of England and France, like their Old Testament predecessors, were subject to, as well as enforcers of, the divine law. These images of powerful law-enforcers were a threat, that any law-breakers would be dealt with, but also a reassurance, since those who were law-abiding could rely on the ruler to keep order and rectify any wrongs done to them. This may not have worked out fully in practice, but it was the public ideal and served to limit royal power.[98] The law united all people, it was 'the general bond between people'. The ruler was above human law but subject to divine law and would be held responsible at the Last Judgement for the operation of justice in the realm.[99]

This doorway (and, as we shall see, the Judgement Portal on the south side of the Angel Choir) are aptly described by Professor Sauerländer: 'The portal separates the secular world outside from an interior which is consecrated, holy and resembles Paradise. For the Faithful the portal is a demand and a promise; a demand for repentance and purification, a promise of forgiveness and salvation.'[100]

38 West doorway and gallery of kings

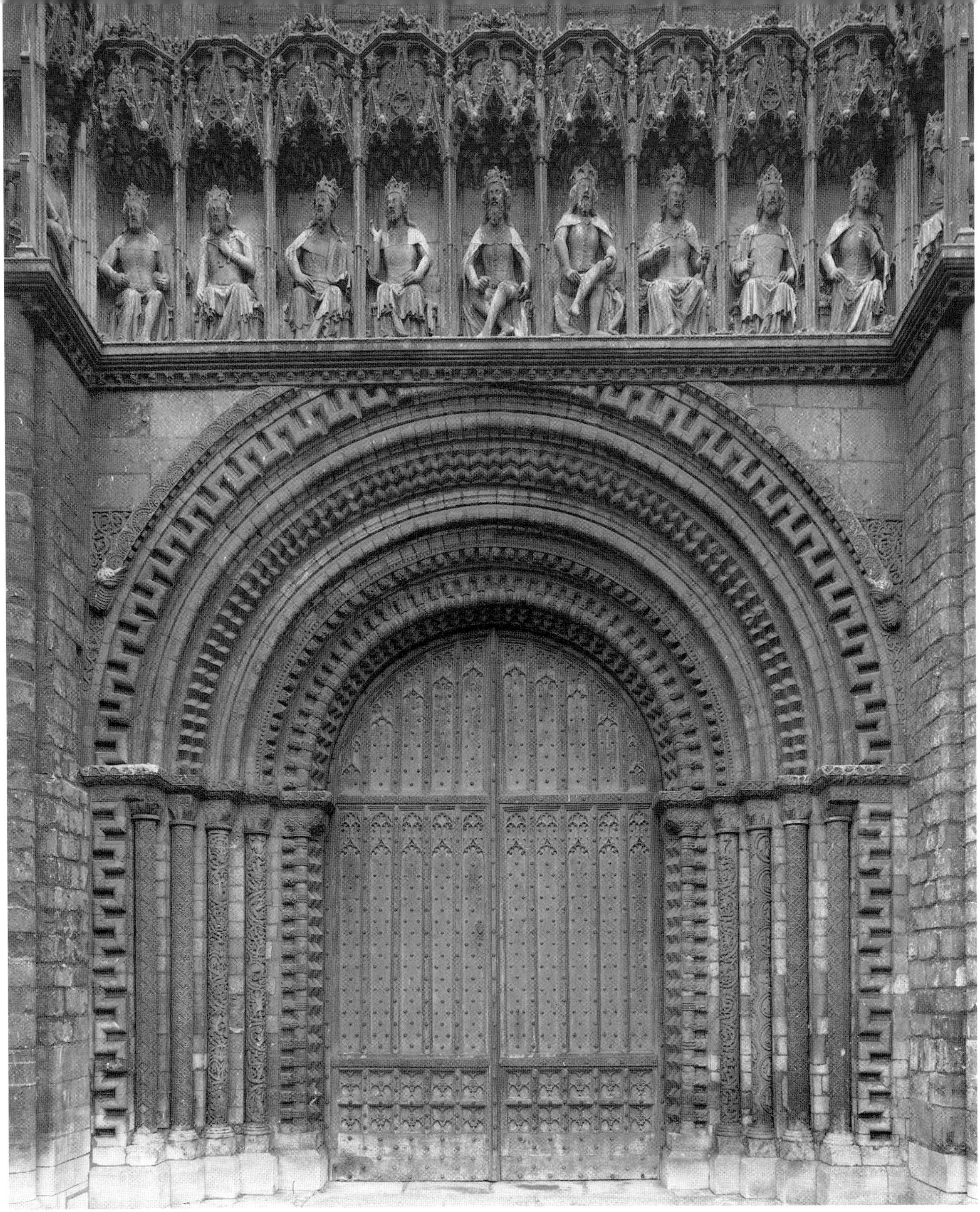

The Font: You were washed, You were sanctified

The pilgrim visiting the cathedral would move through the west doors to enter the nave. The imagery of the west front made clear the importance of this move and the need for purity of intention in those entering the House of God.[101] One of the first objects that meets the eye on entering is the font. There is no certainty as to its original placing but, certainly by the later Middle Ages and possibly earlier, fonts were commonly placed close to the main entrances of churches. Thus they served as a reminder that baptism, which takes place in the font, is the entrance sacrament for the Christian life.[102] This font is made of a dark stone, polished to emulate marble, and the sides of the bowl are carved with animals and grotesques. On the north side two of the figures seem to have books beneath their paws. Professor Zarnecki suggests that these may represent two of the four Evangelists' symbols: the lion of Mark and the ox of Luke. It is not clear what the other figures might represent but such rather fearsome-looking creatures often portray sins or the forces of evil. Such a meaning would be appropriate in a context of the defeat of evil through baptism into the saving grace of Christ.[103]

As with the church building, so the font was itself set apart for its purpose with a special blessing. In the font those to be incorporated into the Christian Church (in medieval times almost invariably babies but in the early centuries both children and adults) were immersed in water and signed with the sign of Christ's cross. Just as the church building and its consecration effected a spiritual transformation by physical means, so also baptism had a spiritual significance. Tertullian, a theologian of the early Church, explained it in this way: 'The body is washed, so that the soul may be made spotless. .. the body is marked with a sign so that the soul also may be fortified'.[104]

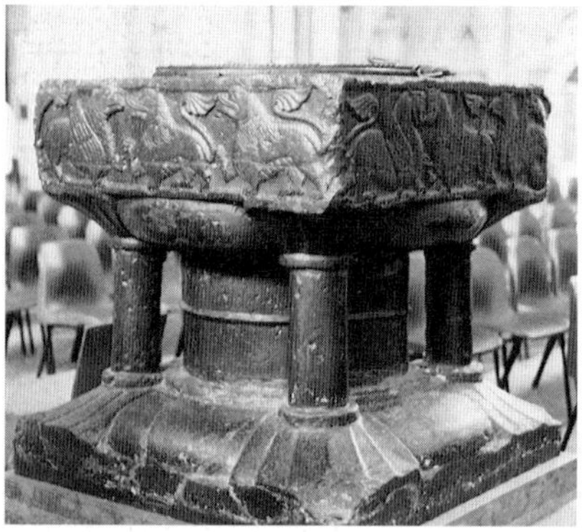

39 Romanesque font

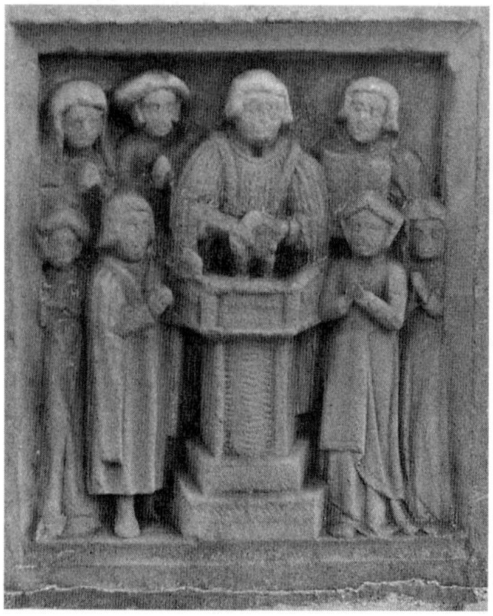

40 Medieval baptism on fifteenth-century Seven Sacrament font, Gresham, Norfolk

41 Beasts with books, perhaps symbols of two Evangelists, on font

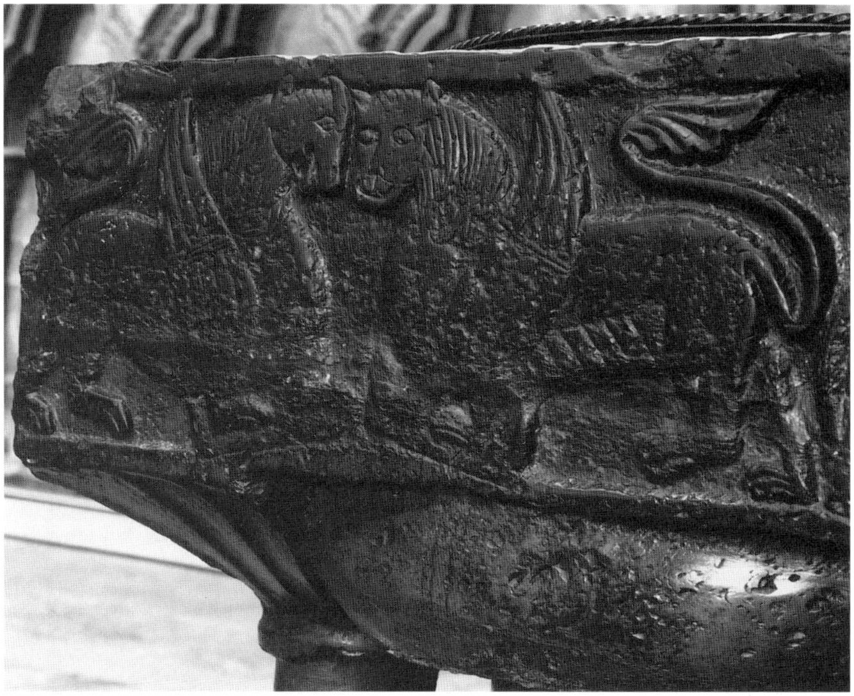

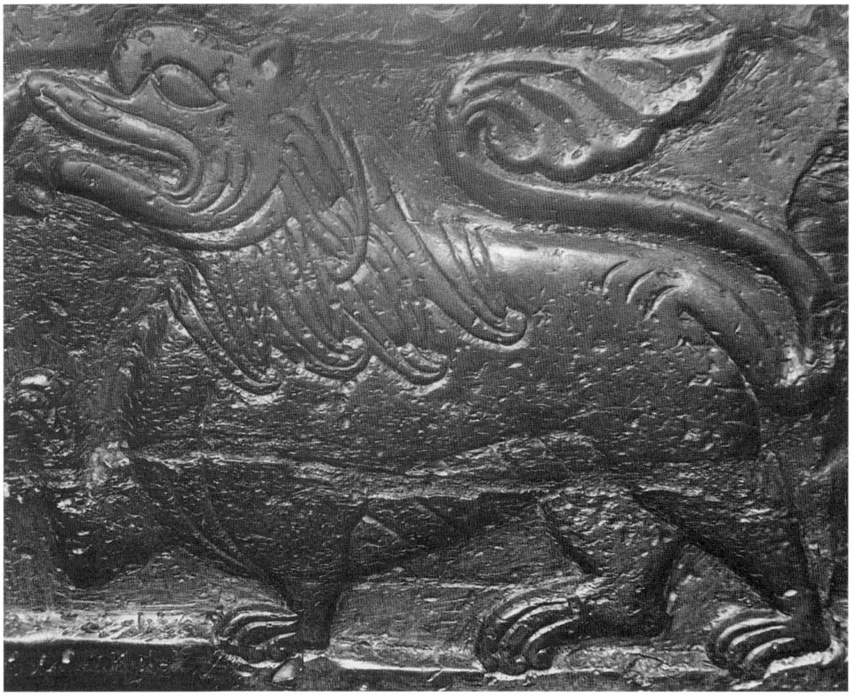

42 Beast, perhaps symbol of St Mark

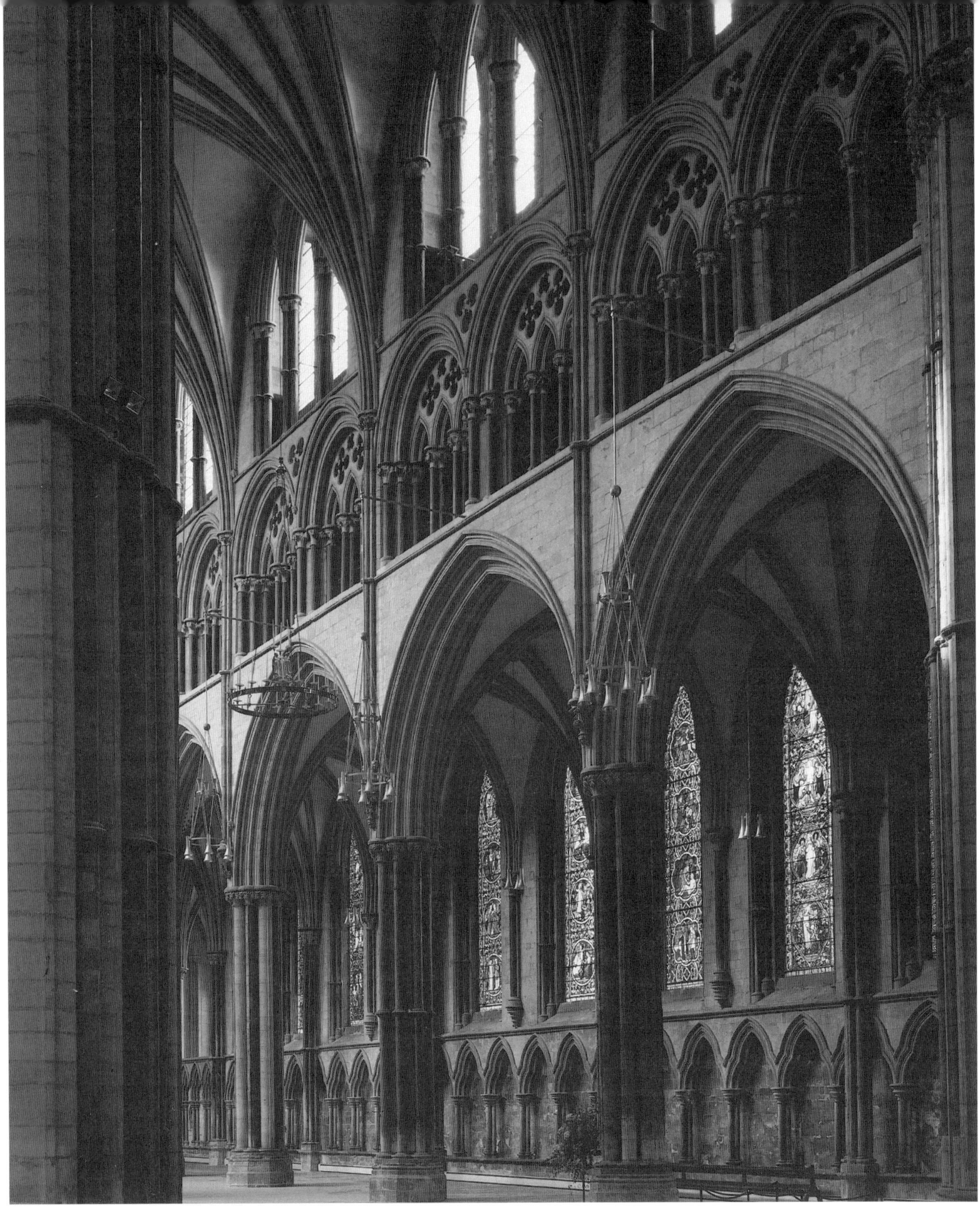

The Nave: Ark of Salvation

From very early times the church building, and in particular the nave, was likened to the ark of Noah which, as we have seen, is portrayed in the frieze over the west doors. This is made clear in the hymn for the dedication feast, 'Hail thee, Festival Day' *(Salve, festa dies)*: 'Here is the ark of God, a refuge of grace to the faithful; Safe to the haven it bears mariners tossed by the waves.'[105] More generally the ark is a type of the Church Militant, the People of God here on earth caught up in the battle against evil. Those who have been baptised into the Christian Church have been brought into this ark of safety. But, as is also shown over the west doors, it is possible to forfeit that safety by wrong-doing. The Flood, from which the inhabitants of the ark are saved, represents the dangers of this world but is also a prefiguration of the Last Judgement. This is expressed in the English thirteenth-century *Song of the Flood* which narrates the biblical story and ends by showing its contemporary relevance: 'The righteous alone are saved in the ark; its security and guard is the mercy of God'.[106]

The ground plan of the cathedral as a whole is cross-shaped, to recall the crucifixion of Christ. As the vehicle of salvation, the cross itself was linked to the ark of Noah. The arms of the cross reach out in the cardinal directions, north, south, east and west, to reach all mankind with the message of salvation, to encourage them into the safety of the ark-church.[107]

The nave of the cathedral was the place of the laity. It was also used for ceremonial processions of the clergy on feast days. In contrast to modern services, the medieval liturgy provided little opportunity for active involvement on the part of lay people. But this does not necessarily mean that they were alienated from it. The services were performed by 'professionals' who spent their lives on prayer and ceremonial duties as the representatives before God of those others who were caught up in the demands of secular life. The liturgy itself was resplendent with colour, movement and music; it has been referred to as 'the high art of medieval ceremonial'.[108] There is ample evidence of the devotion of lay people. Despite their 'passive' part in the liturgy they seem to have

43 Nave, looking west; odd column third from right

found the services inspiring and uplifting, providing a sense of beauty and harmony which enabled them to transcend the fears and anxieties of their everyday lives.

The piers which support the nave arcades seem at first sight to be uniform but closer inspection reveals that there are slight differences between them. This subtle way of obtaining unity in variety is typical of the message of the building; attentive looking gradually leads to further insights worth meditating upon. The piers are mostly arranged in pairs which match each other across the central space but the third from the east on the north side is odd.[109] Why is this? Does it have a meaning? We do not yet know. In the south aisle, almost opposite the odd pier are some bosses carved with figures (all the other nave aisle bosses seem to be simply foliage). In one bay are three such bosses: three heads, perhaps a symbol of the Trinity;[110] the *Agnus Dei* (Lamb of God) a symbol of Christ taken from the Book of Revelation (Rev.14:1); and a man holding up his right hand in blessing with three figures around him, seemingly Christ supported by angels.[111] In the adjacent bay to the west is a boss of a man's head surrounded and attacked by dragons. It would seem that these bays are being marked out for some reason. One possibility is that these bays of the nave may have been used for judicial hearings. The symbolism of the bosses would be appropriate for this. Moreover, it is known that in some churches on the Continent special columns were used to mark the position of such functions.[112] At present this can only be a hypothesis, but it suggests the need for research to find out whether this might indeed be the explanation of the pier and bosses.

As in many other English gothic churches, the piers have capitals carved with foliage, in this case of the early form known as 'stiff-leaf'. This was a fashionable form of decoration but may also have significance. We have seen that the imagery of Exchequer Gate includes a sprouting heart; there the leaves clearly signify the fruitfulness of charity and other good works. Here inside the cathedral the manifold leaf shapes may be meant to convey, albeit less directly, the idea of the continuing abundance of God's creation and re-creation.[113]

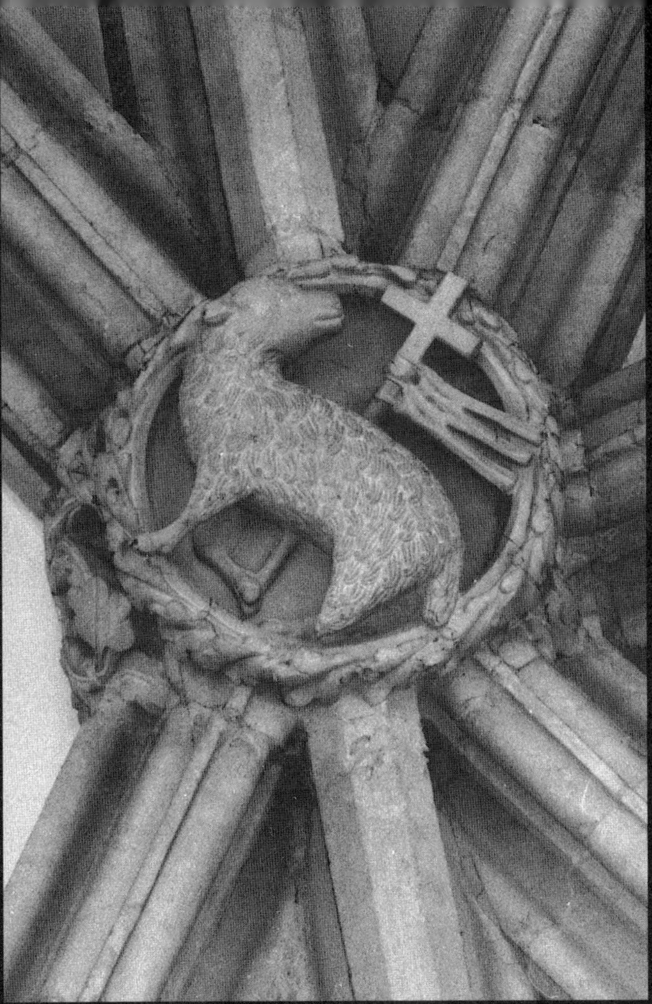

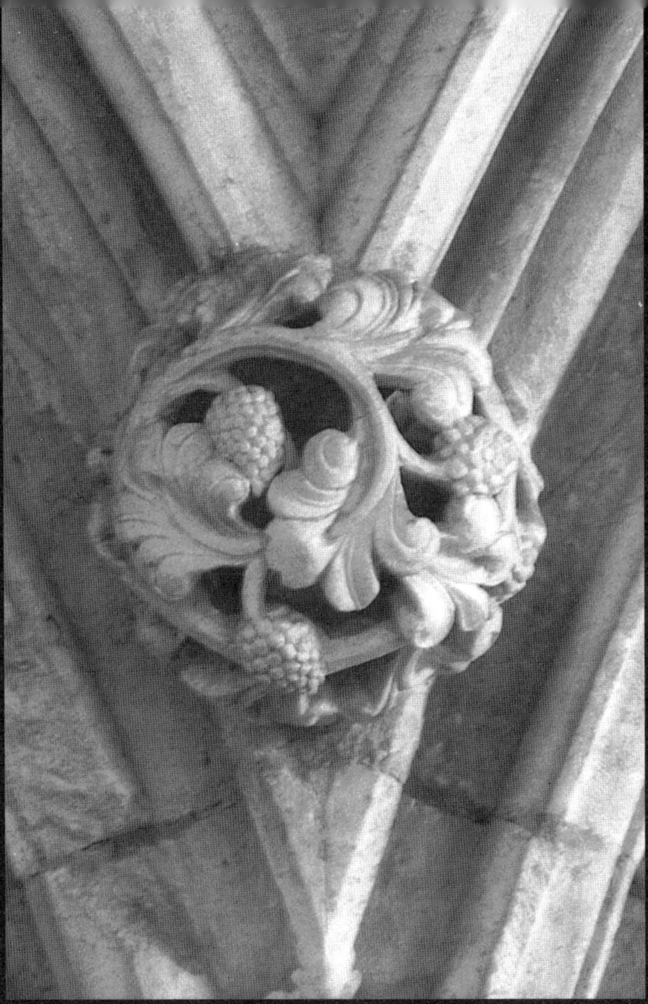

44 *Agnus Dei*, symbol of Christ, boss in vault of south aisle
45 Leaves and fruit, nave arcade spandrel
46 *Christ Blessing*, boss in vault of south aisle

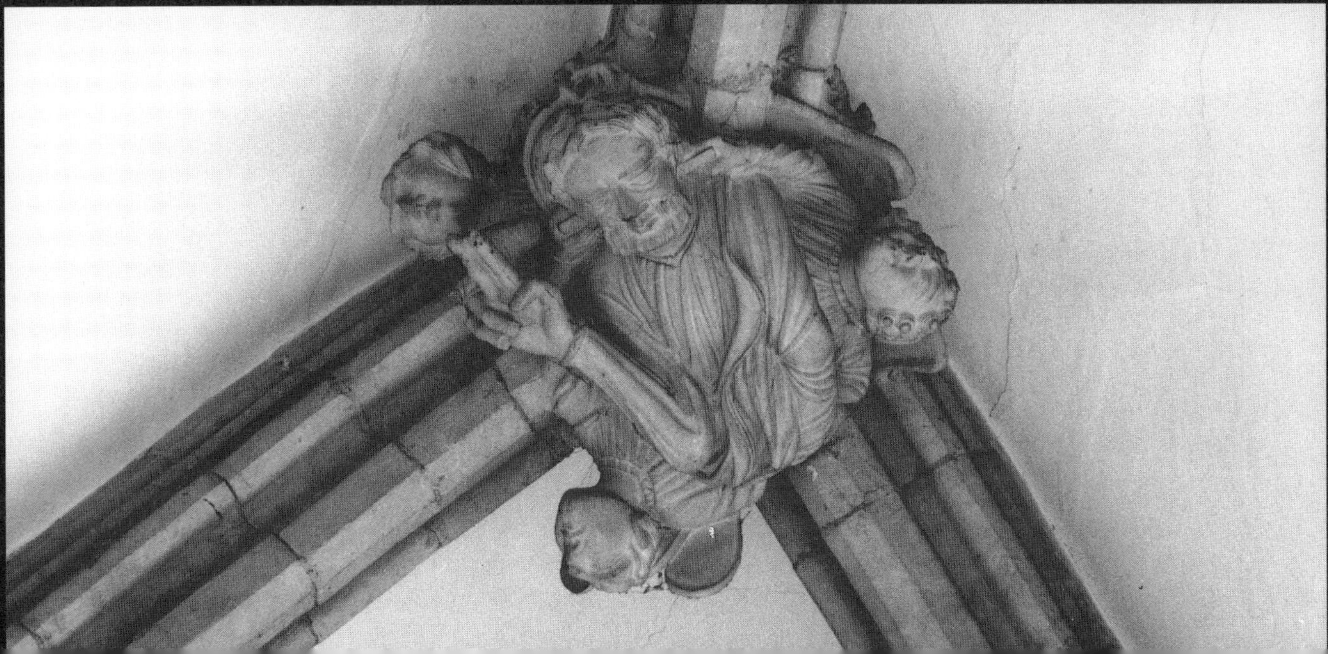

The nave is screened off from the choir and sanctuary so that the latter form almost a separate church within the cathedral. This was done in all the great churches in medieval times. Some cathedrals, such as Ely, Durham and Salisbury, have had their choir screens removed to allow a view along the full length of the building. It may be pleasant to have such a view but the screens had, and still have, a very practical purpose. Regular services of worship are held in every cathedral; the cathedral is also a place for people to visit, look around, find inspiration in the beauty of the architecture and art. These two functions do not fit all that easily together. Visitors do not always want, and are not always able, to join in the services. But if there are people walking around, this can disrupt the prayerful concentration of the services. If the choir retains its screen as at Lincoln, it is possible for both activities to go on simultaneously; visitors may move about the nave without disturbing the services in the choir. Medieval pilgrims seem to have behaved not unlike modern visitors.[114] They wanted to see all the sights and sometimes they were more boisterous than the clergy, and more devout lay people, would have wished. Screens allowed peace and a modicum of privacy so that no one except the

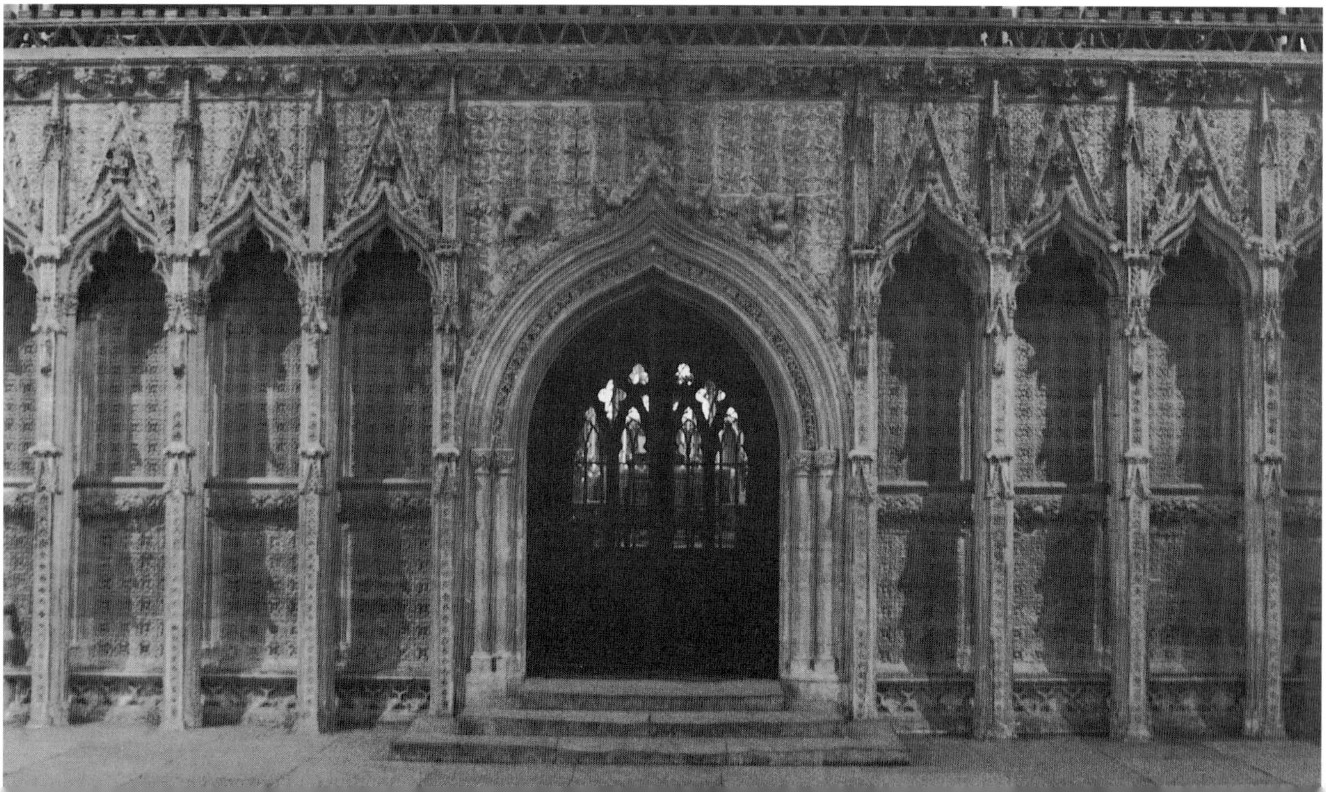

47 Pulpitum

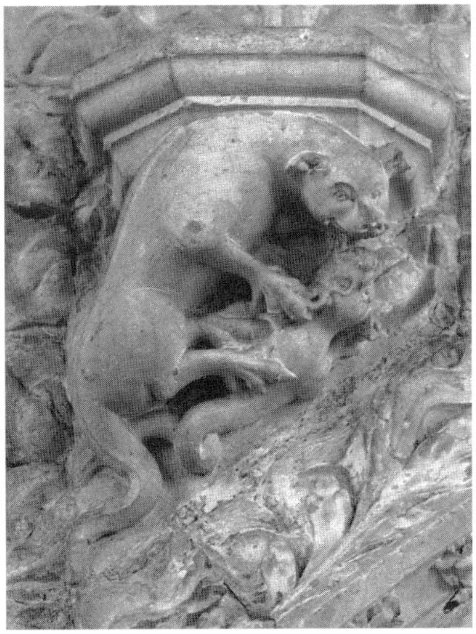

48 Beast corbel on pulpitum

outrageously badly behaved had to be excluded.

The ceremonial entrance to the Choir is through the pulpitum, the screen across the eastern side of the crossing. Above this, or on a second screen in front of it (the Rood screen), there would have been a great crucifix with the figures of Mary and St John the Evangelist to either side. Durandus explains its significance: 'in many places a triumphal cross is placed in the midst of the church; to teach us, that from the midst of our hearts we must love the Redeemer ... [and it] is exalted on high, to signify the victory of Christ.'[115] As in Exchequer Gate, it is beneath the cross that one moves into the sanctuary. Nowadays one can appreciate something of the effect of such placement of a cross in the cathedrals of Peterborough and Southwell, where modern crucifixes have been suspended at the entrance to the Choir.

Normally lay people would move, not through this entrance, but along the aisles to reach the eastern parts of the cathedral, thus preserving the comparative seclusion of the Choir. The entrances to these aisles are spanned by intricately carved arches added at about the same time as the Angel Choir was built. Before these were inserted the aisles will have been more open to visitors. When the Angel Choir was built a new entrance was provided directly to it, as we shall see in discussing the Judgement Porch. It seems as though the building of that entrance and the partial blocking of these two was intended to provide even greater privacy for the Choir while still allowing lay people access to the eastern part of the cathedral.

The pulpitum itself is, as Pevsner noted, 'a gorgeous piece of 1330s decoration'. Its statues have been destroyed in one of the bouts of iconoclasm of the sixteenth or seventeenth centuries but the corbels on which they stood remain. These are carved with grotesque creatures of many kinds. Placed, as these were, beneath the feet of the saints they will have represented the various forms of evil which the saints overcame in their lives. The idea comes from Psalm 110:1: 'The Lord said unto my Lord, Sit thou at my right hand, until I make thine enemies thy footstool.' This text was taken[116] as referring to Christ and, by extension, to those whose courage and purity of life made them fit to take their seats with him in heaven.

St Hugh's Choir: Through a glass darkly

49 Entrance to south Choir aisle, capital with man fighting Satan in the form of a dragon

At the entrance to the Choir aisles, on each side, are elaborately carved archways. That on the south has carved capitals showing a series of little men fighting diminutive dragons. The dragon was used as a symbol of evil; slaying one represented the overcoming of evil. It is not that dragons themselves were considered to be evil, but rather that, since they were the largest and most fearsome of creatures, they were an apt disguise for Satan himself. Moreover their ability to spout fire was appropriate for the flames of hell. This is how a twelfth-century Bestiary explains it: 'The Devil...is like this dragon. He is often borne into the air from his den, and the air around him blazes, for the Devil in raising himself from the lower

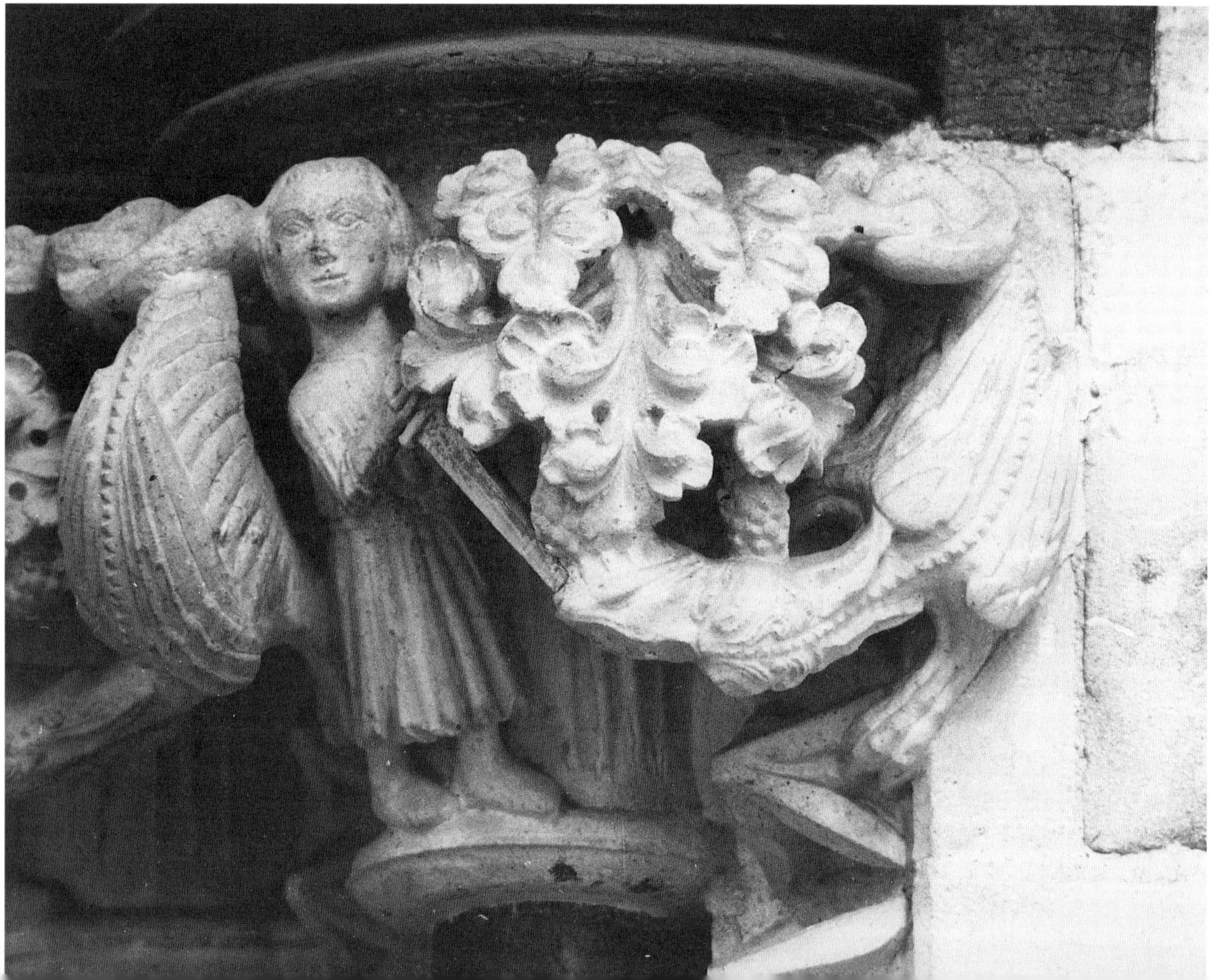

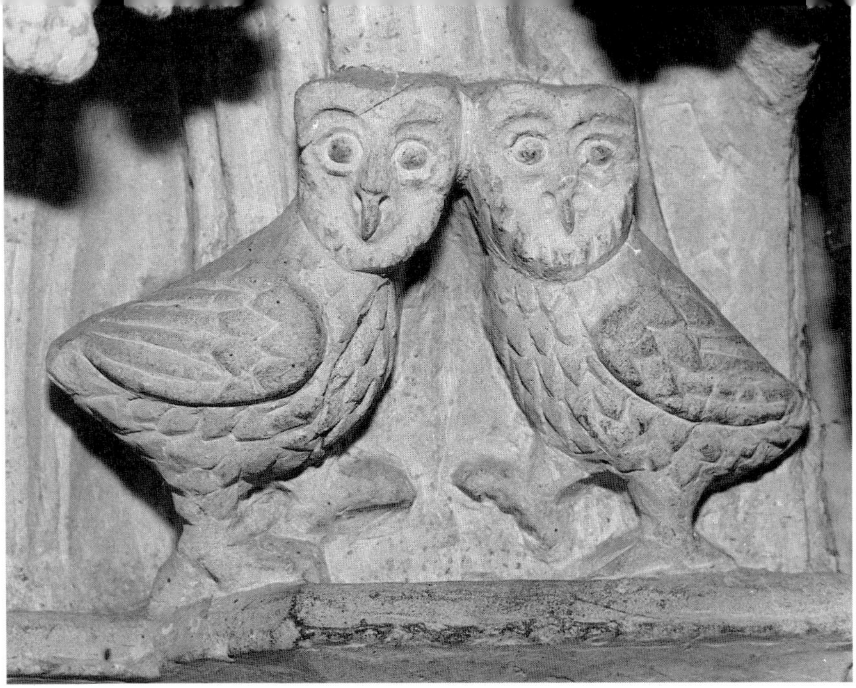

50 Entrance to south Choir aisle, capital with owls, symbolising Ignorance

regions translates himself into an angel of light and misleads the foolish with false hopes of glory and worldly bliss... He lies hidden around the paths on which they saunter, because their way to heaven is encumbered by the knots of their sins, and he strangles them to death. For if anybody is ensnared by the toils of crime he dies, and no doubt he goes to Hell.'[117]

This understanding of the dragon is taken from yet another part of the Book of Revelation: 'And there was war in heaven: Michael and his angels fought against the dragon; and the dragon fought and his angels, And prevailed not ... and the great dragon was cast out, that old serpent, called the Devil...' (Rev. 12:7–9) So these capitals are a further reminder, as one moves toward the sanctuary of the church, of the demand that the Christian should be prepared to combat evil and the assurance that the effort of each individual is part of a cosmic conflict in which good will prevail. Notice that the left, north capital of this doorway has unhindered dragons and a pair of owls. The owl, a night bird, symbolises sinners who prefer the darkness of ignorance to the light of divine truth.[118]

To our left as we move along the south aisle of the choir is a reminder of a sinister aspect of the cathedral's history. It is the remains of the shrine of little St Hugh, a child said to have been ritually murdered by the Jews in 1255. Similar accusations were

above, opposite
52 Double arcading, south aisle. The spandrel figures are not part of the original design
53 Spandrel figure, Choir aisle, not part of original design

below, opposite
54 Double arcading, north-west transept; outer arch is too low to show in the niches
55 Double arcading, south-west transept, with apex of outer arch showing in niches

made in other cities in England, among them York, Norwich and Gloucester, and in many parts of continental Europe. It is unlikely that Jewish people had anything to do with these murders, but they were used as pretexts for savage attacks on the local Jewish people. It is as well for us to remember such unpleasant facts about our history in the hope of preventing repetition of them. Despite this sinister aspect, the shrine itself must have been quite beautiful. It had a tabernacle canopy, traceried and gabled and surmounted with a spire. It is still possible to see how the canopy swung out from the screen wall; the dark rectangle of stone below it was the tomb base.[119]

The choir itself is known as St Hugh's Choir after bishop Hugh of Avalon, the saintly Carthusian monk during whose episcopacy this part of the cathedral was reconstructed. It is one of the most famous and controversial designs in the history of gothic architecture, with its eccentric vault known to art historians as the 'Crazy' vault.[120] This vault is unique in its asymmetry. The designer deliberately emphasised the way in which the ribs swing to and fro across the space and that swing would originally have carried the eye to the eastern end of the choir to be resolved over the original apse (which has since been replaced by the Angel Choir). The eccentricity of the vault is only part of a strongly eccentric design. Although at first sight the building seems to be quite orderly, an attentive look at details will uncover extraordinary variety. There are piers of different shapes and materials; the arcading around the walls has been deliberately designed not to fit evenly into the spaces between vaulting shafts nor between corners: the windows are set asymmetrically in the end walls of the transepts and are of different widths.

All these factors have greatly puzzled art historians; the general consensus seems to be that the designer simply liked eccentric effects and in some places, such as the corners, produced a muddle through miscalculation.[121] I am convinced that there is no muddle but rather a deliberate and unique attempt by the designer to reflect in his architecture a set of theological ideas which were widely current in his time.

To put it very simply the theological point was that humans can

51 'Crazy Vault', St Hugh's Choir

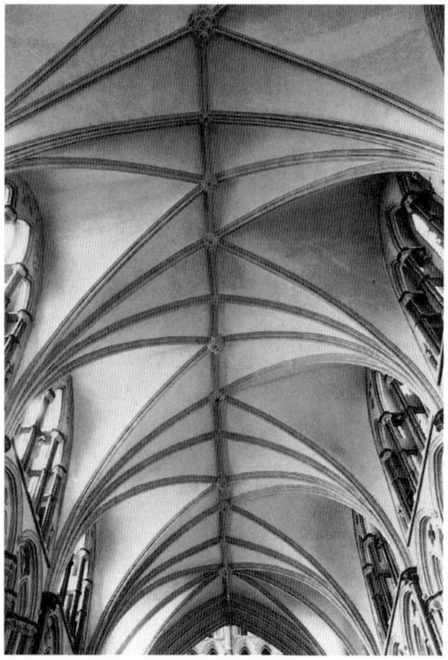

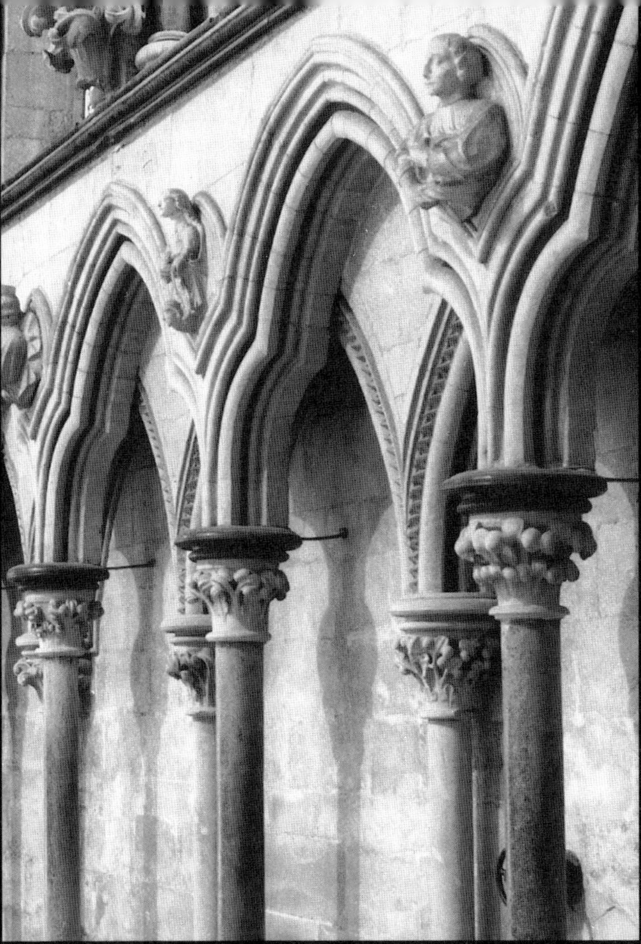
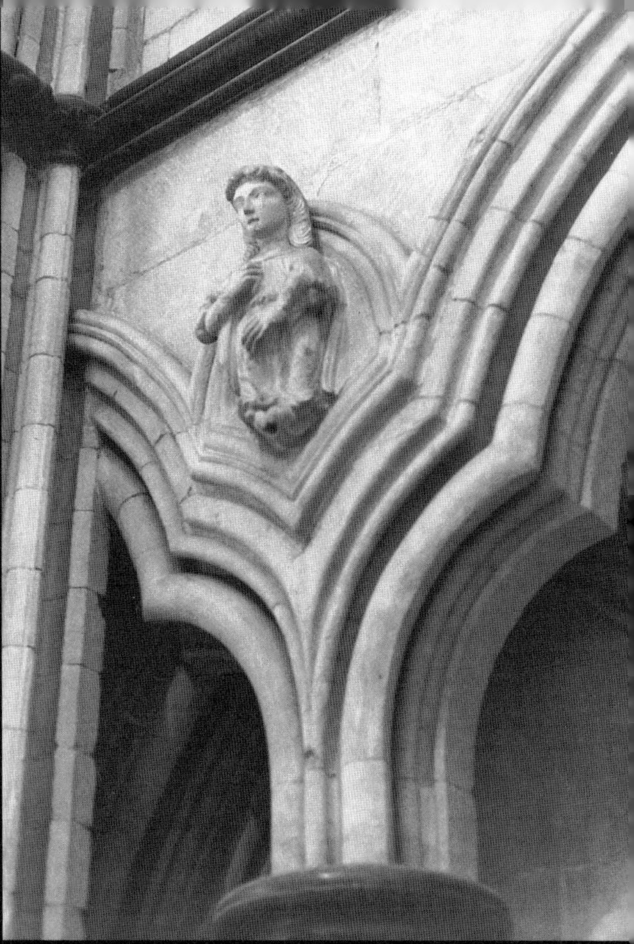
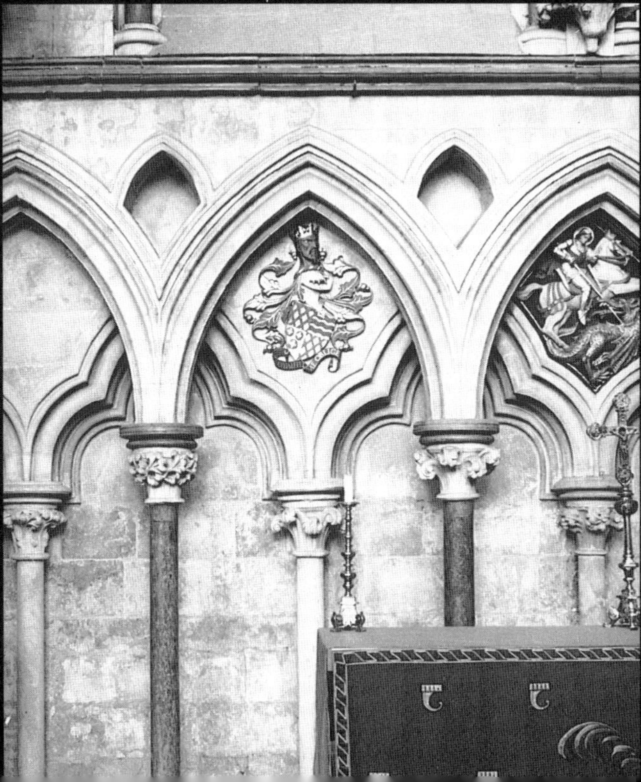
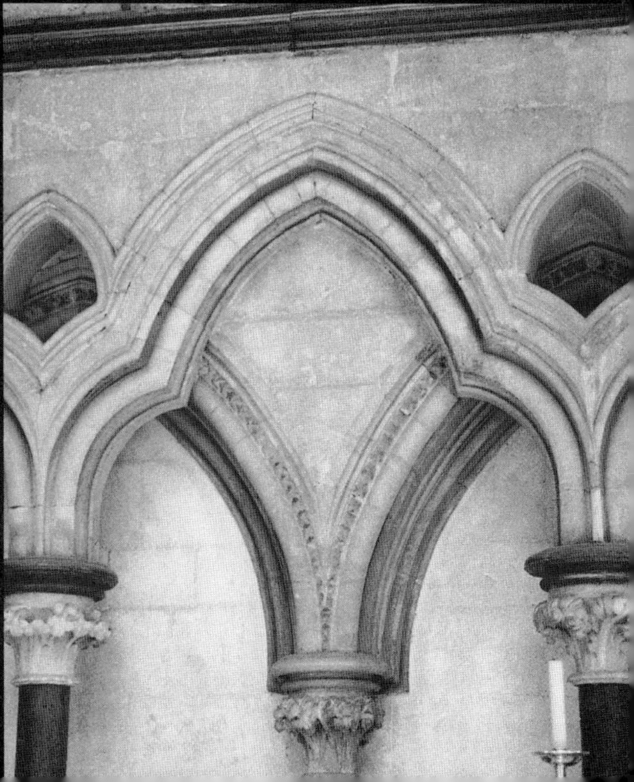

come to an understanding of the nature of God in two ways. In the affirmative way our concepts of goodness, beauty, justice and so forth are considered to apply to God but with the proviso that he represents the greatest perfection of these attributes; we can, as it were, move through these human concepts to grasp something of the divine nature. In the negative way all human concepts must constantly be denied of God lest we rest in the erroneous belief that the divine creator of all that exists can be grasped by finite, imperfect human ideas; this requires a movement away from, rather than through that which is humanly produced. These two ways are contraries but it was always held that they must go together. The attempt to know something of the nature of God requires both that we use what we have available and that we remember how inadequate it is to the task.

These ideas were attributed to a disciple of St Paul, Dionysius the Areopagite. In fact we now know that they were written down by an anonymous author some five centuries later than this, but the attribution to Dionysius (whose conversion by Paul is recorded in the New Testament; Acts 17:16–34) was accepted throughout the Middle Ages and so the Pseudo-Dionysian writings enjoyed great prestige.[122]

56 Detail of sprouts on pier

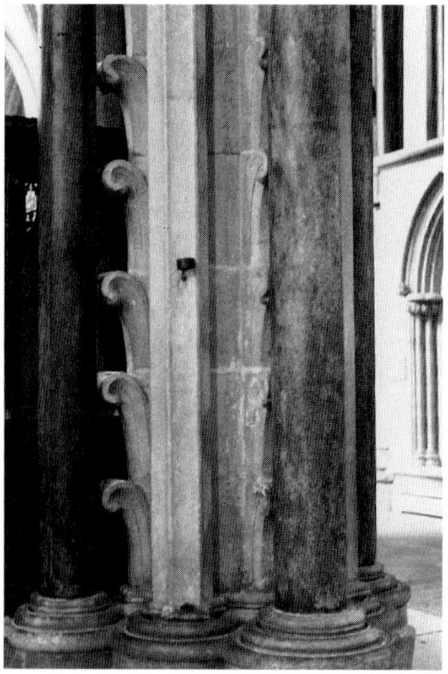

How might these very abstract theological ideas be embodied in a building? To explain this we need to move through St Hugh's Choir twice, once to show how the affirmative way was used and then again for the negative way.

As was pointed out above, there is a clear sense of movement into the cathedral from the outside; there is also a progression within the building from the less to the more sacred parts. The sanctuary, where the altar stands, is the most sacred part of every church. From ancient times the altar has been taken to symbolise the continuing presence of Christ himself with his people. It is on the altar, during the service of the Eucharist, that the elements of bread and wine are transformed for the faithful into the body and blood of Christ. Shrines of local saints were, by the time that St Hugh's Choir was designed, commonly placed in the vicinity of the High Altar thus enhancing the importance of this part of the building.

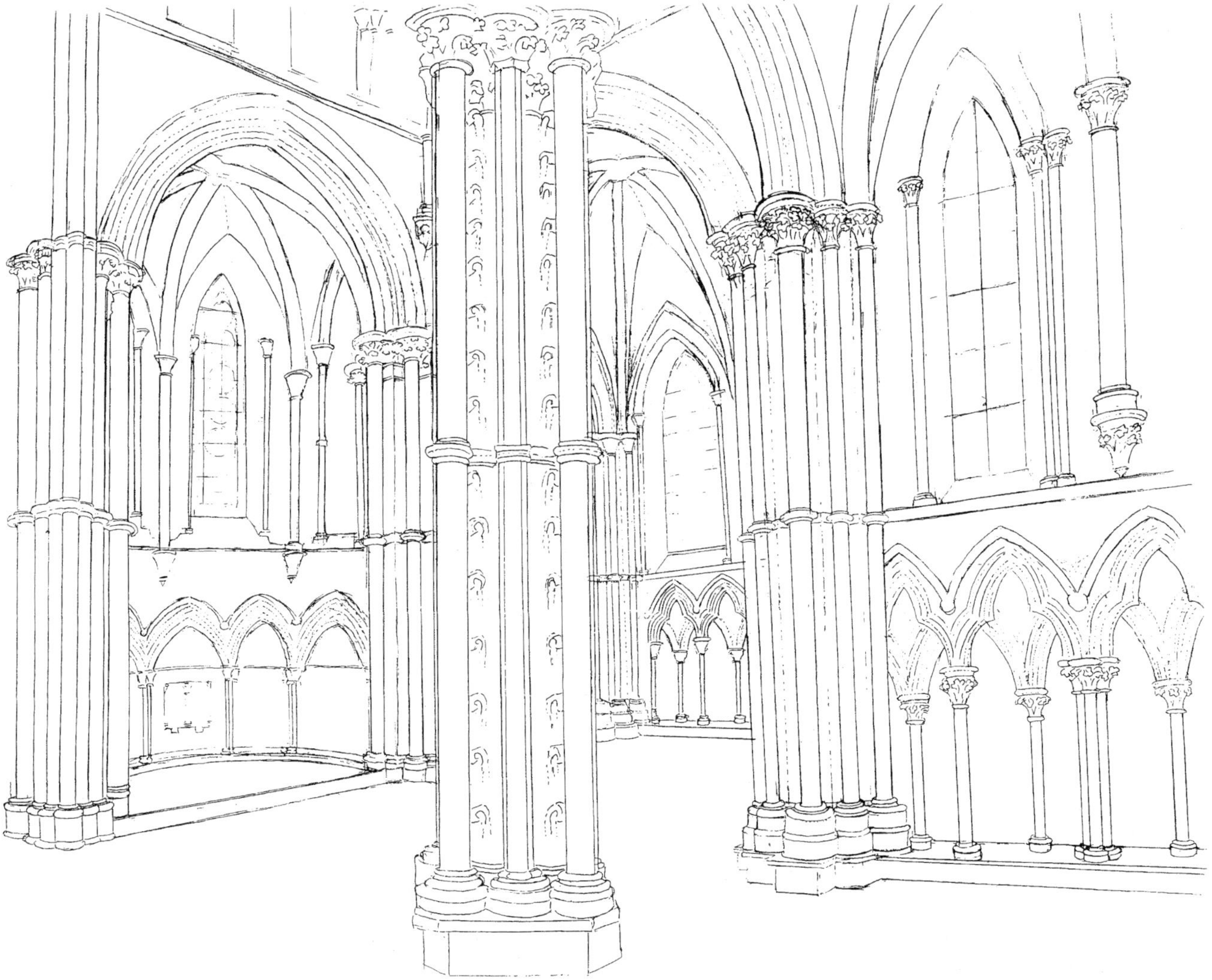

57 Reconstruction of original view into south-east transept showing free-standing sprouting pier.
Drawn by Allan Smith

We begin in the great west transept. One bay of each arm of this transept was built by the designer of St Hugh's Choir. The mason who replaced him changed the design, as is evident from the arcading in the outer bays of each arm of the transept. In the south arm of the transept the original designer placed overlapping, syncopated arcades along the eastern wall. The arches of the front layer are trefoil; those behind are plain and rise higher. Into the spandrels (the triangular sections between the arches) of the front arcade openings have been cut, through which the tops of the back arches are visible. It is a unique 'peek-a-boo' effect.

This arcading continues around the walls on both sides of the choir, running uninterrupted around corners and behind the shafts which run up to the corners of the vault; but when it reaches the

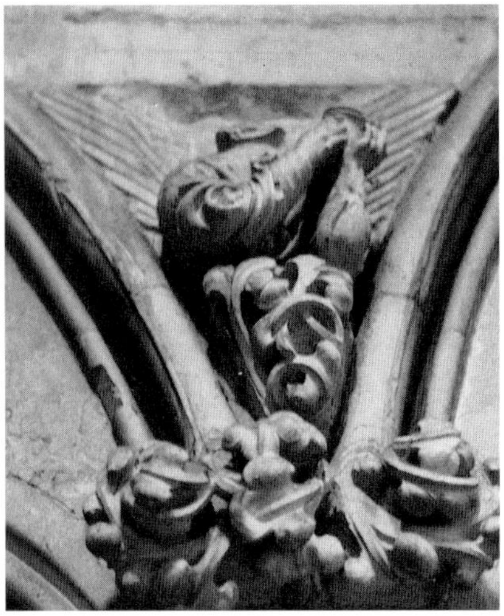

58 Original angel; south-east transept

north-west corner it transposes so that on the north transept east wall the lower trefoil arches are behind the higher plain ones and only blank wall is visible in the spandrel openings. The viewer's justified expectations have been contradicted; one feels that the designer was teasing his audience. These openings were obviously an important part of the design and I will return later to their significancc. Along the north and south walls of the choir the spandrel openings are filled with carved figures. These, however, are not original.[123] It seems that these openings were intended to be like those in the south west transept, allowing a view of the tops of the back arches.

At the east end of each of these walls is an elaborate pier which was originally free-standing although now abutted by later walling. These piers are extraordinarily elaborate and they incorporate rows of stone crockets which seem to sprout from their core. The sprouts are of a form which is found in contemporary manuscript paintings of the cross as the Tree of Life[124] which symbolise the life-giving fruitfulness of Christ's death on the cross and subsequent resurrection. They may also recall the palm trees with which the 'holy of holies' in the Old Testament Temple was decorated. An even more suggestive comparison is with St John's vision of the river of life: 'And he showed me a pure river of water of life, clear as crystal, proceeding out of the throne of God and of the Lamb. In the midst of the street of it, and on either side of the river, was there a tree of life...' (Revelation 22: 1–2). The altar in the midst of a church represents the throne of God and the presence of Christ, the Lamb. These piers, which will have been much more visible when they were free-standing, marked the entrance to the sanctuary of the cathedral.[125]

If we think away the spandrel angels in the aisles and imagine these elaborate piers as standing alone our walk through this part of the building will provide a gradual sense of approaching the Sacred. In the west transept and the aisles the design is quite austere but as we reach the eastern transept the space opens out, marked by the special piers, and there are carvings of angels on the walls.[126] The form of the piers and the angels are reminders that we have drawn near to the altar, the place of meeting with God.

opposite, from top to bottom

59 Quatrefoil on choirstalls; fox preaching to birds
60 Misericord on choirstalls; knight fighting griffin
61 Quatrefoil on choirstalls; green man

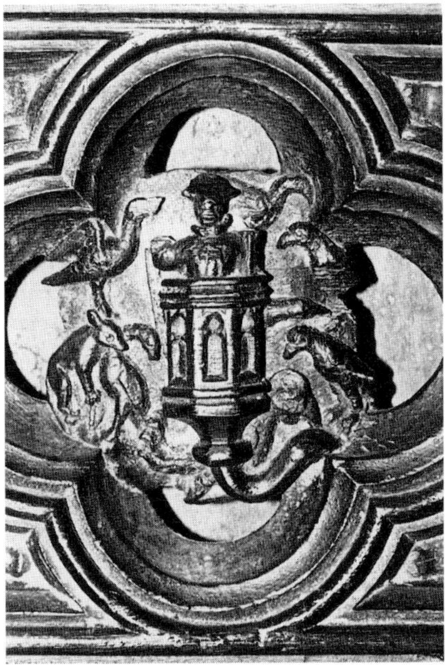

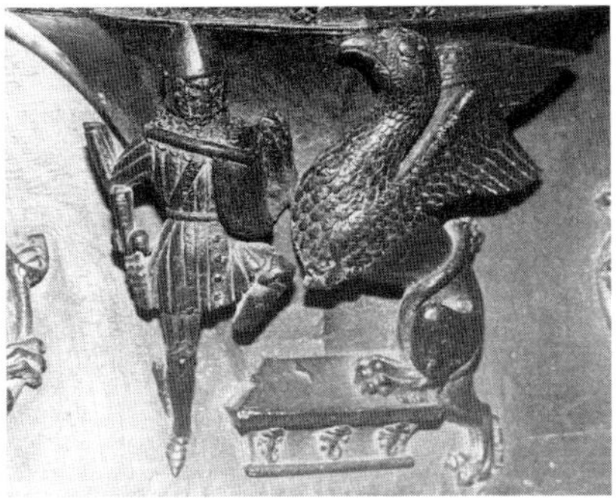

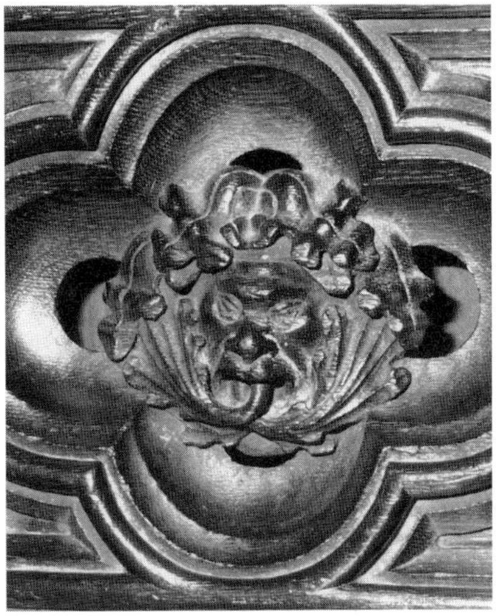

The architecture has led us beyond itself by a gradual movement, a crescendo of beauty and of human symbols: the affirmative way. Those who stay with or return to the building may be led into a rather different experience. Sustained attention to St Hugh's Choir brings into focus its more eccentric features. Its beauty can seem to be undermined by the asymmetries; the solidity of the building can seem to be denied by the way the arcading is scooped out of the wall; the designer seems to be deliberately teasing the beholder with effects such as the crazy vault and the arcading that sometimes does and sometimes does not show the tops of the back arches.

When this aspect of the design becomes dominant one feels wrong-footed: the movement through human artifacts to the Divine is contradicted and there is a need to rethink. This represents the negative way, denying any simple equation of the divine with the perfection of human concepts or artefacts. This stage of uncertainty tends to be resolved by the recognition that the beauty of the building can contain and even be enriched by the seeming imperfections. One's experience of the Divine has been extended to encompass what originally seemed incompatible with it.

Lining the western bays of St Hugh's choir are the magnificent seats for the clergy and choir, dating from around 1370.[127] There is so far no detailed study of the meaning of the carvings on these stalls[128] but it is quite likely that they were originally intended to convey, if not a theological then a moral message. Among the images are, on the outer desk fronts, musician angels and kings. On the inner fronts are various figures, some comic. They include St George and the dragon, a bear with a sore head, a fox with a bird in its mouth, a bat-winged devil and a snail eating a leaf together with various lions and dragons. Among the misericords are religious scenes, including the Resurrection of Christ, and others which may represent vices; the tumbling knight flanked by dragons seems to represent Pride taking a fall.

The Easter Sepulchre: On the third day He rose again

Inside the sanctuary area on the north side is the so-called Easter Sepulchre, added about 1300. Structures representing the tomb of Christ were built in churches from the ninth century, if not earlier.[129] They were used during the Easter services as the focus, or stage prop, for acting out the burial of Christ on Good Friday and then the visit of the three Maries to the tomb on Easter Sunday morning (Mt. 27:57–28:8). There is evidence that such a play was enacted at Lincoln from the twelfth century onwards.[130] These short dramatic sequences, especially when they were in English rather than Latin,[131] were intended to make real for ordinary people the basic facts of their faith. In the vast majority of churches a temporary structure was all that was needed or provided for this purpose. Such structures would be stored away for most of the year, to be brought out and erected for the ceremonies of Holy Week and Easter.

The Lincoln example is unusual both in being a permanent part of the presbytery and in its position. Set, as it is, in the closed-off part of the church reserved for the clergy, it can hardly have been meant as a teaching aid for lay folk. Veronica Sekules has suggested another, related, purpose for which it may have been built: as a Sacrament shrine.[132] The consecrated wafer which was understood to be the body of Christ had from early times been kept reserved within the church building. It was available to be taken for the sick

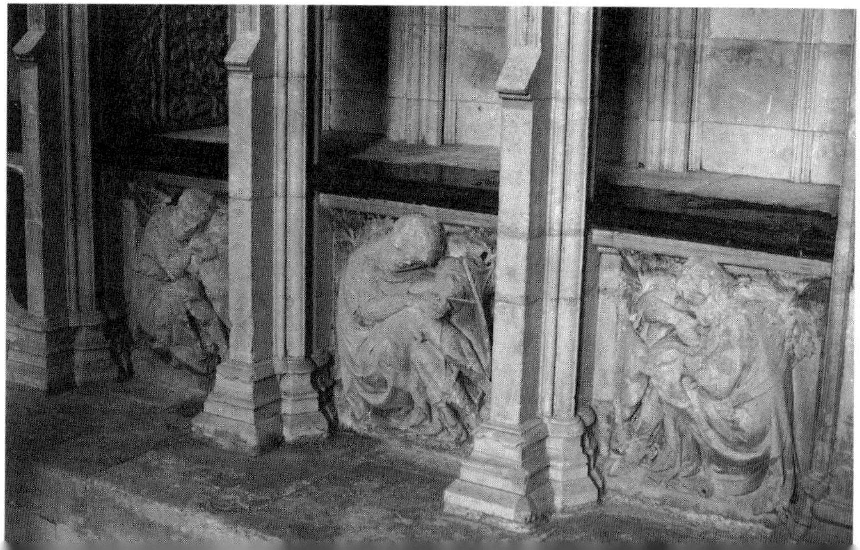

62 *Easter Sepulchre*; sleeping guards

or dying who could not attend services. From the twelfth century it became a focus of prayer for anyone entering the church out of service time.[133] Gradually, devotion to the Blessed Sacrament took on greater importance as the doctrine of transubstantiation was accepted. According to this doctrine the elements consecrated during the Mass were not merely tokens or signs but had undergone a change of substance, becoming actually the body and blood of Christ although their outer appearances remained those of bread and wine. The special feast day, Corpus Christi, was initiated in the second half of the thirteenth century and was celebrated throughout Western Christendom by the middle of the fourteenth century.[134]

A replica of the tomb in which the body of the dead Christ was briefly laid to rest could easily be regarded as an apt place to reserve his sacramental body; it seems that the Lincoln Easter Sepulchre may well have been used for this purpose. It certainly inspired copies, a number of which have survived in good condition. Those at Heckington, Navenby (Lincs), Hawton, Sibthorpe (Notts) and Patrington (Yorks) share a range of features with the Lincoln example. All have some sculpture relating the Easter story; all are situated next to or near a tomb of similar style and date (at Lincoln what seems most likely to be the tomb of bishop Remigius); and all but Lincoln incorporate an aumbry for reservation of the Sacrament.

At Lincoln the sleeping soldiers are depicted on the base. The plain ashlar back wall of the Sepulchre does not look original and it is possible that, like the other examples, it once had more sculpture and an aumbry set there. So it is worth visiting at least one of these parish churches to compare its Easter sepulchre with that at Lincoln. Hawton has the most elaborate: as at Lincoln, the sleeping soldiers occupy the base. Interestingly, their shields are carved with devilish faces, the heraldry of Satan, in whose service they are thus shown to be.[135] Such imagery was a way of giving vent to anger at the misuse of secular power; the soldiers in the Mystery Plays are often portrayed as bullies and oppressors of the poor and innocent.[136] Beside the aumbry above the soldiers are the three Maries visiting the tomb, the angel greeting them and the resurrected Christ appearing to Mary Magdalene; above the canopy at the top of the monument is represented the Ascension. These complex images of the death, burial and resurrection of Christ displayed the significance of the sacramental bread consecrated each day during the Mass (the Host) and always present contained, if not within the structure itself, then somewhere nearby in the chancel of the church.

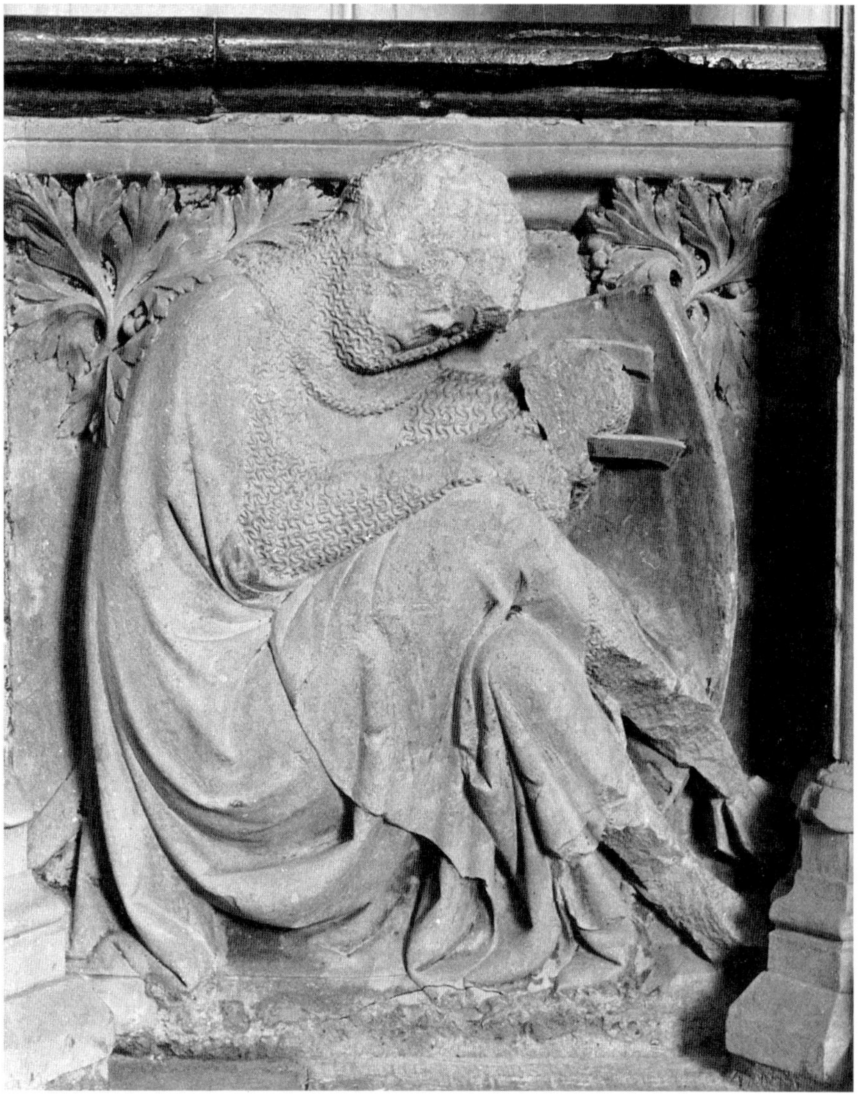

63 Sleeping guard

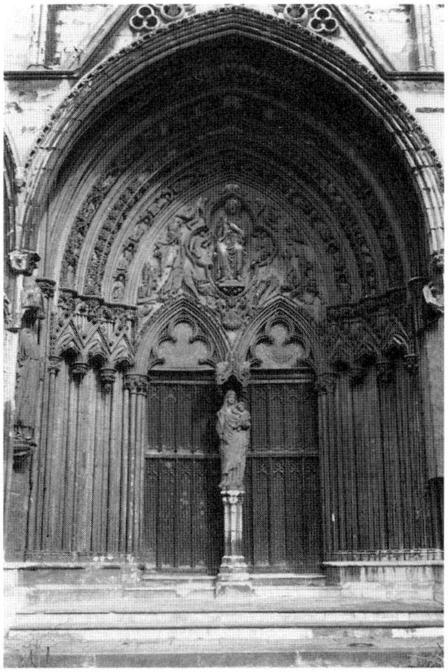

64 Judgement Portal

The Judgement Porch: Blessed are they that keep His commandments

The east end of St Hugh's Choir was replaced between 1256 and 1280 by the so-called Angel Choir. This was built to increase the accommodation behind the altar, where the shrine of the saint was placed. Since pilgrims would come to pray at the shrine, perhaps in large numbers, easy access was required. So this part of the building was given its own entrance, the south or Judgement Porch, in order to allow direct access to the shrine without the need for visitors to move through the nave and choir aisles. In order to understand the meanings of this part of the building we must start again on the outside, commencing at the Judgement Porch. This forms the transition between the outer, secular, world and the sacred space inside the cathedral just as the great west doorway does for those who enter through it into the nave.

The sculptures on the porch portray the Last Judgement, when Christ will divide those who have done good from those who have pursued evil and when all will receive the rewards due to them. At the centre of the tympanum, the arched panel immediately above the door itself, the figure of Christ is shown seated in a quatrefoil (a four-petalled frame) supported by angels. On each side within the quatrefoil is an angel with a censer sending up the sweet-smelling smoke of incense which is an appropriate offering to God, mentioned as such in the Old Testament. The censers, however, are nineteenth-century restorations as are many of the details of other figures on the tympanum. It has been suggested that originally these angels held the Instruments of the Passion. These consisted of the cross, nails, crown of thorns and other objects associated with the sufferings of Christ: motifs even more suitable to the theme of the portal.[137]

The figure of Christ holds open the side of his robe, displaying the wound in his side with his pierced hand. This signifies the Redemption achieved by the suffering, death and resurrection of Jesus. An early thirteenth-century book *The Ancrene Riwle* (Anchoresses' Rule) expresses it very movingly: 'Let His beloved see by that how He bought her love, allowing His shield to be

65 *Christ the Judge* on tympanum of Judgement Portal

pierced, His side opened, to show her His heart, to show her how completely He loved her, and to win her own heart.'[138] It is from this side that the water and the blood flowed, the water to wash away the sins of humanity, the blood to feed them in the Eucharist.[139]

It is interesting that this passage refers to the heart of Jesus, since the carving on the tympanum shows the wound as in his right side. gothic art is sometimes described as 'realistic' and this description has something to recommend it. If we compare the Lincoln tympanum with that of the Romanesque 'Prior's door' at Ely it is clear that the figures on the latter are more distorted; the sculptor's interest was in the expressiveness of his composition rather than in having the figures look like 'real people'. But gothic realism was

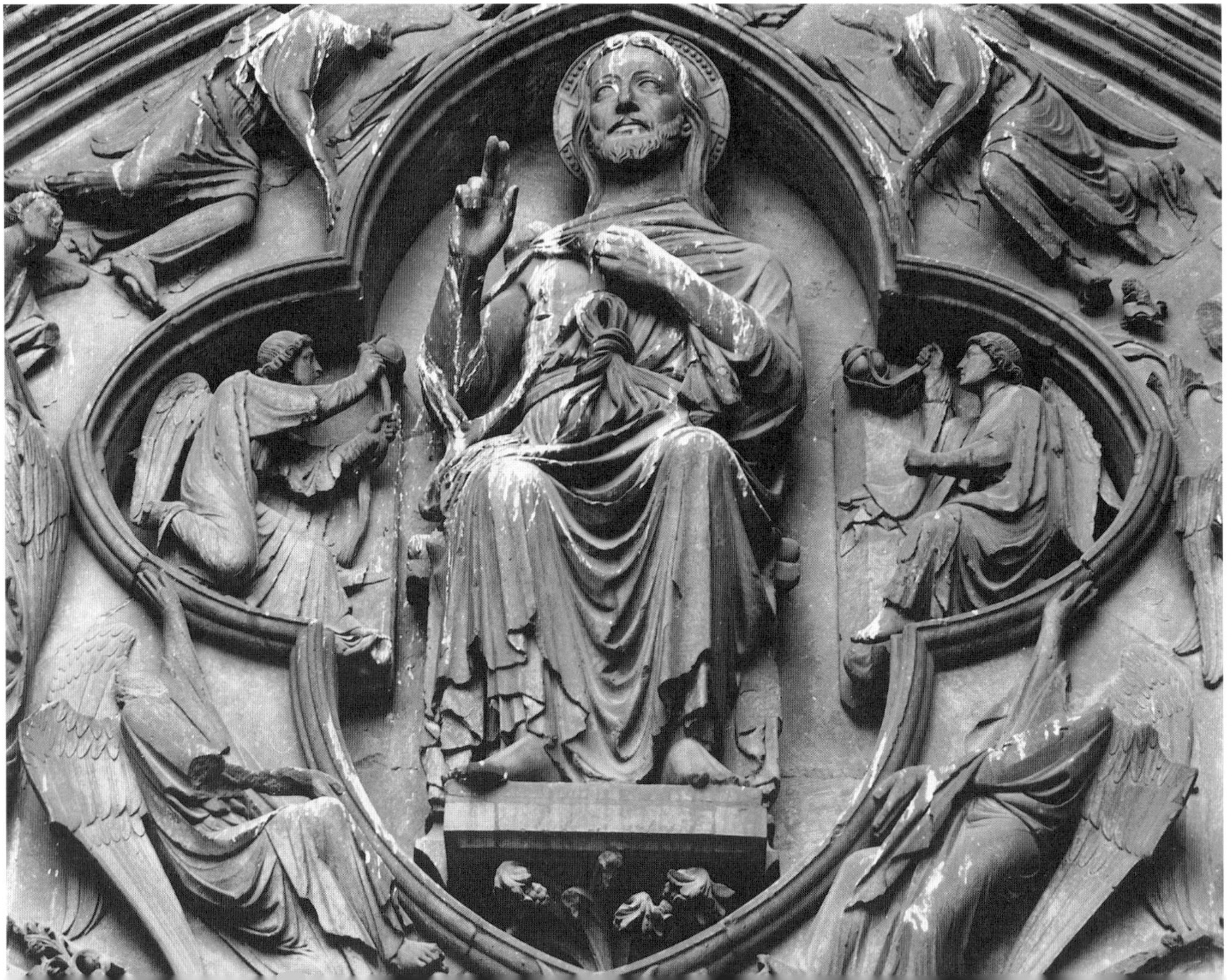

66 Ely cathedral, Prior's Door tympanum with figure of Christ

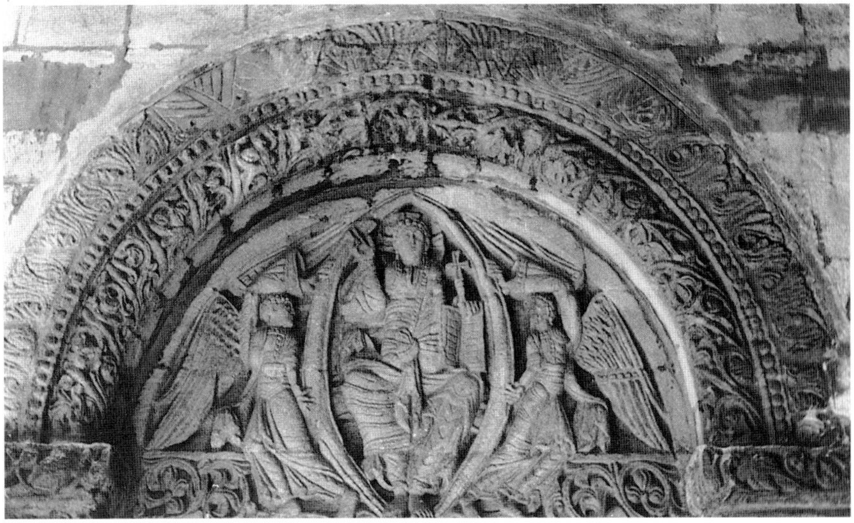

always moderated by symbolic meanings and the wound in Christ's side is an example of this.

The relevant Gospel passage (John 20:34) does not mention which side was pierced. Since the heart was thought to be the seat of compassion the wound in the side was taken as the touching of the deepest feelings of the incarnate God. But the body of Christ was also the new Temple ('Destroy this Temple' he had prophesied, 'and in three days I will raise it up.' John 2:19) seen by the prophet Ezekiel (Ezekiel 47:1 'I saw the waters flowing down onto the right side of the Temple').[140] Since the water flowed onto

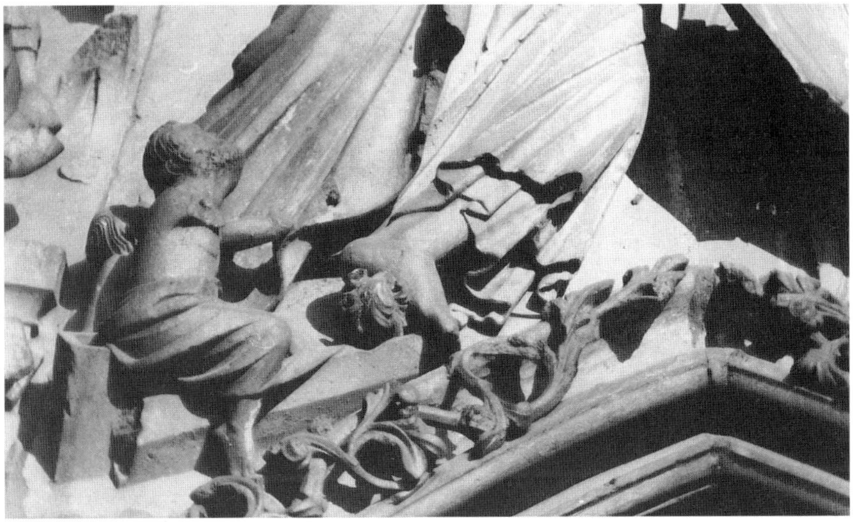

67 Man rising from grave

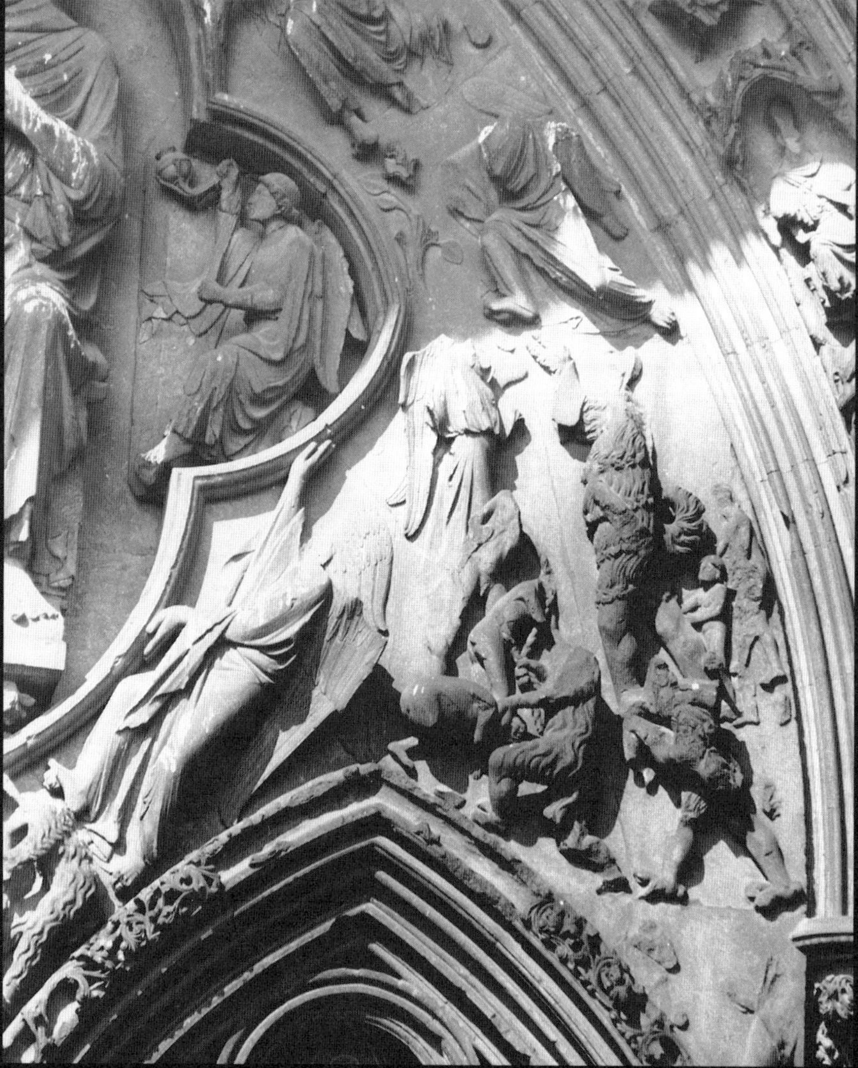

68 Devils taking the wicked to Hell, on tympanum of Judgement Portal

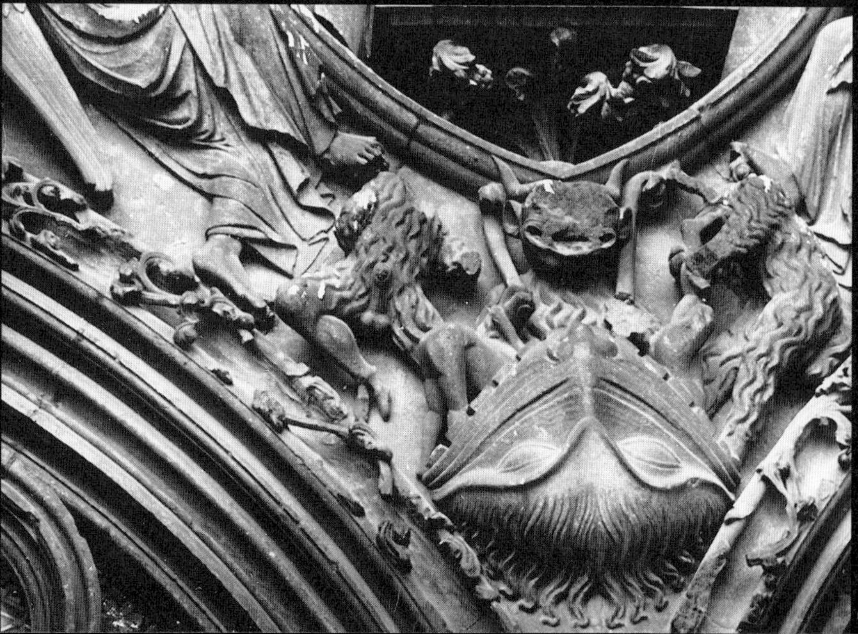

69 ***The Mouth of Hell***

the right side of the Temple, the water and blood which flowed from the side of Christ should also issue from his right. In all representations of the crucified Christ throughout the Middle Ages the wound is shown on the right side, to emphasise the prophetic, biblical meaning of his sufferings and as a reminder of how the Old Testament foreshadowed the Christian sacraments.[141]

Under his feet are the Jaws of Hell like those in the death of Dives and Lazarus panel on the west front. Portraying Hell in this way as a monstrous mouth seems to have been a typically English motif. It is a vivid expression of overwhelming force; a powerful sign of the violence and destructiveness of evil.[142] On the Judgement Porch at Christ's left, or sinister, side are the wicked being grabbed and pushed down towards Hell-mouth by fiercely energetic devils. On His right at the bottom are people arising from their graves, while above them the virtuous are guided upward by angels.

Christian theology has for centuries tried to find ways of expressing effectively two seemingly incompatible doctrines: God's perfect justice and his mercy. Justice requires a hatred of wickedness and determination to eliminate evil. Mercy remits the punishment earned by the sinful. The Church has always held these together by distinguishing between the evil deed and the evil-doer. God hates the evil deed but will extend his mercy to those who turn away from their wickedness. Although the human race suffers from an inherited tendency to sin, Christ, by his death and resurrection, has overcome the power of evil. As a fourteenth-century lyric has Christ say:

> The spear has smitten my heart in two
> For love of thee my blood is spilt
> If thou wilt from thy sinning go
> My mercy is ready when thou wilt.[143]

The Judgement Portal tympanum portrays the just and merciful God of Christian belief. It was intended, as were the sculptures on the west front, to remind visitors of the seriousness of their moral choices. That such sculptures were used for instructive purpose is made clear in the story of the life of St Hugh, who reprimanded John Lackland for his misbehaviour by drawing his attention to just such a representation of the Last Judgement.[144]

T. A. Heslop[145] has pointed out that in this sculpture the normal symbolism of direction has had to be modified, as it seems to have been in the north passageway of Exchequer Gate. Here on the tympanum of the Judgement Porch there is a clash between the east–west direction, west being more secular and east more sacred, and the right and left hands of Christ which symbolise respectively Heaven and Hell. Because the porch is on the south side of the building his right hand is to the west and his left to the east. So the designer has partially resolved this clash by putting Hell's Mouth under his feet and having the blessed at his right side guided upward to heaven by angels. An upward-downward symbolism is substituted for that of east–west, and this symbolism is continued by the figures in the voussoirs (the carved stones around the curve of the arch) of the doorway.[146]

These form three concentric carved bands: on the inner and outer arches are sculpted figures, the middle arch consists of a roll of open-work foliage. To the right of Christ on the outer arch are female figures, four wise and four foolish virgins. According to such theologians as Hugh of St Victor the maidens represent all of humanity waiting for the Last Days. The wise virgins hold their full

70 Female saint
71 Foolish virgin on arch of Judgement Portal
72 Patriarchs

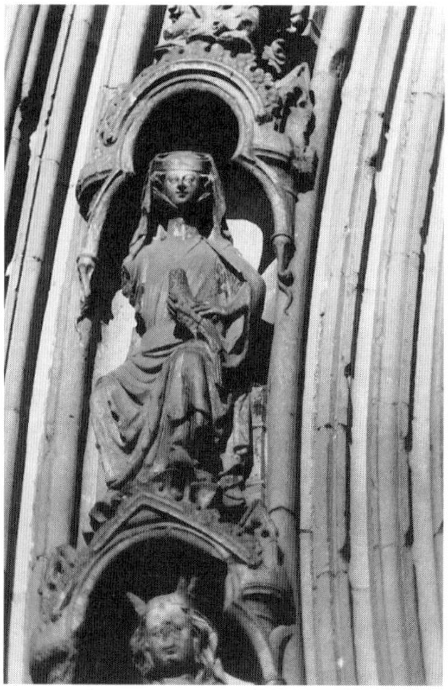

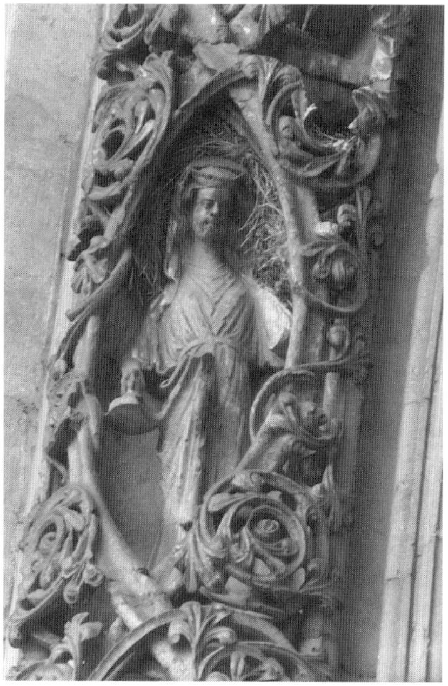

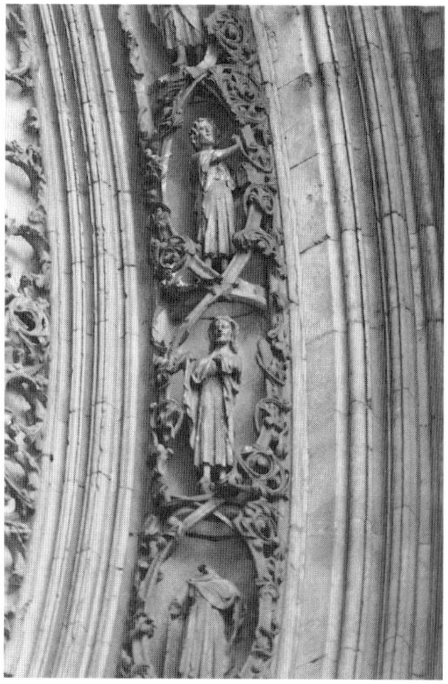

lamps upright; they are the ones who had kept the flame of charity burning and they symbolise the Elect who will be rewarded in heaven. The foolish virgins carry their empty lamps upside down, showing that they let their lamps go out; they symbolise the Damned who do good works only out of pride and for the sake of earthly reputation.[147] On the west doorways of French churches the wise virgins are shown on the right hand of Christ, the foolish on the left. Here at Lincoln the wise are placed above the foolish.[148]

To Christ's left are eight standing, bearded male figures, in interestingly varied postures. All of them grasp, or seem to have grasped, the vine which is entwined around them. All of them seem to have originally carried books, of which some remain. According to Lethaby[149] they represent either prophets or apostles; he suggests that they are almost certainly the latter. But since the apostles are generally shown as the twelve this does not seem very likely. Their grasp of the vine probably provides the key to their significance. The other figures, both male and female, are surrounded by the vine and foliage decoration but do not touch it. Grasping the vine brings the standing males into a different relation with it. For them it is not a mere decoration; so the gesture might be meant to mark them as the ancestors of Christ, inhabitants of the 'Tree of Jesse'. The Tree of Jesse represented the genealogy of Christ, given in the Gospels and related to the prophecy in the Old Testament book of Isaiah: 'And there shall come forth a rod out of the stem of Jesse, and a branch shall grow out of his roots...' (Is.11:1) This was understood as forecasting the birth of Christ from the Virgin Mary and was frequently illustrated as a tree or vine growing from a recumbent figure of Jesse, with his descendants depicted on the branches and Mary and Christ at the top.[150]

On the inner arch are, to the left six women some of whom are crowned and, to the right six kings. Lethaby suggests that the women represent queens and Virgins (i.e. virgin saints) and the men are king-martyrs of England. It may be so but there seems insufficient evidence at present to be sure of their significance. What is of significance is the placing of female figures to the right of Christ and of male figures to his left. In scenes of the crucifixion, such as that in the north passage of Exchequer Gate, Christ is

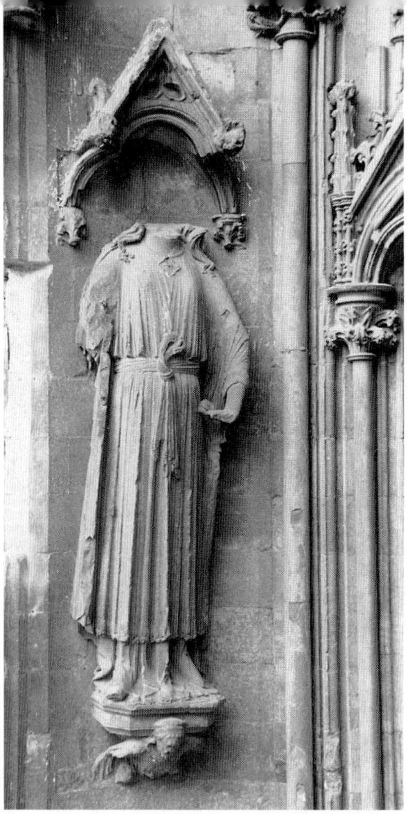

73 Synagogue, on west side of Judgement Portal
74 Church, on east side of Judgement Portal

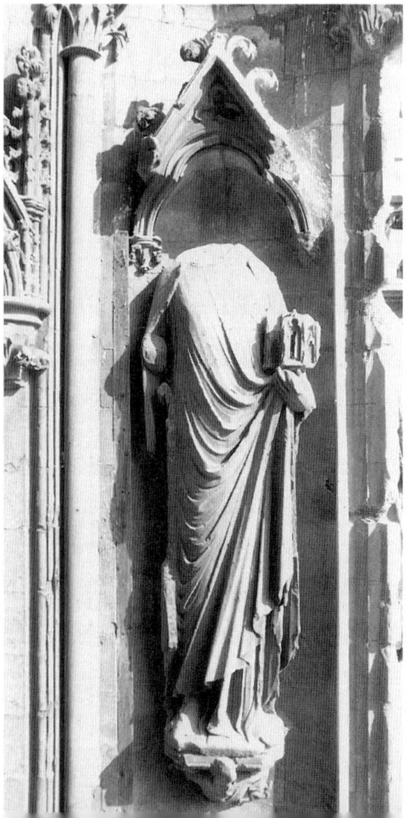

flanked by two figures: Mary on his right and John on his left. In churches and nunneries women often took their place on the north side. This placed them at the right hand of the figure of Christ on the great crucifix, which looked westwards down into the nave of every church from a position above the entrance to the sanctuary.[151]

To either side of the doorway stand the figures of Church and Synagogue, represented as beautiful women. Church will originally have been crowned, looking toward Christ; Synagogue was shown blindfold and looking downwards away from Christ to show that the people of the Old Law did not recognise Christ as the fulfilment of that Law. Church is on Christ's left hand, Synagogue on his right even though that places the latter on the 'holier' side. Her place to the west of Christ, her attitude of turning away and looking down show that, while the normal east–west symbolism is operative, the placing on the right hand of Christ does not have its usual significance.

Between Church and Synagogue, on the trumeau (door post) between the two doors, stands the Virgin Mary holding the child Jesus.[152] Mary is the patron of this church as well as symbolising in herself the Church. In her Christ received human flesh, becoming the brother of all people. It was her response of active obedience ('And Mary said, Behold the handmaid of the Lord; be it unto me according to thy word.' Luke 1:38) which enabled the process of redemption to begin.

All of these carvings around the entrance are meant to prepare those entering for an experience of ultimate realities, both here and in heaven. 'The City of God ... lies not beyond these doors, but beyond the limit of time, encompassed only by the wisdom of God. Yet the living man who enters here may experience, if he has the imagination for it, what it means to pass from profane to sacred, from self to love, from Satan to Christ, from the City of Man to the City of God.'[153]

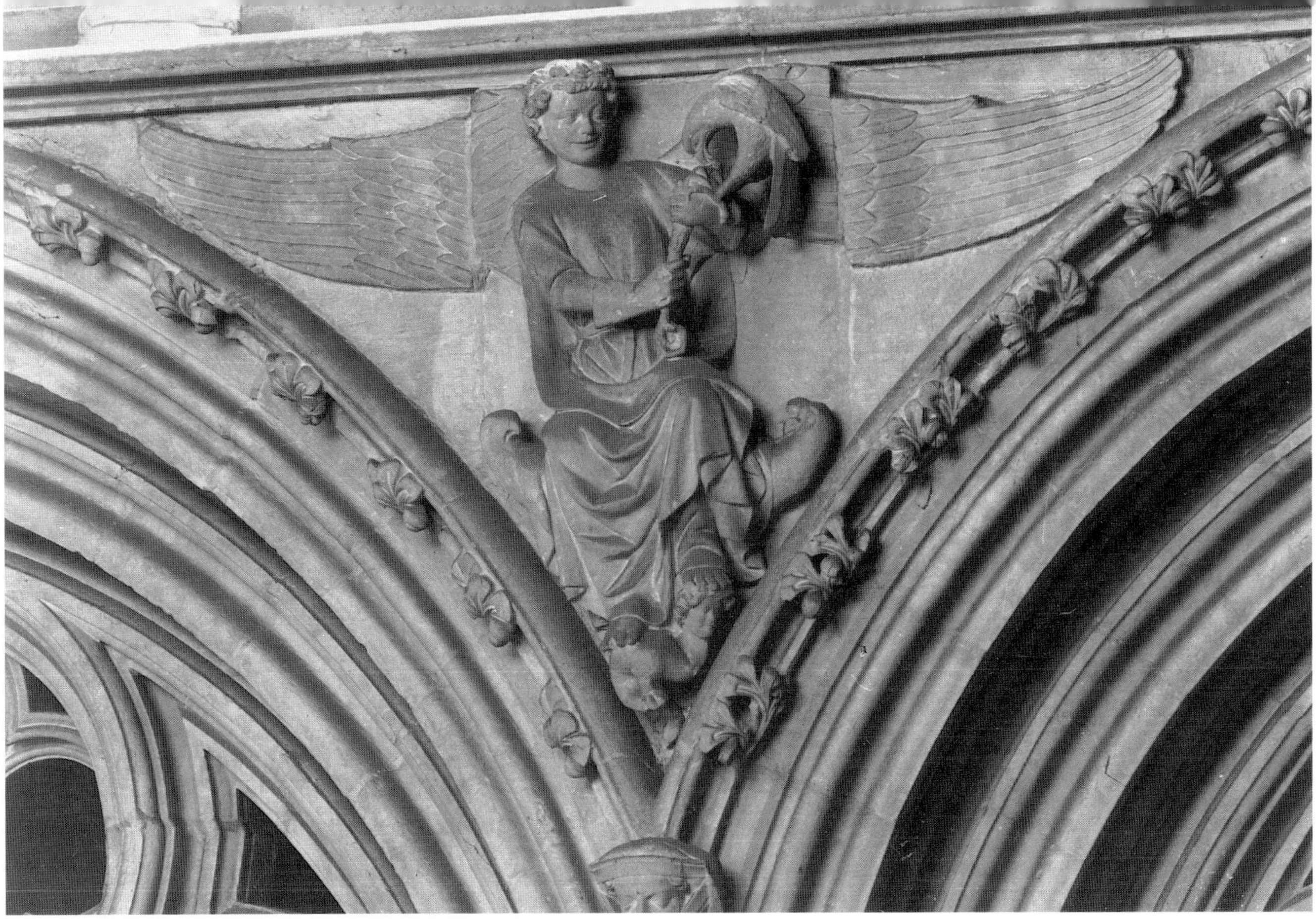

75 Angel with bird and lure. Angel Choir triforium

The Angel Choir: With Angels and Archangels

Within the Angel Choir the east–west symbolism is reasserted. In the south aisle, immediately inside the entrance, are figured vault bosses. To the west of the doorway are dragons, monsters and humans in combat. To the east the bosses are carved with aspects of the story of Redemption; among them are the Coronation of the Virgin and King David in the Tree of Jesse. King David was the best-loved of the ancestors of Christ, famous especially as a musician and considered to be the composer of the Book of Psalms. The Coronation of the Virgin boss shows Mary the mother of Christ in heaven being given the crown of eternal life. Mary stood for the Church and so this scene represents the final joy in heaven of all faithful Christians and the completion of God's purposes in creation and redemption. As Georges Duby puts it: 'the scholars considered her the symbol of the New Testament and the fulfillment of the Old. In her person mankind was united with God, the soul was mystically wed to its creator. Mary was the concrete image of the assembled body of the Church...'.[154] Her crowning thus was symbolic of the Church's final triumph and the heavenly joys awaiting all the faithful. Although not strictly a biblical scene, it is based on the visions in the Book of Revelation of the woman who bears a male child and is threatened by the dragon. Mary was identified with this woman, who is also symbolically the Church.

Those entering through the south door would be coming to visit the shrine of St Hugh. This would have been visible as they entered, more or less directly ahead of them, set to the east of the screen behind the high altar. Above it, in the triforium (the middle storey) of the Angel Choir, are the carved angels from which it takes its name.[155] The screen in fact divides the Angel Choir into two parts. To its east are angel musicians, not so much a choir as an orchestra, together with a bearded, winged figure playing a harp generally interpreted as King David.[156] This is the holiest part of the building, representing Heaven itself where saints and angels sing praises to their God.

76 Retro-choir with musician angels in spandrels of triforium and the Shrine of St Hugh bottom right

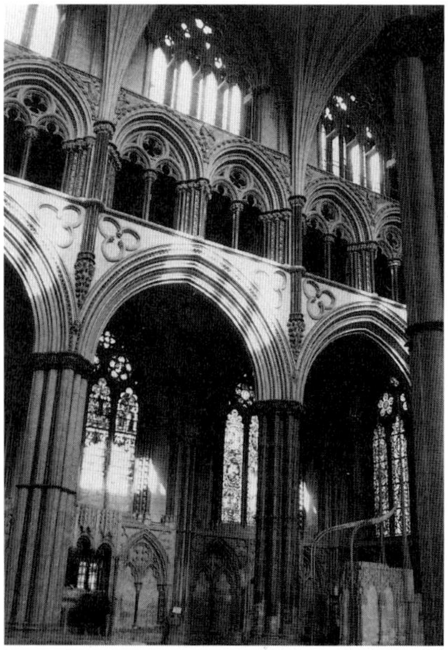

To the west the figures are not all angels and none of the angels are singing or otherwise making music, because this section represents the Last Days. The cosmic significance of the human pilgrimage is represented by an angel on the north side holding up the sun and moon. The inevitability of judgement is shown by an angel with scales (probably St Michael who weighs each person's good and bad deeds) and by two angels on opposite sides of the westernmost bay. The image of Michael the archangel weighing souls at the Last Day is a quaint medieval image but it was not simply a whimsical idea. It, like so much of the imagery in the cathedral, is scripturally based. For instance Psalm 62:9 speaks of the wicked: '...laid in the balance, they are altogether lighter than vanity.' And in the book of Daniel, Daniel says to Belshazzar, interpreting the writing on the wall: 'Thou art weighed in the balances and art found wanting.' (Dan. 5:27)

On the south side of the Choir an angel carries a soul to Heaven; on the north, an angel brandishing a sword pushes two towards

77 Christ showing his wounds; angel presenting a soul to him. Angel Choir triforium

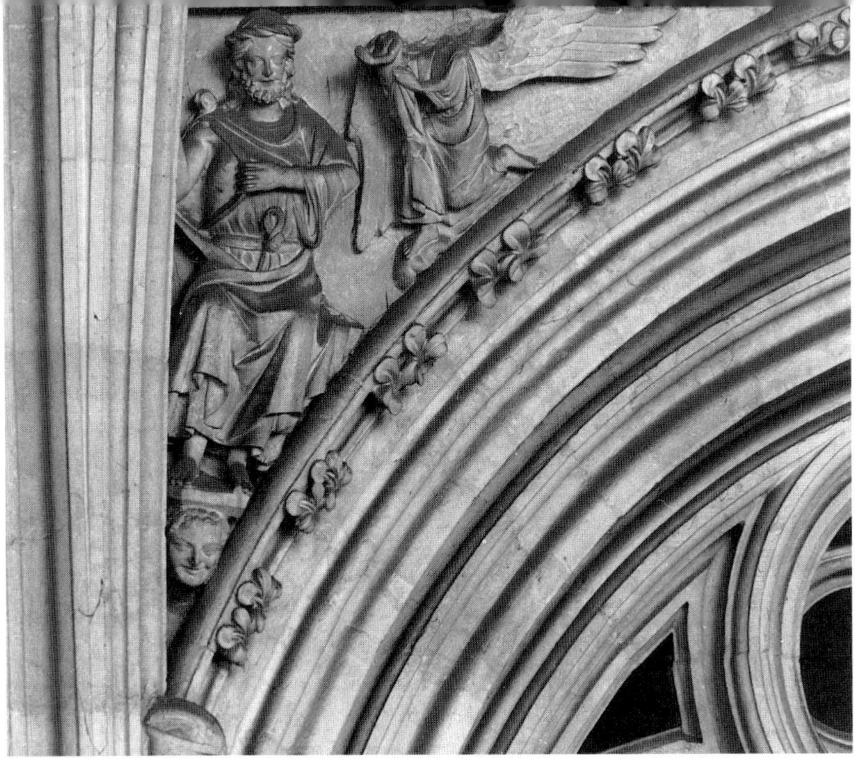

Hell. The latter scene is very similar to representations of the Expulsion of Adam and Eve from Paradise, an apt comparison since it was their defection that brought sin into human life.

But the Last Judgement is not simply about human merit; more important is the redemptive work of Christ. It is only through faith in Him that human beings become able to act well. So in this area are also the figures of Christ showing his wounds and an angel feeding a bird with raw meat. Christ's wounds are the vehicles of redemption, the signs of his victory over all the powers of evil and reminders of His unchanging love for humankind. They, together with the 'Instruments of the Passion' held by two of the angels, were a popular focus of meditation in the late Middle Ages and their theological significance was widely understood.[157] To quote again from *The Ancrene Riwle:* '"Can a mother", He says, "forget her child?" And even if she should, I can never forget you – and then He gives the reason ... "I have painted you," He says, "in my hands." This He did with red blood, upon the cross. People tie knots in their belts to remind them about things, but our Lord, because He wished never to forget us, put marks of piercing in both His hands, to remind Him of us.'[158] In response to this, human art is used to paint and engrave the Christian message as a reminder of

Christ's redeeming work.[159] The meaning of this devotion was evident to the Wesleys, who use it in some of their hymns; the most well-known example is probably that in the hymn, 'Lo! He Comes', in which Charles Wesley wrote: 'With what rapture/ Gaze we on those glorious scars!'[160]

The angel with the bird is more enigmatic. Hunting with a trained bird of prey, such as a falcon, was a fashionable pastime for the medieval upper classes. It seems that when a trained bird would not return to the falconer's hand he would hold out a lure of raw meat for which it would return. This image was used in the thirteenth century by Dante: 'Like the falcon, that first gazes at his feet, then turns at the call, and spreads his wings with desire of the repast which draws him there, such I became...'.[161] By the fifteenth century, if not before, it was being used as an example by preachers in England.[162]

Just as the falconer lures his bird, so Christ offers his own flesh, in the Eucharist, to draw straying sinners back to their true home in God. It is fitting that this image is close to the High Altar where the Eucharist is celebrated and to the Easter Sepulchre where the Host, the body of Christ, was probably kept.

In discussing the tympanum of the Judgement Porch it was

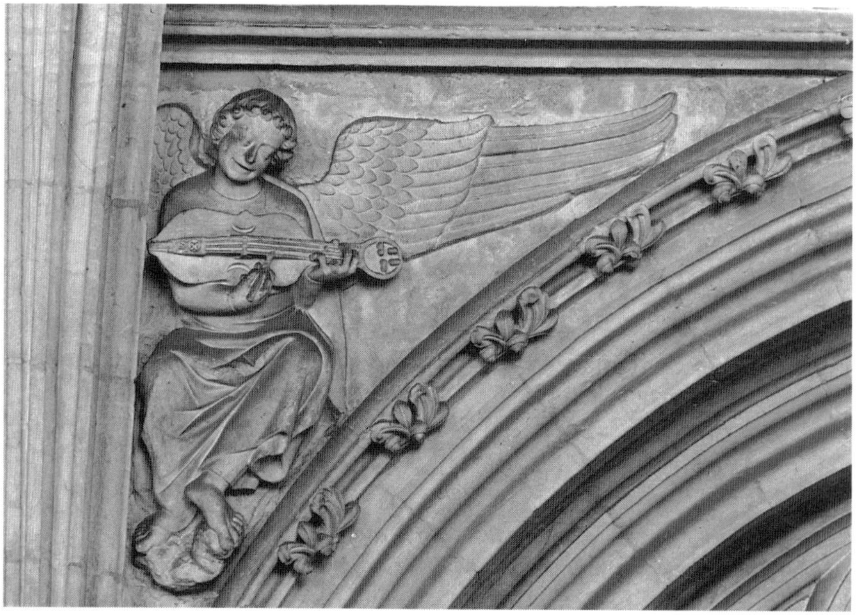

78 Angel playing gittern

noted that the angels flanking Christ would originally have carried the Instruments of the Passion and, as we have seen, these are also carried by angels in the Angel Choir. A further use of them can be seen on the putative shrine of St Hugh. Carved around the top of this structure are small angels together with heraldic shields. These show, not the coats of arms of earthly families, but the heraldry of Christ. Some of the earliest blazons on shields are said to have represented objects related to some courageous act of the knight in battle; these were known as his 'achievements'. Throughout the later Middle Ages, as indeed later, there was much interest in chivalry. Stories of heroic deeds were very popular among all classes of society. Since Christ's redemption of humankind was the greatest of all deeds it came to be sung in similar style to the popular chivalric romances.[163] Christ was portrayed as a lover-knight who battled with the Devil to save the human soul.[164] 'As a valiant warrior You robbed hell and led out Your dear love, that is to say: man's soul, to your bright bower, full of all bliss, to live in Your embrace always without end.'[165] Those objects that were instrumental in his suffering and death became his 'achievements', were shown on shields and were used as a focus for meditation upon his Passion.[166] They were also worn by people wishing to show their allegiance to Christ rather than, as with the soldiers at his tomb, to the Devil.

79 Instruments of the Passion: nails, spear and sponge

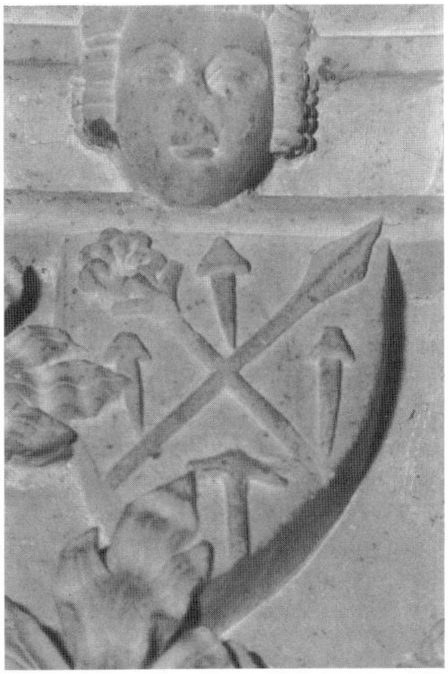

Another of the images in this part of the triforium is the Virgin and Child which encapsulates the doctrine of the Incarnation, God taking on human form. The couple are censed by an angel, for this child is both human and divine, and Mary offers the child her breast. This quintessentially maternal gesture was understood as a token of intercession. Mary is often shown in representations of the Last Judgement baring her breast before Christ the Judge as if reminding her son of his humanity which needed the nurture of her body. Just as she cared for Him so she cares for all of sinful humanity, pleading their cause at the last day. She is shown thus on the fourteenth-century painting over the chancel arch of Ickleton church in Cambridgeshire. It seems that the sculpture in Lincoln also carries this meaning, which fits so well the judgement theme of this western part of the Angel Choir.[167]

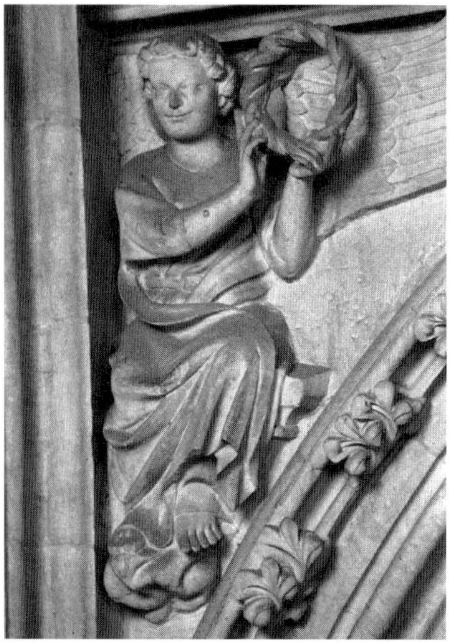

80 Angel with Crown of Thorns

The easternmost part of the Angel choir is known as the Retro-Choir because it lies behind the liturgical Choir (St Hugh's Choir) where the choir sings the services. Here the carved angels are making music, as is appropriate for the inhabitants of Heaven. How real was this sense of heavenly music can be seen from the reactions of medieval people. Margery Kempe, the fourteenth-century mystic of (Kings) Lynn, envisioned heaven as filled with music: 'On a night, as this creature lay in her bed with her husband, she heard a sound of melody so sweet and delectable, that she thought she had been in Paradise. And therewith she started out of her bed and said, "Alas, that ever I did sin! it is full merry in Heaven."'[168] In the same century, in Germany, Henry Suso experienced a joyous vision in which he was taken by angels to dance and sing with the company of Heaven the carol '*In dulci jubilo*'.[169] Such a dance was shown by Fra Angelico in a fifteenth-century painting of the Last Judgement where angels and the blessed join hands in a circle.[170]

The carvings in the Angel Choir are a reminder that the cathedral was built to be filled with music, colour and movement.[171] The stone vaults provide a fine acoustic and music was not considered merely an optional elaboration, as it unfortunately tends to be nowadays.[172] As mentioned earlier, the psalms were sung daily as the earthly Church's contribution to the heavenly music. They still are sung on most days at the Office of Evening Prayer and on Sundays also at Morning Prayer, for the Church of England's moderate reformation retained the main features of the traditional daily Office and of the Mass.[173] Richard Rolle held that this singing of the psalms was itself a means of participating in the joys of heaven while still on earth: 'The song which gives delight to hearts and instructs the soul has become a sound of singing: with angels whom we cannot hear we mingle words of praising, so that any one would be right to reckon himself exiled from true life if he does not in this way experience the delightfulness of this gift of wonderful sweetness...'.[174]

During the Eucharist, as the service moves towards its climax, the earthly choir sings 'with angels and archangels and with all the company of Heaven'. The Christian does not pray alone but together with all the faithful who have lived and died as well as with the angelic inhabitants of Heaven. On earth, as in Heaven, songs of praise are sung in honour of the goodness and faithfulness of God. And this music is the very essence of reality.[175] The orderliness of the universe, and of the human soul which reflects the universe, is a musical harmony.[176] As Shakespeare's Lorenzo expresses it:

> There's not the smallest orb which thou behold'st
> But in his motion like an angel sings,
> Still quiring to the young-eyed cherubins;
> Such harmony is in immortal souls;
> But, whilst this muddy vesture of decay
> Doth grossly close it in, we cannot hear it.[177]

While still in our earthly bodies we cannot hear the 'music of the spheres' but we are continually reminded of our small part in it by the Church's liturgy and by these carved figures decorating a part of the cathedral which represents heaven. 'If this heavenly music is indeed "real", then to share in it is not a metaphoric experience; it is rather our earthly music that is the metaphor.'[178]

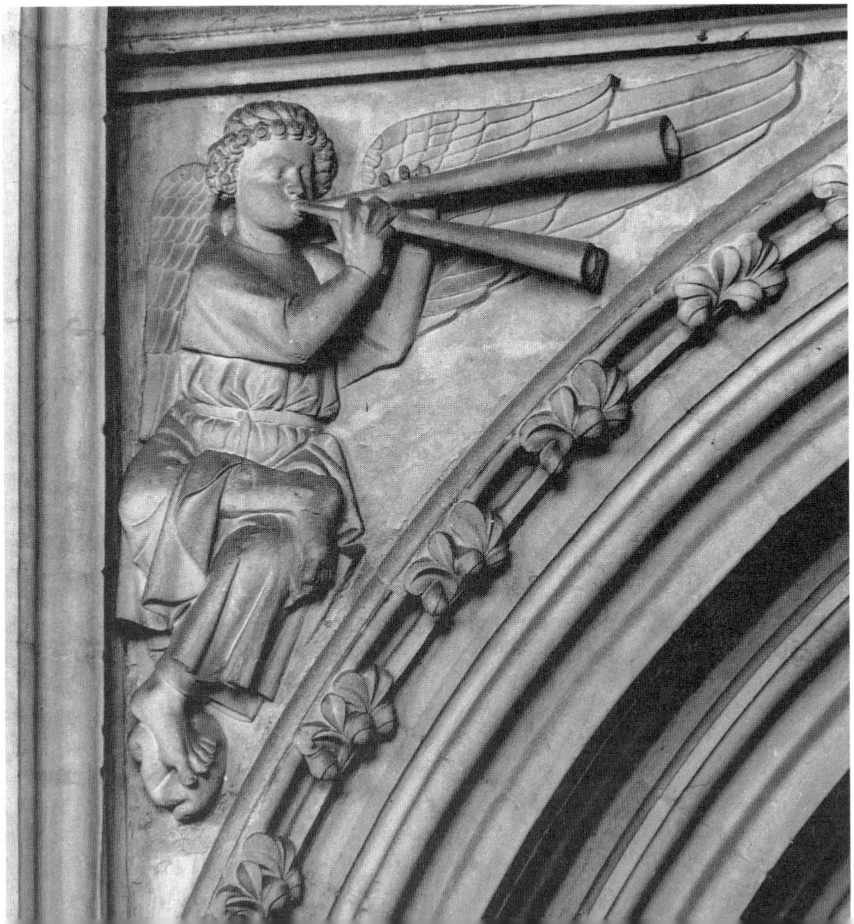

81 Angel playing pipes

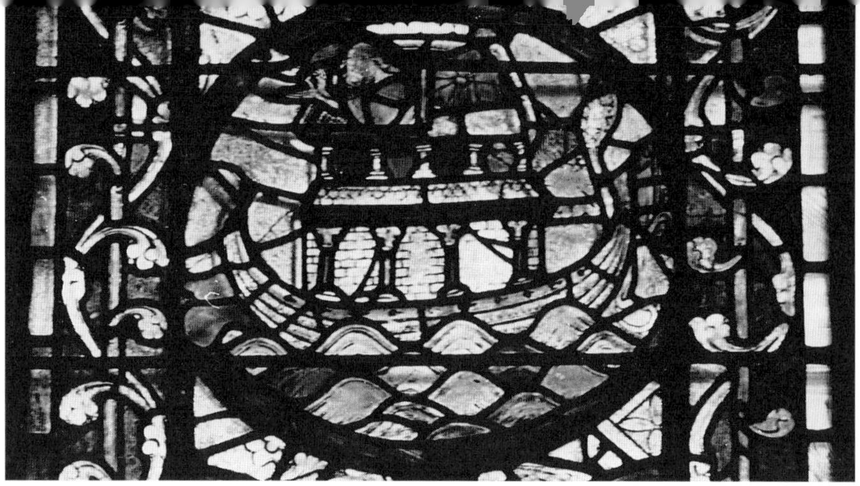

82 Noah sends forth the dove, panel in east window, south aisle

Stained glass: The Light Shone in the Darkness

Stained glass held a particularly revered place in the system of imagery within a medieval church. Light was considered the best image of God. The prevailing neo-platonist theology, transmitted by that same Dionysius whose two ways of approaching the divine were discussed in the chapter on St Hugh's Choir, drew on the theology of St John's Gospel and of the Book of Revelation for this idea: 'And the city had no need of the sun, neither of the moon, to shine in it: for the glory of God did lighten it, and the Lamb is the light thereof.' (Rev. 21:23). This view is already present in embryo in the psalms: 'in thy light shall we see light' (Ps. 36:9). Abbot Suger, of the Abbey of St Denis just outside Paris, has left us a commentary on his own newly-built (in the mid twelfth century) gothic church which emphasises this.[179] The light which comes through windows is itself akin to the divine nature. When those windows contain pictures of biblical, or other Christian, stories the message is all the more powerfully conveyed. According to Durandus: 'The glass windows in a church are Holy Scriptures, which expel the wind and the rain, that is all things hurtful, but transmit the light of the true Sun, that is, God, into the hearts of the faithful.'[180]

Lincoln retains a considerable quantity of its medieval glass, although unfortunately not much of it has remained in the situation for which it was designed.[181] The most impressive survivals are the windows in the end walls of the main, west, transept. Each wall contains a circular 'rose' window with, below it, a series of lancets. Both of the roses portray the Last Judgement. In the north rose, known as 'The Dean's Eye', the glass dates from around 1200. The south rose, known as 'The Bishop's Eye', was reconstructed, it is thought, about 1340 with the characteristic flowing tracery of that time. A verse biography of St Hugh suggests the symbolism of these two windows.[182] The Bishop's Eye looks south towards the sunlight which represents the Holy Spirit and the Dean's Eye faces the north, dark, side which symbolises the Devil. The Bishop's Eye invites the Spirit in while the Dean's Eye watches to keep the Devil at bay. This directional symbolism is both ancient and pervasive. It is present in the Bible and is one of the reasons why, in most medieval churchyards in England, parishioners preferred to be buried on the south side.[183]

The lancets below these windows contain a mixture of panels taken from various other windows, as do the windows at the east end of the south and north aisles of the Angel Choir. From a study of these panels Professor Nigel Morgan has been able to establish what kind of subjects were in many of the lost windows. It seems that by the time of the completion of the Angel Choir the entire cathedral was glazed. Many of the windows contained pictures; some were filled with grisaille, silver-grey glass with ornamental plant designs and small enlivening spots of colour. The so-called Five Sisters windows in the north-west transept of York Minster are particularly fine examples of this latter style of glass.

83 Bishop's Eye

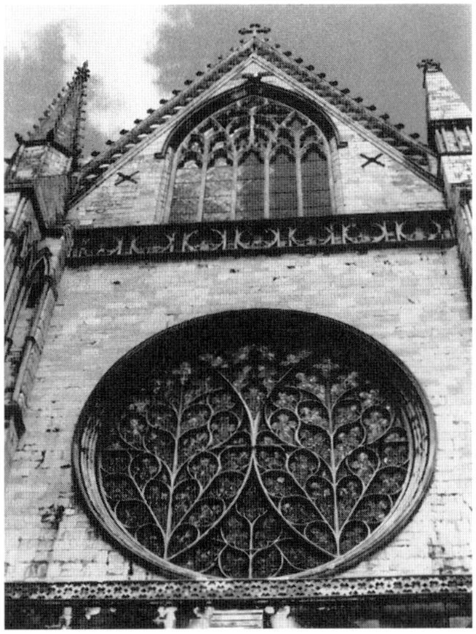

Of the pictorial windows, some will have shown scenes from the lives of the saints. The cathedral had many small chapels, in each of which the altar would have been dedicated to a particular saint. Generally the life of that saint was portrayed in a window above the altar. There survive scenes from the lives of St John the Evangelist, St Nicholas, St Denis (alias Dionysius, discussed above) and St James, each of whom had an altar in the cathedral. There are also scenes from the lives of saints to whom no altar is known to have been dedicated, such as St Etheldreda of Ely who was particularly venerated in East Anglia and the east Midlands. Also surviving are some scenes from the Old Testament, the New Testament parable of The Prodigal Son, and the legend of Theophilus who, like Faust, made a pact with the Devil but who, unlike Faust, was finally saved because of his devotion to the Virgin Mary.[184]

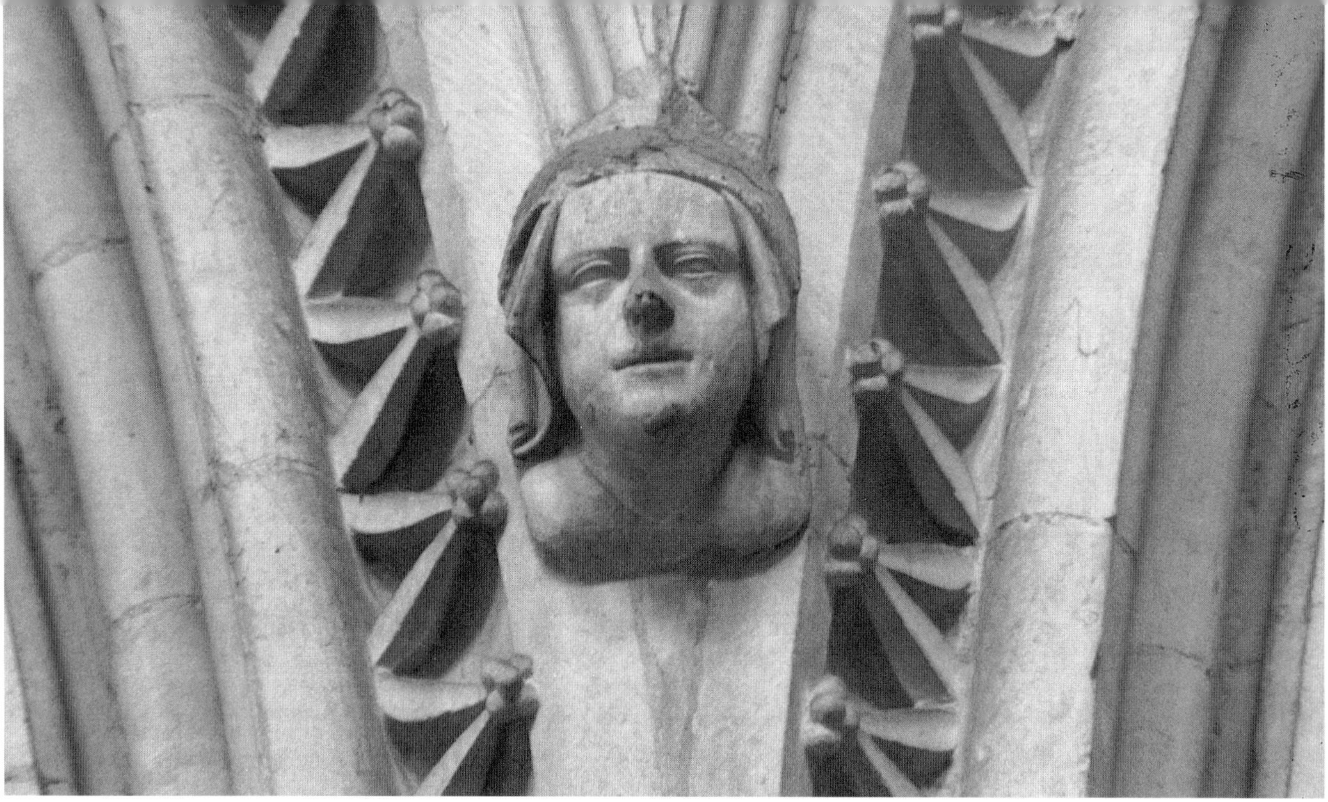

84 Head, Angel Choir

85 Head, Angel Choir

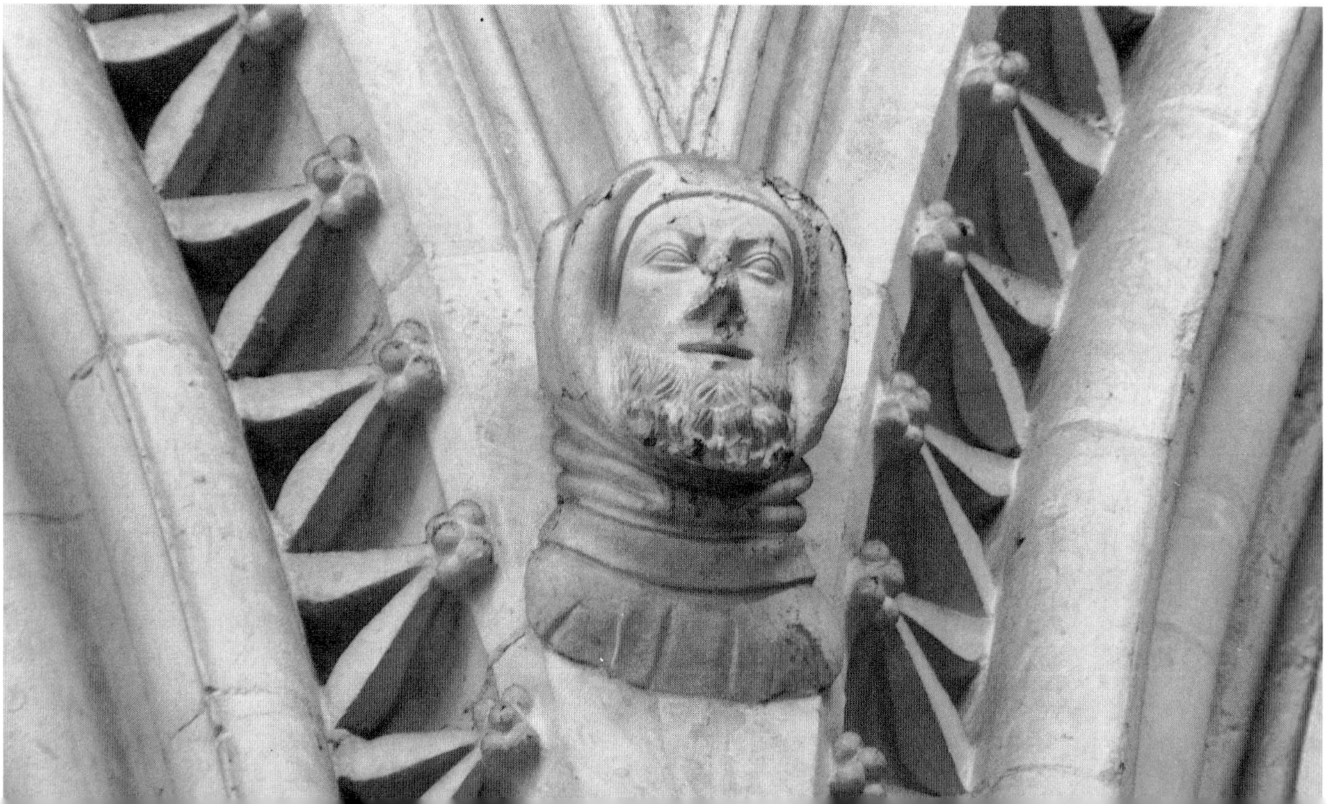

Inhabitants: The Whole Company of Earth and Heaven

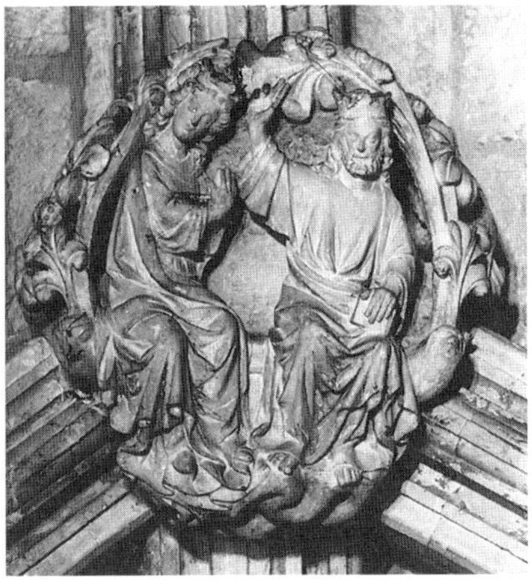

86 *Coronation of the Virgin*, boss in vault of Angel Choir, south aisle

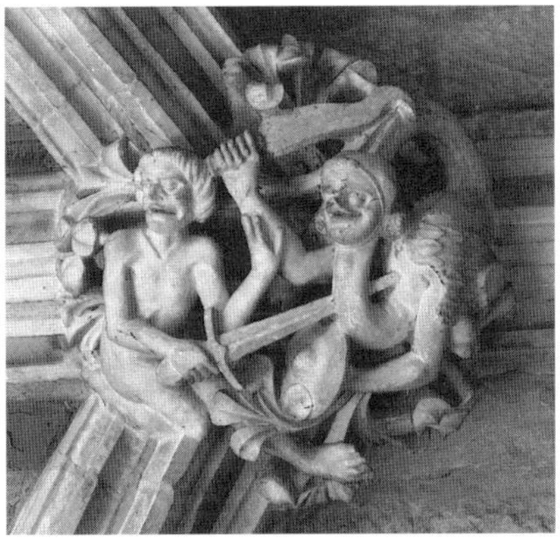

87 Man fighting monster

88 Dragons fighting

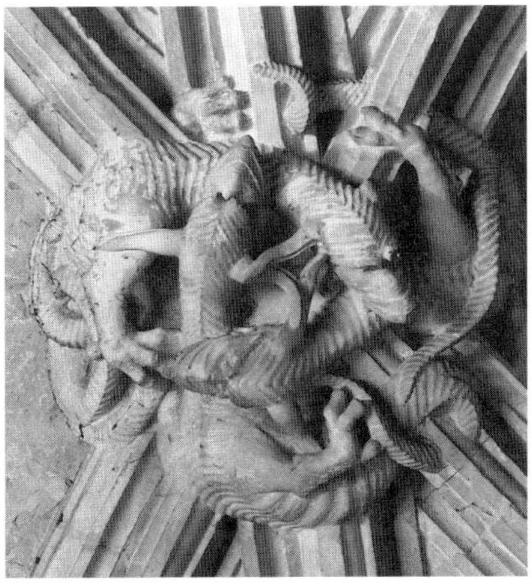

In some medieval manuscript illuminations God the creator is shown as an architect/geometer, drawing with a massive pair of compasses the outlines of the universe, as for instance in the *Holkham Bible Picture Book.*[185] According to the biblical account of the Creation (Genesis 1: 1–31), after dividing the elements and forming the world God filled it with a great variety of creatures. It seems that the human architect also expected to fill his handiwork with diverse creatures since it was to be a microcosm, an image of God's creation in all its wonderful diversity.[186]

Throughout the cathedral can be seen faces, busts and full-length human figures. This seems to be an English speciality.[187] It is not entirely clear what these represent, nor have they been thoroughly studied but there is sufficient evidence to suggest that they are not just random decoration. Salisbury cathedral has a sequence of heads so carefully arranged that it must have some significance.[188] Many cathedrals have series of kings and bishops which, as 'expressing the alliance between "regnum" and "sacerdotium" [secular and religious authority], were a commonplace in medieval art.'[189] Others may represent the inhabitants of heaven, ordinary people from all walks of life who have obtained the promised reward. In other places, such as the passage from the north-east transept to the cloister, are vigorously carved figure corbels of men holding up the shafts of the vault. They are shown in contorted poses as if the weight of the vault did indeed rest on their shoulders and represent the plight of humankind still struggling on earth, weighed down by sin and suffering.[190]

In various parts of the cathedral there are images which have a personal, private meaning for individuals. Monuments frequently proclaim the Christian faith and hopes of those who are commemorated by them. The mid fourteenth-century Fleming and Burghersh monuments on the north side of the Retro-Choir are particularly interesting examples. The Fleming monument is two-storied with, on top, an effigy of the bishop in his episcopal vestments and, behind the arcading below, his emaciated corpse in a winding-sheet. It is the earliest example in England of such a figure and, as Pevsner comments, intended to shock.[191] It might seem to twentieth-century sensibilities that this is hardly an example of Christian faith and hope. But it was meant as a reminder that all humans, including the rich and powerful, are mortal.[192] The late-medieval church encouraged people to prepare for death; to live well in order to die well and be fit for heaven. There were books explaining the art of dying (*ars moriendi*). This thought, that one should study to die well, did not fade with the end of the Middle Ages nor with the religious Reformation in the mid sixteenth century. In the seventeenth century the Anglican Jeremy Taylor wrote a popular and much reprinted pair of treatises entitled *The Rule and Exercises of Holy Living* and *The Rule and Exercises of Holy Dying*. Chapter Two of the latter begins: 'He that would die well, must always look for death, every day knocking at the gates of the grave, and then the gates of the grave shall never prevail upon him to do him mischief.'[193] Bishop Fleming's shocking monument was meant to open to the spectator the gates of the grave, not to provoke horror or despair but in order to encourage a true and constructive view of what is worthwhile in this life.[194]

At the feet of Lord Burghersh's effigy are two angels holding a cloth in which is a small naked figure with hands held up in prayer. All three figures have lost their heads but this is still a fine example of what this fourteenth-century aristocrat hoped and prayed for himself: that at the Last Day he might be judged worthy to be carried by angels into heaven,[195] there to be welcomed with angelic song, as in a contemporary lyric in the *Pilgrimage of the Soul*:

Right welcome are you, blessed creatures!
It's time your pack and burden to forsake,
For now you shall no longer journey make;
And after work it's time to be quiet,
And heaviness and anguish to forget.[196]

A much earlier example is the grave slab of Bishop Nigel[197] (c. 1140) in Ely cathedral on which St Michael the Archangel is shown bearing Nigel's soul. Nigel was related to that Bishop Alexander who beautified the west front of Lincoln cathedral.

89 Curled dragon above woman's head, arcade spandrel of Angel Choir

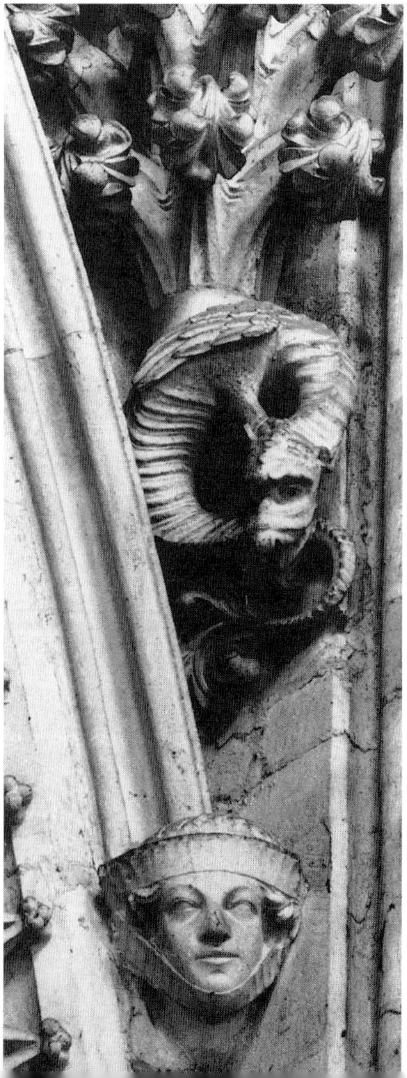

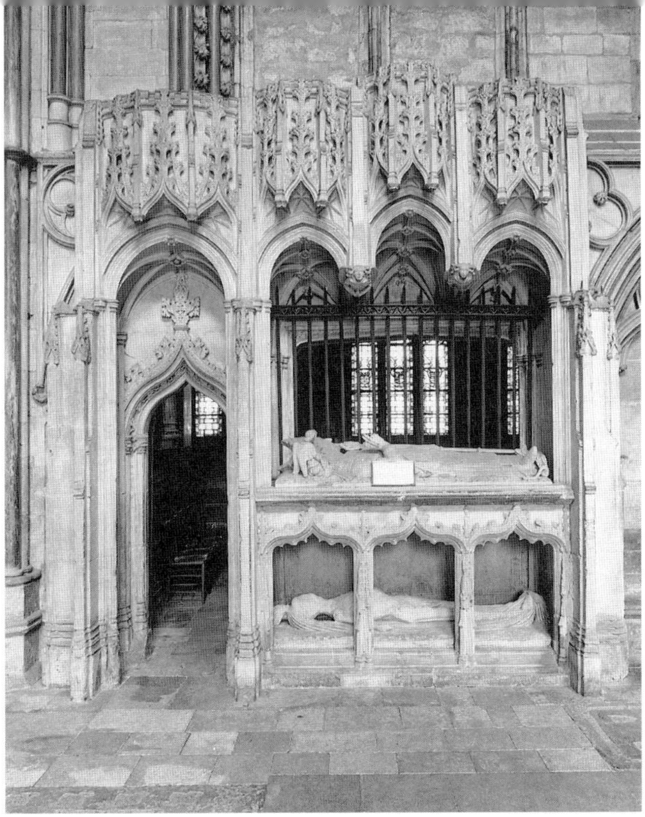
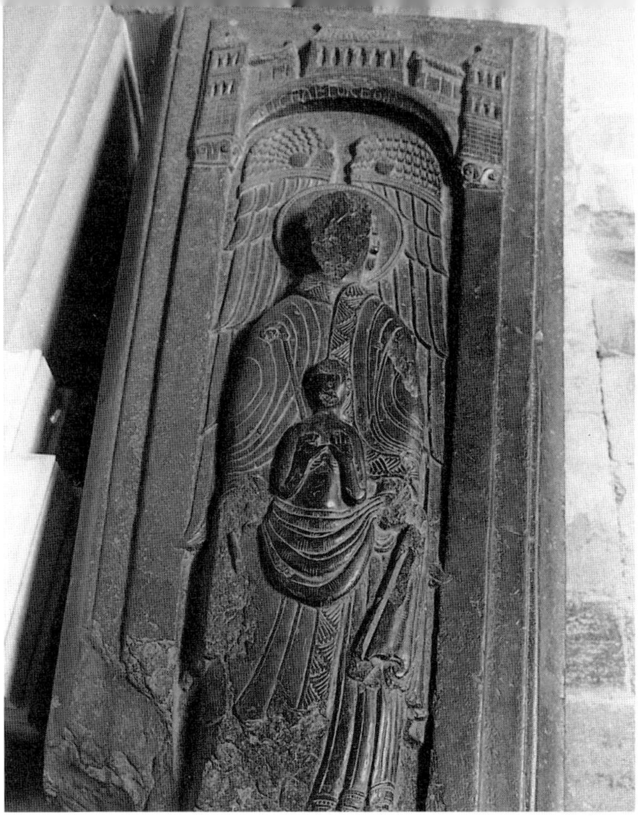

90 Bishop Fleming's monument
91 Ely Cathedral, tombstone of Bishop Nigel; Archangel Michael holding the bishop's soul
92 Lord Burghersh's monument
93 Two angels carrying Lord Burghersh's soul

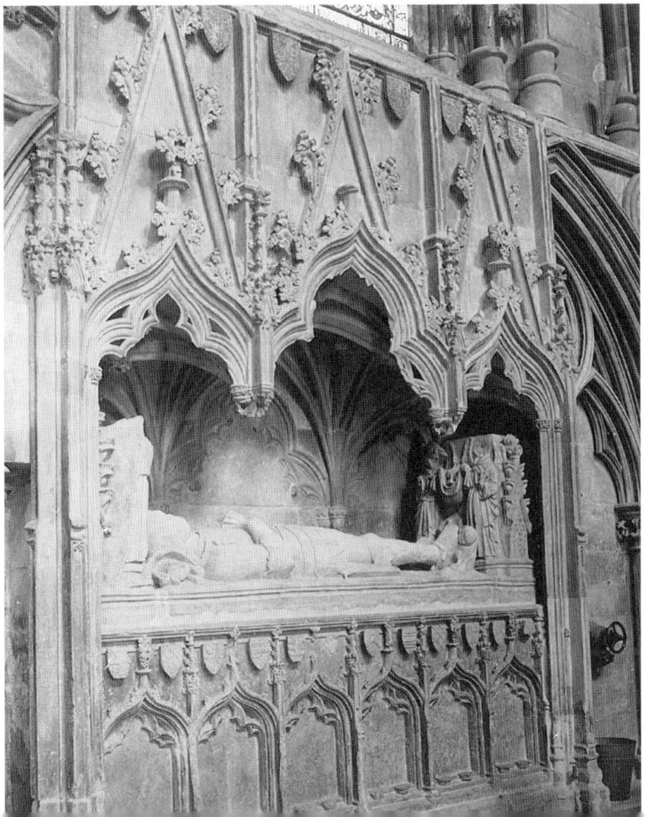
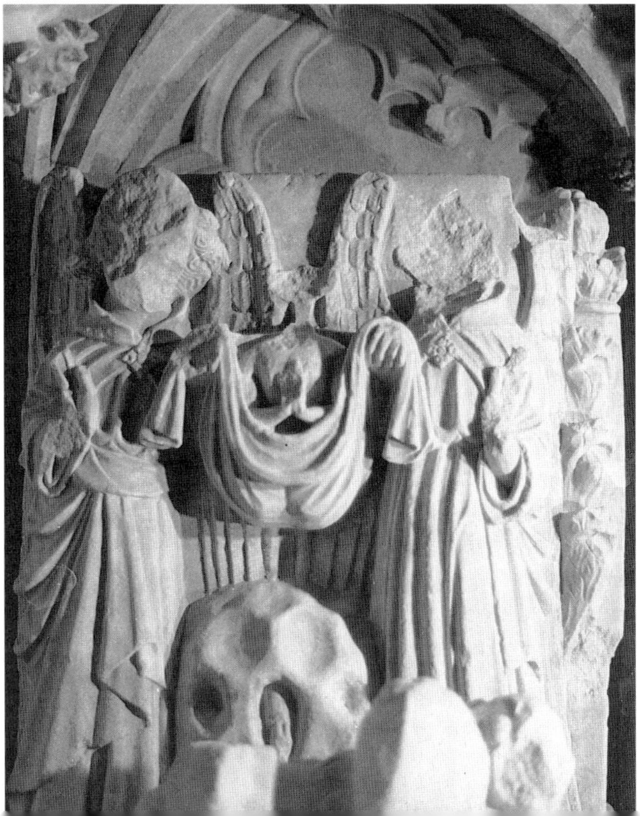

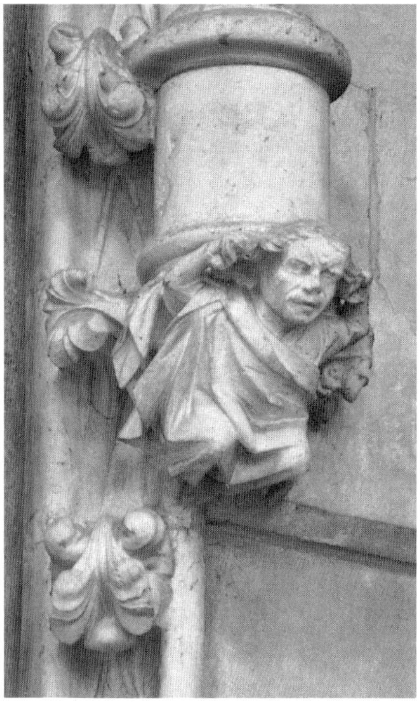

94 Man supporting vault

Indeed it seems likely that Alexander may have ordered the Ely slab together with his own, the slab containing a Tree of Jesse now set into the north nave arcade (and wrongly inscribed as the tomb of bishop Remigius).[198] As we have seen, one of the panels on his frieze on the west front shows the souls of the Righteous, held in the bosom of Abraham in much the same way as the angels carry Lord Burghersh.

The juxtaposition of the Fleming and Burghersh tombs might put one in mind of the fourteenth-century English mystic Julian of Norwich's passage on death: 'I saw a body lying on the earth which appeared heavy and horrible, and without shape and form, as it were a swollen pit of stinking mud, and suddenly out of this body there sprang a most beautiful creature, a little child, fully shaped and formed, swift and lively and whiter than a lily, which quickly glided up to heaven.'[199] The imagery of these tombs, although private, echoes the message of the sculptural programme of the cathedral in which they are set: individuals understood their own lives and deaths in terms that the Church taught, and undoubtedly obtained some comfort in the face of death.[200]

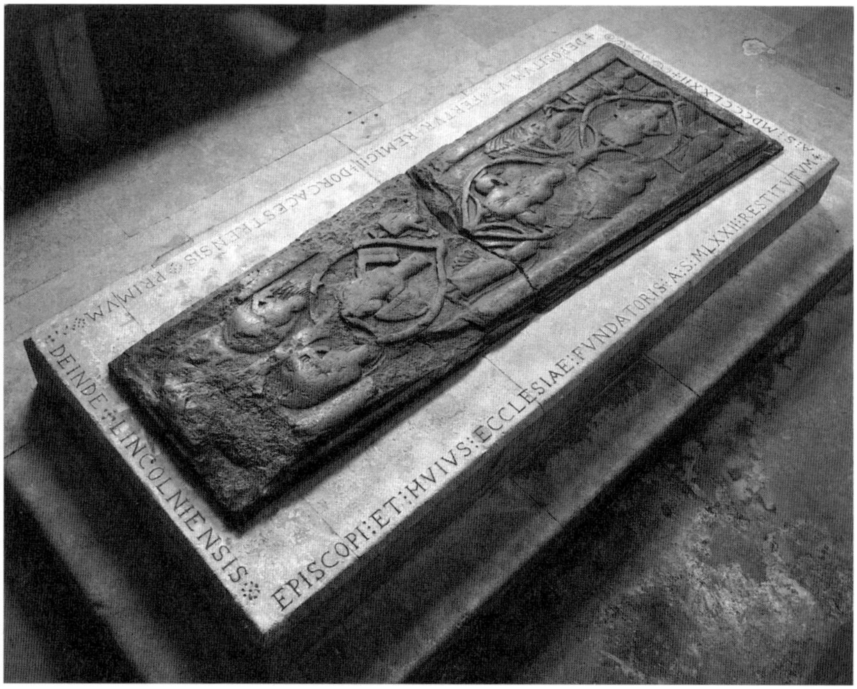

95 Tombstone of Bishop Alexander

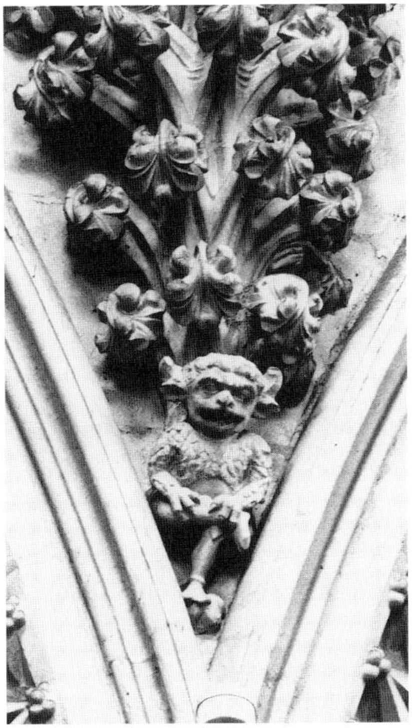

96 Imp, Angel Choir triforium

The Imp and other Beasts: Let all that hath breath Praise the Lord

One final feature is worth our attention; one that Lincoln shares with most other medieval cathedrals and churches in England. Throughout the building, in accessible and inaccessible spots, are innumerable creatures both real and fabulous. The Lincoln Imp has uniquely caught the public imagination, but he has plenty of companions: imps and devils both charming and grotesque, animals of many recognisable kinds together with weird or humorous monsters. The cathedral teems, not only with angels and the hosts of Heaven, nor just with human figures but with a veritable menagerie of beasties as well. These have been explained in various ways.

Nineteenth-century Romantics such as Victor Hugo portrayed them as sinister, devilish forms spewed out of the fearful and superstitious imagination of benighted medieval man. A similar attitude has been expressed recently in charges of Satanic influence; the Imp is considered by some to represent the power of the devil within the building.[201] But if the Imp is indeed devilish he most likely represents a warning to those who do not concentrate on their prayers. Many medieval sermons refer to Tutivilus, whose task is to gather up the fragments of psalms slurred over or omitted by lazy clerics during the daily services. He also takes notes of the similar misdeeds of the laity who tended to gossip in church rather than pay attention to the service.[202] Tutivilus would appear at the Last Judgement with his sacks of fragments to be weighed in St Michael's scales against the good deeds of each 'church-chatterer'.[203] Medieval preachers used him, and other devilish specialists, as a humorous way of making a serious point. It is noteworthy that the Imp sits cross-legged, a sign of authority shown by the Kings on the west front. Satan, as seen in the mystery plays, fell through pride, through trying to usurp the true authority of God. Devilish authority is a lust for power whose result is pain and destruction,[204] whereas true authority comes from God and is recognisable in its happy and harmonious effects.

Some beasts also are devilish. Satan in dragon form has already been mentioned. The *Ancrene Wisse* refers to the devil both as 'the dogge of helle'[205] and as 'the cat of helle'; in the *Ayenbite of Inwyt* (*Remorse of Conscience*) the devil is said to play with the sinner as the cat does with the mouse; in *The Castle of Perseverance* Belial threatens to bind Mankind in hell 'as catte dothe the mows'.[206] The cat with a mouse in its claws in the arcading of the Chapter House vestibule may well be a reminder of the wiles of Satan. But most animals have dual meanings, both good and bad, as well as sometimes being simply themselves.[207]

Another modern interpretation sees such images as examples of secular humour, the caprices of sculptors who had grown tired of depicting serious religious matters and when free to do so would resort to irreverence and caricature. On this view they are, to use the title of a recent book which is concerned with such figures, 'images on the edge'.[208] They were a means of joking about, even subverting, the serious message of the Church. Alternatively, they are simply the result of the masons' fanciful play.[209]

97 Fox carrying cub, choirstalls

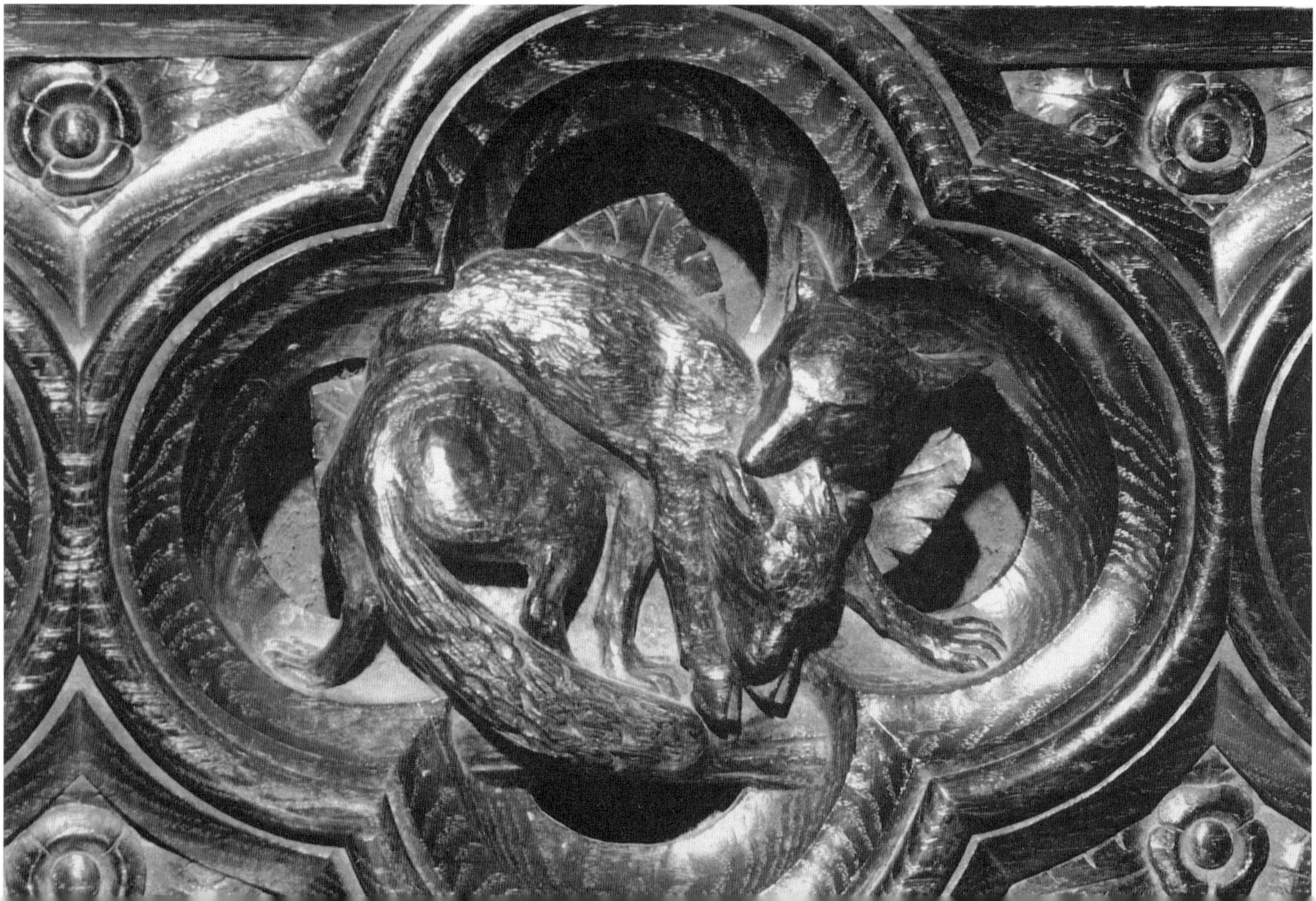

98 Fox, Angel Choir exterior

That there is humour in these figures is very likely, for medieval religion did not consider all forms of humour to be purely secular. Not all forms of humour are meant to be subversive. One might remember that Dante in the thirteenth century portrayed the inhabitants of Paradise as singing and dancing for joy.[210] Medieval preachers made much use of humorous stories, often about animals, to make their moral points.[211] The 'mystery plays' also made use of humour, sometimes of the lowest comedy, to very good effect in heightening by contrast their serious message.[212] Devils in these plays were generally portrayed as comic and grotesque.[213] They were frightful creatures making a dreadful cacophony with fireworks, loud instruments played out of tune[214] and the beating of pots and pans;[215] scary, perhaps, but always overcome by the good characters in the end. In this way was shown the aggressiveness of evil, which needs to be taken seriously and avoided, but also the comforting promise of Christian faith.[216] For the Christian story is itself a comedy. It is a comedy not in the

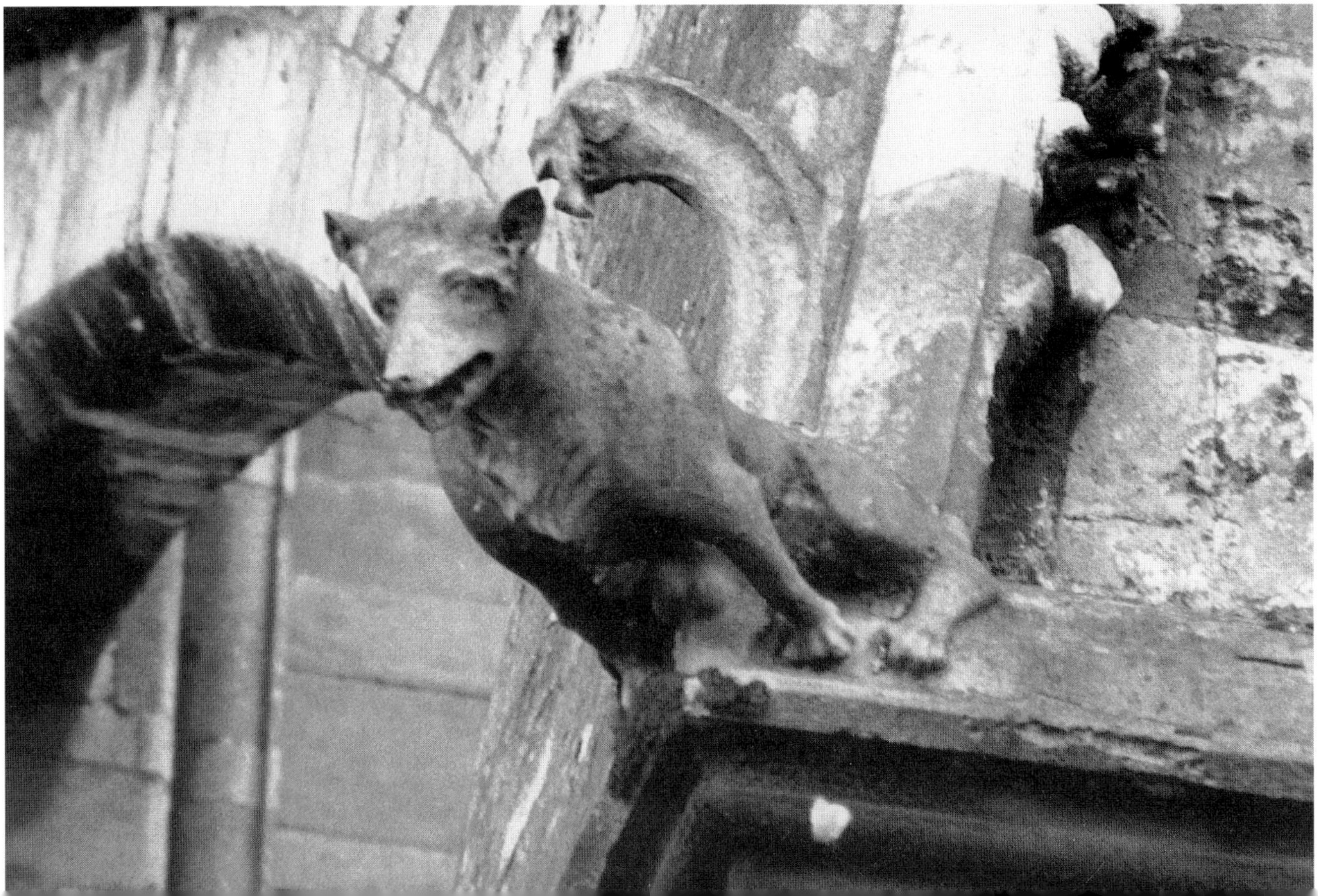

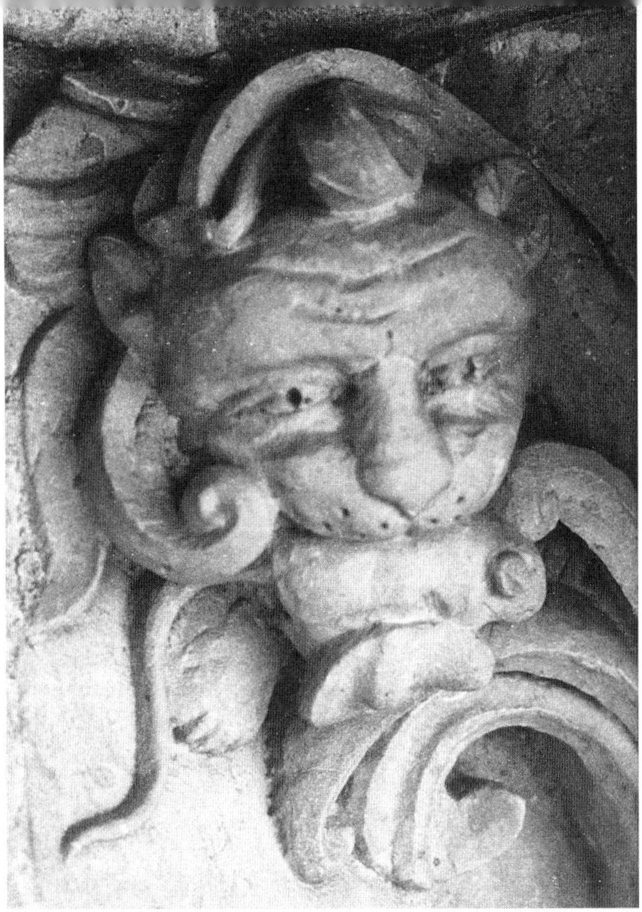

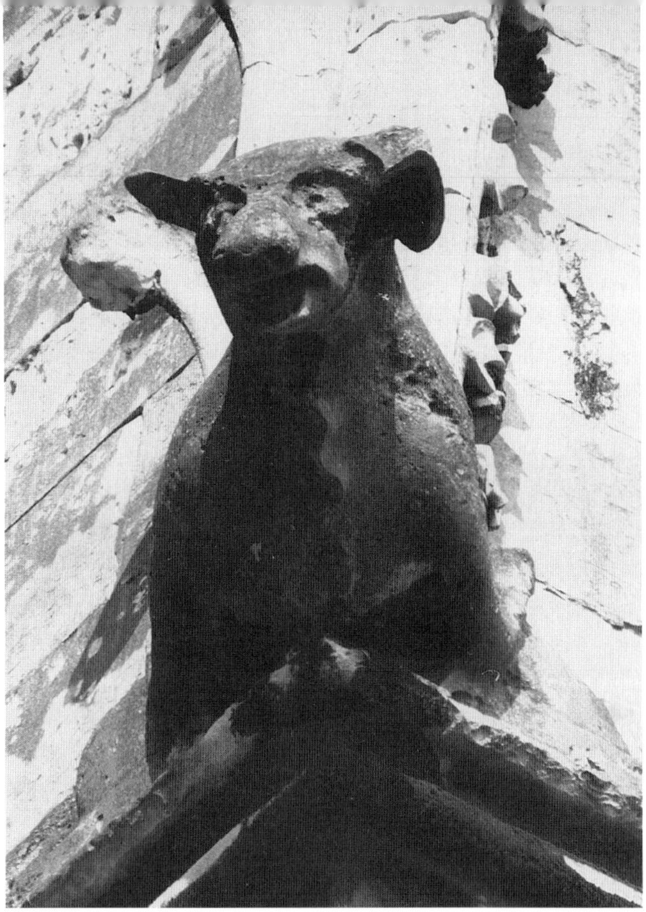

superficial sense of slapstick and jokery but in the deeper classical sense of a story in which, although many dangerous, grim and unpleasant things might happen, though everything might seem lost in death and despair, all turns out well in the end.[217] Thus was Dante able to call his serious poem about Hell, Purgatory and Heaven *The Divine Comedy*[218] and Julian of Norwich could recognise the full depths of evil in this world and yet understand Christ as saying to her that ultimately 'all shall be well'.[219]

Many of the small sculptures in the cathedral display an evident delight in the diversity of creatures.[220] Medieval natural historians, knowing less than we do the extent of the earth's inhabitants, allowed for the existence of many creatures which we know to be fabulous: not only allowed their existence but valued them as part of God's creation.[221] Some monsters are partly, or wholly, human such as, for instance, the manticore which has a human head but the body of a lion and the tail of a scorpion.[222] St Augustine

99 Cat and mouse, Chapter House

100 Dog, Angel Choir exterior

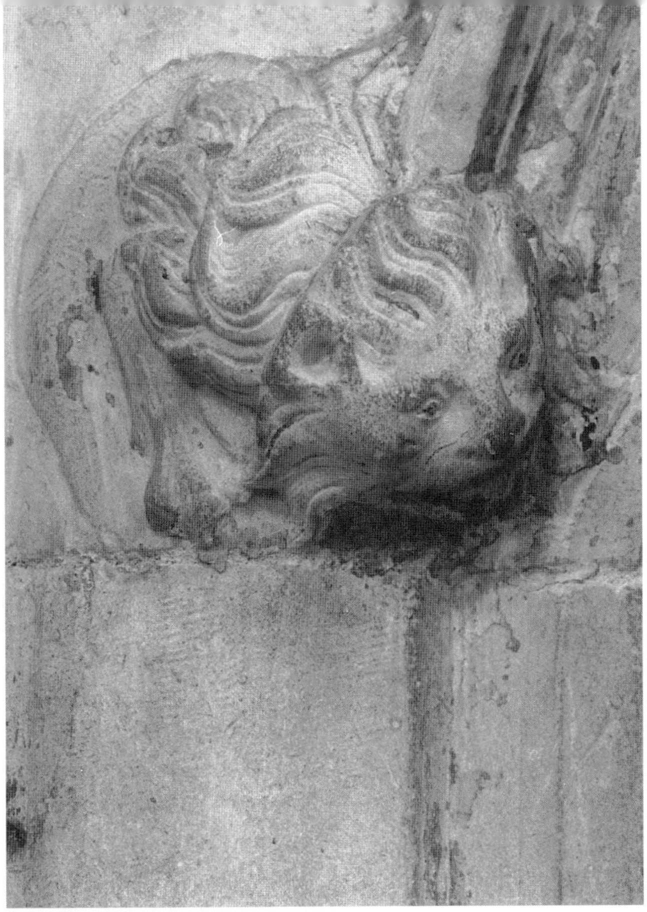

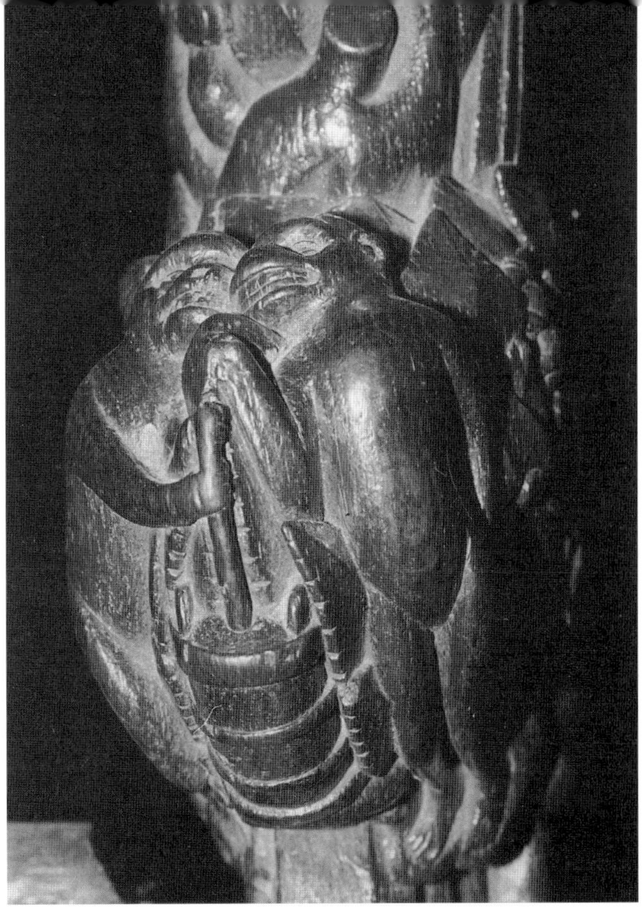

101 Lion, pulpitum

102 Apes churning, choirstalls poppy-head

addressed the question of whether, if such monstrous creatures exist, they are or are not human. He replied that if there is any doubt they should be treated as human; that is, they should be allowed the same moral status as human beings.[223] This enlightened view was certainly not always carried into practice by medieval people but it was repeated by many theologians throughout the Middle Ages and shows how the teaching of the Church aimed at encouraging the humane treatment of those who looked strange or outlandish.[224] It contrasts very favourably with the view expressed in the sixteenth and seventeenth centuries that monsters, even deformed human births, are creations of the Devil.[225]

As we have seen, the Church was likened to Noah's ark, which saved not only humans but also other creatures. For that reason alone they would require a place in the ark-church. In the Bestiaries they were generally given a moralising interpretation, and Lincoln seems to have been a centre for illustrated Bestiary manuscripts in the twelfth century.[226] But they also, simply as themselves, have a place in the prayers of the faithful. Already in the fourth century St Ambrose was extolling the wonders of God's creation. The full marvels of His creation are revealed only to those who diligently study its particular manifestations. Contemplation of the details of his glorious works draws the human mind to God.[227]

Even in the times of the Viking and Danish invasions of Britain, when Christianity and its values were almost destroyed, it was possible for hermit saints to take delight in animals of all kinds as fellow creatures of God.[228] The *Lives* of the Celtic and Northumbrian saints contain stories of their kindness; St Madoc fed a starving wolf, St Columba admonished a brother to care for an exhausted, storm-tossed crane, St Cuthbert rebuked, but did not otherwise harm, the birds who had ravaged his newly-sown fields.[229] The Northumbrian painters who adorned the great Gospel books with miniatures seem to have carefully observed the birds, cats and other animals portrayed so decoratively in their work.[230]

Later saints also showed concern for beasts. Of St Godric of Finchale, who died in 1170, it is related that 'in winter when all about was frozen stiff in the cold, he would go out barefoot, and if he lighted on any animal helpless with misery of the cold, he would set it under his armpit or in his bosom to warm it'.[231] It is recorded of St Hugh of Lincoln that a swan became devoted to him.[232]

Our modern tendency is to consider such behaviour merely an attractive sign of these saints' liking for animals,[233] but there is more to it than that. Another story of St Cuthbert narrates how he had gone to pray one night, standing in the icy waters of the sea. When he emerged onto the beach '...there came forth two beasts, vulgarly called otters, from the depth of the sea, which stretched on the sand before him, began to warm his feet with their breath, and busily to wipe them dry with their hair'.[234] This is understood by the onlooker and by the biographer as a sign of Cuthbert's sanctity: in him the enmity between man and animal, which is a result of sin, has been overcome. God's peaceable kingdom is restored as the animals minister to the saint.[235]

The influential twelfth-century theologian Hugh of St Victor

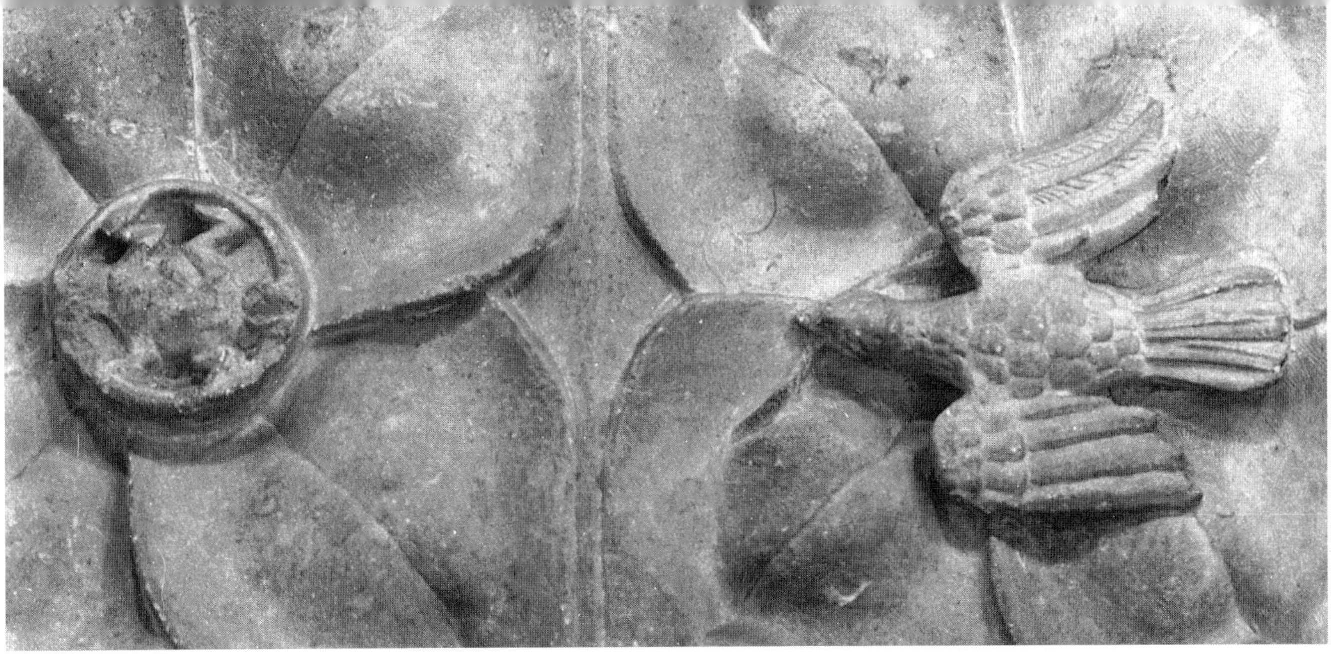

103 Bird flying back to nest with chicks, screen wall, south-east transept

104 Two dragons

recommends meditation on the variety of creatures and writes with wonder about those which are seemingly useless or even harmful to humankind.[236] They were created by the boundless outpouring of God's goodness. The later master, Richard of St Victor, in one of his works on contemplation, *The Mystical Ark* or *Benjamin Major*, writes that 'when the form and image of those visible things are brought into consideration in amazement we contemplate them and in contemplation we are amazed how many, how great, how diverse, how beautiful and joyful are these bodily things that we take in by means of our bodily senses. Marvelling we venerate and

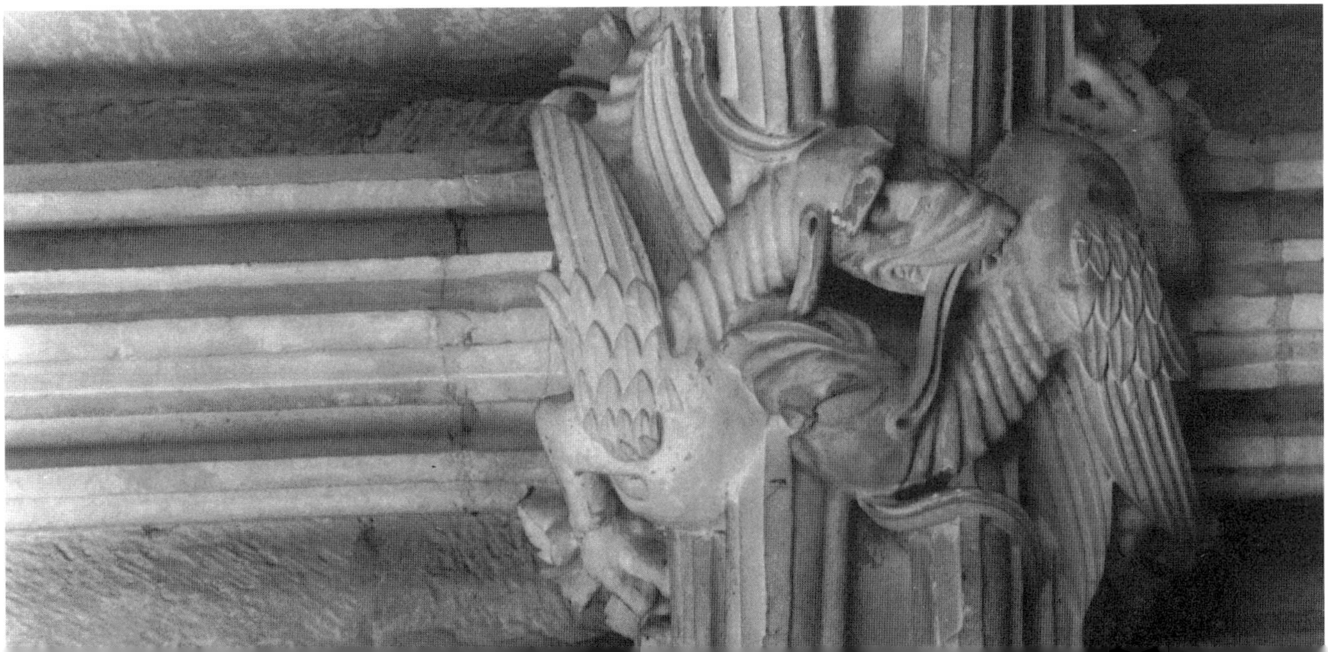

105 Otter, pulpitum

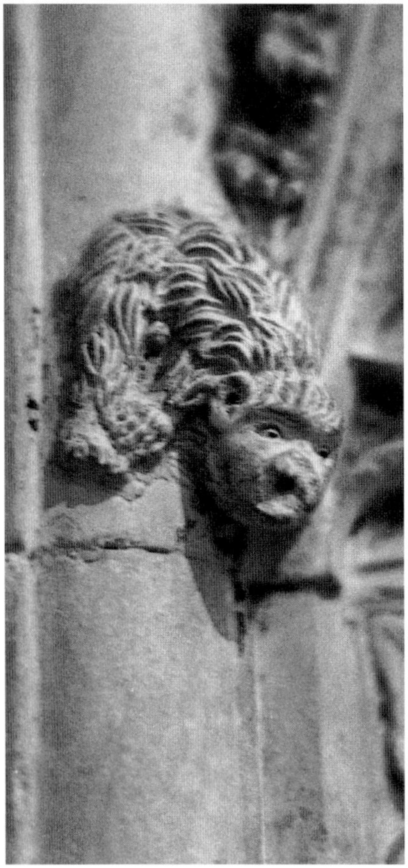

venerating we marvel at the power, wisdom and generosity in all these things of that creative superessence.'[237]

St Francis of Assisi was another contemporary who expressed such attitudes. In his 'Canticle of the Sun' he envisaged all created beings as praising God; the well-known stories of his preaching to the birds and conversion of the wolf show this delight in all of God's creation.[238] St Thomas Aquinas also argued that 'meditation on the divine works' is useful for building up our faith and that such consideration moves us to admiration of the wisdom and power of God and inflames us with love of his goodness.[239]

The first chapter of the Book of Genesis portrays the delight that God took, first in creating the variety of creatures, and then in seeing that they are good. Many of the psalms have this as their theme; Psalm 104 is a lengthy and lovely meditation upon the wonders of God's world, including Leviathan the sea-dragon whom God created for his own amusement.[240] Psalm 148 calls upon all the various parts of creation to praise the Lord.[241] And the Book of Revelation envisages a final consummation in which all creatures join in praising their creator with a great song of joy: 'And every creature which is in heaven, and on the earth, and under the earth, and such as are in the sea, and all that are in them, heard I saying, Blessing and honour, and glory, and power, be unto him that sitteth upon the throne, and unto the Lamb for ever and ever.' (Rev. 5:13) Following these examples, Christian people can find that contemplation of his creatures deepens their understanding of the nature of God.[242]

At the end of the Middle Ages Sir Thomas More, in his *Utopia,* summed up this attitude of wonder thus: '[the people of Utopia] assume that [God] has the normal reactions of an artist. Having put the marvellous system of the universe on show for human beings to look at – since no other species is capable of taking it in – He must prefer the type of person who examines it carefully, and really admires His work, to the type that... remains quite unimpressed by the whole astonishing spectacle.'[243] The world, and the cathedral which is a world in miniature, is full of the grandeur of God. But its wonders become apparent only to those who pay attention, who are willing to take time and study it.[244]

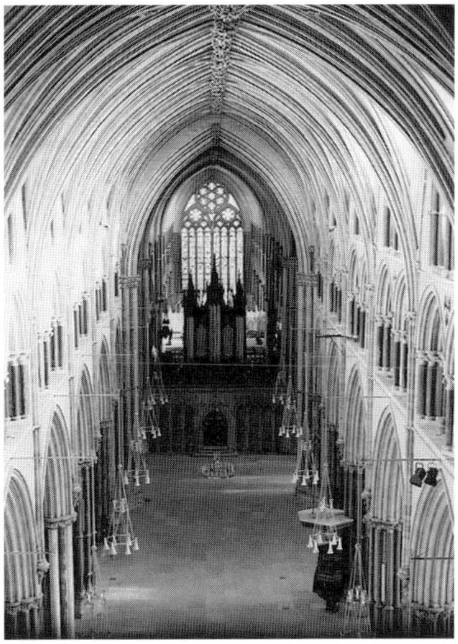

106 View of nave, looking east

Epilogue: Out of Zion, the perfection of Beauty, God hath shined

Although the cathedral has changed a great deal since the end of the middle ages, much has survived. The change in religious belief and practice at the Reformation, although great, left much intact. At the centre of the life of the cathedral is still the worship of God and the celebration of the Christian message. The modern liturgies of the Eucharist, the daily offices of Morning and Evening Prayer, and the occasional offices have all developed out of their medieval predecessors; their contents and structure remain very similar to the medieval services. The stories from the Bible, which are portrayed on various parts of the building, remain basic to Christian belief. And visitors of many sorts and conditions continue to make their way here hoping for inspiration and perhaps even a blessing.

The cathedral is a still very special place. For those who look attentively it is not just a representation or picture of heaven but a foretaste, a place of intersection where heaven and earth meet; here, now. The Kingdom of God is both present and yet to come. The hymn for the feast of Dedication, 'Hail thee, Festival Day', which contains the comparison of the church with Noah's Ark, also has the image of Jacob's Ladder. 'Ladder of Jacob, by none but by thee we can mount to the heavens; Grant that thy people, O Lord, thither ascending may reign.'[245] This refers to the Old Testament story (Genesis 28:11– 17) of how the patriarch Jacob, one of the ancestors of Christ, dreamt that in the very place where he lay a ladder stretched from earth to heaven. Angels were climbing up and down the ladder; it was a place of connection between earth and heaven, between the bodily and the spiritual worlds.[246] The Consecration and Dedication liturgies also incorporated Jacob's words when he awoke: 'How dreadful is this place! this is none other but the house of God, and this is the gate of heaven'.[247]

This building, made with imperfect human hands, was designed and built as an image of the wonder of God's universe in this world and the next.

Notes

INTRODUCTION

1. For a concise account of the context for the building of such cathedrals see Brooke 1969; 1.
2. Classic examples of an iconographical approach to medieval buildings are: Mâle, Krautheimer, Simson. Mâle and Simson, however, restrict their discussion to French buildings.
3. Nolan, pp. 43–4.
4. For useful introductions to these changes see Brooke 1969; 2, which deals with the period during which Bishop Alexander's changes were made to the west front and then St Hugh's Choir was built; Rowley, which is a concise coverage of the later period.
5. See Fowler, for a concise account of the use of the Bible in the liturgy and its wider influence in the Middle Ages. A more comprehensive account can be found in Smalley.
6. For a concise account of the medieval liturgy see Harper, pp. 1–42. Lincoln's liturgy seems to have been a variant on that of Salisbury; see *ibid.* p. 203, Pfaff and the forthcoming pamphlet in the Lincoln series by Nicolas Alldrit.
7. This is what should have happened. In reality the complexities of building and rebuilding could sometimes cause the delay of the consecration. See, for instance, Gransden. But this does not detract from the influence of the imagery of the consecration service on the way in which a church building was understood.
8. For a brief history of this practice see Muncey. For the history of the early development of the rite see Duchesne, Ch. XII, pp. 399–418.
9. The Sarum rite, which was used extensively in England, is available in Legge, pp. 202–4. Some earlier rites are in Martène. For a discussion of the relevance of these rites to gothic architecture and translations of selected texts, see Stookey. See also Neale, pp. 196–203 for a compact version of the rite in English translation.
10. See Sperber, esp. Chs 5 & 6.
11. Coldstream, p. 11.
12. For a brief description of the medieval use of the psalms see Ward 1992, XV, pp. 15–18; Harper pp. 67–72.
13. Prologue to *The English Psalter*, in Rolle 1989, p. 67: 'Sothely þis shinand boke es a chosen sange bifor God, als laumpe lyghtenand oure lyf, hele of a seke hert, huny til a bitter saule...In þaime es...mekil fairehede of vnderstandynge and medicyne of wordes...' Rolle 1931/1988, p. 5. See also *The Ludus Coventriae* (Block, p. 96) ll. 437–48 where the Virgin Mary speaks similarly about the psalms.
14. At Lincoln this practice of dividing the psalms among the clergy for private recitation can be traced back to the 1130s: Pfaff, p. 21. Lists of the stalls and psalms can be found in Wickenden, pp. 56–7.
15. Second Prebend Sermon, in Donne, p. 91.
16. All scriptural quotations are from the Authorised (King James) version of the Bible [hereafter AV]. Where this differs significantly from the Vulgate Latin which was in use in the medieval church I shall provide the latter in a footnote.
17. *English Hymnal* no. 362 and *Hymns*, no.114.
18. English translation in *English Hymnal*, nos. 169 & 170 and in *Hymns* no. 332. Latin original in Henry, pp. 344–50.
19. Nolan, p. 49.
20. Martène quotes (p. 258) a sermon of Archbishop Ecgbert of York mentioning this as part of the rite. He does not give a date for this sermon but evidently it is pre-Conquest.
21. The Epistle to the Ephesians, although now thought not to have been written by St Paul, has been traditionally considered his work.
22. 'et dicebat Simpliciano, non palam sed secretius et familiarius, "noveris me iam esse christianum." et respondebat ille, "non credam nec deputabo te inter christianos, nisi in ecclesia Christi videro." ille autem inridebat dicens, "ergo parietes faciunt christianos?"' Augustine, 8.2.4, in O'Donnell, vol. 1, p. 89.
23. The works of Hugh, and also Richard, of St Victor will have been known in Lincoln by the late twelfth century through the then chancellor, William de Montibus, who had studied and taught in the Paris schools, in the milieu of the Victorines. See MacKinnon and Goering.
24. Neale and Webb, Supplement: 'The Mystical Mirror of the Church' by Master Hugh of St Victor, Ch. II, p. 171. 'Quae autem hic fiunt visibiliter, omnia in anima per invisibilem virtutem Deus operatur, quae verum templum Dei est, ubi fides fundamentum facit, spes erigit, charitas consummat.' PL CLXXVII col. 339. See also Durandus' own comment, Neale and Webb, p. 17: 'For the material church, wherein the people assemble to set forth God's holy praise, symboliseth that Holy Church which is built in heaven of living stones.' 'Siquidem Ecclesia materialis, in qua populus ad laudandum Deum convenit, sanctam significat Ecclesiam, quae in coelis vivis ex lapidibus

construitur....' Durandus Bk 1, Ch. 1, § 9.

25. Neale and Webb p. 196. '...haec festivitas specialiter significat aeternam dedicationem, in qua Ecclesia illa, scilicet anima sancta, ita Deo dedicabitur, id est copulabitur, ut non possit ad alios usus transferri...' Durandus Book VII, Ch. 48 S3. Rabanus Maurus in *de Universo* has a similar comment: 'Lapides ergo diversi generis in structuris apti sunt, quorum significatio...et in bonam et in contrariam partem ponitur, quia dicuntur lapides vivi, hoc est sancti, qui ad coelestem constructionem habiles sunt...' PL CXI col. 561.
26. Donne p. 136.
27. 'As symbol of the heavenly city, it united the finite and mortal with the infinite and perfect, the body with the soul, natural with supernatural, man with God.' Dougherty, p. 49.

EXCHEQUER GATE

28. For the symbolism of gateways in early Christian times see Milburn, pp. 121–2.
29. In Pevsner 1989, p. 484. Also noted are two of the carved bosses but their significance is not commented on.
30. That the west front of the cathedral should be understood as a triumphal arch is suggested in Zarnecki 1988, p. 38. Fritz Saxl had earlier considered this suggestion but rejected it on the grounds that it was unlikely that such a far-off exemplar could have influenced the work at Lincoln. However, since that paper was published much evidence has been found of the influence of the triumphal arch on Christian architecture. For general accounts of this symbolism see Onians Ch. V, and Smith. Mr John Goodall has kindly informed me that the late fourteenth-century gatehouse of Thornton Abbey, in the north of Lincolnshire, has a carving of a devil so placed as to be seeming to usher visitors towards the outside world.
31. The only works of which I am aware are Ferguson amd Morant. Dr V. A. Sekules has recently studied the gates of Norwich cathedral and found evidence that they also carried messages: I am grateful to have been allowed to read her paper 'The Gothic Sculpture' before its publication; Sekules 1996.
32. See Major, p. 26. Permission was given by Edward I in 1285 for walls to be completed around the north and east sides of the Close. This had been requested by bishop Oliver Sutton in order to improve the safety of its inhabitants.
33. Jones, Major, and Varley, p. 92. An illustration of the outer gate is in Hill, plate 5.
34. One of the most famous and dramatic examples of this is the entrance to the west Choir of Naumberg cathedral, illustrated in Stratford, vol. 2, plate 1 of Peter Kidson's article.
35. Durandus Ch. 1, § 26, p. 24.
36. See below p. 23.
37. *English Hymnal* 258, *Hymns* 4. The hymn continues: 'Christ, the true, the only Light/Sun of righteousness, arise,/Triumph o'er the shades of night'; indeed, the entire hymn is an extended development of this image.
38. See 'The Religious Meaning of the Ruthwell Cross' in Schapiro 1980, p. 153.
39. A later sprouting heart can be seen on a panel of the font in Earl Stonham church in Suffolk and there is also one carved on a spandrel of the doorway to the rood-loft stair at Horseheath church, Cambridgeshire.
40. PL XXXV col. 1993: 'Quasi agrum invenit [deus] corda hominum...Plantare ibi vult arborem: charitatem.' col. 2020: 'Opus ergo suum probet unusquisque nostrum, utrum de vena charitatis emanet, utrum de radice dilectionis rami bonorum operum pullulent.' My translation.
41. The detailing is very similar to that of the castle on the brass of Bishop Wyville (died 1375) in Salisbury cathedral. See sketch of the brass in Pevsner 1963, p. 373.
42. Originally there was an outer gate (see above **p. 8)** but the upper parts of the castle were higher than they are now and would most likely have been visible from this spot just within the west end of the present Exchequer Gate.
43. See Cornelius.
44. *The Castle of Perseverance*, in Eccles 1969, lines 2011ff. Coldstream p. 101 refers to other writers who 'used the castle as a metaphor for the body. The castle, its outer walls and towers reflecting its inner strength, was an apt image...'
45. For an introduction to the life and work of Grosseteste see Srawley. For more detail see Southern; special reference to *Le Château d'Amour*, can be found on pp. 225–9.
46. Middle English text in Horstmann 1892, pp. 355–406.
47. See Rolle, 1989 p. 16 and pp. 25–41. But, in monastic circles, the devotion dates back at least to the twelfth century when the hymn on the Holy Name, 'Dulcis Jesu Memoria', seems to have been written. See Ward 1992, XIX, p. 194; Gray 1972, p. 79.
48. Fourth Prebend Sermon, as quoted in Ward 1992, XIX.

EXTERIOR

49. Freedberg, p.100 'fundamental to every pilgrimage is the element of hope. The focus of every pilgrimage journey is the shrine. The journeys are undertaken in the expectation, however weak, of physical and spiritual benefit...'
50. For late medieval pilgrimage see Brewer, p. 25: 'The pilgrimage was the climax of travelling in the Middle Ages...Anxious, uncomfortable and disappointing as it so often was, the pilgrimage was a great liberation, a holiday that was also a holy-day.' Also Gray 1990, pp. 6–7: 'It was a solemn occasion – it was the image of man's earthly pilgrimage to "Jerusalem celestial", and of his journey to death – and highly emotional, and also a holiday, with an element of that 'game' and merriment which is...a common element in "popular religion".' For modern interpretations of pilgrimage see Turner and Sumption. A classic Christian account is Kötting, esp. Abschnitt IV. See also Duffy, pp. 190–200; Aston 1993, pp. 3–4.
51. Kempe 1940, p. 68: 'þe forseyd creatur wept & sobbed so plentyvowsly as þow sche had seyn owyr Lord wyth hyr bodyly ey sufferyng hys Passyon at þat tyme. Befor hir in hyr sowle sche saw hym veryly be contemplacyon, & þat cawsyed hir to haue compassyon.' Modernisation taken from Kempe 1936, p. 107.
52. For an introduction to the Church's calendar of special days see Cobb, pp. 403–19.
53. For a concise introduction to liturgical processions see Harper, pp. 127–33; For a detailed account see Bailey.
54. Cobb notes that 'Primitively it [ie the Palm Sunday procession] always began at some place outside the main church; at Canterbury, for example, it began at the parish church of St Martin and made its way to the cathedral...' p. 408.
55. Excellent discussions of this can be found in Holloway, pp. 63, 145–162 and in Wilkinson.
56. This incident is reported in all four Gospels (Mt. 21: 1–11; Mk 11: 1–11; Lk. 19: 29–40; Jn 12: 12–16).
57. See Franklin.
58. Baldovin, p. 268: 'A procession is a most intentional act, heightening a sense of participation in leading its partakers to a goal. On the other hand, such movement also suggests incompleteness. This incompleteness or pilgrim nature of the Christian community is well expressed by the supplicatory and penitential motifs used in the liturgical processions...They were a means of expressing the public and cultural nature of Christianity and an expression of that faith as pilgrimage and process.'
59. See Kahrl, pp. 228–9.
60. For a concise account of the Lincoln evidence see Harris 1994; Nelson, Ch. 6; for a more general account of the development, meaning and staging of the plays see Harris 1992, Wickham and Tydeman.
61. Rubin 1991, p. 268.
62. Hill, p. 147 estimates that there were forty-six parish churches in Lincoln, of which forty-three were in existence by the mid twelfth century.
63. Miri Rubin, in Abulafia and others, p. 12. This was the ideal; the practice generally also emphasised that not all were included. The craft guild processions left 'women, foreigners, youngsters, journeymen, visitors from the countryside' outside as onlookers. But see Palliser, pp. 144–9, who argues that such displays did in fact promote a sense of unity even in those who were merely onlookers.
64. The 'visitatio sepulchri' mentioned in the *Regularis Concordia* of Bishop Aethelwold. Also the Winchester tropes, cited in Berry, pp. 149–160. See also Harper pp. 137–8, Wickham, pp. 38–41.
65. Owen, p. 154; Harris 1994, p. 32.
66. Owen, p. 140.
67. Sekules, 1995.
68. For a discussion of the meaning of some common figures see Aberth, pp. 37–45. That such figures were generally understood as having meaning is suggested by the C13 *Roman de la Rose*, in which the garden walls display images of Hate, Felony, Villainy, Covetousness, Avarice, Envy, Sorrow, Old Age, Hypocrisy and Poverty. See Chaucer's C14 translation, *The Romaunt of the Rose*, II, 132–474. Some of these figures are Vices, commonly found on or in churches.
69. See Harris 1992, pp. 10–14, 145–6; for a more general discussion, Geremek, Ch. 5.
70. This is their significance in late medieval paintings of the Passion of Christ (see Melinkoff, Chs 10 & 11). The interpretation of such gestures as insults is incontrovertible. It is hard to see how they came to be on the outside of church buildings unless their meaning related in some such way to the Christian message.
71. Coldstream p. 82: 'There was constant awareness that any object represented both itself and some deeper meaning. The church building represented the kingdom of Heaven; but...the same concept could be embodied in a small, canopied niche.'
72. Wickham, p. 26. For an illustration see the tympanum panel in Wenhaston church in Suffolk, illustrated in Tasker, p. 75.

THE WEST FRONT

73. In Gem, pp. 9–28. There is a reconstruction drawing here and also in Pevsner 1989, p. 447. Doubt has recently been thrown upon Gem's reconstruction and Zarnecki's dating of the frieze by the findings of the west front restoration project, reported in Baily 1995. These suggest that the frieze is part of the original build, rather than having been added later. It is likely to be some time before the implications of this evidence have been fully assimilated by art historians. Since it is sure to cause a great deal of controversy it seems wisest to present here the currently accepted dating.
74. For further thoughts on this, see Bates, pp. 17–19. Dorothy Owen in Owen pp. 8–9 points out that William would have needed to be alert for Viking raids such as Harold had repulsed at Stamford Bridge as well as possible internal insurrections.
75. Brooke in Crook, p. 5.
76. For a general discussion of the fortification of churches see Bonde, Ch. 1, pp. 11–52; for Lincoln in particular pp. 151–6.
77. Verzar, p. 122, points to some carvings with inscriptions on north Italian churches suggesting that they were commissioned 'during the Investiture Controversy, by patrons strongly allied to Papal Rome' to announce their allegiance. Alexander was not strongly allied to the Papacy but, after his imprisonment on suspicion of treason and the confiscation of his castles he is unlikely to have been a strong supporter of the royal cause. (See Zarnecki 1988, p. 16.) Moreover, as Richard Gem points out, the cathedral seems to have been commandeered by King Stephen as a base from which to attack the castle prior to the battle of Lincoln in 1141. Dorothy Owen, in Owen pp. 122–3, suggests that this will have 'made the vicinity of the cathedral for a long period no better than a battleground'. It would be little wonder if, after this, Alexander wished to distance himself and his cathedral from secular power.
78. In view of Bishop Alexander's nickname 'the Magnificent' it could be thought that such elaboration of the building was rather an assertion of his own importance. These two insights are not totally at odds. The bishop's elaborate changes to the entrance of his cathedral would no doubt show how munificent he was. But the imagery, as far as it survives (or can be reconstructed), is entirely religious with no direct reference to Alexander himself. If his desire was to commemorate himself one would expect some clear reference to his generosity.
79. Kidson 1994 suggests that Bishop Alexander probably did not live to see this work completed although he most likely initiated it.
80. Heslop 1986, pp. 111–18. This meaning is also suggested for twelfth-century continental carvings of apes entangled in vines in Janson, p. 47. Verzar, p. 134, quotes a similar carved inhabited scroll at Sagra di San Michele which has an accompanying inscription: 'hoc opus ortatur sepius ut aspiciatur'; 'this work demands frequent consideration'. My translation.
81. Illustrated in Heslop 1986 and in Williamson, colour plate 6.
82. Francis Klingender, in his discussion of the Northumbrian crosses, points out that the hunter figures shooting their arrows upwards symbolise the persecutors of the Christian faith. (Klingender, p. 133.) Dante, in *The Inferno* Canto XII, has centaurs tormenting those damned for violence and brutality.
83. Camille, p. 106; but Camille does not see the possibility that these images might symbolise a particular sin.
84. For a detailed discussion and illustrations of the frieze carvings see Zarnecki 1988, Chs 4–7.
85. For a clear and concise explanation of the meaning of these episodes and their place in the play cycle see Harris 1994, pp. 18–21.
86. 'The story of Noah's flood actually describes evil overcoming itself. The waters were allowed to rise and blot out an evil world.' Margaret Barker, *The Lost Prophet*, London, 1988, p. 82. The biblical view of the sea as representing evil and chaos is found explicitly in Pss 46 & 69 and Rev. 21:1.
87. This way of understanding the Bible began in the earliest Christian times and has continued into the post-Reformation church. For a discussion of its use by the Wesleys see Ward 1992, XIII, pp. 14–25, 'A Converting Ordinance: Some reflections on the hymns of Charles Wesley in the light of medieval biblical commentary'; also *ibid.* XIX: 187–95, 'St Bernard and the Anglican Divines: Reflections on Mark Frank's sermon for the Circumcision'. Typology is not currently fashionable among biblical scholars but, given its prevalence in the New Testament, this situation can hardly continue indefinitely. Even during the Middle Ages some scholars questioned the usefulness of typological interpretation. For instance, William of Auvergne (early C13) took the analogies between the two Testaments as simply descriptive or metaphorical; see Schapiro 1973, p. 35.
88. Carpenter, p. 58: 'None of these people could have failed to be impressed by the clear-cut message that

the rich would have a harder time getting...into paradise than the poor'. See also Duffy pp. 357–61. For an account of how the inhabitants of one town responded (not ideally well) to this message see Rubin 1987.

89. For an analysis of the history and significance of this message see Sheingorn.

90. See Zarnecki 1988 plate 82, p. 61.

91. 'et nunc ille vivit in sinu Abraham, quidquid illud est quod significatur sinu, ibi Nebridius meus vivit, dulcis amicus meus.' Augustine 9.3.6. My translation.

92. Henderson, Inhumatio Defuncti; pp. 97–8: 'Obsecramus misericordiam tuam, omnipotens aeterne Deus...ut [famulus tuus]...in sinu Abrahae Patriarchae collocatus, locum lucis et refrigerii se adeptum esse gaudeat...' The image is also used in other parts of the service, see pp. 94 & 101. Sheingorn (p. 278) quotes another passage, which makes explicit the reference to Lazarus, from the monastic breviary of Hyde Abbey.

93. The date of *c.*1380 is suggested in the first footnote to Russell, p. 88.

94. See Steane, pp. 18–22.

95. Kings are also on the West Front of Exeter cathedral, which also was originally dedicated to the Virgin Mary. Of these Paul Williamson writes that they are almost certainly the Kings of Judah; Swanson 1991, p. 76.

96. Wilson, Introduction and p. 191.

97. King David is often portrayed thus, as in the Glazier Psalter, New York, Pierpoint Morgan Library: Ms. G25, reproduced in Schapiro 1980, p. 339, fig.11.

98. Gurevich, pp. 163–5 & 168. This is clear, for instance, from the advice to the king in Gower's *Vox Clamantis*: 'You are above the laws but live as a just man under them and because of you there will be hope of welfare for us.' Book 6, ch. 8, translation from Coleman, p. 154.

99. This is well put in Horrox p. 13.

100. Sauerländer, p. 21: 'The portal stands as the ubiquitous symbol of transformation. It is the icon of metamorphosis and revelation.'

THE FONT

101. 'Once through the gates, the Christian worshiper entered the centre of the world, a...unified space arranged progressively from the laity in the nave to the clergy in the chancel and the celebrant priest before the altar, where the power of God came down on men.' Dougherty p. 50.

102. For the early development and meaning of the rite see Duchesne Ch. IX, pp. 292–341.

103. There is a similar font in Winchester cathedral, imported from Tournai in what is now Belgium by Bishop Henry of Blois. It seems likely that Bishop Alexander, who visited Winchester in 1141, saw it and was inspired to obtain one for his own cathedral. The font and Alexander's tomb slab, also of Tournai marble, have been plausibly dated to the mid 1140s. See Zarnecki 1988, pp. 90–2; Zarnecki 1986, p. 160 and Schwartzbaum, pp. 89–97.

104. 'Caro abluitur, ut anima emaculetur...caro signatur, ut anima muniatur...' quoted in Duchesne, p. 335. My translation.

THE NAVE

105. 'Haec est arca Dei credentibus auxiliatrix/Quae vehit ad portum quos vehit unda maris' Henderson 1875, p. 202. Translation taken from *English Hymnal*, no. 634. This hymn may be no earlier than thirteenth century but the simile is already present in an English rite of *c.*900 described in Martène p. 262.

106. Text, music and translation given in Stevens 1986, pp. 144–52: 'Solos salvat archa justos cuius fides est et custos dei misericordia'.

107. See McEntire.

108. Harper, p. 121. Also Coldstream, p. 108.

109. For a detailed description and plan of the nave piers see Hoey.

110. However, one of these is a woman's head, clearly delineated with a wimple. It is very rare, but not entirely unknown, for one member of the Trinity (the Holy Spirit) to be depicted as female.

111. Cave suggests this, p. 3.

112. Crossley, pp. 39–48.

113. Cp. Heslop in Buckton and Heslop, pp. 36–45: 'The combination of foliage detailing superimposed on a spiral clearly conveys the notion of burgeoning increase because of its association with the natural unfurling of a plant.' Although the leaves on capitals are not exactly spiralling, their place at the top of a trunk-like pier surely has a similar effect; the leaves on bosses are frequently spiralling.

114. See Furnivall, pp. 5–6.

115. Neale and Webb, p. 28: 'Crux triumphalis in plerisque locis in medio Ecclesiae ponitur, ad notandum quod de medio corde Redemptorem nostrum diligimus...Crux autem in altum dirigitur per quod Christi victoria designatur.' Durandus Ch. 1 § 41.

116. In the New Testament itself, as well as by later theologians, see Heb. 1:13.

ST HUGH'S CHOIR

117. White, p. 167.
118. Janson, p. 178. For the devilish significance of the north side see below **p. 38** and fn. 184.
119. There is a reconstruction drawing of it by David Stocker in Stocker, p. 113.
120. It seems to have been Robert Willis, in the mid nineteenth century, who first characterised the vault as 'crazy'; the term was taken up by Paul Frankl in Frankl 1953 and Frankl 1962.
121. See Baily 1991, pp. 1–35 for a survey of the major interpretations of the building since the early nineteenth century. Professor Peter Kidson has published two magisterial papers on Lincoln (Kidson 1986 and Kidson 1994). It is only after long pondering on his argument and much time spent in the building that I have reached an interpretation which differs from his.
122. These are readily available in English with useful introductory material in Dionysius 1987.
123. So I argue in Broughton 1992.
124. For example in the St Albans Psalter (probably before 1123) the illustration to the Canticle from Isaiah 12 (p. 327) shows a cross with just such crockets, with a lamb on the arm and the fount of salvation flowing at its base. Pächt, Dodwell and Wormald, Plate 91d.
125. For evidence of the symbolic use of columns see Deshman, pp. 261–82.
126. These are part of the original design, as can be seen from the fact that they are carved directly on the stones of the walling rather than being set into a niche, as are the aisle figures.
127. For a concise description and evidence of dating see Pevsner 1989, pp. 475–6; for a general introduction to misericords see Laird; for a more detailed account see Bond, both volumes.
128. The only studies of which I am aware are those by Wickenden and Anderson. Wickenden's interpretations are by no means reliable but he does provide a list of the subjects of the carvings. Anderson's interpretations are more reliable and her plans indicate the extent of medieval, and later, work.

THE EASTER SEPULCHRE

129. For the ceremonies of Good Friday and Easter see Young 1920 and Young 1933, vol. 1, Chs III–XIII.
130. Woolf 1972, p. 18, referring to the *Vision of the Monk of Eynsham*, Huber, p. 653.
131. Woolf 1972, p. 43.
132. Sekules 1986, passim. See also Coldstream, pp. 96–7.
133. For the various understandings of the Sacrament as they developed during the early medieval centuries see Macy. For the development of devotion to the Sacrament see *ibid.* pp. 86–93.
134. See Rubin 1987, esp. pp. 294–97.
135. One of the soldiers is shown thus on a mid fourteenth-century English enamelled triptych in the Victoria and Albert Museum; illustrated in Campbell, p. 41. It also appears in at least one version of the popular *Speculum Humanae Salvationis*, copied in England in the late fourteenth century (Yale University, The Beinecke Rare Book and Manuscript Library, MS 27) illustrated in Wilson and Lancaster, p. 38.
136. Observation made to me by Sr Julia Bolton Holloway, N.CHF. See Stevens 1987, p. 78–87 for this and other aspects of the York plays which served as criticism of contemporary misuse of power.

THE JUDGEMENT PORCH

137. See Roberts.
138. Quoted from *Ancrene Riwle* 1955, p. 174. 'His leofmon bihalde þron, hu he bohte hire luue. lette þurlin his scheld openin his side, to shawin hire his heorte, to shawin hire hu inwardliche he luuede hire, & to ofdrahen hire heorte.' *Ancrene Wisse* 1962, p. 200. See also the fifteenth century *Fervor Amoris*: '[Christ] suffred...his gloryous herte to be thorugh-percyd with a sharpe spere for to gyve his herte-blood to bye man body and soule into Ioye without ende.' (in Horstmann 1896, p. 73); also Julian of Norwich, Ch. 12, pp. 14–15.
139. For the eucharistic overtones of devotion to the wounds of Christ see Rubin 1991, pp. 302–6. Glasscoe, p. 103, refers to 'the sign of the unfailing creativity of God – life-blood.'
140. Vulgate: 'aquae...descendebant in latus templi dextrum...'. AV: '...the waters came down from under from the right side of the house'.
141. The earliest occurence of this seems to be in the Rabbula Gospels (586); see Gurewich, pp. 358–62. See also the discussion in O'Reilly.
142. For further discussion of the history and meaning of this image see Meyer Schapiro, 'Cain's jawbone That did the First Murder', in Schapiro 1980, pp. 257–9.
143. 'The spere hat smiten myn herte ato–/For love of the my blod is spilt./Yif thu wilt fro thi senne go,/ My merci is redi quan thu wilt.' Quoted in Gray 1972, p. 141; my modernisation.
144. Hugh *Magna Vita*, 2, 137.
145. Heslop, in Fernie and Crossley.

146. For the upward–downward symbolism in plays see Twycross, pp. 48 & 60.
147. PL CLXXV Cols 799–800.
148. In this interpretation of the directional symbolism I, following Dr Heslop, part company with Roberts.
149. Lethaby 1906.
150. The Tree of Jesse survives more often in glass than in sculpture in English churches. However, the reredos of Christchurch, Hampshire, still retains its figures of Jesse, David and Solomon (with crossed legs); illustrated in Pevsner 1967/1973, plate 32. In the text (p. 175) the figure of David, with harp, is mis-identified as Daniel. The abbey church at Dorchester, Oxfordshire, has a window which combined sculpted figures on the mullions with others portrayed in the glass; illustrated in Sherwood 1974, plate 30. Both of these examples are fourteenth century.
151. See Gilchrist, pp. 139–43.
152 The statue is early twentieth century but, in view of the dedication of the cathedral to the Virgin, it is very likely that the original statue was also of the Virgin and Child.
153. Dougherty p. 51. See also Seidel, p. 52 discussing the carvings of the Wise and Foolish Virgins around the doorway arches of some twelfth-century Aquitainian churches: 'On one level then, the archivolt on which the parable of the wise and foolish virgins is shown is a visual metaphor for the Gate of Paradise at which Christ welcomes the well-prepared souls. The story is not simply illustrated along this arcuated backdrop; the key feature of the drama, the heavenly door, is literally identified with the central element of the actual portal structure and transforms it, thereby, into something more imposing. The archivolt does not merely stand for the celestial gate; in this place, it becomes the very gate itself.'

THE ANGEL CHOIR

154. Duby, p. 158.
155. In the following analysis of the sculptures I will be drawing heavily upon Heslop in Fernie and Crossley and Glenn. My analysis differs from their's in some respects.
156. There exists at least one other example of bearded angels, on the arcade of the north chancel chapel of Stalbridge church in Dorset (probably early sixteenth century). The puzzling fact is that angels are supposed to be sexless, so signs of masculinity are out of place. As far as I know no detailed research has been done on the prevalence or meaning of medieval bearded, winged figures. The unusualness of the Lincoln figure must raise a question as to its authenticity. Is the head original? Unfortunately this question cannot be answered without close scrutiny of the stonework, which will not be possible until the next occasion when scaffolding is erected. Meanwhile it is worth pointing out that figures in the nave triforium at Chichester are said to have been heavily restored.
157. Devotion to the Wounds of Christ developed in monastic circles in the eleventh and twelfth centuries, spreading more widely in the late Middle Ages. It was especially popular in England. See Rubin 1991, pp. 302–6; Horsfield, pp. 212–13; Duffy, pp. 234–47 and plates 85, 98–100, 110. The religious community of Brigittines, who had a house at Syon Abbey west of London, were devoted to the Five Wounds. They wore five red circles on a white cross above their veils to signify this devotion. There is what I take to be an illustration of the Syon habit in Sargent, plate 23.
158. *Ancrene Riwle* 1955, p. 175. 'Mei Moder he seið forȝeoten hire child? ant þah heo do: ich ne mai þe forȝeoten neauer, ant seið þe resun efter...Ich habbe he seið depeint te i mine honden. swa he dude mid read blod up o þe rode. Me cnut his gurdel to habben þoht of a þing, ah ure lauerd for he nalde neauer forȝeoten us, dude mearke of þurlunge in ure munegunge i ba twa his honden.' *Ancrene Wisse* 1962, p. 202.
159. The Pilgrimage of Grace, the northern protest/rebellion against Henry VIII's dissolution of the monasteries, mustered under banners of the Five Wounds. It is thus probable that the Reformers' objections to the portrayal of the Wounds was politically rather than religiously motivated.
160. *English Hymnal* 7; *Methodist Hymn Book* 264. See also Ward 1992, XXI.
161. 'Quale il falcon, che prima ai pie si mira,/ indi si volge al grido e si protende/per lo disio del past che la il tira/tal me fec' io...' Dante; *Purgatorio*, Canto XIX: 64–6, pp. 232–3.
162. For instance in a sermon in Cambridge University Library Ms. Gg. vi.16, fol.36 'Those that have gentyll hawkys when thei have lete them flye after the game thei call them agen to hande. But when thei wyll not redely come, the meyster hathe a reclamatory...a parte of rawe flesche of some best or fowle that the hawke the rather wyll come down to hande. Ryght so owr mercyful lorde Christe Jesus...'. For a detailed discussion of this imagery see Holloway, Appendix II: Pilgrimage and Falconry.
163. Wickham pp. 151–56 has a concise account of the growth and meaning of this trend.
164. See Rosemary Woolf, 'The Theme of Christ the

Lover-Knight' in Woolf 1986, pp. 99–117. Camille, p. 51 and illustration 51, cites a marginal image in an English Psalter which depicts a scene of a knight rescuing a lady, below a picture of the elevation of the Host at Mass. He is unable to suggest what might be the connection between the two images but it is surely not unlikely that it refers cryptically to the redemptive work of Christ, the lover-knight.

165. 'And as a kene kempe robbedest helle/and laddest out þi deore leef/þat is monnes soul/to þi briȝte boure ful of all blisse, to wonin in þi cluppying/ever wiþ outen end.' Westra, pp. 34–35.

166. For background to the Arms of Christ see also Lewis, pp. 183, 189.

167. For detailed discussions of Marian imagery, with extensive bibliographical notes, see Morgan 1991 and 1993.

168. 'On a nygth, as þis creatur lay in hir bedde wyth hir husband, sche herd a sownd of melodye so swet & delectable, hir þowt, as sche had ben in Paradyse. And þerwyth styrt sche owt of hir bedde & seyde, "Alas, þat evyr I dede synne, it is ful mery in Hevyn."' Kempe, 1940, p. 11; modern version Kempe 1936, p. 30. This text might go some way towards counteracting the modern tendency to assume that medieval penitence was due merely to a fear of Hell.

169. Suso, pp. 29–30.

170. In the Museo di San Marco, Florence; it dates from around 1431. Illustrated in Pope-Hennessy, p. 12. Its representation of the difference between heaven and hell shows very nicely the distinction as one of orderliness vs chaos, which I suggested above.

171. For an insight into the riches of plate and vestments in a medieval cathedral see Swanson, R. N.; Williamson passim, and especially the colour plates.

172. 'The Christian liturgy was born singing, and it has never ceased to sing.' 'The Christian liturgy can be celebrated without singing or music; but this is to mutilate it.' J. Gelineau, 'Music and Singing in the Liturgy', in Jones *et al.*, 1978, pp. 440 & 442.

173. '...it is remarkable that in England rather than anywhere else in Europe the corporate singing of a daily Office has continued in choral foundations.' Harper p. 184.

174. Rolle 1989, p. 67. 'þe sang þat delites tille hertes and leres þe saule es made a voyce of syngand; and with aungelis wham we may noght here we menge wordes of lovynge, swa þat worthily he may trow hym alien fra verray lyf wha sa haves noght þe delitabilte of þis gifte of wonderfulle swetnes...', Rolle 1931/1988, p. 5.

175. For an extensive general discussion of medieval cosmology see Lewis 1967; for a brief introduction see Hamilton, pp. 87–95. For music see Winn, Chs 2 and 3; Stevens 1986, pp. 394–99; Stevens 1987 p. 159 'Music...was...one of the four highest subjects of learning, and in the form of *musica ecclesiastica*, it was the essential expression, among the arts, of cosmic harmony.' See also *ibid*, p. 172 and 178–9 for the significance of the move from musical dissonance to harmony in the Wakefield *Secunda Pastorum* play. For the contrast between heavenly harmony and hellish cacophony see below pp. 44–5.

176. Thus for Hildegarde: 'The human soul is symphonic, and any symphony of voices and instruments on earth, which is directed heaven-wards, is a means of reintegration, of bringing the lost human-heavenly condition alive again.' Dronke, p. 198.

177. *The Merchant of Venice*, Act V Scene I lines 60–65.

178. Stevens 1986, p. 397.

STAINED GLASS

179. Extracts translated by Panofsky 1946, esp. pp. 62–7. See also Radding and Clark, Chs 4 and 5.

180. Neale and Webb, Ch. 1 § 19, p. 23.

181. The major reference is Morgan 1983. A detailed analysis of the Bishop's Eye and its context can be found in King, pp. 132–45.

182. Hugh, *The Metrical Life*, lines 937–945, pp. 58–9.

183. See, for instance, Neale, vol. II, pp. 138–39: '...the north, all through the Old Testament, is taken, even as village tradition has made it in our churchyards, to be the especial possession of Satan.' *The Castle of Perseverance* has Belial's scaffold on the north side, Milton also has the armies of Satan coming from the north, see *Paradise Lost*, VI, 78–86.

184. For the Theophilus legend see Fryer.

INHABITANTS

185. Ed. W. O. Hassall, London, 1954, fols 2 and 2v.

186. A marvellous example of an image of this fecundity can be found in the Hours of St Omer in the British Library, reproduced in Camille, ill. 66.

187. So Hausherr suggests.

188. Whittingham 1979, pp. 9–13.

189. Whittingham 1973, p. 8.

190. Verzar, pp. 130–3, refers to such figures at Modena and Piacenza which have inscriptions suggesting this meaning. Janson, p. 46, refers to images of apes in such poses: 'Their demonic character is conveyed by their pose and expression: they are oppressed by a heavy load from which they cannot free themselves...there are [also] numerous examples of

human, or semi-human, beings treated in this manner....obviously sinners or personified vices...' Michael Camille in Cassidy, p. 49, argues that 'this heaviness is the weight of the flesh that bears down upon the human soul, preventing its ascendance.'

191. Pevsner 1989, p. 473.

192. And Gray 1990, p. 180, points out that: '...the decomposing corpse is only half of the total visual ensemble and...the effigies of the dead persons are often portrayed with a fineness and sad beauty which seem to defy the ravages of death.'

193. First published 1650 & 1651. Recent edition 1989; quotation from p. 49.

194. For an insightful discussion of these matters see Aston 1993. Horrox p. 11, has a rather different interpretation, seeing 'a horrified fascination with physical corruption which expresses an underlying sense that the pleasures of worldly success are guilty pleasures'. See also Binski 1996.

195. The burial service contains a prayer that this be done; Henderson p. 94. See also Sheingorn esp. pp. 279–83.

196. 'Ryght welcome be ye, blessid creatures!/Tyme is that scrippe and burdoun ye forsake,/For now ye schul no lenger journey make;/And after labour time is of quiete,/And hevynesse and angwysshe to foryete.' Quoted in Gray 1972, p. 219. My modernisation.

197. This is the date suggested by both Schwarzbaum and Pevsner 1989. Zarnecki 1988, p. 96, thinks post-1145 more plausible.

198. See Schwartzbaum.

199. See Julian of Norwich, Ch. 64, pp. 78–9; 'I saw a body lyand on the erth which body shewid hevy and ogyley, withoute shappe and forme as it were a bolned quave of styngand myre. And sodenly out of this body sprang a ful fair creature, a little childe ful shapen and formid, swifte and lively, whiter than lilly, which sharpely glode up onto hevyn.'

200. The imagery of angels carrying the soul is often used in books of Hours to illustrate the Commendation of Souls, a series of psalms recited after the Office of the Dead. This seems especially characteristic of English books; see Wieck, pp. 131–2.

THE IMP AND OTHER BEASTS

201. In recent years there was some dissension within the cathedral Chapter which the Press unfortunately made much of. It was suggested by some Christians of rather extreme views that the troubles were caused by the presence of and attention paid to the Imp.

202. Goldberg points out (p. 118) that women were generally considered to be the paradigm church-chatterers; a characteristic piece of medieval misogyny. Tutivilus is usually shown between two gossiping women, as in a wall-painting at Melbourne, Derbyshire.

203. See Owst, pp. 512–15 for Tutivilus and other comic devils with a moral purpose. Tutivilus turns up among the other devils in the Towneley play of the Last Judgement. Although he rejoices in all forms of ill-doing, his special role is not forgotten: 'yit of thise kyrkchaterars/here ar a menee.../god castys thaym out, trulee, ffrom his temple; all sich mysdoers/I cach thaym then to me ffull soyn.' England, p. 304.

204. Stevens 1987, p. 166: 'The demons betray their lust for power, much like earthly tyrants...'

205. *Ancrene Wisse* 1962, p. 149.

206. *Ancrene Wisse* 1962, p. 54; Morris, p. 179; Eccles, p. 31, II.951–2.

207. If it seems surprising that images should have different, even contradictory meanings one need only compare them with linguistic units. As Meyer Schapiro succinctly puts it: 'Two senses of the same view may exist then in one style like the variable senses of a word, a grammatical category, or syntactical form in different contexts.' Schapiro 1973, p. 45.

208. Camille, passim.

209. For instance, this is the interpretation given by Gardner (pp. 226–7) of the gargoyles on the exterior of such churches as Heckington: 'In these the mason was able to give free play to his fancy'.

210. Dante: *Paradiso*, Canto XIII: 19–30, pp. 158–9.

211. For a brief discussion of this see Harris 1992, pp. 89–90.

212. See Tydeman, p. 26: '...these texts should be regarded as essentially exercises in popularising what the medieval mind perceived as constituting the truths necessary for human survival in this world and the next, and no literary or theatrical strategies are deemed too down market in their associations to be rejected.' See also his discussion, on p. 31, of the play *Mankind*, which he characterises as a 'racy and scatological piece which has only recently been accorded its true importance as a piece of excellent didactic drama.' The implications of this comment throw some doubt on the argument in Camille that the scatological features of medieval visual imagery are of largely secular inspiration. See also Wentersdorf, pp. 1–19.

213. This treatment of devils was not confined to the plays; see, for instance, Peter Dronke's comment: 'when she gives her demon words, Hildegard [of Bingen] resorts to a lower or comic register of speech...(So too in

Hrotsvitha's writings, evil, about to be confounded, always showed itself as comic and grotesque.)' Dronke, p. 165. The depiction of devils as winged, bestial figures seems to have been developed by Anglo-Saxon artists between *c.*970 and 1070; see Jordan.

214. Stevens 1987, p. 159, points to the strong, deliberate contrast in the Wakefield cycle between the musical harmonies of heaven and the Church's liturgy, and 'the cacophony of demonic voices that rings forth from devils and the unregenerate. At its most extreme, this contrast is expressed throughout the medieval popular religious drama on the one hand by divine music, the language of the spirit, and on the other by obscenity...'

215. For instance the directions for Belial in *The Castle of Perseverance*: '...and he that shall play Belial, look that he have gunpowder burning in pipes in his hands and his ears and in his arse when he goeth to battle.' Harris 1994, p. 12; also p. 30 for devilish music. Harris 1992, p. 142 has a description of a performance in which Satan's costume caught fire – not an intentional effect.

216. See Kolve, Ch. 6.

217. For an approach to this aspect of the Christian 'story' see J. R. Tolkein, *Tree and Leaf*, London, 1964, the essay on 'Fairy Stories' esp. pp. 61–63. 'The Christian still has to work, with mind as well as body, to suffer, hope and die; but he may now perceive that all his bents and faculties have a purpose, whch can be redeemed.' p. 63. See also Stevens 1987, pp. 305–7 for the relation between 'play' and 'earnest' in the mystery plays and in Chaucer.

218. Dante also wrote into his poetry a sense of the chaos of Hell and the harmony of Heaven; see Ferrante, esp. p. 170: 'With all the chaos and all the apparent variety, Hell is finally much more a realm of sameness, of aggressive selfishness with different trappings, while Paradise, with all the harmony, is, poetically, the realm of greatest variety. It is the diverse voices in *Paradiso* that create its sweet harmony.'

219. Julian of Norwich, Ch. 27, pp. 28–9: '...Jesus...seyd: "Synne is behovabil, but al shal be wel, and al shal be wel, and al manner of thyng shal be wele".' See also Ward 1992, XXV:29, 'For her the Cross is the revelation of the love that is God; and having faced steadily all the implications of this, in the end she can write, "Love was our Lord's meaning".'

220. It is often said that medievals had little sense of, or interest in, the real nature of other animals, but recently it has been argued that their knowledge was more accurate than has been recognised. See Clark and McMunn.

221. See Friedman 1981, pp. 184–5. The *Liber Monstrorum* shows extreme hostility towards exotic races, but this attitude seems to have fallen out of favour in the twelfth century, when all kinds of monstrous creatures begin to be portrayed as accessible to preaching and conversion; see Friedman 1986, pp. 319–41.

222. At least, according to the twelfth-century Bestiary edited and translated by T. H. White (White pp. 51–53). He notes, however, that there is some confusion among bestiaries and among theological commentators as to the exact nature of this beast.

223. For the moral implications of this acceptance of diversity see 'Monsters and the Antipodes in the Early Middle Ages and Enlightenment' in Flint, pp. 65–80.

224. A contrary view was expressed by Albertus Magnus, who argued that pygmies were sub-human, but his ideas were not widely accepted; see Janson, pp. 83–94.

225. For an extensive account of the natural history of the monstrous races see Friedman 1981; pp. 90–2 have a discussion of Augustine's views.

226. See Muratova.

227. See Klingender, p. 152.

228. See Tilley.

229. Bede, Ch. XIX, pp. 220–23.

230. See Backhouse.

231. See Klingender pp. 140 and 344. The translation of this quotation from the *Life of St Godric* is taken from Waddell, pp. 87–8. 'Nam algentibus circumquaque brumae rigoribus, ipse nudipedalis incessit, et si forte aliquid animal glaciali inquietudine dissolutum repperisset, inter ascellas suas, vel certe in sinu suo, refocillandum, componere consuevit.' Godric of Finchale, Ch. 40, p. 98.

232. Hugh *Magna Vita* pp. 103–9.

233. Muratova p. 131: '...in September 1186, St Hugh of Avalon had been installed in Lincoln, arousing everyone's curiosity with his pet swan.'

234. Bede, Ch. X, pp. 188–91. 'Quod dum ageret, uenere continuo duo de profundo maris quadrupedia, quae uulgo lutraeae vocantur. Haec ante illum strata in arena, anhelitu suo pedes ejus fouere coeperunt ac uillo satagebant extergere.'

235. This point is made in greater depth by Ward 1989, pp. 65–76. See also Schapiro 1980, pp. 154–60 & 175.

236. As discussed in Cizewski, pp. 65–88. See also Muratova p. 122: 'ideas on knowledge of the material world leading to knowledge of God...were widely current among English scholars of the twelfth century.'

237. *De Gratia Contemplationis*, Liber Primus, Cap. 6, in *Richardi Sancti Victoris: Opera*, Vol. I, p. 154: 'quando rerum istarum visibilium forma, et imago in

considerationem adducitur, cum obstupescentes attendimus, et attendentes obstupescimus, corporalia ista quae sensu corporeo haurimus quam sint multa, quam magna, quam diversa, quam pulchra, vel iucunda, et in his omnibus creatricis illius superessentiae potentiam, sapientiam, munificentiam mirando veneramur et venerando miramur.' Translation adapted from that in *Richard of St Victor*, p. 161.

238. For some less well-known examples see St Bonaventure's *Life of St Francis*, Ch. 8. A readily available edition is that trans. T. Okey, Everyman's Library, London, 1910, repr. 1950, pp. 350–56.
239. SCG II: Ch. 2. Trans. in Aquinas, p. 30.
240. This is the way the Vulgate took the meaning of this passage: 'Illic naves pertransibunt: Draco iste quem formasti ad illudendum ei' (in the Vulgate numbering 103:26). This is the meaning of the original Hebrew text according to Seybold, pp. 79 & 188. Other translations have understood it otherwise; AV has: 'There go the ships: there is that leviathan, whom thou hast made to play therein.' I am grateful to Professor John Emerton for confirming that the Hebrew allows both translations.
241. Including dragons, about whom St Augustine commented: '...magna quaedam sunt animantia dracones, majora non sunt super terram...et laudant Deum? Absit. Sed vos considerantes dracones, attendite artificem draconum, creatorem draconum; et cum miramini dracones, et dicitis, Magnus Deus qui haec fecit, dracones laudant Deum de vocibus vestris...' (dragons are certain large creatures, there are none larger on earth...and they praise God? Far from it. But you who think of dragons, pay attention to the maker of dragons, to the creator of dragons; and when you marvel at dragons, and say, 'Great is God who has made these', the dragons praise God through your voices....) *Enarratio in Psalmum CXLVII*, PL XXXVII Col. 1943. My translation.
242. Chapter 175 of the popular fourteenth-century book *Gesta Romanorum*, which deals with the monstrous races is headed: 'Concerning the Diversity and Marvels of the World...' Friedman points out (p. 125) that this 'focuses on the "showing forth" by the races of God's plenitude and creative imagination.' In the seventeenth century George Herbert took up the theme of all creatures praising God in his poem *Providence*.
243. More 1965, Book 2, pp. 100–101. 'quem caeterorum more artificum arbitrantur: mundi huius visendam machinam homini (quem solum tantae rei capacem fecit) exposuisse spectandam: eoque chariorem habere: curiosum ac sollicitum inspectorem, operisque sui admiratorem: quam eum qui velut animal expers mentis: tantum ac tam mirabile spectaculum, stupidus immotusque neglexerit.' From More 1966, i3 recto.
244. 'But the cathedral itself is still only a building, a work of art. The spiritual edification which it is to effect requires the concentrated effort of the observer meditating on the images and relationships among the parts of the artistic model.' Nolan, p. 54.

EPILOGUE

245. 'Haec est scala Jacob, per quam conscendere solam/Credenti populo dat bona vita polum.' Henderson p. 202 fn. Translation *English Hymnal* no. 634 v.9.
246. Bath Abbey has on its west front sculpted angels climbing ladders, an explicit example of this imagery.
247. Precisely this text was inscribed over the Apsidal arch of the pilgrimage church of St Martin at Tours. See MacCormack.

Bibliography

Aberth, J., 'The Sculpted Heads and Figures Inside the Chapter House of York Minster', *Journal of the British Archaeological Association*, CXLII 1989

Abulafia, David, Michael Franklin, and Miri Rubin, eds, *Church and City 1000–1500: Essays in Honour of Christopher Brooke*, Cambridge, 1992

Ancrene Riwle, The (*The Corpus MS: Ancrene Wisse*), translated into modern English by M. D. Salu, London, 1955

Ancrene Wisse, ed. J. R. R. Tolkien, EETS, London, 1962

Anderson, M. D., *The Choir Stalls of Lincoln Minster*, Lincoln, 1951

Aquinas, St Thomas, *Summa contra Gentiles*, trans. James F. Anderson, Notre Dame and London, 1975

Aston, Margaret, 'Death', in Horrox, pp. 202–28

Aston, Margaret, *Faith and Fire*, London, 1993

Atherton, Ian, Eric Fernie, Christopher Harper-Bill and Hassell Smith, eds, *Norwich Cathedral: Church, City and Diocese, 1096–1996*, London, 1996

Augustine of Hippo, *Confessions*, ed. James J. O'Donnell, Oxford, 1992

Backhouse, Janet, 'Birds, Beasts and Initials in Lindisfarne's Gospel Books', in Gerald Bonner, David Rollason and Clare Stancliffe, eds, *St. Cuthbert, his Cult and his Community to AD 1200*, Woodbridge, 1989

Bailey, T. W., *The Processions of Sarum and the Western Church*, Toronto, 1971

Baily, John, 'Lincoln Cathedral: Progress on the Romanesque Frieze', *Church Building*, 1995, pp. 16–21

Baily, John, 'St. Hugh's Choir at Lincoln', *Architectural History*, 1991, pp. 1–35

Baldovin, J. F., *The Urban Character of Christian Worship*, Rome, 1987

Bates, David, *Bishop Remigius of Lincoln*, Lincoln, 1992

Beadle, Richard, ed., *The Cambridge Companion to Medieval English Theatre*, Cambridge, 1994

Bede, *Two* Lives *of Saint Cuthbert, A Life by an Anonymous Monk of Lindisfarne* and *Bede's Prose Life*, ed. and trans. Bertram Colgrave, Cambridge, 1940, repr. 1985

Berry, Mary, 'What the Saxon Monks Sang: Music in Winchester in the Late Tenth Century', in Yorke, pp. 149–60

Binski, Paul, *Medieval Death: Ritual and Representation*, London, 1996

Block, K. S., *Ludus Coventriae: or, The Plaie Called Corpus Christi*, 1922, repr. Oxford, 1960

Boitani, Piero and Anna Torti, eds, *Religion in the Poetry and Drama of the Late Middle Ages in England*, Cambridge, 1990

Bond, Francis, *Wood Carvings in English Churches: Misericords*, Oxford, 1910

Bond, Francis, *Wood Carvings in English Churches: Stalls and Tabernacle Work*, Oxford, 1910

Bonde, Sheila, *Fortress-Churches of Languedoc: Architecture, Religion and Conflict in the High Middle Ages*, Cambridge, 1994

Bonner, Gerald, David Rollason and Clare Stancliffe, eds, *St. Cuthbert, his Cult and his Community to AD 1200*, Woodbridge, 1989

Brewer, Derek, *Chaucer and his World*, London, 1978

Briscoe, Marianne G. and John C. Coldewey, eds. *Contexts for Early English Drama*, Bloomington and Indianapolis, 1989

Brooke, Christopher, 'Bishop Walkelin and his Inheritance', in Crook, pp. 1–12

Brooke, Christopher, 'The Cathedral in Medieval Society', in Swaan 1969, pp. 13–20

Brooke, Christopher, *The Twelfth Century Renaissance*, London, 1969

Broughton, Lynne, 'The Metaphysics of Light and the Metaphysics of Contradiction', *Seminaria Niedzicka* VII, Cracow, 1992, pp. 27–36

Buckton, David and T. A. Heslop, *Studies in Medieval Art and Architecture*, Stroud, 1994

Camille, Michael, *Image on the Edge: The Margins of Medieval Art*, London, 1992

Campbell, Marion, *An Introduction to Medieval Enamels*, London, 1983

Carpenter, Christine, 'The Religion of the Gentry of Fifteenth-Century England' in Williams, pp. 53–74

Cassidy, Brendan, ed., *Iconography at the Crossroads*, Princeton, 1993

Cave, C. J. P., *Lincoln Roof Bosses* (Lincoln Minster Pamphlets, No. 3), 1973

Cizewski, Wanda, 'Reading the World as Scripture: Hugh of St. Victor's *De Tribus Diebus*', *Florilegium* , vol. 9, 1987, pp. 65–88

Clark Willene B. and Meredith McMunn, eds, *Beasts and Birds of the Middle Ages*, Philadelphia, 1989

Cobb, Peter G., 'The History of the Christian Year', in Jones, Wainwright and Yarnold, pp. 403–19

Coldstream, Nicola, *The Decorated Style*, London, 1994

Coleman, Janet, *English Literature in History*, London, 1981

Cornelius, Roberta D., *The Figurative Castle*, Bryn Mawr Pennsylvania, 1930

Crook, John, ed., *Winchester Cathedral: Nine Hundred Years 1093–1993*, Chichester, 1993

Crossley, Paul, 'Kasimir the Great at Wisliça', in Stratford, pp. 39–48
Dante Alighieri, *The Inferno of Dante Alighieri*, London, 1900, repr. 1962
Dante Alighieri, *The Purgatorio of Dante Alighieri*, London, 1901, repr. 1962
Dante Alighieri, *The Paradiso of Dante Alighieri*, London, 1899, repr. 1962
Davidson, Clifford, ed., *Word, Picture and Spectacle*, Kalamazoo, 1984
Deshman, Robert, 'The Imagery of the Living Ecclesia and the English Monastic Reform', in Szarmach, pp. 261–82
Dionysius the Areopagite, *Pseudo-Dionysius: The Complete Works* (The Classics of Western Spirituality Series), trans. Colm Luibheid, New York, 1987
Donne, John, *Donne's Prebend Sermons*, ed. Janel M. Mueller, Cambridge Massachusetts, 1971
Dougherty, James, *The Fivesquare City*, Notre Dame, 1980
Dronke, Peter, *Women Writers of the Middle Ages*, Cambridge 1984, repr. 1991
Duby, Georges, *The Age of the Cathedrals: Art and Society 980– 1420*, trans. Eleanor Levieux and Barbara Thompson, London, 1981
Duchesne, L., *Christian Worship: Its Origin and Evolution*, fifth edn, London, 1923
Duffy, Eamon, *The Stripping of the Altars*, New Haven and London, 1992
Durandus of Mende, *Rationale Divinorum Officiorum a Rev.^{mo} Domino Gulielmo Durando*, ed. Joseph Dura, Naples, 1859
Durandus of Mende, translation in Neale and Webb
Eccles, Mark, ed., *The Macro Plays*, EETS OS 262, Oxford, 1969
England, George, ed., *The Towneley Plays*, EETS ES 71, Oxford, 1897
English Hymnal, The, 1st edn, 1906, repr. 1933
Ferguson, Peter, '"Porta Patens Esto": Notes on Early Cistercian Gatehouses in the North of England', in Fernie and Crossley, pp. 47–59
Fernie, Eric and Paul Crossley, eds, *Medieval Architecture and its Intellectual Context*, London, 1990
Ferrante, Joan, 'A poetics of chaos and harmony', in Jacoff, pp. 153–71
Flint, Valerie I. J., *Ideas in the Medieval West: Texts and their Contexts*, London, 1988
Fowler, David C., *The Bible in Early English Literature*, London, 1977
Frankl, Paul, 'Lincoln Cathedral', *The Art Bulletin*, 1962, pp. 29–39
Frankl, Paul, 'The "Crazy" Vaults of Lincoln Cathedral', *The Art Bulletin*, 1953, pp. 95–107
Michael Franklin, 'The Cathedral as Parish Church', in Abulafia, Franklin, and Rubin, pp. 173–198
Freedberg, David, *The Power of Images*, Chicago, 1989
Friedman, John Block, *The Monstrous Races in Medieval Art and Thought*, Cambridge Massachusetts, 1981
Friedman, John Block, 'The Marvels-of-the-East Tradition in Anglo-Saxon Art', in Szarmach, pp. 319–41
Fryer, Alfred C., 'Theophilus, the Penitent, as represented in Art', *The Archaeological Journal*, XCII, 1936, pp. 287–333.
Furnivall, F. J., ed., *The Tale of Beryn*, London, 1887
Gardner, Arthur, *A Handbook of English Medieval Sculpture*, New York and Cambridge, 1935
Gem, Richard, 'Lincoln Minster: Ecclesia Pulchra, Ecclesia Fortis', in Heslop and Sekules
Geremek, Bronislaw, *The Margins of Society in Late Medieval Paris*, Cambridge, 1987
Gilchrist, Roberta, *Gender and Material Culture*, London, 1994
Glasscoe, Marion, *English Medieval Mystics: Games of Faith*, London, 1993
Glenn, Virginia, 'The Sculpture of the Angel Choir at Lincoln', in Heslop and Sekules, pp. 102–8
Godric of Finchale, St, *Libellus de Vita et Miraculis S. Godrici, Heremitae de Finchale*, London (Surtees Society), 1845
Goering, Joseph, *William de Montibus (c. 1140–1213): The Schools and the Literature of Pastoral Care*, Toronto, 1992
Goldberg, P. J. P., 'Women', in Horrox, pp. 112–31
Goldman, Bernard, *The Sacred Portal*, Detroit, 1966
Gransden, Antonia, 'The question of the consecration of St Edmund's church', in Wood and Loud, pp. 59–86
Gray, Douglas, 'Popular Religion and Late Medieval English Literature', in Boitani and Torti, pp.1–28
Gray, Douglas, *Themes and Images in the Medieval English Lyric*, London, 1972
Gurevich, A. J. *Categories of Medieval Culture*, London, 1985
Gurewich, V., 'Observations on the Iconography of the Wound in Christ's Side, with Special Reference to its Position', *Journal of the Warburg and Courtauld Institutes*, 1957, pp. 358–62
Hamilton, Bernard, *Religion in the Medieval West*, London, 1986
Harper, John, *The Forms and Orders of Western Liturgy*, Oxford, 1991
Harris, John Wesley, *Medieval Plays at Lincoln*, Lincoln, 1994
Harris, John Wesley, *Medieval Theatre in Context*, London,

1992
Hausherr, Reiner, 'Zu Auftrag, Programm und Büstenzyklus des Prager Domchores', *Zeitschrift für Kunstgeschichte* 34, 1971, pp. 21–46
Henderson, W. G., ed., *Manuale et Processionale ad usum insignis ecclesia Eboracensis* (Surtees Soc. vol. LXIII) Durham, 1875
Henry, H. T., ed., *The Hymns of the Breviary and Missal*, London, 1922
Heslop, T. A. and V. A. Sekules, eds, *Medieval Art and Architecture at Lincoln Cathedral: The British Archaeological Association Conference Transactions for the Year 1982*, Leeds, 1986
Heslop, T. A., 'Brief in Words but Heavy in the Weight of its Meaning', in *Art History*, 9, 1986, pp. 1–11
Heslop, T. A., 'The Iconography of the Angel Choir at Lincoln Cathedral', in Fernie and Crossley
Heslop, T. A., 'Towards an Iconology of Croziers', in Buckton and Heslop, pp. 36–45
Hill, Francis, *Medieval Lincoln*, Cambridge, 1948, repr. Stamford, 1990
Hoey, Laurence, 'Pier Alternation in English Gothic Architecture' *Journal of the British Archaeological Association*, 139, 1986, pp. 45–67
Holloway, Julia Bolton, *The Pilgrim and the Book*, New York, 1987; repr. 1992
Horrox, Rosemary, ed., *Fifteenth Century Attitudes*, Cambridge, 1994
Horsfield, Robert A., '*The Pomander of Prayer*: Aspects of Late Medieval English Carthusian Spirituality and its Lay Audience', in Sargent, pp. 205–13
Horstmann, Carl, *The Minor Poems of the Vernon Manuscript*, EETS OS vol. 117, London 1892
Horstmann, Carl, *Yorkshire Writers*, ii, London, 1896
Huber, P. M., ed., *The Vision of the Monk of Eynsham* (*Visio Monachi de Eynsham*), *Romanische Forschungen*, xvi, 1903
Hugh, St, Bishop of Lincoln, *Magna Vita Sancti Hugonis*, ed. Decima L. Douie and David Hugh Farmer, corr. repr. Oxford Medieval Texts, 1985
Hugh, St, Bishop of Lincoln, *The Metrical Life of St. Hugh*, trans. Charles Garton, Lincoln, 1986
Hymns Ancient and Modern: New Standard, London, 1983
Jacoff, Rachel, ed., *The Cambridge Companion to Dante*, Cambridge, 1993
Janson, H. W. *Apes and Ape Lore*, London, 1952
Jones, Cheslyn, Geoffrey Wainwright and Edward Yarnold, eds, *The Study of Liturgy*, London, 1978
Jones, Stanley, Kathleen Major, and Joan Varley, *The Survey of Ancient Houses in Lincoln II: Houses to the south and west of the Minster*, Lincoln, 1987
Jordan, Louis, 'Demonic Elements in Anglo-Saxon Iconography', in Szarmach, pp. 283–317
Julian of Norwich, *A Revelation of Love*, ed. Marion Glasscoe, 1976, rev. repr. 1986
Kahn, Deborah, ed., *The Romanesque Frieze and its Spectator*, London, 1992
Kahrl, Stanley J., 'Medieval Staging and Performance', in Briscoe and Coldewey, pp. 219–37
Kempe, Margery, *The Book of Margery Kempe*, ed. Sanford Brown Meech and Hope Emily Allen, Oxford, EETS 212, 1940
Kempe, Margery, *The Book of Margery Kempe*, modern version by W. Butler-Bowden, London, 1936
Kidson, Peter, 'St Hugh's Choir', in Heslop and Sekules 1986, pp. 29–42
Kidson, Peter, 'Architectural History', in Owen 1994, pp. 14–46
King, David J., 'The Glazing of the South Rose of Lincoln Cathedral', in Heslop and Sekules, pp. 132–45
Klingender, Francis, *Animals in Art and Thought to the End of the Middle Ages*, Cambridge, Massachusetts, 1971
Kolve, V. A., *The Play Called Corpus Christi*, London, 1966
Kötting, Bernhard, *Peregrinatio Religiosa: Wallfahrten in der Antike und das Pilgerwesen in der alten Kirche*, Regensberg, 1950
Krautheimer, Richard, 'Introduction to an "Iconography of Medieval Architecture"', *Journal of the Warburg and Courtauld Institutes*, 5, 1942, pp. 1–33
Laird, Marshall, *English Misericords*, London, 1986
Legge, J. Wickham, *The Sarum Missal Edited from Three Early Manuscripts*, Oxford, 1916
Lethaby, W. R., 'Notes on the Sculptures in Lincoln Minster: The Judgement Porch and the Angel Choir', *Archaeologia*, 1906, pp. 379–90
Lewis, C. S., *The Discarded Image*, Cambridge, 1967
Lewis, Flora, 'Rewarding Devotion: Indulgences and the Promotion of Images', in Wood, pp. 179–94
MacCormack, Sabine, 'Loca Sancta: The Organization of Sacred Topography in Late Antiquity', in Ousterhout, pp. 7–40
MacKinnon, H., 'William de Montibus, a Medieval Teacher', in Sandquist and Powicke, pp. 32–45
Macready, Sarah and F. H. Thompson, eds, *Art and Patronage in the English Romanesque*, London, 1986
Macy, Gary, *The Theologies of the Eucharist in the Early Scholastic Period*, Oxford, 1984
Major, Kathleen, *Minster Yard*, Lincoln, 1974
Mâle, Emile, *The Gothic Image*, trans. Dora Nussey, London, 1961

Martène, E., *De Antiquis Ecclesiae Ritibus*, III, Rouen, 1702
McEntire, Sandra, 'The Devotional Context of the Cross Before A. D. 1000', in Szarmach, pp. 345–76
Melinkoff, Ruth, *Outcasts: Signs of Otherness in Northern European Art of the Late Middle Ages*, 2 vols, Berkeley and Los Angeles, 1991
Milburn, Robert, *Early Christian Art and Architecture*, Aldershot, 1988
Morant, Roland W., *The Monastic Gatehouse and Other Types of Portal of Medieval Religious Houses*, Lewes, 1995
More, Sir Thomas, *Utopia*, facsimile of the first (1516) edition, Leeds, 1966
More, Sir Thomas, *Utopia*, trans. P. Turner, London, 1965
Morgan, Nigel, *The Medieval Glass of Lincoln Cathedral*, Corpus Vitrearum Medii Aevi, Great Britain-Occasional Paper III, London, 1983
Morgan, Nigel, 'Texts and Images of Marian Devotion in Fourteenth Century England', in Rogers 1993, pp. 34–57
Morgan, Nigel, 'Texts and Images of Marian Devotion in Thirteenth Century England', in Ormrod 1991, pp. 69–103
Morris, Richard, ed., *The Ayenbyte of Inwyt, or, Remorse of Conscience*, EETS OS 23, London, 1866
Muncey, R. W., *A History of the Consecration of Churches and Churchyards*, Cambridge, 1930
Muratova, Xenia, 'Bestiaries: an Aspect of Medieval Patronage', in Macready and Thompson, pp. 118–44
Neale, J. M., *A Commentary on the Psalms from Primitive and Medieval Writers*, third edn London, 1874
Neale, J. M., and B. Webb, trans., *The Symbolism of Church Ornaments*, London, 1893
Nelson, Alan H., *The Medieval English Stage*, Chicago and London, 1974
Nolan, Barbara, *The Gothic Visionary Perspective*, Princeton, 1977
Onians, John, *Bearers of Meaning*, Cambridge, 1988
O'Reilly, Jennifer, 'St John as a Figure of the Contemplative Life', in Ramsay, Sparks and Tatton-Brown 1992, pp. 165–85
Ormrod, W. M., ed., *England in the Thirteenth Century*, Harlaxton, 1985
Ormrod, W. M., ed., *England in the Thirteenth Century*, Stamford, 1991
Ousterhout, Robert, ed., *The Blessings of Pilgrimage*, Urbana and Chicago, 1990
Owen, Dorothy, ed., *A History of Lincoln Minster*, Cambridge, 1994
Owst, G. R., *Preaching in Medieval England*, Cambridge, 1926
Pächt, O., C. R. Dodwell and F. Wormald, *The St. Albans Psalter*, London, 1960
Palliser, D. M., 'Urban Society', in Horrox, pp. 144–9
Panofsky, Erwin, *Abbot Suger on the Abbey of St.-Denis and its Art Treasures*, Princeton, 1946
Pevsner, Nikolaus and David Lloyd, *The Buildings of England: Hampshire and the Isle of Wight*, 1967 repr 1973
Pevsner, Nikolaus and John Harris, *The Buildings of England: Lincolnshire*, 2nd ed. rev. Nicholas Antram, London, 1989
Pevsner, Nikolaus, *The Buildings of England: Wiltshire*, Harmondsworth, 1963
Pfaff, Richard W., '*De Cella in Seculum*: the Liturgical Aspects', in Sargent
PL, *Patrologiae Cursus Completus, series latina*, ed. J. P. Migne, 221 vols, Paris, 1857–66
Pope-Hennessy, John, *Fra Angelico*, Florence, 1981
Radding, Charles M., and William W. Clark, *Medieval Architecture, Medieval Learning: Builders and Masters in the Age of Romanesque and Gothic*, New Haven and London, 1992
Ramsay, Nigel, Margaret Sparks and Tim Tatton-Brown eds, *St Dunstan: His Life, Times and Cult*, Woodbridge, 1992
Richard of St. Victor, ed. and trans. Grover A. Zinn, New York, 1979
Richardi Sancti Victoris: Opera quae hactenus apparuere omnia, Venice, 1592
Roberts, M. E., 'The Relic of the Holy Blood and the Iconography of the Thirteenth Century North Transept Portal of Westminster Abbey', in Ormrod 1985, pp. 129–142
Rogers, Nicholas, ed., *England in the Fourteenth Century*, Stamford, 1993
Rolle, Richard, *Richard Rolle: The English Writings*, trans., ed. and intr. Rosamund S. Allen, London, 1989
Rolle, Richard, *The English Writings of Richard Rolle, Hermit of Hampole*, ed. Hope Emily Allen, Oxford, 1931, repr. 1988
Rowley, Trevor, *The High Middle Ages*, London, 1986
Rubin, Miri, *Charity and Community in Medieval Cambridge*, Cambridge, 1987
Rubin, Miri, *Corpus Christi: The Eucharist in Late Medieval Culture*, Cambridge, 1991
Russell, Georgina, 'The Thirteenth Century West Window of Lincoln Cathedral', in Heslop and Sekules, pp. 83–89
Salisbury, Joyce E., ed., *The Medieval World of Nature*, New York and London, 1993
Sandquist, T. A. and M. R. Powicke, *Essays in Medieval History Presented to Bertie Wilkinson*, Toronto, 1969
Sargent, Michael G., ed., *De Cella in Seculum: Religious and*

Secular Life and Devotion in Late Medieval England, Cambridge, 1989
Sauerländer, Willibald, 'Romanesque Sculpture in its Architectural Context', in Kahn, pp. 17–43
Saxl, Fritz, 'Lincoln Cathedral: The Eleventh Century Design for the West Front', *Archaeological Journal* 103 1946, pp. 105–117
Schapiro, Meyer, *Late Antique, Early Christian and Medieval Art*, London, 1980
Schapiro, Meyer, *Words and Pictures*, The Hague, 1973
Schwartzbaum, E., 'Three Tournai Tombslabs in England', *Gesta*, 1981, Vol. XX, pp. 89–97
Seidel, Linda, *Songs of Glory*, Chicago, 1981
Sekules, Veronica, 'Beauty and the Beast: Ridicule and orthodoxy in architectural marginalia in early fourteenth-century Lincolnshire', *Art History*, 1995, pp. 37–62
Sekules, V. A., 'The Gothic Sculpture', in Atherton, Fernie, Harper-Bill and Smith, pp. 197–209
Sekules, V. A., 'The Tomb of Christ at Lincoln and the Development of the Sacrament Shrine: Easter Sepulchres Reconsidered', in Heslop and Sekules, pp. 118–31
Seybold, Klaus, *Introducing the Psalms*, trans. R. Graeme Dunphy, Edinburgh, 1990
Sheingorn, Pamela, 'The Bosom of Abraham Trinity: A Late Medieval All Saints Image', in Williams, pp. 273–295
Sherwood, Jennifer, and Nikolaus Pevsner, *The Buildings of England: Oxfordshire*, Harmondsworth, 1974
Simson, Otto von, *The Gothic Cathedral*, New York, 1956, 3rd edn expanded 1989
Smalley, Beryl, *The Study of the Bible in the Middle Ages*, Oxford, 1952, repr. 1983
Smith, E. Baldwin *Architectural Symbolism of Imperial Rome and the Middle Ages*, Princeton, 1956
Southern, R. W., *Robert Grosseteste*, Oxford, 1986
Sperber, Daniel, *Midrash Jerushalem: A Metaphysical History of Jerusalem*, Jerusalem, 1982
Srawley, J. H., *Robert Grosseteste*, Lincoln, repr. 1966
Steane, John, *The Archaeology of the English Monarchy*, London, 1993
Stevens, John, *Words and Music in the Middle Ages*, Cambridge, 1986
Stevens, Martin, *Four Middle English Mystery Cycles*, Princeton, 1987
Stocker, David, 'The Shrine of Little St. Hugh', in Heslop and Sekules, pp. 109–17
Stookey, Laurence Hull, 'The Gothic Cathedral as the Heavenly Jerusalem: Liturgical and Theological Sources', *Gesta*, VIII, 1969, pp. 35–41
Stratford, Neil, ed., *Romanesque and Gothic*, Bury St Edmunds, 1987
Sumption, J., *Pilgrimage, an Image of Medieval religion*, London, 1975
Suso, Henry, *The Life of the Servant*, trans. James M. Clark, Cambridge, 1952, repr. 1982
Swaan, Wim, *The Gothic Cathedral*, London, 1969
Swanson, M. ed., *Exeter Cathedral: A Celebration*, Exeter, 1991
Swanson, R. N., 'Liturgy as Theatre: The Props', in Wood, pp. 239–53
Szarmach, Paul E. ed., *Sources of Anglo-Saxon Culture*, Kalamazoo, 1986
Tasker, Edward G., *Encyclopaedia of Medieval Church Art*, London, 1993
Taylor, Jeremy, *The Rule and Exercises of Holy Living* and *The Rule and Exercises of Holy Dying*, two volumes ed. P. G. Stanwood, Oxford, 1989
Tilley, Maureen A., 'Martyrs, Monks, Insects and Animals', in Salisbury, pp. 145–163
Towneley Plays, The, ed. George England, EETS es 71, Oxford, 1897
Turner, Victor and Edith, *Image and Pilgrimage in Christian Culture: Anthropological Perspectives*, Oxford, 1978
Twycross, Meg, 'The theatricality of medieval English plays', in Beadle, pp. 37–84
Tydeman, William, 'An introduction to medieval English theatre', in Beadle, pp. 1–36
Verzar, Christine B., 'Text and Image in North Italian Romanesque Sculpture', in Kahn, pp. 121–40
Waddell, Helen, *Beasts and Saints*, London, 1934
Ward, Benedicta, *Signs and Wonders*, Variorum Press, 1992
Ward, Benedicta, 'The Spirituality of St. Cuthbert', in Bonner, Rollason and Stancliffe, pp. 65–76
Wentersdorf, Karl P., 'The Symbolic Significance of *Figurae Scatologicae* in Gothic Manuscripts', in Davidson, pp. 1–19
Westra, M. Salvina, ed., *A Talking of the Love of God*, The Hague, 1950
White, T. H., trans. and ed., *The Book of Beasts*, New York, 1954, repr. 1984
Whittingham, Selby, *A Thirteenth Century Portrait Gallery at Salisbury Cathedral*, Salisbury, 1979
Whittingham, Selby, *Medieval Portrait Busts at New College Oxford*, London and Chichester, 1973
Wickenden, J. F., 'The Choir Stalls of Lincoln Cathedral', *The Archaeological Journal*, XXXVIII, 1881, pp. 42–61
Wickham, Glynne, *The Medieval Theatre*, Cambridge 1974, rev. 1987
Wieck, Roger S., *Time Sanctified*, New York, 1988

Wilkinson, John, 'Jewish Holy Places and the Origins of Christian Pilgrimage', in Ousterhout, pp. 41–53

Williams, Daniel, ed., *England in the Fifteenth Century*, Woodbridge, 1987

Williamson, Paul, ed., *The Medieval Treasury: The Art of the Middle Ages in the Victoria and Albert Museum*, London, 1986

Wilson, Christopher, *The Gothic Cathedral*, London, 1990

Wilson, Adrian and Joyce Lancaster, eds, *A Medieval Mirror: The Speculum Humanae Salvationis*, Berkeley and Los Angeles, 1984

Winn, James Anderson, *Unsuspected Eloquence: A History of the Relations between Poetry and Music*, New Haven and London, 1981

Wood, Diana, ed., *The Church and the Arts*, Oxford, 1992

Wood, Ian and G. A. Loud, eds, *Church and Chronicle in the Middle Ages*, London, 1991

Woolf, Rosemary, *Art and Doctrine: Essays on Medieval Literature*, London, 1986

Woolf, Rosemary, *The English Mystery Plays*, Berkeley and Los Angeles, 1972

Yorke, Barbara, ed., *Bishop Aethelwold: His Career and Influence*, Woodbridge, 1988

Young, Karl, *The Drama of the Medieval Church*, Oxford, 1933

Young, Karl, *The Dramatic Associations of the Easter Sepulchre*, Madison, 1920

Zarnecki, George, 'Henry of Blois as a Patron of Sculpture', in Macready and Thompson, pp 159–72

Zarnecki, George, *Romanesque Lincoln*, Lincoln, 1988

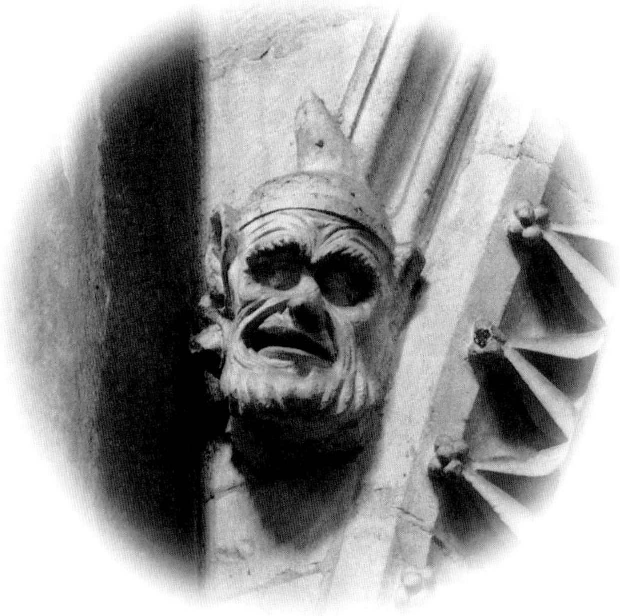

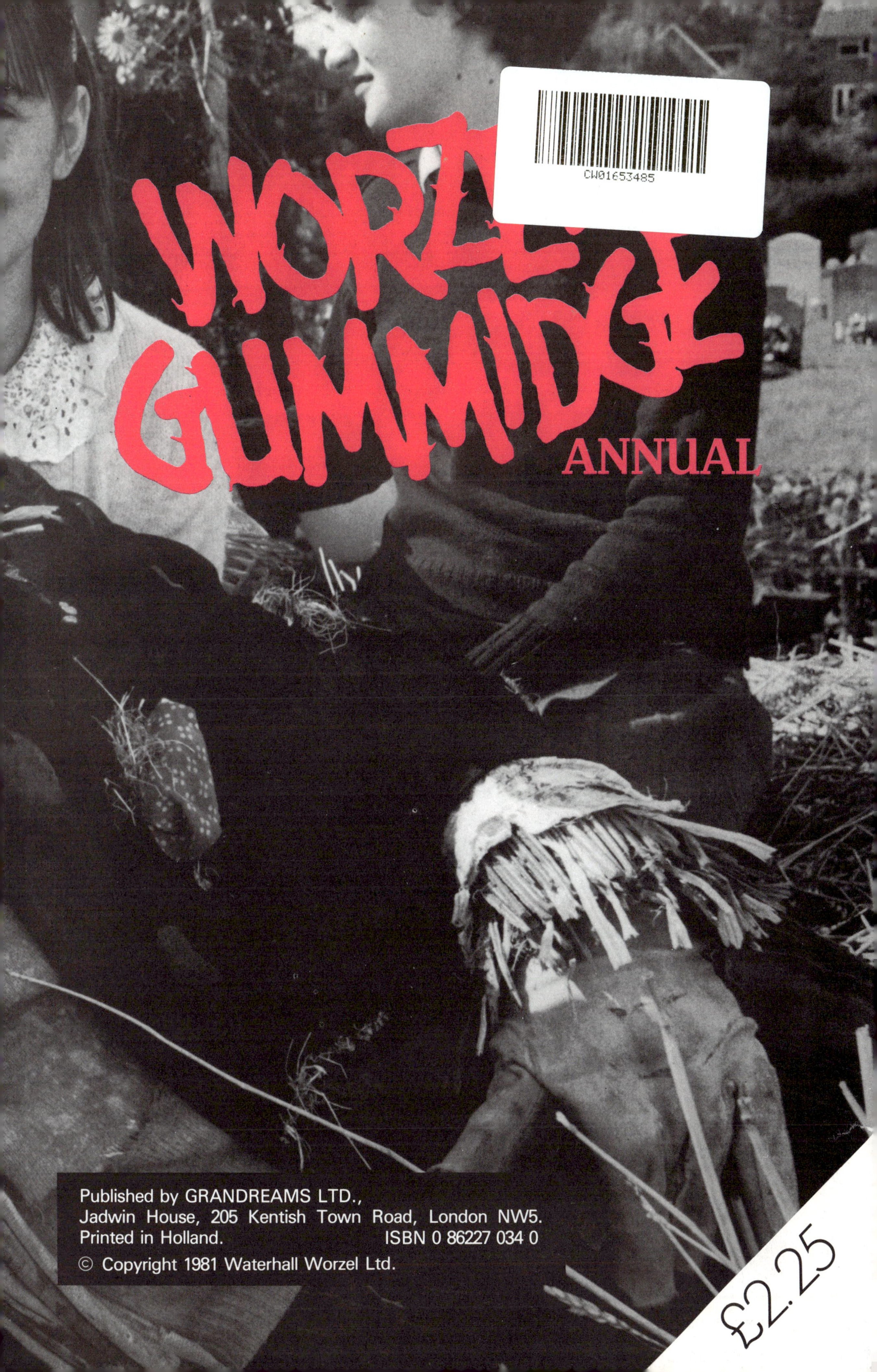

Published by GRANDREAMS LTD.,
Jadwin House, 205 Kentish Town Road, London NW5.
Printed in Holland. ISBN 0 86227 034 0

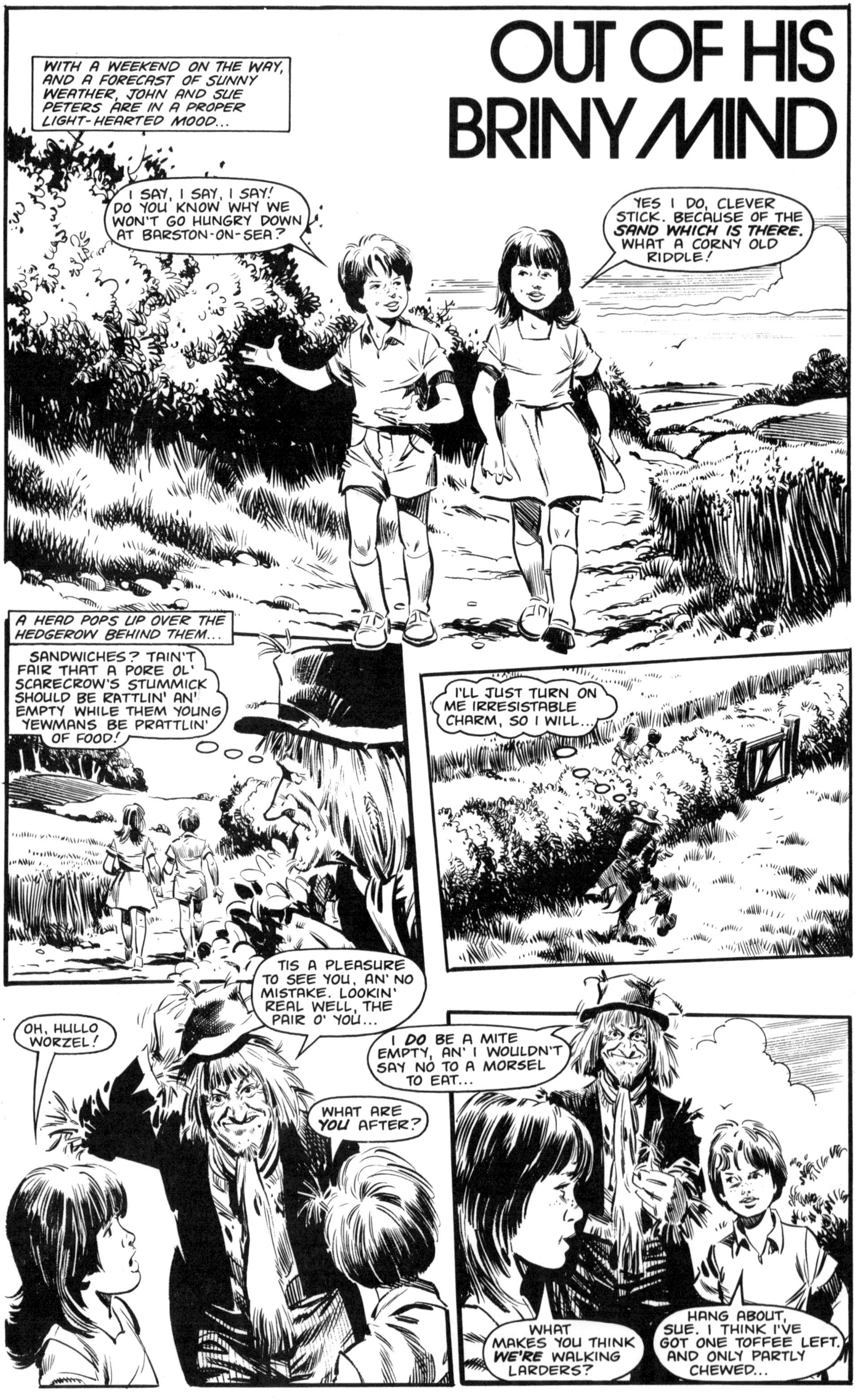
OUT OF HIS BRINY MIND
WITH A WEEKEND ON THE WAY, AND A FORECAST OF SUNNY WEATHER, JOHN AND SUE PETERS ARE IN A PROPER LIGHT-HEARTED MOOD...
I SAY, I SAY, I SAY! DO YOU KNOW WHY WE WON'T GO HUNGRY DOWN AT BARSTON-ON-SEA?
YES I DO, CLEVER STICK. BECAUSE OF THE SAND WHICH IS THERE. WHAT A CORNY OLD RIDDLE!
A HEAD POPS UP OVER THE HEDGEROW BEHIND THEM...
SANDWICHES? TAIN'T FAIR THAT A PORE OL' SCARECROW'S STUMMICK SHOULD BE RATTLIN' AN' EMPTY WHILE THEM YOUNG YEWMANS BE PRATTLIN' OF FOOD!
I'LL JUST TURN ON ME IRRESISTABLE CHARM, SO I WILL...
TIS A PLEASURE TO SEE YOU, AN' NO MISTAKE. LOOKIN' REAL WELL, THE PAIR O' YOU...
OH, HULLO WORZEL!
WHAT ARE YOU AFTER?
I DO BE A MITE EMPTY, AN' I WOULDN'T SAY NO TO A MORSEL TO EAT...
WHAT MAKES YOU THINK WE'RE WALKING LARDERS?
HANG ABOUT, SUE. I THINK I'VE GOT ONE TOFFEE LEFT. AND ONLY PARTLY CHEWED...

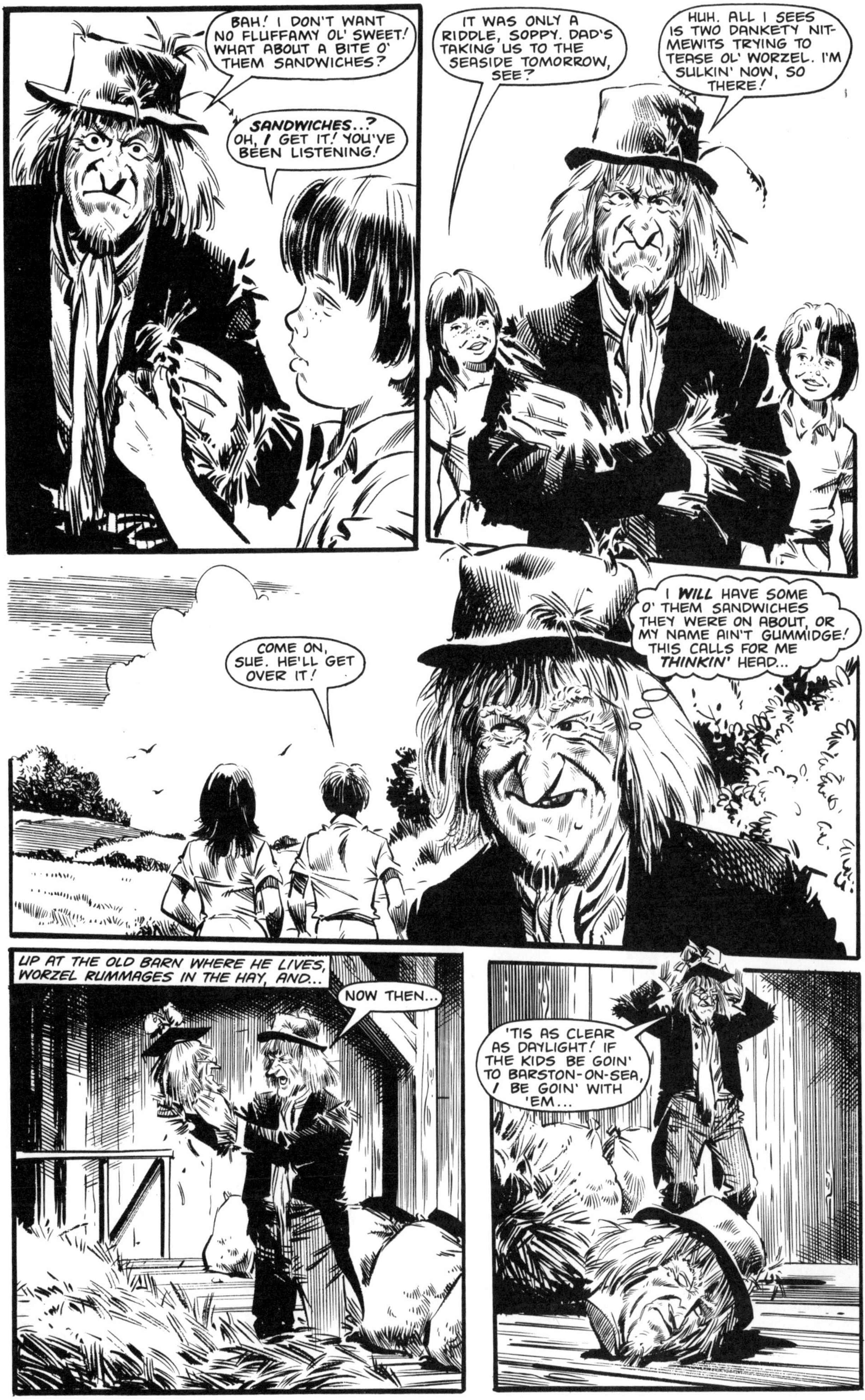

BAH! I DON'T WANT NO FLUFFAMY OL' SWEET! WHAT ABOUT A BITE O' THEM SANDWICHES?
SANDWICHES..? OH, I GET IT! YOU'VE BEEN LISTENING!
IT WAS ONLY A RIDDLE, SOPPY. DAD'S TAKING US TO THE SEASIDE TOMORROW, SEE?
HUH. ALL I SEES IS TWO DANKETY NIT-MEWITS TRYING TO TEASE OL' WORZEL. I'M SULKIN' NOW, SO THERE!
COME ON, SUE. HE'LL GET OVER IT!
I WILL HAVE SOME O' THEM SANDWICHES THEY WERE ON ABOUT, OR MY NAME AIN'T GUMMIDGE! THIS CALLS FOR ME THINKIN' HEAD...
UP AT THE OLD BARN WHERE HE LIVES, WORZEL RUMMAGES IN THE HAY, AND...
NOW THEN...
'TIS AS CLEAR AS DAYLIGHT! IF THE KIDS BE GOIN' TO BARSTON-ON-SEA, I BE GOIN' WITH 'EM...

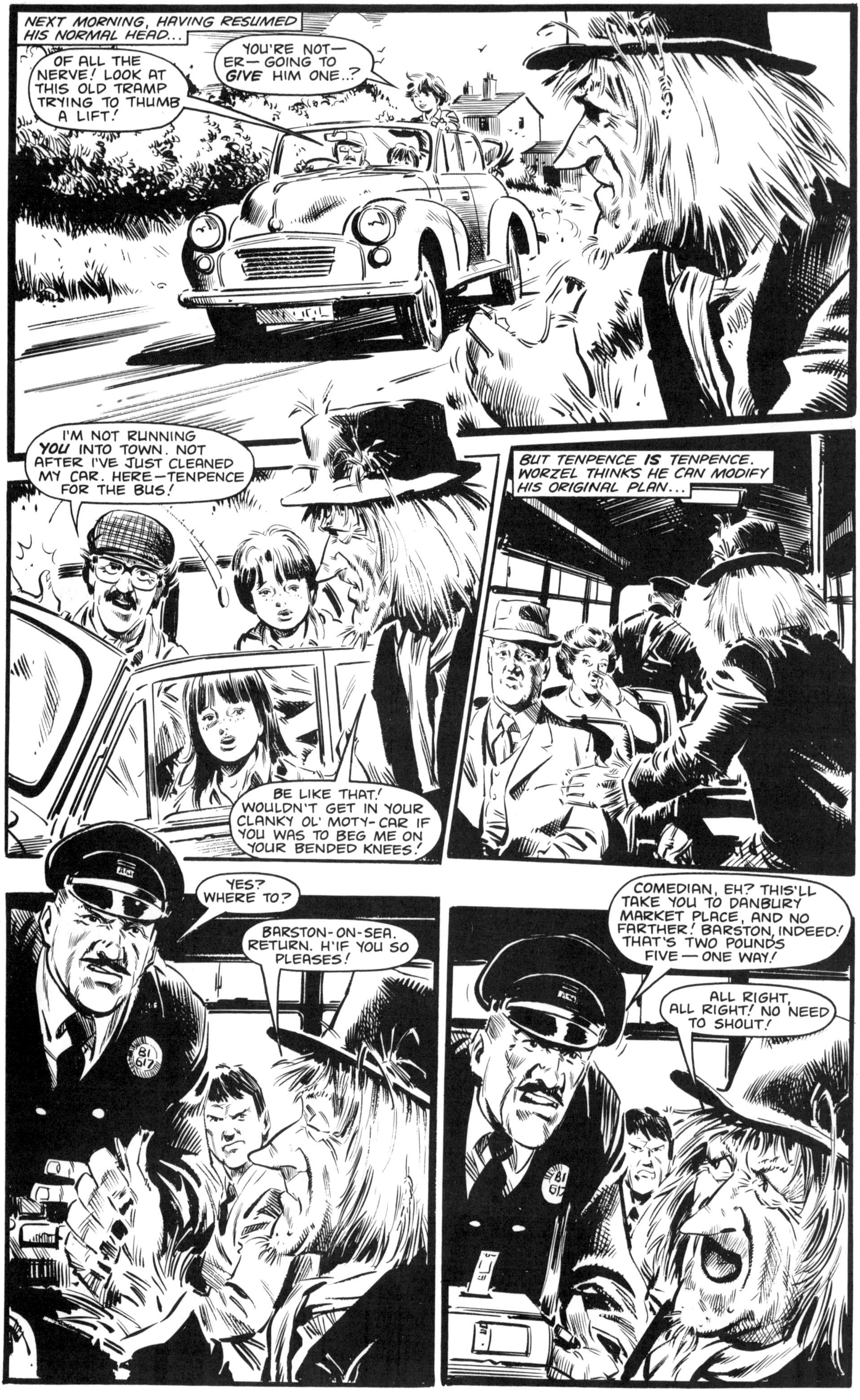
NEXT MORNING, HAVING RESUMED HIS NORMAL HEAD...
OF ALL THE NERVE! LOOK AT THIS OLD TRAMP TRYING TO THUMB A LIFT!
YOU'RE NOT— ER— GOING TO GIVE HIM ONE..?
I'M NOT RUNNING YOU INTO TOWN. NOT AFTER I'VE JUST CLEANED MY CAR. HERE—TENPENCE FOR THE BUS!
BE LIKE THAT! WOULDN'T GET IN YOUR CLANKY OL' MOTY-CAR IF YOU WAS TO BEG ME ON YOUR BENDED KNEES!
BUT TENPENCE IS TENPENCE. WORZEL THINKS HE CAN MODIFY HIS ORIGINAL PLAN...
YES? WHERE TO?
BARSTON-ON-SEA. RETURN. H'IF YOU SO PLEASES!
COMEDIAN, EH? THIS'LL TAKE YOU TO DANBURY MARKET PLACE, AND NO FARTHER! BARSTON, INDEED! THAT'S TWO POUNDS FIVE—ONE WAY!
ALL RIGHT, ALL RIGHT! NO NEED TO SHOUT!

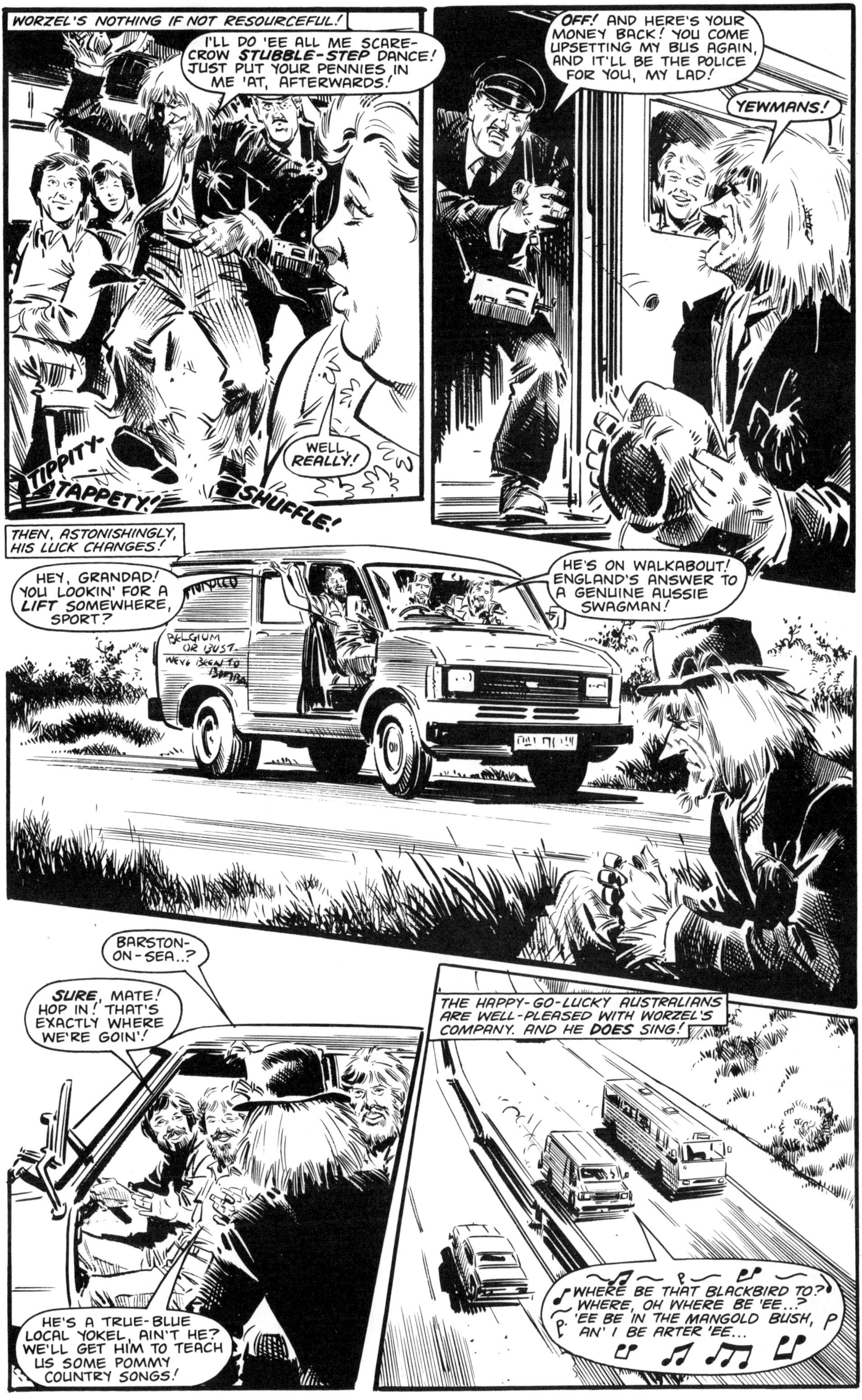
WORZEL'S NOTHING IF NOT RESOURCEFUL!
I'LL DO 'EE ALL ME SCARE-CROW STUBBLE-STEP DANCE! JUST PUT YOUR PENNIES IN ME 'AT, AFTERWARDS!
TIPPITY-TAPPETY!
SHUFFLE!
WELL, REALLY!
OFF! AND HERE'S YOUR MONEY BACK! YOU COME UPSETTING MY BUS AGAIN, AND IT'LL BE THE POLICE FOR YOU, MY LAD!
YEWMANS!
THEN, ASTONISHINGLY, HIS LUCK CHANGES!
HEY, GRANDAD! YOU LOOKIN' FOR A LIFT SOMEWHERE, SPORT?
HE'S ON WALKABOUT! ENGLAND'S ANSWER TO A GENUINE AUSSIE SWAGMAN!
BELGIUM OR BUST.
BARSTON-ON-SEA..?
SURE, MATE! HOP IN! THAT'S EXACTLY WHERE WE'RE GOIN'!
HE'S A TRUE-BLUE LOCAL YOKEL, AIN'T HE? WE'LL GET HIM TO TEACH US SOME POMMY COUNTRY SONGS!
THE HAPPY-GO-LUCKY AUSTRALIANS ARE WELL-PLEASED WITH WORZEL'S COMPANY. AND HE DOES SING!
WHERE BE THAT BLACKBIRD TO? WHERE, OH WHERE BE 'EE..? 'EE BE IN THE MANGOLD BUSH, AN' I BE ARTER 'EE...

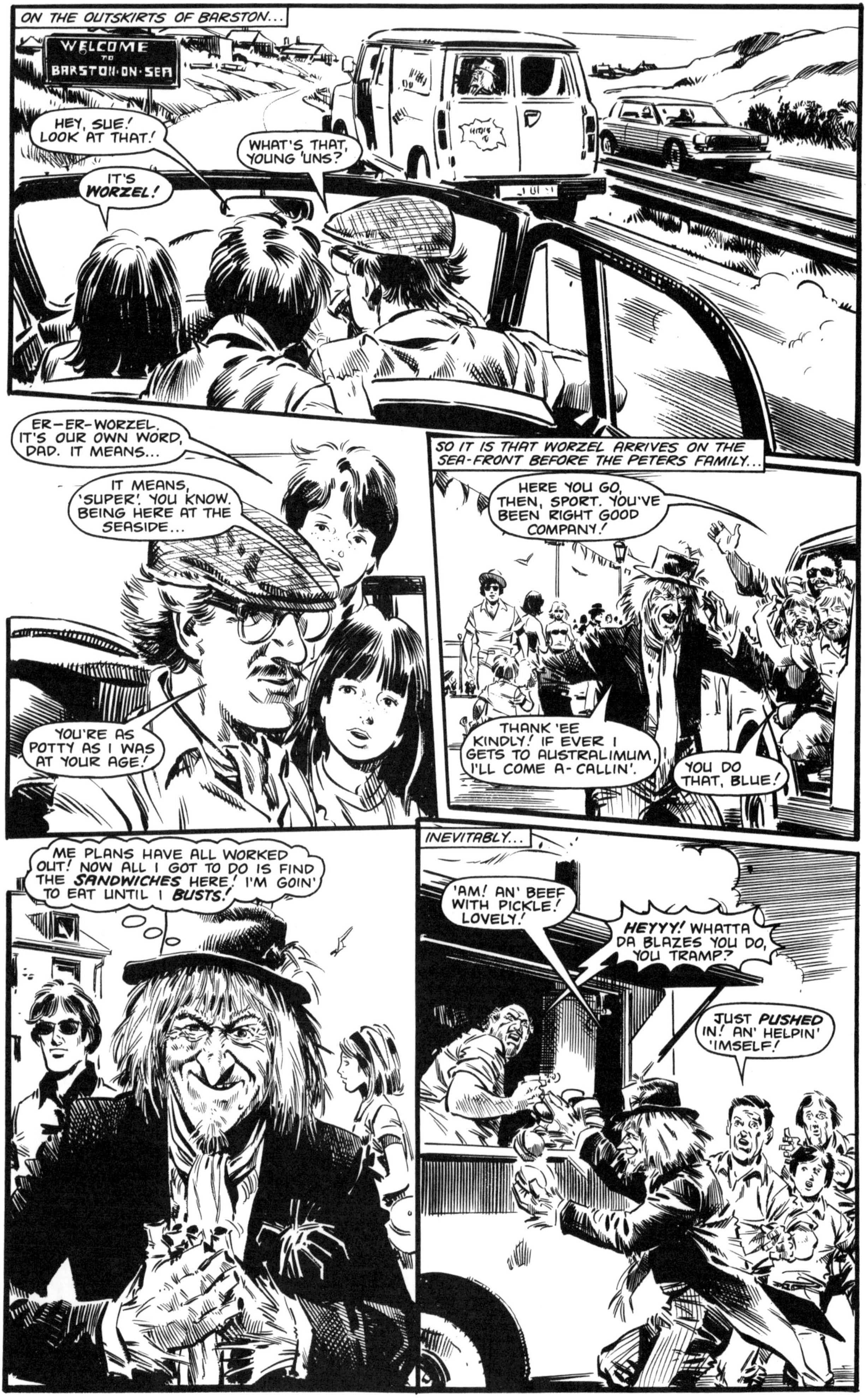
ON THE OUTSKIRTS OF BARSTON...
WELCOME TO BARSTON-ON-SEA
HEY, SUE! LOOK AT THAT!
IT'S WORZEL!
WHAT'S THAT, YOUNG 'UNS?
ER-ER-WORZEL. IT'S OUR OWN WORD, DAD. IT MEANS...
IT MEANS, 'SUPER'. YOU KNOW. BEING HERE AT THE SEASIDE...
YOU'RE AS POTTY AS I WAS AT YOUR AGE!
SO IT IS THAT WORZEL ARRIVES ON THE SEA-FRONT BEFORE THE PETERS FAMILY...
HERE YOU GO, THEN, SPORT. YOU'VE BEEN RIGHT GOOD COMPANY!
THANK 'EE KINDLY! IF EVER I GETS TO AUSTRALIMUM, I'LL COME A-CALLIN'.
YOU DO THAT, BLUE!
ME PLANS HAVE ALL WORKED OUT! NOW ALL I GOT TO DO IS FIND THE SANDWICHES HERE! I'M GOIN' TO EAT UNTIL I BUSTS!
INEVITABLY...
'AM! AN' BEEF WITH PICKLE! LOVELY!
HEYYY! WHATTA DA BLAZES YOU DO, YOU TRAMP?
JUST PUSHED IN! AN' HELPIN' 'IMSELF!

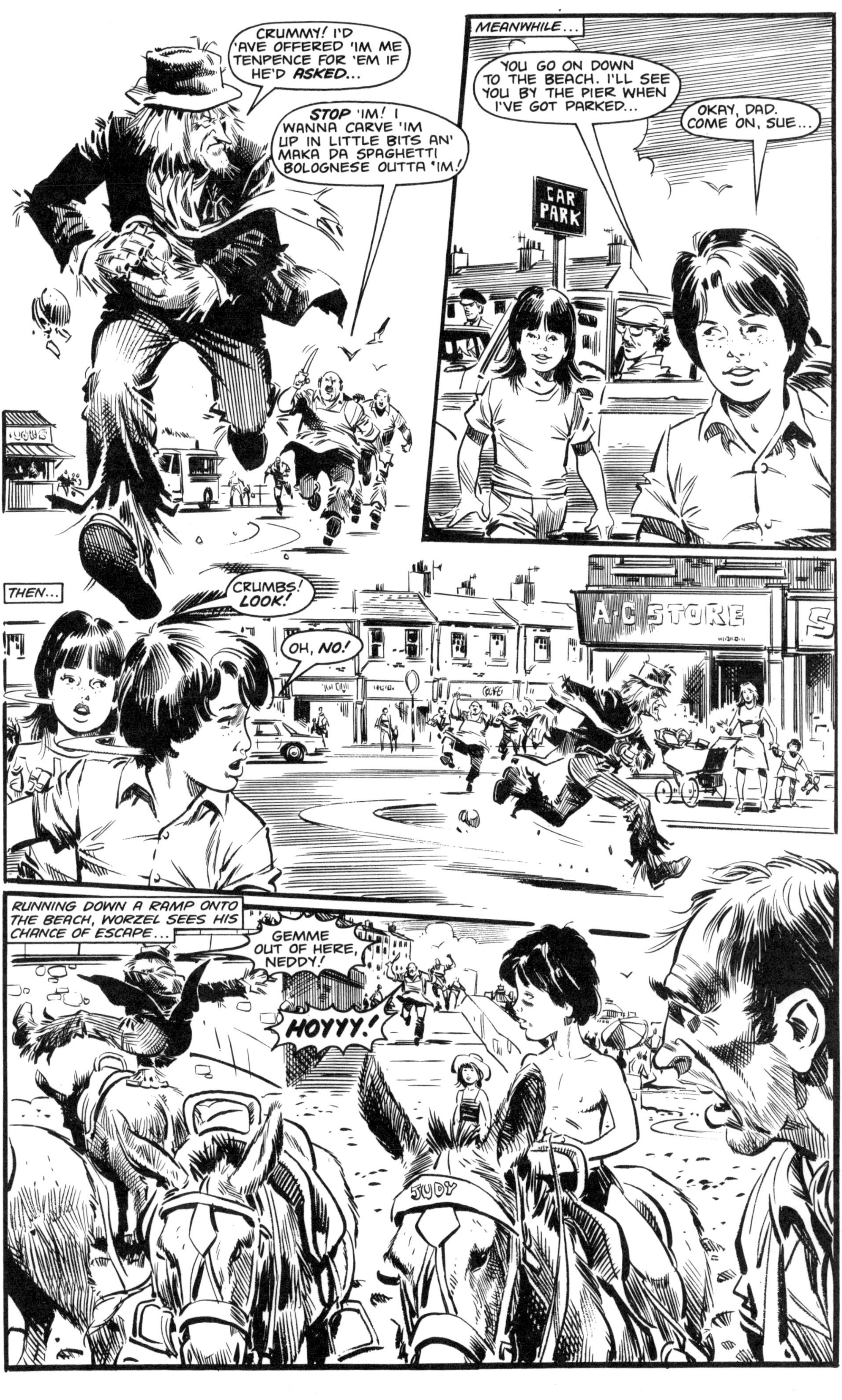
CRUMMY! I'D 'AVE OFFERED 'IM ME TENPENCE FOR 'EM IF HE'D ASKED...
STOP 'IM! I WANNA CARVE 'IM UP IN LITTLE BITS AN' MAKA DA SPAGHETTI BOLOGNESE OUTTA 'IM!
MEANWHILE...
YOU GO ON DOWN TO THE BEACH. I'LL SEE YOU BY THE PIER WHEN I'VE GOT PARKED...
OKAY, DAD. COME ON, SUE...
CAR PARK
THEN...
CRUMBS! LOOK!
OH, NO!
A-C STORE
RUNNING DOWN A RAMP ONTO THE BEACH, WORZEL SEES HIS CHANCE OF ESCAPE...
GEMME OUT OF HERE, NEDDY!
HOYYY!
JUDY

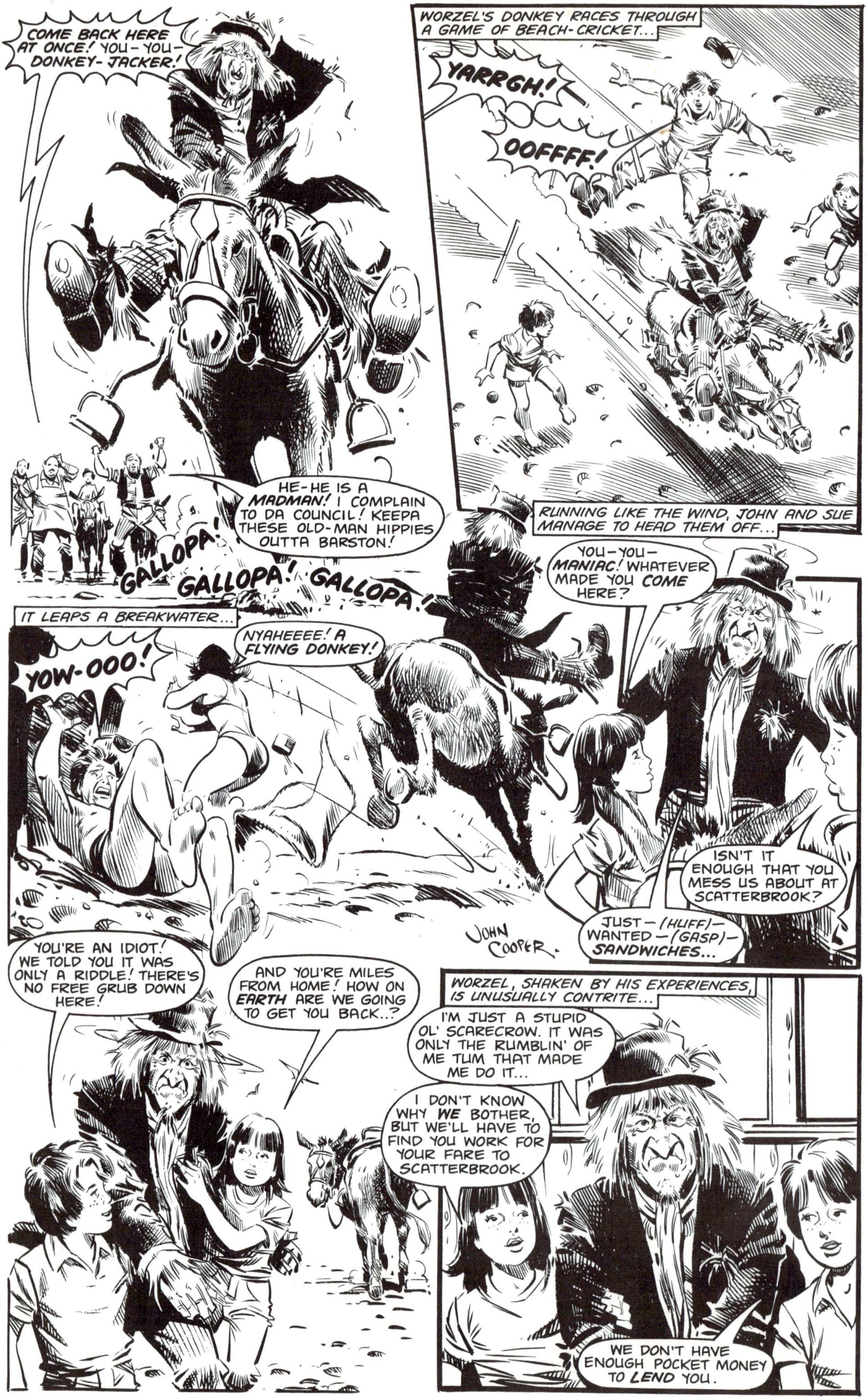

COME BACK HERE AT ONCE! YOU—YOU—DONKEY-JACKER!
HE-HE IS A MADMAN! I COMPLAIN TO DA COUNCIL! KEEPA THESE OLD-MAN HIPPIES OUTTA BARSTON!
GALLOPA! GALLOPA! GALLOPA!
WORZEL'S DONKEY RACES THROUGH A GAME OF BEACH-CRICKET...
YARRGH!
OOFFFF!
IT LEAPS A BREAKWATER...
YOW-OOO!
NYAHEEEE! A FLYING DONKEY!
RUNNING LIKE THE WIND, JOHN AND SUE MANAGE TO HEAD THEM OFF...
YOU—YOU—MANIAC! WHATEVER MADE YOU COME HERE?
ISN'T IT ENOUGH THAT YOU MESS US ABOUT AT SCATTERBROOK?
JUST—(HUFF)—WANTED—(GASP)—SANDWICHES...
JOHN COOPER.
YOU'RE AN IDIOT! WE TOLD YOU IT WAS ONLY A RIDDLE! THERE'S NO FREE GRUB DOWN HERE!
AND YOU'RE MILES FROM HOME! HOW ON EARTH ARE WE GOING TO GET YOU BACK..?
WORZEL, SHAKEN BY HIS EXPERIENCES, IS UNUSUALLY CONTRITE...
I'M JUST A STUPID OL' SCARECROW. IT WAS ONLY THE RUMBLIN' OF ME TUM THAT MADE ME DO IT...
I DON'T KNOW WHY WE BOTHER, BUT WE'LL HAVE TO FIND YOU WORK FOR YOUR FARE TO SCATTERBROOK.
WE DON'T HAVE ENOUGH POCKET MONEY TO LEND YOU.

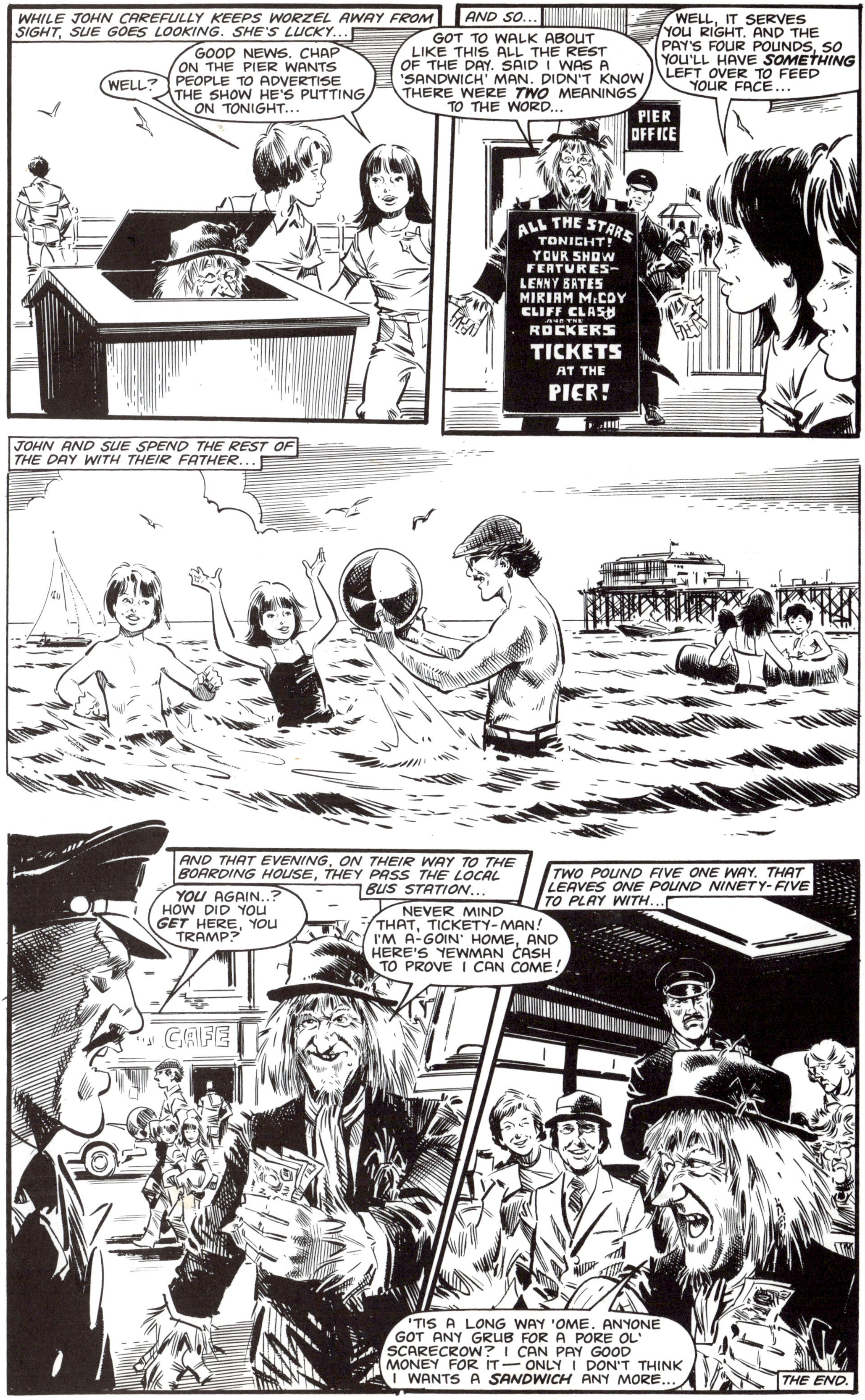
WHILE JOHN CAREFULLY KEEPS WORZEL AWAY FROM SIGHT, SUE GOES LOOKING. SHE'S LUCKY...
WELL?
GOOD NEWS. CHAP ON THE PIER WANTS PEOPLE TO ADVERTISE THE SHOW HE'S PUTTING ON TONIGHT...
AND SO...
GOT TO WALK ABOUT LIKE THIS ALL THE REST OF THE DAY. SAID I WAS A 'SANDWICH' MAN. DIDN'T KNOW THERE WERE TWO MEANINGS TO THE WORD...
PIER OFFICE
ALL THE STARS TONIGHT! YOUR SHOW FEATURES- LENNY BATES MIRIAM McCOY CLIFF CLASH AND THE ROCKERS TICKETS AT THE PIER!
WELL, IT SERVES YOU RIGHT. AND THE PAY'S FOUR POUNDS, SO YOU'LL HAVE SOMETHING LEFT OVER TO FEED YOUR FACE...
JOHN AND SUE SPEND THE REST OF THE DAY WITH THEIR FATHER...
AND THAT EVENING, ON THEIR WAY TO THE BOARDING HOUSE, THEY PASS THE LOCAL BUS STATION...
YOU AGAIN..? HOW DID YOU GET HERE, YOU TRAMP?
NEVER MIND THAT, TICKETY-MAN! I'M A-GOIN' HOME, AND HERE'S YEWMAN CASH TO PROVE I CAN COME!
CAFE
TWO POUND FIVE ONE WAY. THAT LEAVES ONE POUND NINETY-FIVE TO PLAY WITH...
'TIS A LONG WAY 'OME. ANYONE GOT ANY GRUB FOR A PORE OL' SCARECROW? I CAN PAY GOOD MONEY FOR IT — ONLY I DON'T THINK I WANTS A SANDWICH ANY MORE...
THE END.

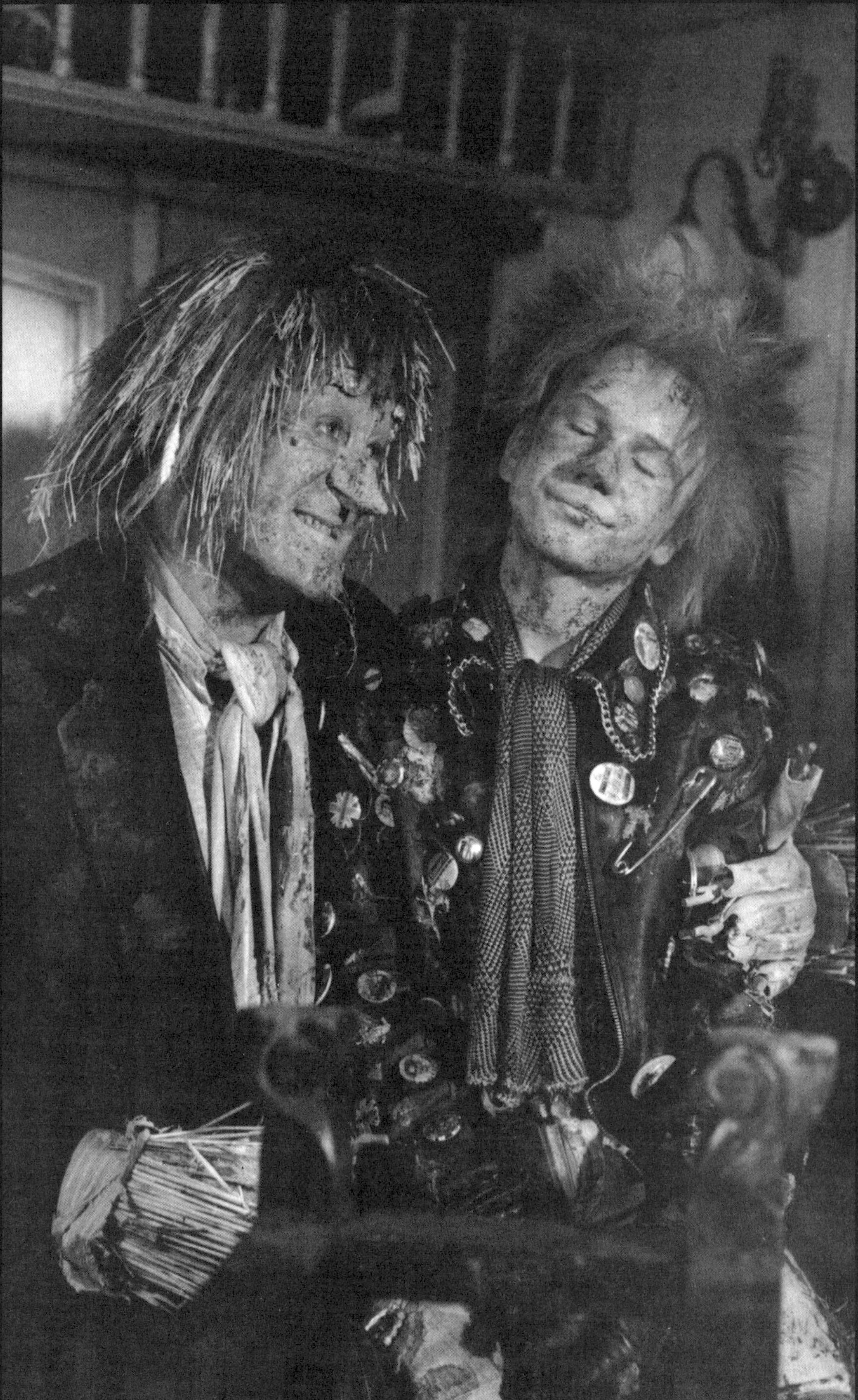

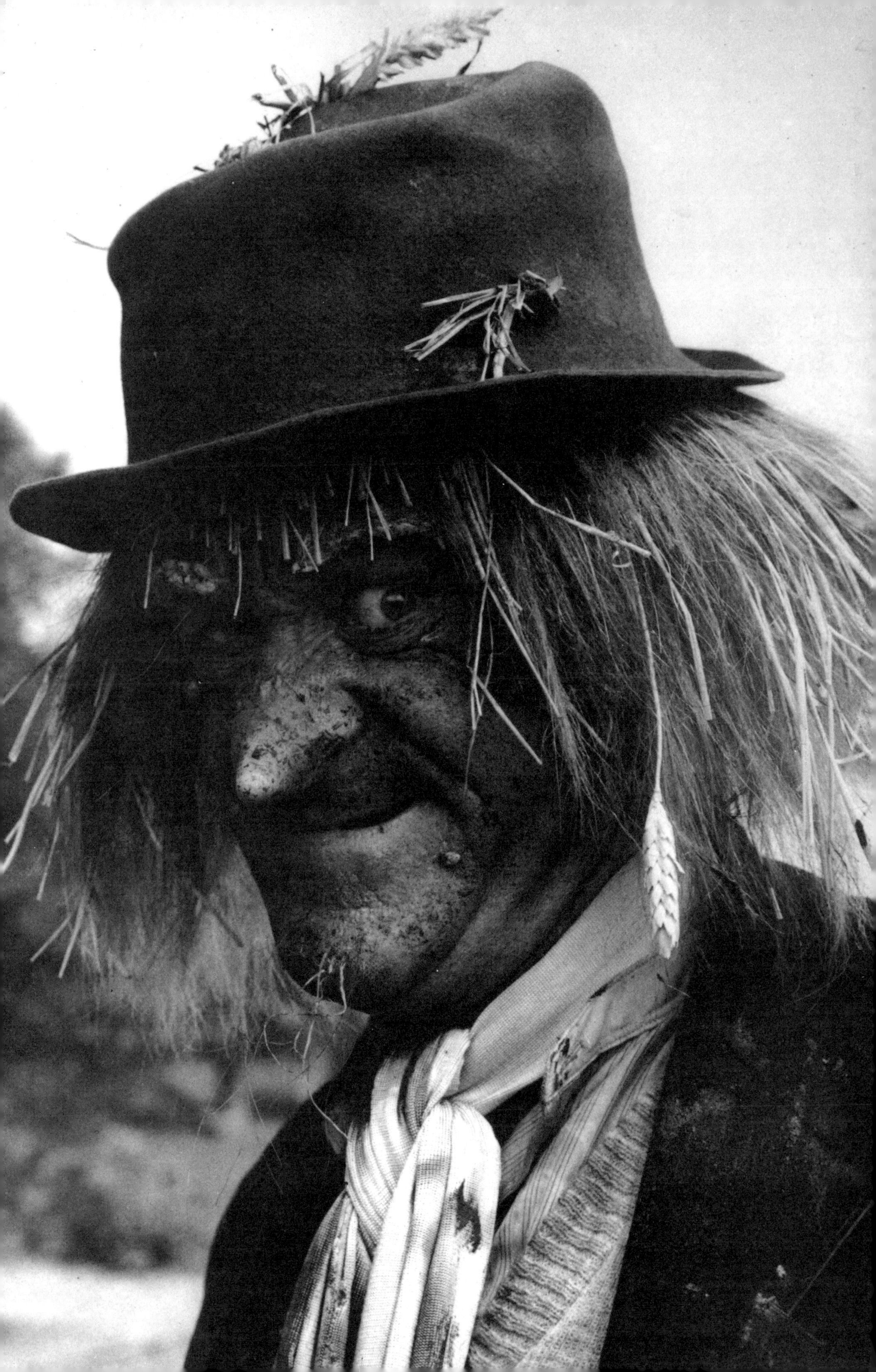

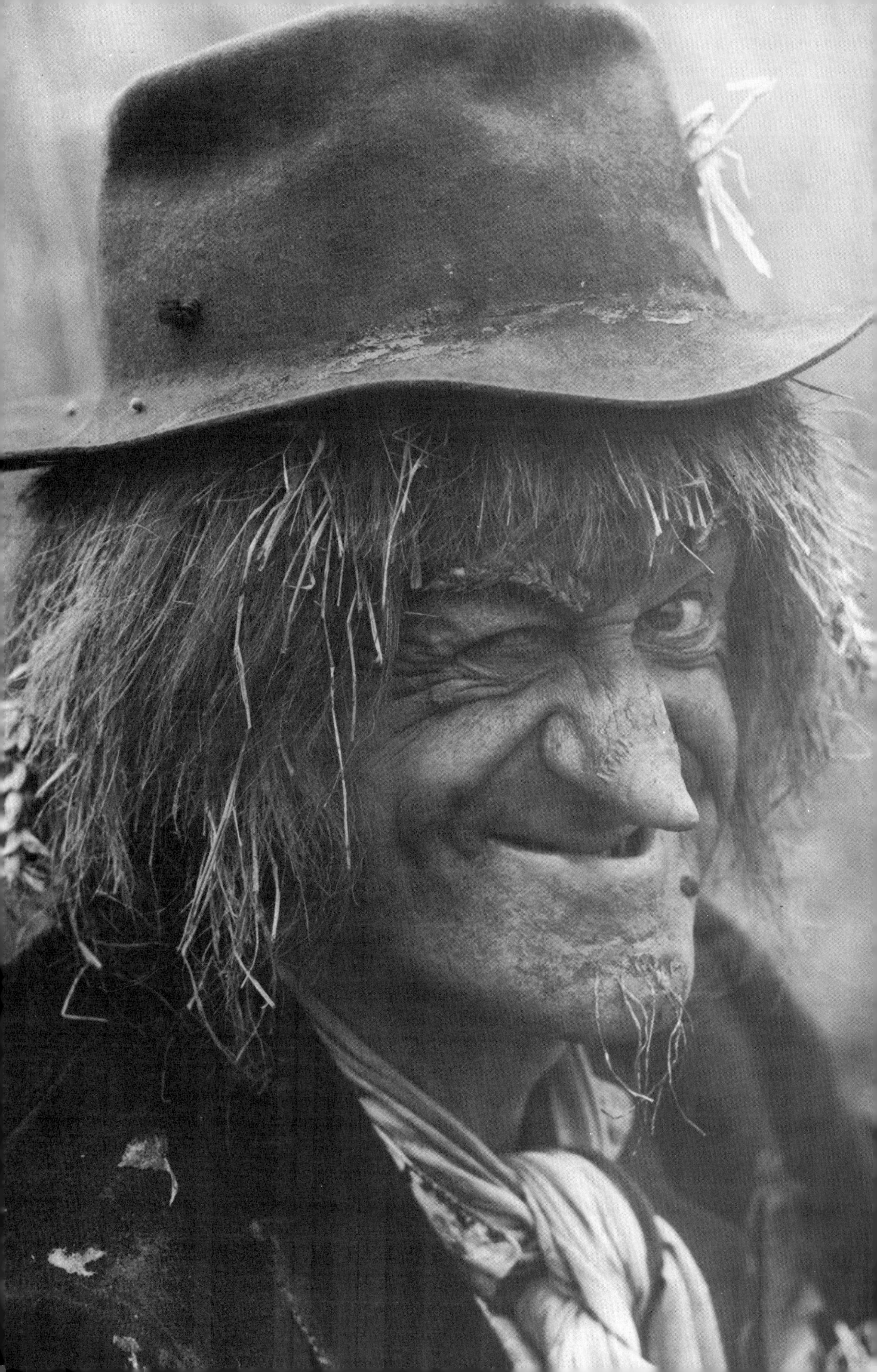

SPEAK AND SAY, THE WORZEL WAY

"Peewor Yewwor Esswor Aitchworzel Ohwor Effwor Effwordip."

"I beg your pardon?" said the scholarly-looking man in Ten Acre Field.

"You 'eard," said Worzel.

"I did *not* hear. And I most decidedly did not come across the furrows to have a string of impertinence spouted at me by a tramp!"

"Aywor Eyewor Ennwor Teeworzel Ennwor Owordip Teewor Arrwor Aywor Emmwor Peeworzel," said the scarecrow, defiantly.

The man swallowed. "I came to ask you if you could direct me to Braithwaite's Farm. I have some research to do there."

"Straight down the lane, matey. Unless you wants to go over the field an' climb the stile," said Worzel amiably. "Don't mind me. Don't h'apologumise. 'Tis only my land you'm a-crossin'."

"Silly fool," spluttered the academic. "But look here. What was that gibberish you were spouting at me just then?"

"Ah!" Worzel put a straw finger to his nose. "That there were *Worzelese,* guv'nor. 'Tis what I uses to confuse loony yewmans like you."

The professor — for such he was, all the way from Oxford to collect an example of country dialect from the Braithwaites' oldest farmhand on his tape-recorder — went on his way, muttering. He little realised that he has just passed up the unique opportunity of learning one of *the* most secret local languages in the world! The language of that most taciturn tribe — the scarecrows!

As he watched the man go, Worzel thought back to the days when he'd been no more than a parcel of chaff. Lumped together on the Crowman's bench, about to be made into a genuine, bird-staggering, rook-baiting caretaker-of-the-corn!

"I mind you he used to croon at me," said Worzel to himself. "When you wants to talk to 'em — them yewmans, like — put a 'wor' behind the letters of each word, 'e said. 'course, I had to take me books an' learn to read, I did. Still got me learnin' 'ead, I 'ave. Up in the old barn."

He chuckled. "First, it was 'the cat sat on the mat'. That were easy. Cat. C-A-T. So it became Ceewor Aywor Teewor. But it were only three letters, so it were Ceewor Aywor Teewor*dip.* You puts 'dip' on the end of any word o' three letters or less. More than three — say it were 'cats', then it would be Ceewor Aywor Teeworzel. You shoves 'worzel' on the end o' words o' more than three letters, see?"

Worzel pondered as a large black crow fluttered down and paused, as if considering whether or not to try its luck. "Now," he mused, as he flapped the bird away, "I've got meself a right eddikayshun. I can spell big words, an' all. Like — er — er — turnip. That's — teewor yewwor arrwor ennwor eyewor peeworzel." He smiled smugly. "Nobody else around here knows as much about Worzelese as me. Not even them two dafty yewman brats

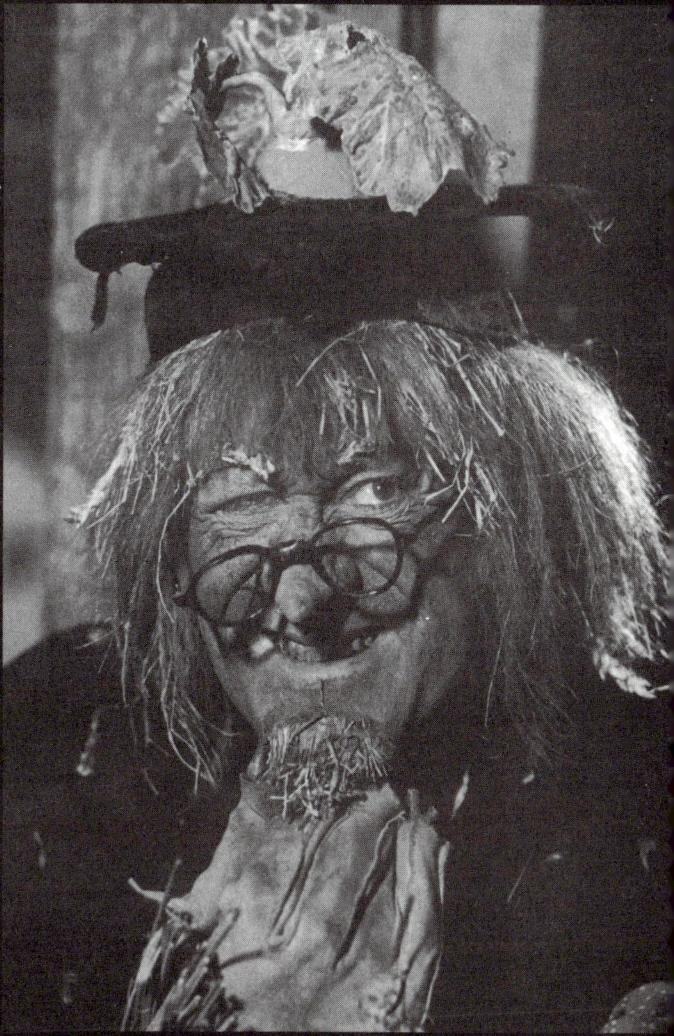

what calls 'emselves me friends."

An hour later, the academic gentleman from Oxford returned the way he had come, looking decidedly irritated. He passed Worzel without a sideways glance, but Worzel called out to him. "Ain't you got what you came for, teacher-man?"

"I found the fellow," snapped the professor. "But for the life of me, I couldn't make him understand what I wanted, and as far as he was concerned, he just gabbled a load of nonsense at me."

"That's cause old Jarge is deaf," said Worzel, equably. "I could've told 'ee that if you'd asked."

"What's that you said?" queried the man.

"Peewor ohwor ohwor arrworzel effwor eewor ellwor ellwor ohwor dubbleyouworzel eyewor esswordip deewor eewor aywor effworzel," answered Worzel, laughing. And the man wandered off, his mind reeling. It'd be a long time before *he* left Oxford again . . .

Now. Working from Worzel's language, above, can *you* make sense out of the following Worzelese? Remember — the letters are written as they sound. 'A' is 'ay', and 'B' is 'bee' and so on . . .

Dubbleyouwor ohwor yewwor ellwor deeworzel wywor ohwor yewordip esswor teewor aywor ennwor deeworzel eyewor ennwordip aywordip effwor eyewor eewor ellwor deeworzel aywor ennwor deewordip teewor aywor ellwor kayworzel teewor ohwordip aywordip esswor ceewor aywor arrwor eewor ceewor arrwor ohwor dubbleyouwordip? Wywor ohwor yewordip emmwor yewor esswor teeworzel beewor eewordip beewor aywor arrwor emmwor wyworzel!

(Now turn the page upside down to check your answer.)

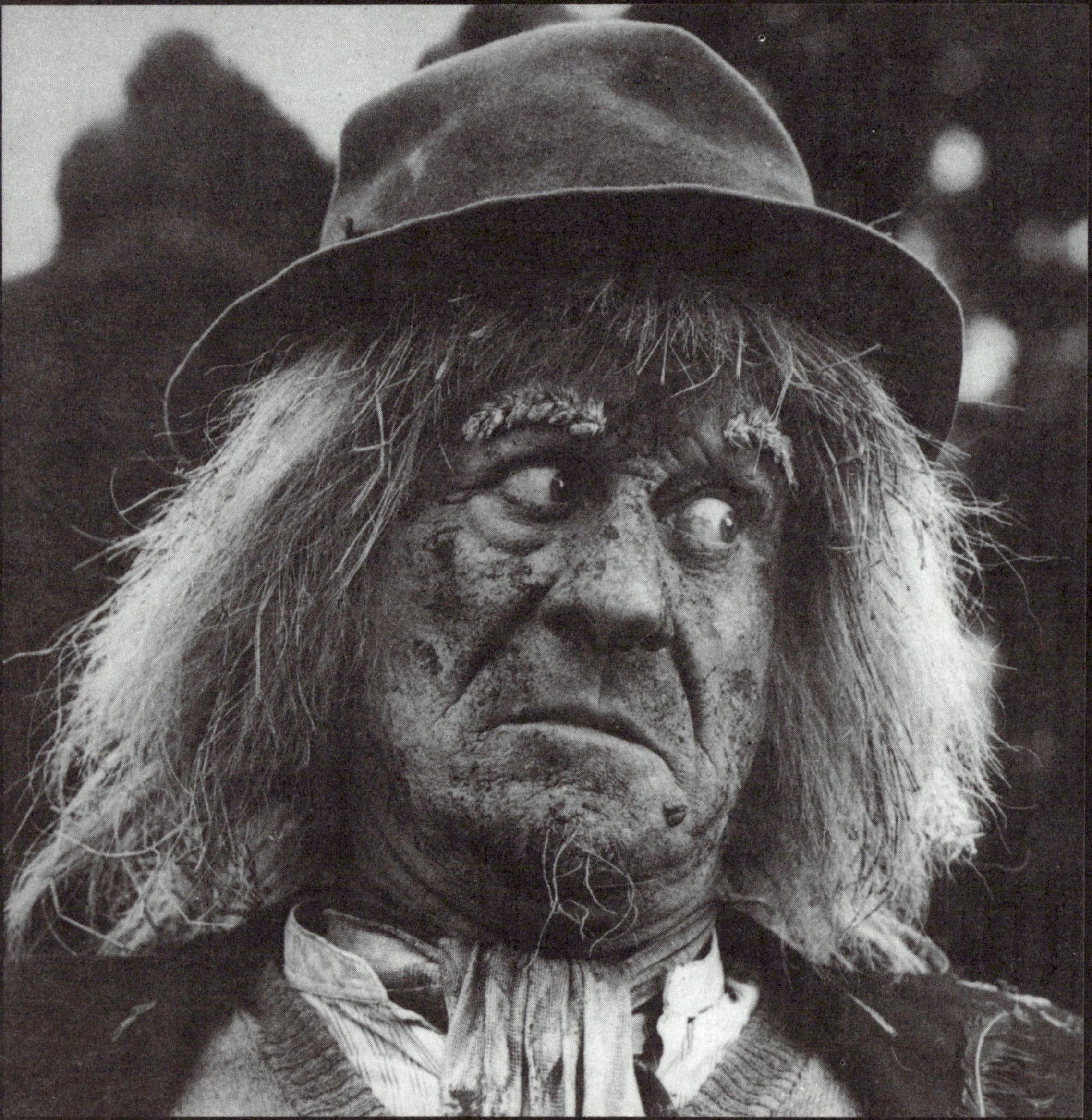

Would you stand in a field and talk to a scarecrow? You must be barmy!

SCRAPHEAP SCARECROW

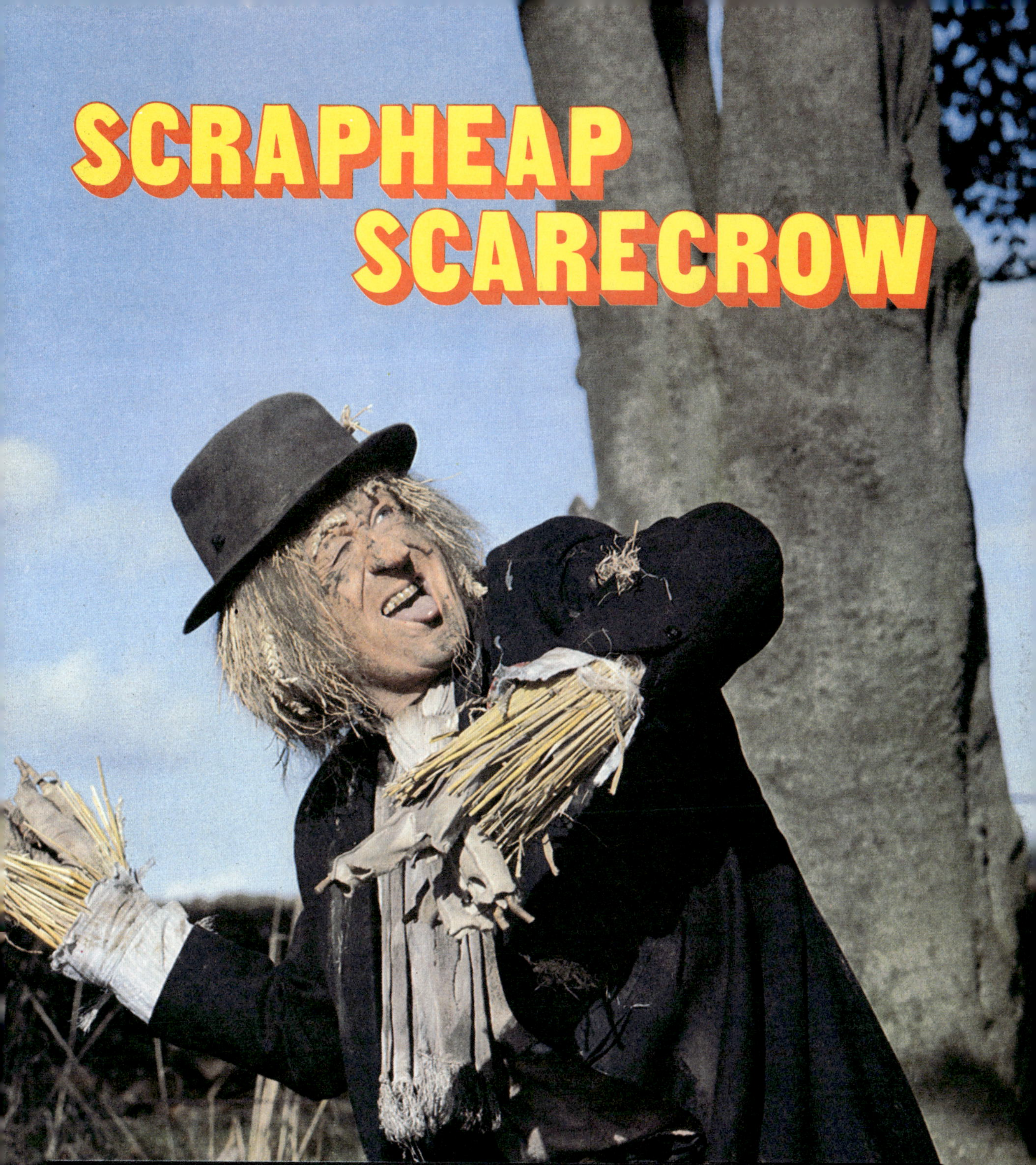

Nobody liked a sunny summer day more than Worzel Gummidge. It made him think about his work. To be more accurate, it made him think about dodging it. "Ain't a bit o' sense standin' here wavin' me arms at them flappity black crows, when I ought to be stretched out in a garding 'ammock with a comic an' a nice cool drink," he grumbled. "'Course, I ain't got no 'ammock, nor no comic neither," he said to himself. "But it's the principle of the thing. Least I can go up the brook an' get a mouthful o' clear water an' stretch out on the banks for forty winks."

The decision made, Worzel detached himself from his cross-prop and set off through the gate of Ten Acre Field.

It was in the lane that he found himself hailed by a passing motorist, a young man who drew to a halt beside him. "Excuse me, gaffer," said the man. "Can you tell me where Braithwaite's Farm is?"

"Yes," said Worzel.

There was a perplexed pause, and then . . . "Well, where *is* it?"

Always inquisitive, Worzel peered closely at the driver.

"What be your business there, mister?"

"If you *must* know, I'm a representative for Krow-Gon, Limited. I'm going to sell Mr Braithwaite one of our new, multi-action Bird-Scarers. Now, be a good chap and give the directions, eh?"

"Multy-ma-whatsit *bird* scarers?" Worzel was at once appalled and offended. "Yew means summat that puts pore ol' scarecrows out o' work?"

The man sighed. "Trust me to pick a lunatic to ask," he muttered. He let in the gears and drove on, leaving Worzel gaping after him. His outrage slowly gave way to apprehension, and then to real dismay as the full import of what the salesman had said penetrated to his brain. "Lawks an' lumme! I can't 'ave no dankety machine takin' over my job! It'd be beneath me dignity! It ain't that I likes work, but there wouldn't be no fun in playin' truant from doin' *nothin'*!" Worzel wasn't sure he really understood his own logic, but he knew that he'd have to attempt to appear to indispensible, and that was why he scurried back into his field, yelling and waving his arms at the squadrons of wheeling crows that mocked and jeered, as usual, from the safety of the skies.

When he realised that prancing up and down did no good at all, Worzel scurried across to one of Braithwaite's potato clamps in a corner of the hedgerow, broke it open, and began to pelt at the birds for all he was worth!

He scored no hits. At least, not on any of the crows. But one missile, disappearing over the hedge, brought the tinkle of greenhouse glass to his ears. Another potato neatly left its mark on one of Mrs Braithwaite's newly-washed white sheets out on her line. A third scored a direct hit on Farmer Braithwaite himself as he emerged from the house, drawn by the sound of a car coming up the lane . . .

"It's raining taters," he spluttered, picking up his hat and rubbing his stinging pate. But by the time he'd fetched a box to stand on so's he could look over the hedge, there was nothing to be seen. Worzel had heard him, and made a swift tactical withdrawal!

"Dashed funny," muttered Braithwaite. "Must have been some of those hooligans from the village. I'll have to speak to the constable."

Meanwhile, Worzel's attitude had changed once again. This time, properly disgruntled, he wrenched his cross-prop out of the ground, put it over his shoulder, and set off determinedly in the direction of the main road. "Blow ol' Braithwaite an' 'is rotten crows," he grumbled. "There's more than one farmer in these parts, an' dang me if I don't go for hire to another master!"

It was not to be as easy as he thought! A two-mile trek brought Worzel to Swain's Farm, over the hill. He made for the farmhouse, talking aloud to himself, airing his grievances and his hopes over and over again. Which is why Swain's own, long-serving scarecrow, known in such circles as 'The Terrible Turnip' from his habit of flying into instant rages, caught him by the scruff of the neck and the seat of the trousers and ran him back the way he'd come! "Come here and try to do me out my livin', would you, you shambling apology for a badly-stuffed mattress? Shove off!" Worzel found himself flat on his face in one of the mud pools at the bottom of Swain's main field. "And don't" said The Terrible Turnip, dusting his hands, "even *think* of comin' back!"

Worzel cleaned himself off as best he could with some handy dock-leaves, and, with many a baleful glance back at his adversary, went along the road to Dickson's Dairy Farm. There, it was one of Dickson's prize Hereford bulls that chased

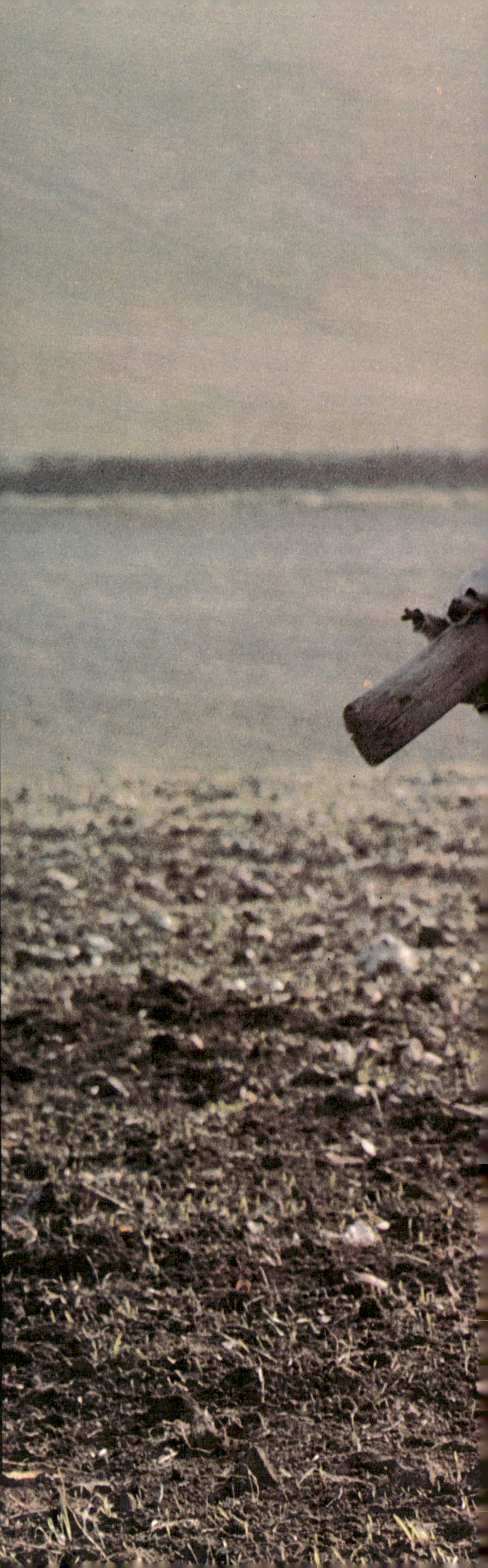

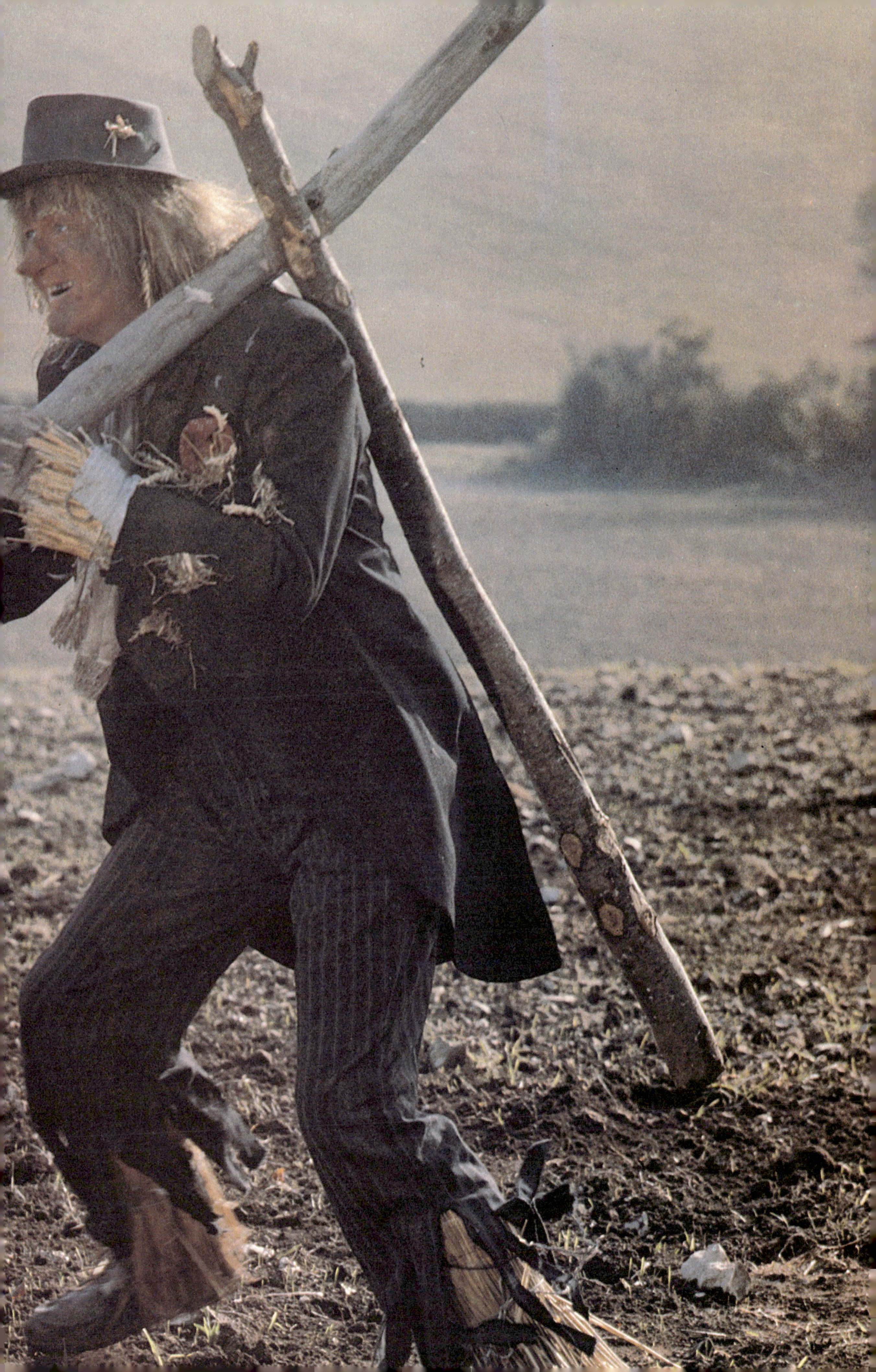

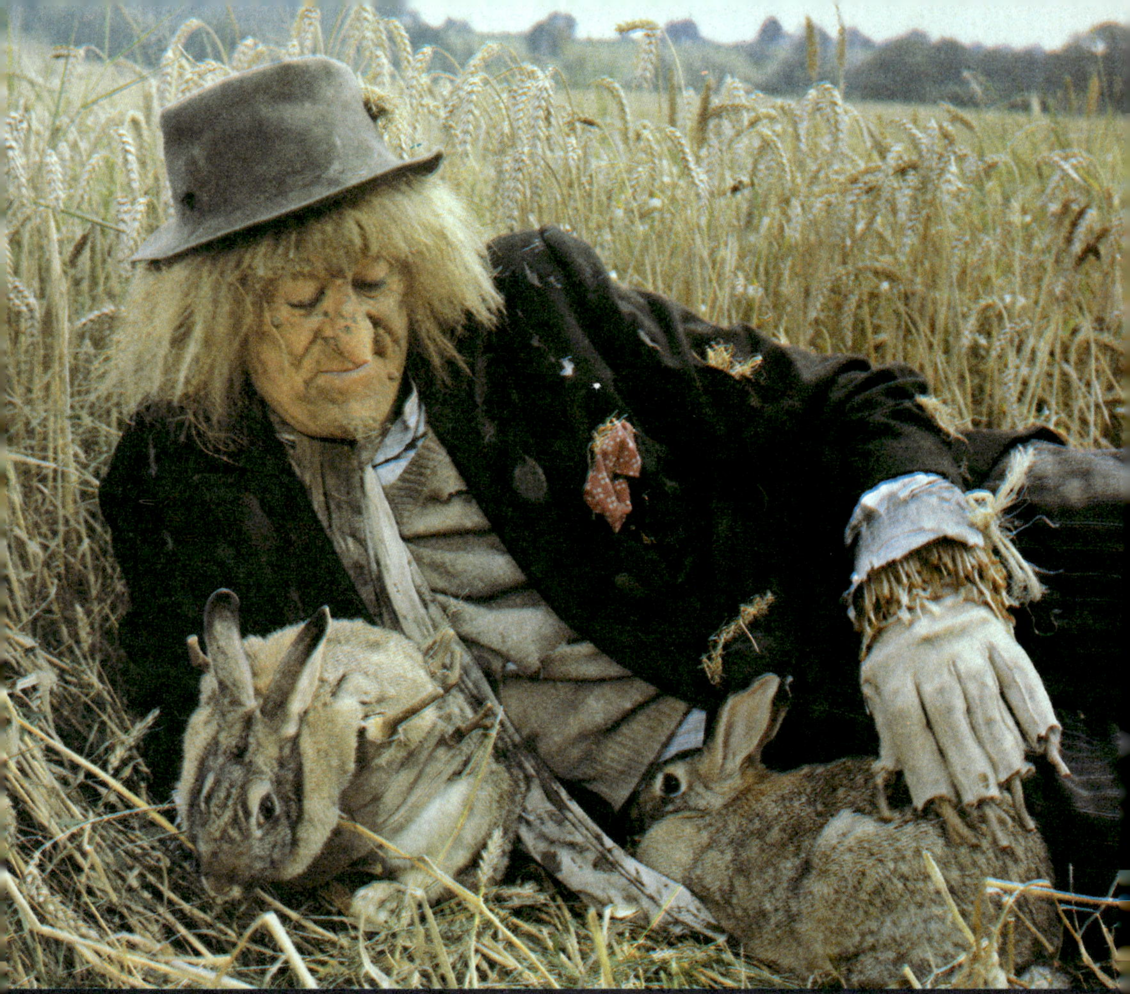

him off. Remembering something that he'd once read in a book, Worzel tried for a moment to play the toreador, with the aid of the red scarf he hastily snatched from his pocket. But it was no contest. Contemptuously, the bull tossed him, scarf and all, out of the field and back into the ditch at the roadside.

He might have had more luck at Waterman's Farm beyond Stile Woods, except that Waterman himself, being short-sighted, and having lost a couple of chickens the day before, took him for a marauding tramp and let him have both barrels of his shotgun! Luckily for Worzel, Waterman's aim was as bad as his eyesight, but Worzel's breath was coming in extremely short pants by the time he stopped running!

He sank down on the heath of Scatterbrook Common, exhausted and depressed. "Ain't no use," he said to himself. "I'm redundyment, that's what I am. Fit for nothin' but the scrap'eap. Nobody wants me at all!" Then, he was aware of something moving near him, and quite suddenly, a rabbit — which had been watching him with its big, dark eyes, loped across and began nibbling at some of his straws.

"Huh." Worzel patted the furry animal. "You thinks I'm some use, do you? Arr. Good to eat. But there ain't no future for me in *that*, cottony-tail."

The rabbit stopped chewing, and looked up at Worzel as if it understood. Worzel sighed. "You've got a big family, no doubt. Pity you can't hire me. I'd become a scare-fox, or scare-ferret, or somethin' like that. Tchah! What am I blatherin' about? I'm just a useless ol' bogle what ain't no bargain to anyone!"

Totally depressed, Worzel gently parted himself from the rabbit and slouched on his way, his shoulders bowed, his heart heavy. "I'll run away an' seek me fortune, that's what I'll do," he said. "I'll join the army. Or the navy. Or even the airforce. Arr! Then I'll be a pilot, an' spend me time shootin' down some o' them blarmy crows!" The trouble was, when it came to the bit, he had no idea at all how to apply to become a recruit. Which was, perhaps, just as well.

Worzel's aimless meanderings took him back to Ten Acre Field, where he gloomily replaced his cross-prop in its hole and sat down at the foot of it. He was too dispirited even to trek up to his old barn and put on his thinking head, which might have helped him dream up a few more ideas. "I'll just sit here until I rots away," he muttered. 'I'll let the crows come down an' pick me to bits if they like. What does it matter?" But in the event, he had to stand up again, rather sharply, and at least pretend he was doing his work as he saw, in the distance, Farmer Braithwaite enter the field in company with the salesman from Krow-Gon Limited. And the younger man was carrying one of the company's automatic, multi-action bird-scarers.

Meanwhile, word had gone round of Worzel's morning journey, and the tale, passed from The Terrible Turnip, through Paddy The Parsnip and Flap-Arm Fitzherbert (one of the classier scarecrows in the neighbourhood) had reached the ears of The Crowman himself — the creator of Worzel and his kind. It was the Crowman who, well-knowing Worzel's cantankerous ways, put two and two together. The arrival of the Krow-Gon Salesman in the area hadn't escaped his notice, either. "Mark my words," said the Crowman to Fitzherbert, "that Gummidge is going to get himself into trouble if I don't do something about it."

"Well," said Fitzherbert, "There's no use *talking* to him, old chappie. You know how he is!"

In Ten Acre Field, the salesman had ably demonstrated the bird-scarer. It worked on the principle of a clock-driven time-mechanism ("No extra electricity bills," the rep had gushed) which fired off blank shotgun cartridges at intervals. And at the very first bang, every crow in the vicinity had quit.

"Absolutely marvellous," beamed Braithwaite. "'Course, I'll need time to think about it."

"By all means, by dear sir! Let's leave it in position, and I'll come back tomorrow." The salesman, hands on hips, let his glance smugly wander round the landscape. "You'll find the Krow-Gon a darned sight more efficient than *that*!" He gestured towards the drooping Worzel . . .

"Aye, lad. I think you're right. Now, come on back to the house. The missus will have the kettle on for a nice cuppa." Farmer Braithwaite and his companion plodded back and out of Worzel's vision.

For a long time, he regarded the set-up contraption with a dismal eye. Then that eye became beady. Then it grew enraged. There was nothing so quick-change as a Worzel Gummidge mood! "Blamed, blinkety-blankety monster-osity," he snarled at last, and detaching himself, marched purposefully towards the thing. As he approached it loosed off one of its cartridges with a cracking report!

When Worzel picked himself warily up from the ground, he was full of that valour which comes from sheer desperation. Gritting his teeth, he ran forward and aimed a hefty kick!

BA-*BLAMMM*! Three of the cartridges went off at once, and with a wild yell of dismay, Worzel was enveloped in a cloud of smoke that only slowly cleared. His last thoughts were of the sensation of flying through the air . . . and then there was nothing!

It was the Crowman who found him — in bits. One leg here, one leg there. His nose down a stoat-hole. He'd been hurled a good ten yards from the Krow-Gon.

"You silly old lummox," chuckled the Crowman as he set about putting Worzel together again. "That weren't no way to beat the system!"

As Worzel's senses returned, he found his maker helping him gently to his feet. "Oh! 'Tis you, yer honour, yer worship, yer majesty!" He put on his most cringing, apologetic air. "I didn't mean no 'arm, sir! Honest I didn't! 'Twas just the thought o' bein' made redundymant!"

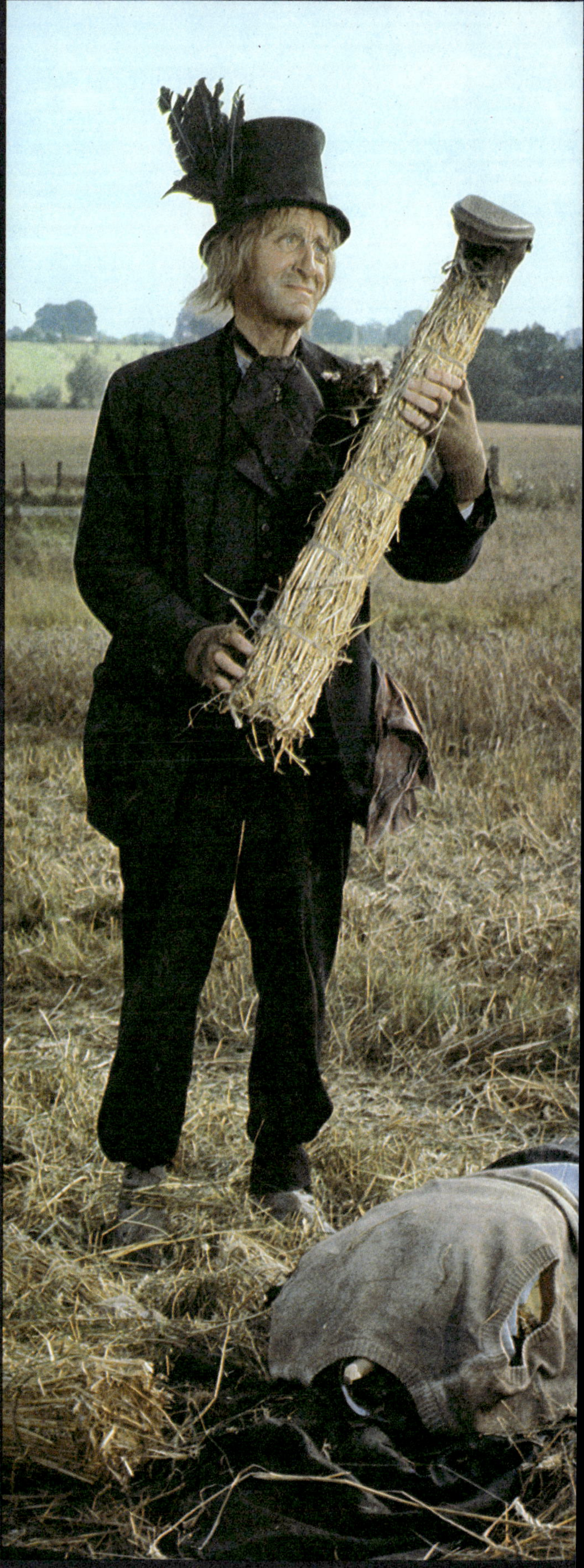

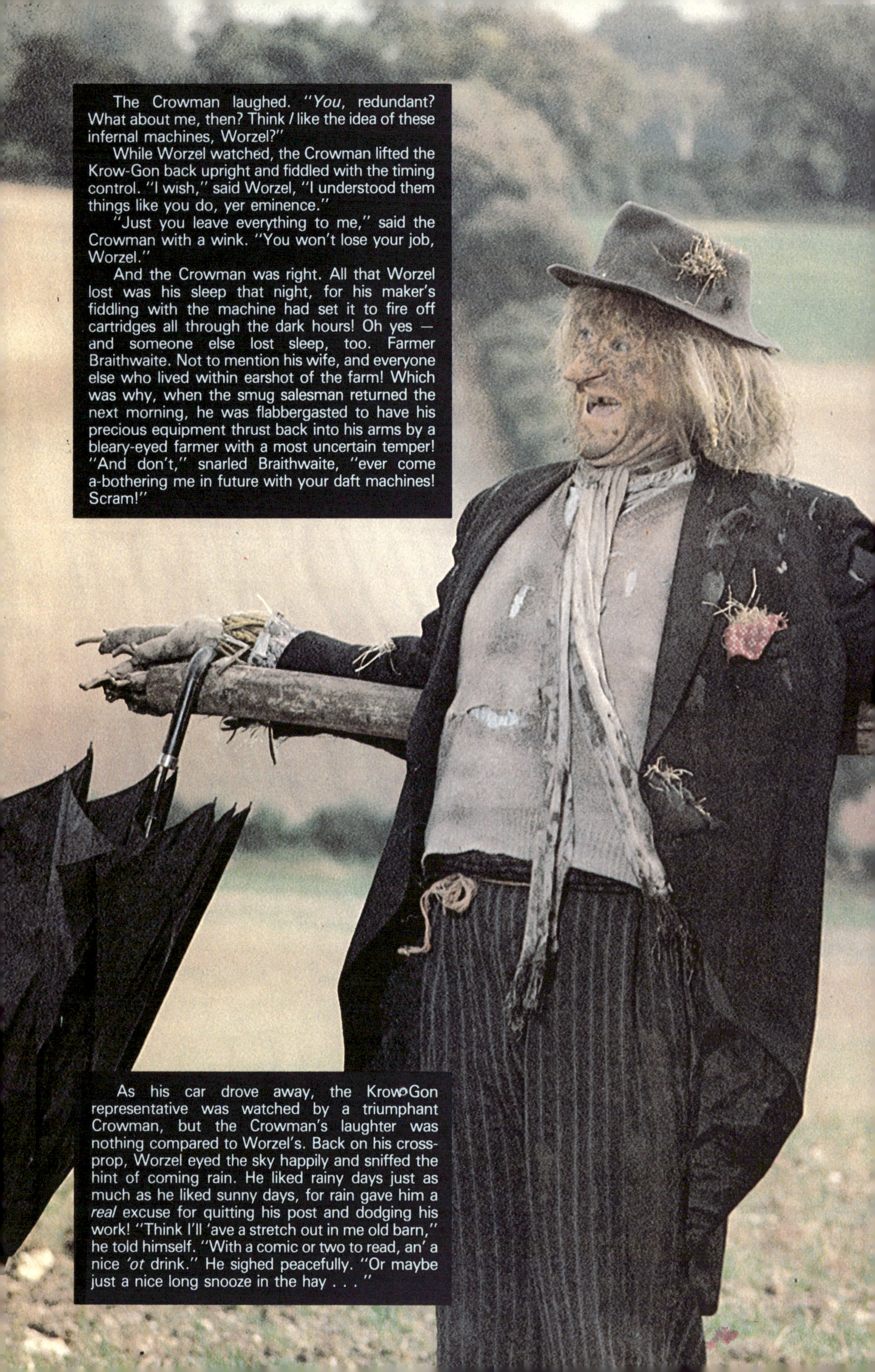

The Crowman laughed. "*You*, redundant? What about me, then? Think *I* like the idea of these infernal machines, Worzel?"

While Worzel watched, the Crowman lifted the Krow-Gon back upright and fiddled with the timing control. "I wish," said Worzel, "I understood them things like you do, yer eminence."

"Just you leave everything to me," said the Crowman with a wink. "You won't lose your job, Worzel."

And the Crowman was right. All that Worzel lost was his sleep that night, for his maker's fiddling with the machine had set it to fire off cartridges all through the dark hours! Oh yes — and someone else lost sleep, too. Farmer Braithwaite. Not to mention his wife, and everyone else who lived within earshot of the farm! Which was why, when the smug salesman returned the next morning, he was flabbergasted to have his precious equipment thrust back into his arms by a bleary-eyed farmer with a most uncertain temper! "And don't," snarled Braithwaite, "ever come a-bothering me in future with your daft machines! Scram!"

As his car drove away, the Krow-Gon representative was watched by a triumphant Crowman, but the Crowman's laughter was nothing compared to Worzel's. Back on his cross-prop, Worzel eyed the sky happily and sniffed the hint of coming rain. He liked rainy days just as much as he liked sunny days, for rain gave him a *real* excuse for quitting his post and dodging his work! "Think I'll 'ave a stretch out in me old barn," he told himself. "With a comic or two to read, an' a nice *'ot* drink." He sighed peacefully. "Or maybe just a nice long snooze in the hay . . . "

Jon Pertwee
the man behind the make-up

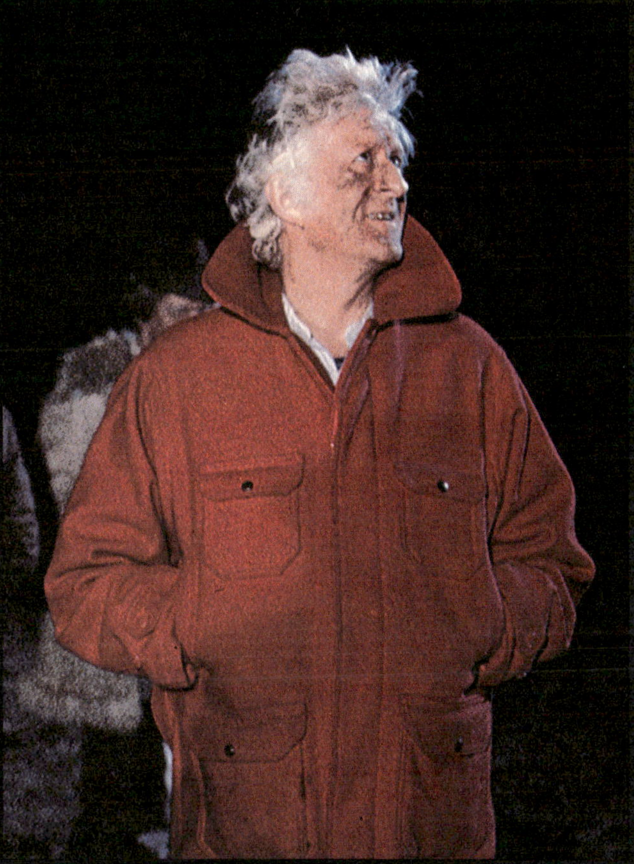

Getting kicked out as incompetent and told to forget showbusiness as a career by the world's most famous drama school, London's Royal Academy of Dramatic Art, isn't exactly the most auspicious start to a career as an actor.

But sometimes the desire to prove others wrong can be as strong an incentive to do well as the most forceful encouragement, which is probably the reason why Jon Pertwee's name is now known and respected all over the world — and not simply as an actor, but also as a singer, comedian, cabaret entertainer and satirist.

His failure at R.A.D.A. came as a blow at the time, but now he simply shrugs it off — he says he was far more worried that his father would go spare when he found out than that he had lost any professional credibility.

His father, in fact, backed him up completely, and he also received some unexpected encouragement from one of the most respected figures in the theatre at the time — Noel Coward.

Coward came to watch the last play that Jon appeared in at R.A.D.A. before his ignominious departure, in which he played two roles. In the first act he played a man who was murdered, and in the last act, the detective who solves the crime. Jon takes up the story;

"After the show the principal asked Noel Coward if he had enjoyed the production and had he perhaps spotted anyone with promise? 'Oh yes, yes very good indeed,' (here Jon gives a perfect imitation of Coward's elegant manner). 'Yes, yes that young chappie who was killed off in the first act, very original performance — Oh yes, and that last chappie who played the detective, remarkable — who were they?'"

That note of encouragement was echoed by his family — which was formidable backing, to say the least. Jon belongs to one of the oldest and most firmly established theatrical families, and the list of guests at the Christmas gatherings he recalls at their South Kensington home as a boy reads like a theatrical Who's Who.

"Let me see....among the older ones, several of my aunts were very famous. My aunt Eva Moore was a Dame

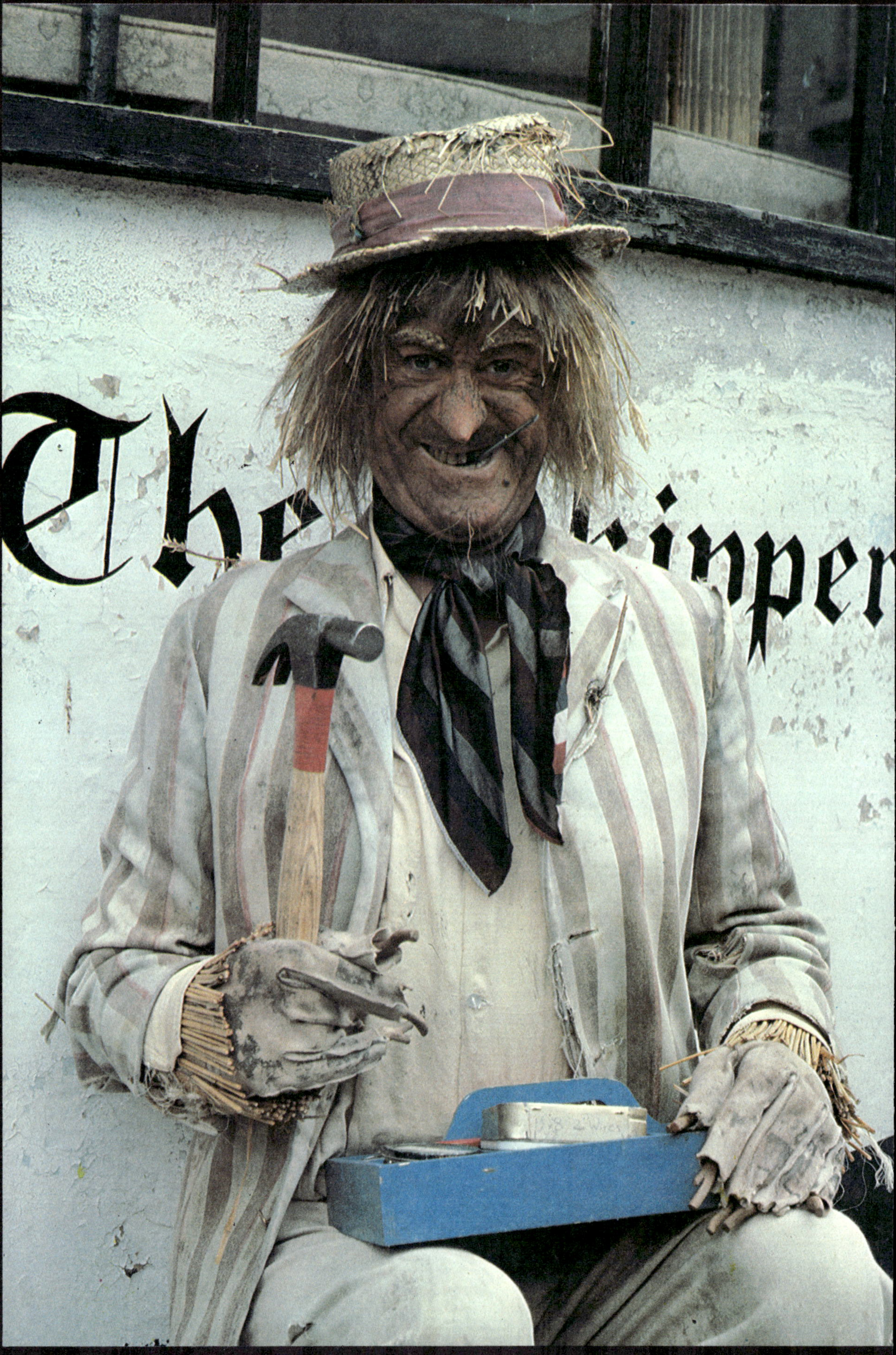

of the theatre, her sister Decima Moore was a doyen of Gilbert and Sullivan and my grandmother was an opera singer.

"Then Sir Laurence Olivier was married to my cousin, my Godfather was Harold Huth, a silent screen star in the early 'thirties, my father and brother were playwrights and my uncle ran the Guildhall School of Music and Drama — and that was just the nucleus of an enormous theatre family.

"We just talked theatre, breathed theatre. There was never any question of what I was going to do — it was accepted that I would be an actor almost from the time I could speak."

But despite his priviledged theatrical background, Jon had to start treading the boards right at the bottom, like any young aspiring actor, not always with very successful results. In the early days he did the rounds of vaudeville theatres, including the notorious Glasgow Empire, known in the business as the 'Comedians Graveyard'. It's horrors are with him yet.

"I went on one night and no one laughed at all. They just sat in dead silence, so eventually I decided to cut my losses and quit. When I asked the manager for my money his reply was, 'Why go home laddie? They dinna give ya the bird'." So he carried on — only to end up being pelted with bags of water and having beer poured over him from the gallery.

Things could only get better — and eventually they did. He joined a pick-up company, performing in a different town every night. Later, he worked in a circus, even appeared on ice!

"Those were good days. I worked in repertory companies getting paid £3.10s a week for working all the hours God gave. I lived in digs that cost thirty bob a week with three meals a day, ran a motorbike, had a girlfriend to take out and still came out with change at the end of the week. Not bad, eh?"

The war broke out soon afterwards and Jon found himself conscripted into the Navy on the lowest deck, where he was rescued from the almost certain misery of death by his cousin who was a Captain.

He moved into his cousin's house in the dock-yard, so everything became quite comfortable except for the poisonous looks he got from a three-badge able- seaman who had to wait on Jon at the table when he was just an ordinary blue-jacket.

The easy life couldn't last forever, and Jon was soon whisked away to join the submarine corps, but was eventually removed because he was too tall. A spell on

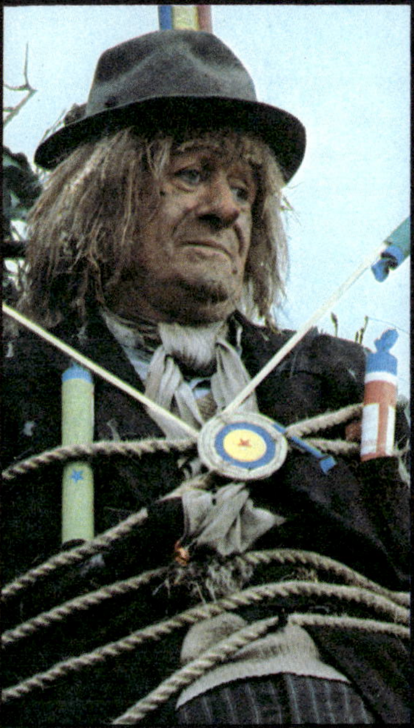

battle-cruisers culminated on the HMS Hood, which was sunk by the Bismark. Luckily, Jon was one of the survivors of the ship and was then ironically posted to the air-sea division. But wasn't that terribly dangerous?

"Not at all," says Jon, laughing. "In fact it was excellent. There was hardly anyone around to rescue at that period in the war, so we just stayed ashore in the Isle of Man.

"We didn't even have rationing. There was petrol, the milk and butter were good and everything was fine until the RAF twigged and sent a squadron of aircraft every Saturday to fill up and fly the supplies over to the mainland."

Serving in Naval Intelligence took him on North Sea Convoys around Denmark, Sweden, Russia and Iceland, then he finished up his service in London, running a section of Naval Broadcasting.

Those wartime experiences provided the basis for the show that turned Jon into a star. He was the originator of a radio show called **"The Navy Lark"** which was so popular that it became, after 18½ years, the longest-running radio show to go on the air anywhere in the world.

Jon became known as the 'Man of a Thousand Voices' because of his phenomenal talent for imitating accents, and he built up a steady reputation for comedy through two more radio shows, **"Up The Pole",** which he made with Jimmy Jewell, and **"Waterlogged Spa"** with Eric Barker.

Jon's favourite character in **"Waterlogged Spa"** was an irascible old postman whose catchphrase (Jon suddenly breaks into broad Worzel as he says it) was, "Well, what does it matter so long as yer tears 'em up!".

The postman was an irritable but lovable old Westcountryman and Jon longed more than anything else to put him on the screen. And it was that character who formed the basis for Worzel Gummidge when the series came about.

"It wasn't difficult at all to bring a scarecrow 'to life' as I already had a whole picture in my head from the postman days. It's fascinating that you can actually build a whole personality around a voice. Playing Worzel was just a question of getting the movements and the make-up right and so on."

Make-up isn't always a straightforward business though. One day, after spending over an hour getting made-up as Worzel, Jon found out that the rain machine needed for the scene he was shooting which would wash the mud from his

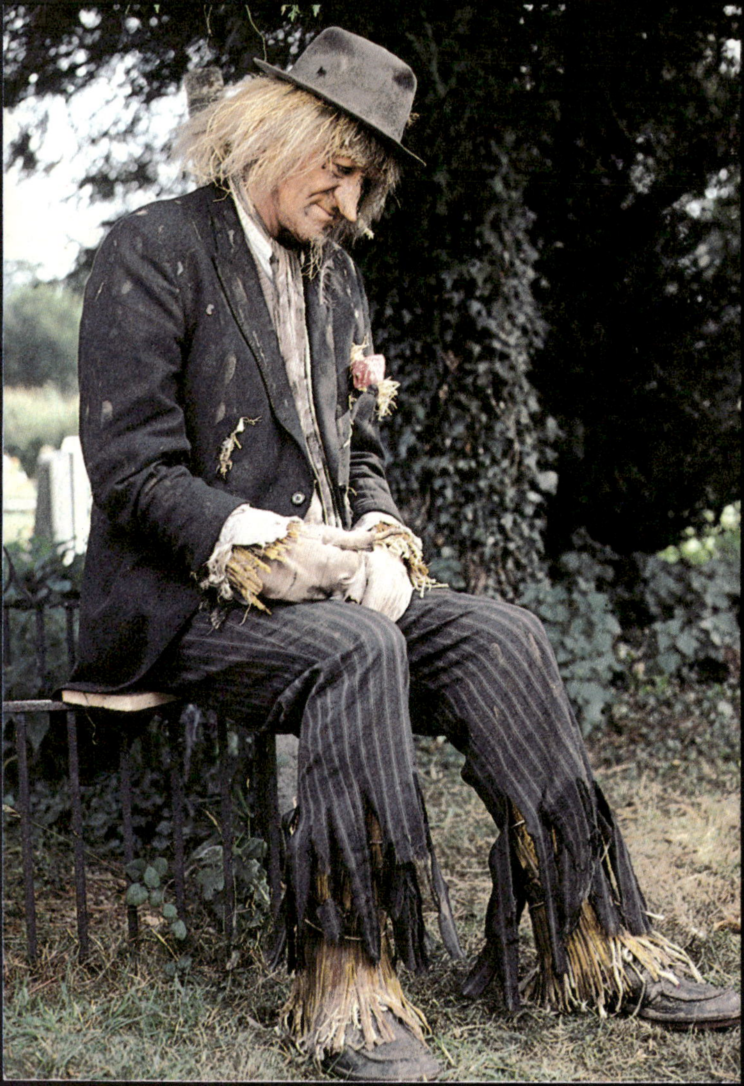

face wasn't working.

He had to sit, with the mud getting harder and harder for over three hours in the middle of a field. The mud was plastered on over an inch thick and he was only able to breathe through a straw stuck in his mouth. Eventually he was saved by the arrival of the local fire brigade who were able to hose him down.

Working on Worzel is normally much more fun.

"The crew have a great affection and understanding for each other, and that's the best — and only — way to work. I have worked with all the people involved in the production before, and the guests are often old friends.

"People like Bill Maynard to whom I gave his first job many years ago and Barbara Windsor, John Le Mesurier and Joan Sims who I made movies with years and years back."

Away from the film-set, Jon likes to spend as much time as possible with his family. He lives with his wife, Inge, who is an author, and their two children, Sean and Dariel, in a huge converted barn by the River Thames.

The house is filled with stacks of antique pictures and books which he collects, as well as many examples of naive and primitive art which he has acquired on his extensive travels.

He spent most of his early life in France and returns there as often as he can. He is descended from an old Hugenot family — their original name was Pertuis de Laillavault — and is extremely proud of his French ancestry.

His passion for skin-diving and shell-collecting began in France too. He was taught to dive by the famous Jacques Cousteau and worked on his boat while they were trying to uncover the wreck of a Danish ship off the French coast.

Since then he has travelled all over the world in pursuit of his hobby — and found himself in some pretty hair-raising situations.

On a boat-trip in Ibiza with a professional explorer the boat hit a freak-storm, so Jon suggested diving to see if the water was calmer below. About 40ft down he was caught by the swell of the water which dropped him on the anchor like a fish on a hook.

He struggled and lost his air-pipe, and when the other diver took his out to share with Jon he panicked and wouldn't give it back. Without air, the other was unable to free him. After a few moments, the explorer's wife dived too and knocked Jon out with a dinghy paddle, as the only way he could be freed was if he were unconscious. He was saved within moments of drowning.

Diving can be pleasant though, even with sharks around. According to Jon, the sharks off South Africa and Australia are nasty and ferocious. "But," he says, "when I have been diving off the coast of India I have often been surrounded by sharks and they merely look on with interest as I make notes on the fish I see. Perhaps it's because they are so well-fed..."

When he wants to completely get away from his hectic life in the theatre, Jon and his wife retreat to their own small corner of paradise — a tiny island of their own in the Indian Ocean, just off Sri Lanka.

"The island is tiny — only about 250 yards long and covered in palm trees," says Jon. "We live Robinson Crusoe-style, fishing every day for food and eating mango, red fruit and pumpkin leaves which are rather like spinach. It is just sheer and total relaxation, cut off from the rest of the world."

Ironic that he has to go so far to escape from the fame that once seemed so elusive itself.

A HEAD FOR ALL OCCASIONS!

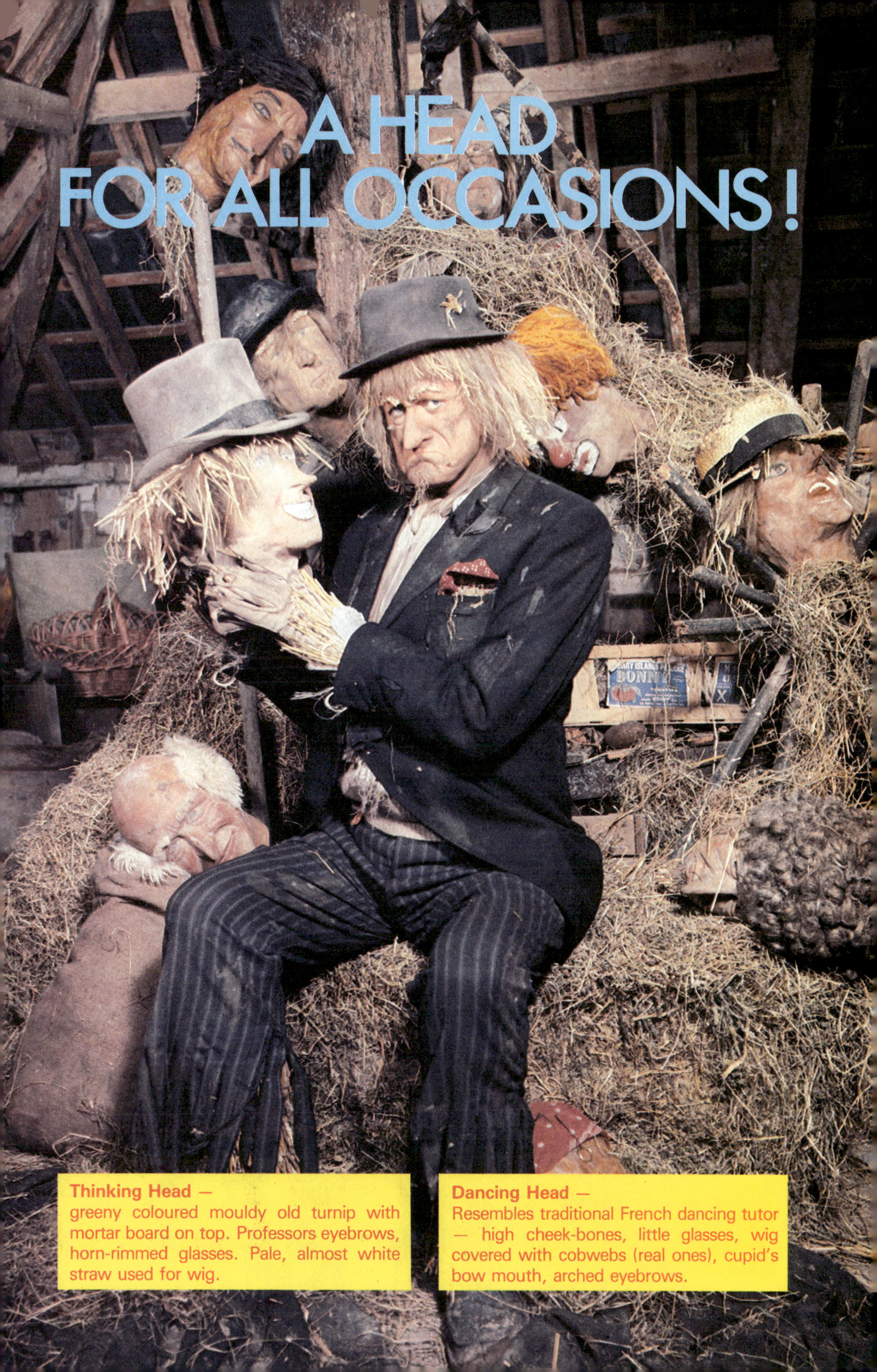

Thinking Head —
greeny coloured mouldy old turnip with mortar board on top. Professors eyebrows, horn-rimmed glasses. Pale, almost white straw used for wig.

Dancing Head —
Resembles traditional French dancing tutor — high cheek-bones, little glasses, wig covered with cobwebs (real ones), cupid's bow mouth, arched eyebrows.

Worzel heads — the facts

1. All heads made of moulded white latex rubber/silicone. Made to Jon's features by freelance special effects man, Ken Lailey.
2. Greatest difficulty was matching Jon's skin tone as normal foundation simply sank into rubber, so now heads are baked.
3. Now simply has to be checked for colour after set people have dressed the head for the scene.
4. All the wigs etc. that Jon wears for the scene must be matched exactly.
5. There are a variety of different wigs, and it is sometimes difficult to get two done. In that case the takes have to be shot separately, and the wig is transferred to Jon's head and vice versa.

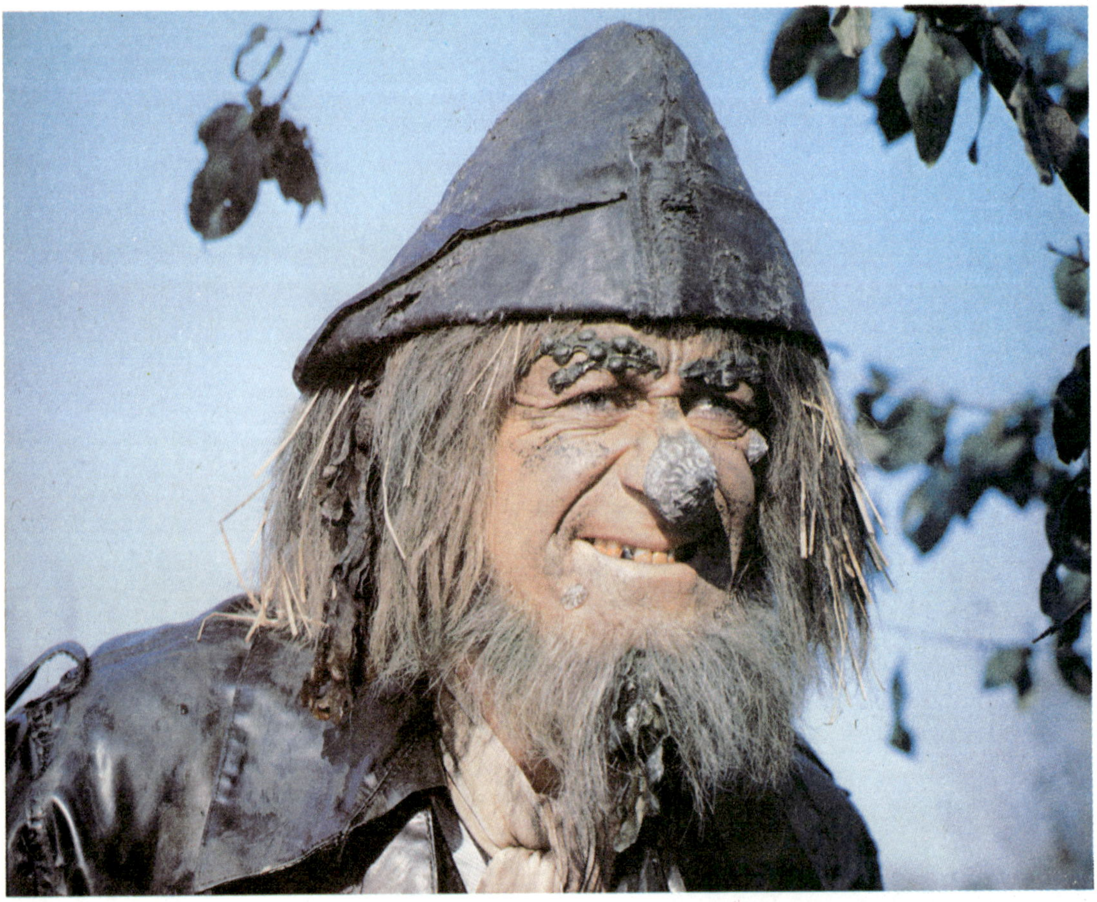

Wrangling Head — transposed from angling head, hay wig, mostly sea-green, covered with sea-weed, topped with souwester hat. limpet shells on face instead of warts, sea-weed for eyebrows.

Handsome Head — Used to attract lady scarecrow, resembles old matinee idol (John Gilbert?) — tatty old black wig with centre parting, latin eye make-up, monocle, big white hideous teeth — kept slipping for comic effect.

Choirboy's Head — blonde corn wig, fresh-faced and innocent-looking rosy-cheeked and innocent, but still dirty old Worzel underneath. Gap between teeth, painted freckles. Like choirboys on Christmas cards.

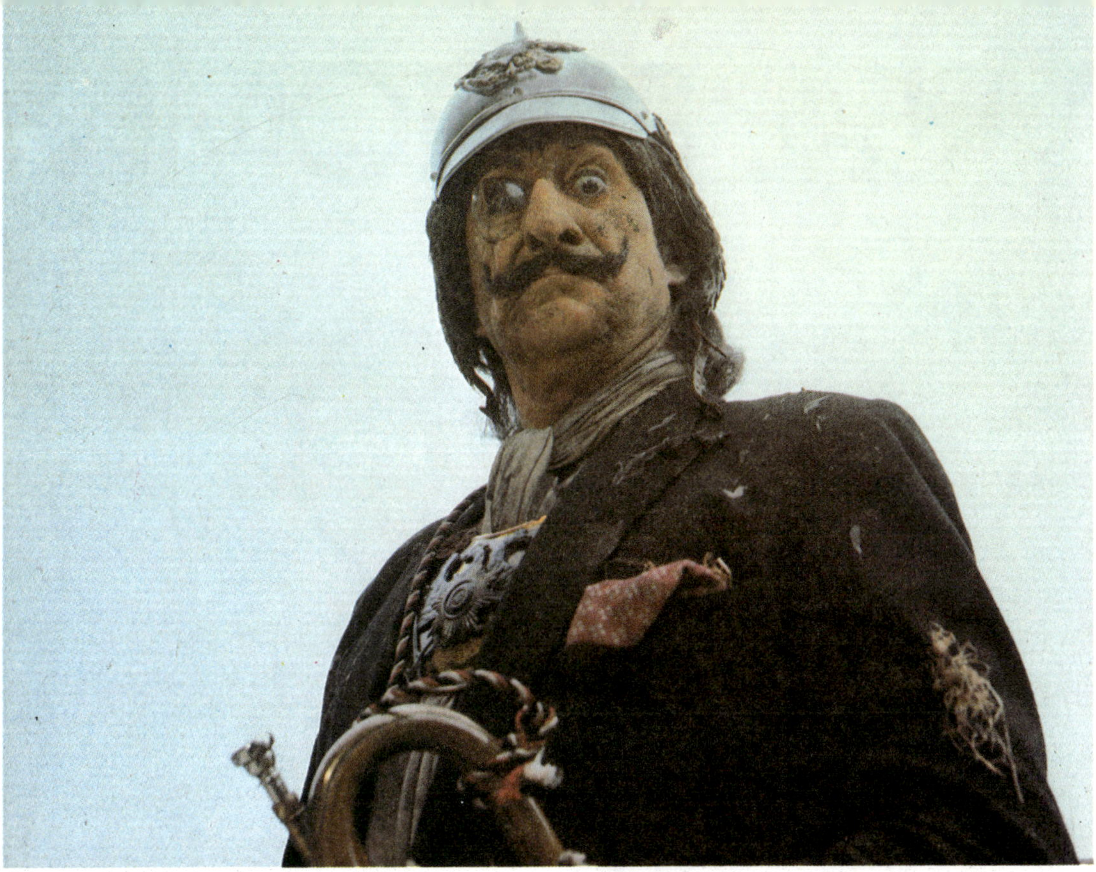

German Hun —
black wig, short back and sides, German moustache of the old Kaiser type, Duke of Wellington nose and monocle.

Butler Head —
Snooty, rather like Edgar in the Aristocats. Had to be careful not to make it too severe. Worzel still has to come through.

Singing Head —
Bud Flanagan type, over made-up, very theatrical eyes, short wig.

Magician Head —
painted moustache (curly) and eyebrows like Marvo — sparkly goatee beard.

Clown Head —
red ping-pong ball for nose, full pierrot make-up. Swede for head (meant to be Swedish clown).

Making Your Own Worzel Head

1. Use a balloon as a base. Cover it with papier mache, then when it is shaped and set, burst the balloon.

2. *Wig* —
use hay which you can buy for rabbit hutches in pet shops. Stick strands on to an elastic wig base which you can get from Woolworths with copydex, let it dry.

3. Paint on flesh colour with water-soluble paints.

4. *Nose* —
either onto papier mache base or mould from plasticine.

5. Stick on wig, and also eyebrows made from sheaths of corn (also from the pet shop).

6. For mud, make your own mixture either with thick brown paint or a mixture of flour and water coloured with paint or gravy browning.

7. *Beard* —
stick strands of hay onto chin as for wig.

A REAL PANTOMIME

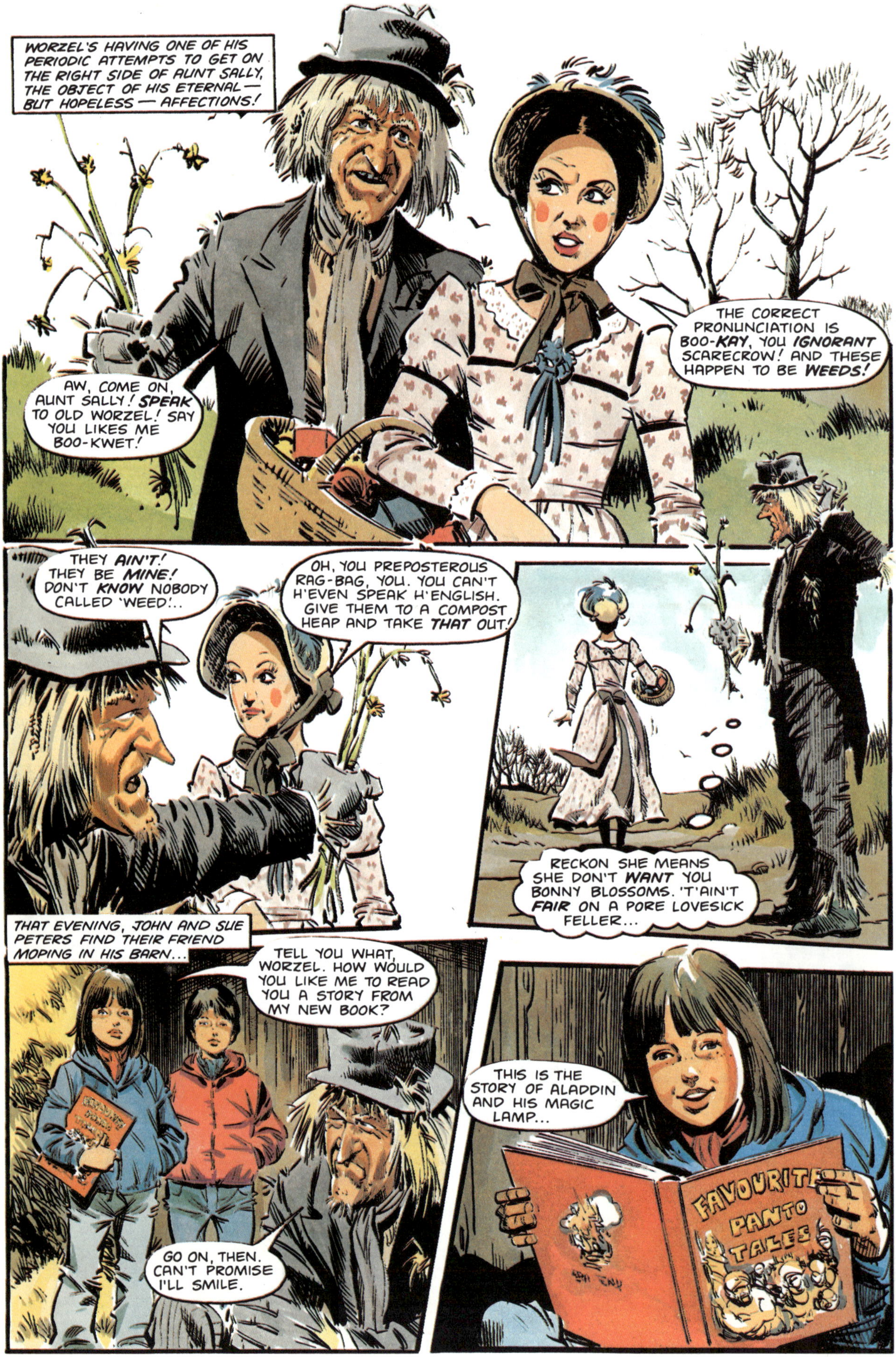

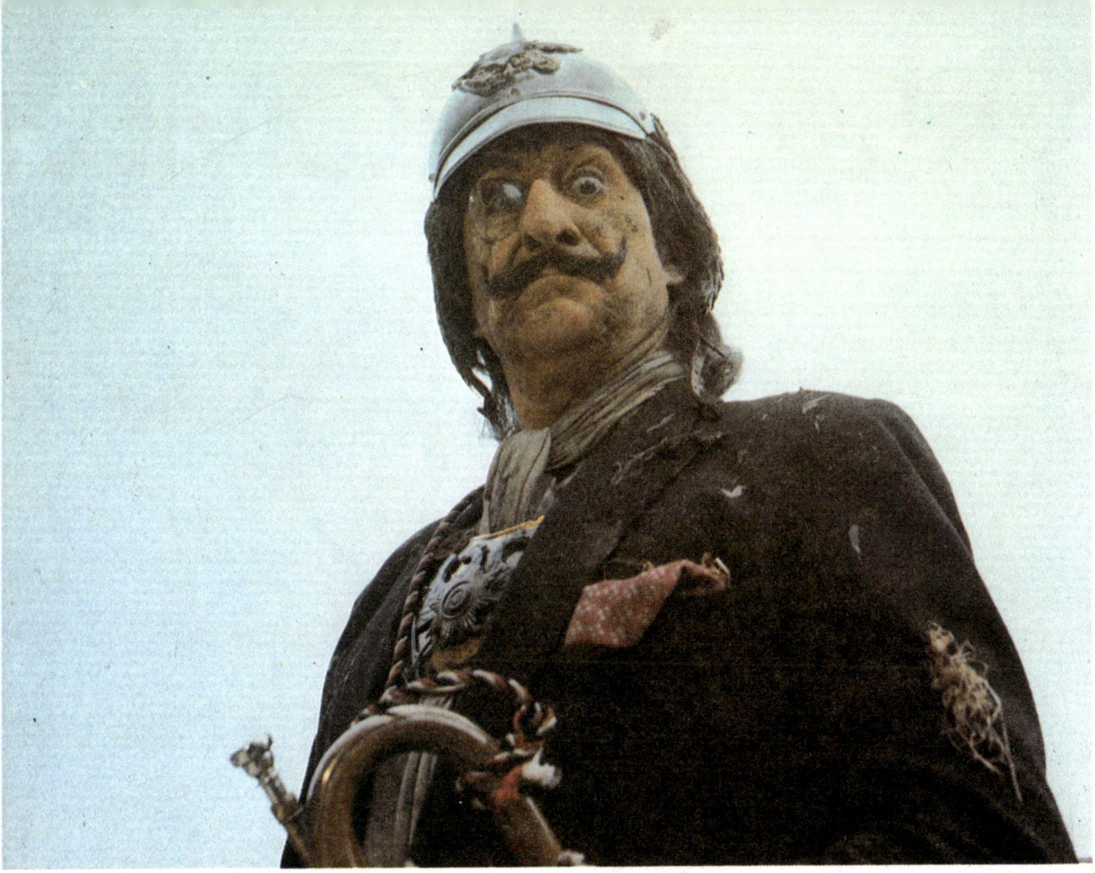

German Hun –
black wig, short back and sides, German moustache of the old Kaiser type, Duke of Wellington nose and monocle.

Butler Head –
Snooty, rather like Edgar in the Aristocats. Had to be careful not to make it too severe. Worzel still has to come through.

Singing Head –
Bud Flanagan type, over made-up, very theatrical eyes, short wig.

Magician Head –
painted moustache (curly) and eyebrows like Marvo – sparkly goatee beard.

Clown Head –
red ping-pong ball for nose, full pierrot make-up. Swede for head (meant to be Swedish clown).

Making Your Own Worzel Head

1. Use a balloon as a base. Cover it with papier mache, then when it is shaped and set, burst the balloon.
2. *Wig* –
   use hay which you can buy for rabbit hutches in pet shops. Stick strands on to an elastic wig base which you can get from Woolworths with copydex, let it dry.
3. Paint on flesh colour with water-soluble paints.
4. *Nose* –
   either onto papier mache base or mould from plasticine.
5. Stick on wig, and also eyebrows made from sheaths of corn (also from the pet shop).
6. For mud, make your own mixture either with thick brown paint or a mixture of flour and water coloured with paint or gravy browning.
7. *Beard* –
   stick strands of hay onto chin as for wig.

A REAL PANTOMIME

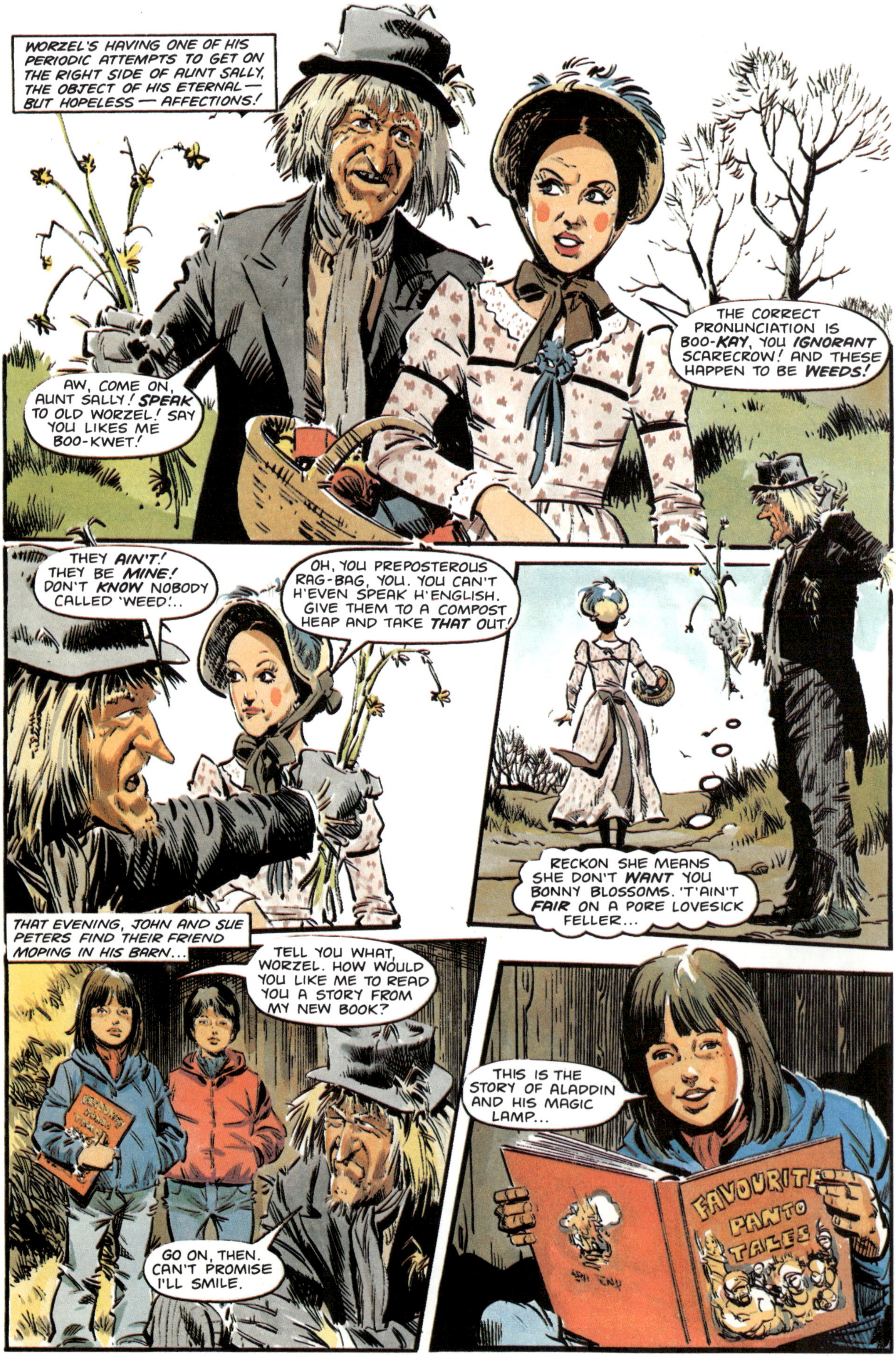

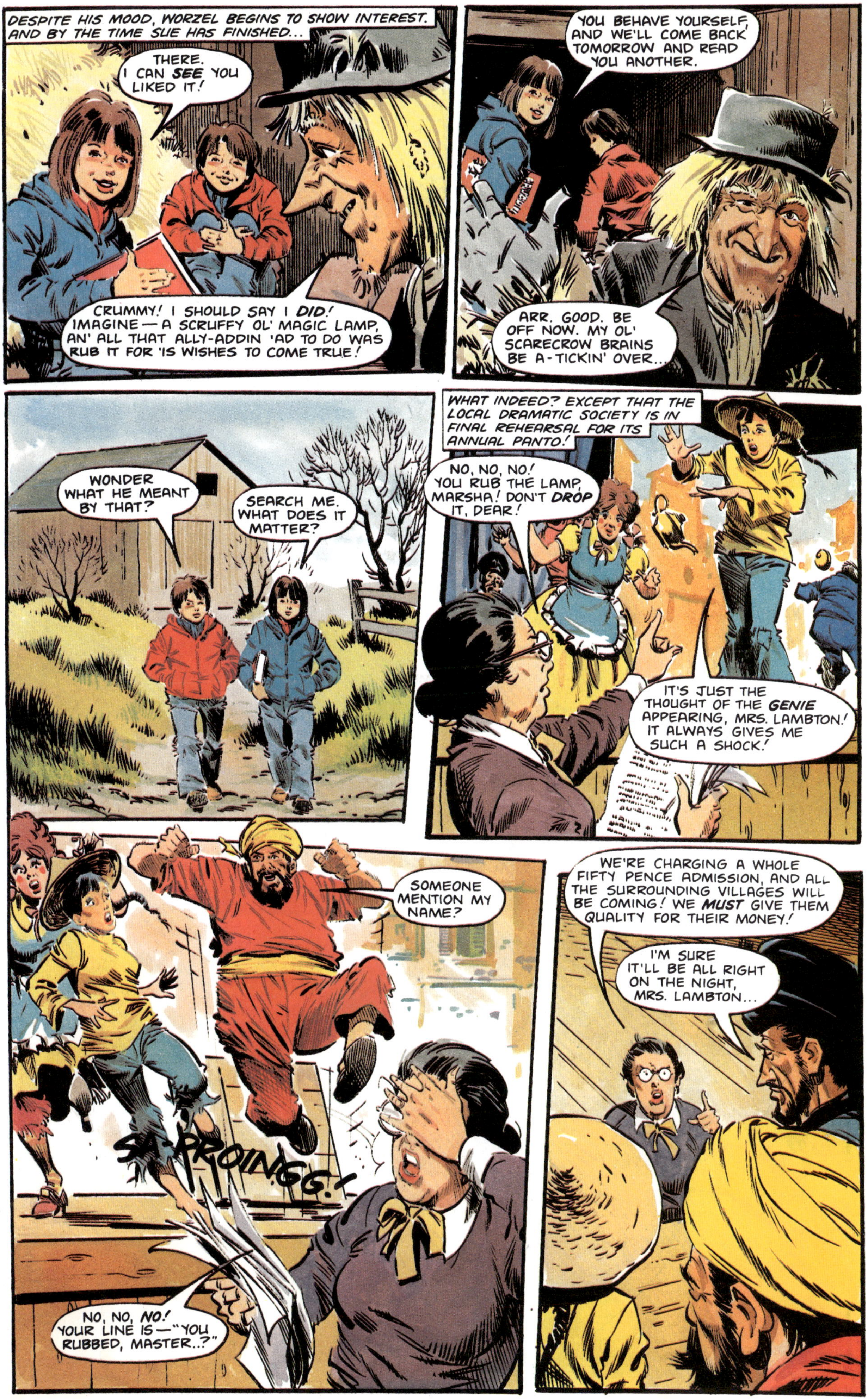

DESPITE HIS MOOD, WORZEL BEGINS TO SHOW INTEREST. AND BY THE TIME SUE HAS FINISHED...
THERE. I CAN SEE YOU LIKED IT!
CRUMMY! I SHOULD SAY I DID! IMAGINE — A SCRUFFY OL' MAGIC LAMP, AN' ALL THAT ALLY-ADDIN 'AD TO DO WAS RUB IT FOR 'IS WISHES TO COME TRUE!
YOU BEHAVE YOURSELF, AND WE'LL COME BACK TOMORROW AND READ YOU ANOTHER.
ARR. GOOD. BE OFF NOW. MY OL' SCARECROW BRAINS BE A-TICKIN' OVER...
WONDER WHAT HE MEANT BY THAT?
SEARCH ME. WHAT DOES IT MATTER?
WHAT INDEED? EXCEPT THAT THE LOCAL DRAMATIC SOCIETY IS IN FINAL REHEARSAL FOR ITS ANNUAL PANTO!
NO, NO, NO! YOU RUB THE LAMP, MARSHA! DON'T DROP IT, DEAR!
IT'S JUST THE THOUGHT OF THE GENIE APPEARING, MRS. LAMBTON! IT ALWAYS GIVES ME SUCH A SHOCK!
SOMEONE MENTION MY NAME?
SA-PROINGG!
NO, NO, NO! YOUR LINE IS — "YOU RUBBED, MASTER..?"
WE'RE CHARGING A WHOLE FIFTY PENCE ADMISSION, AND ALL THE SURROUNDING VILLAGES WILL BE COMING! WE MUST GIVE THEM QUALITY FOR THEIR MONEY!
I'M SURE IT'LL BE ALL RIGHT ON THE NIGHT, MRS. LAMBTON...

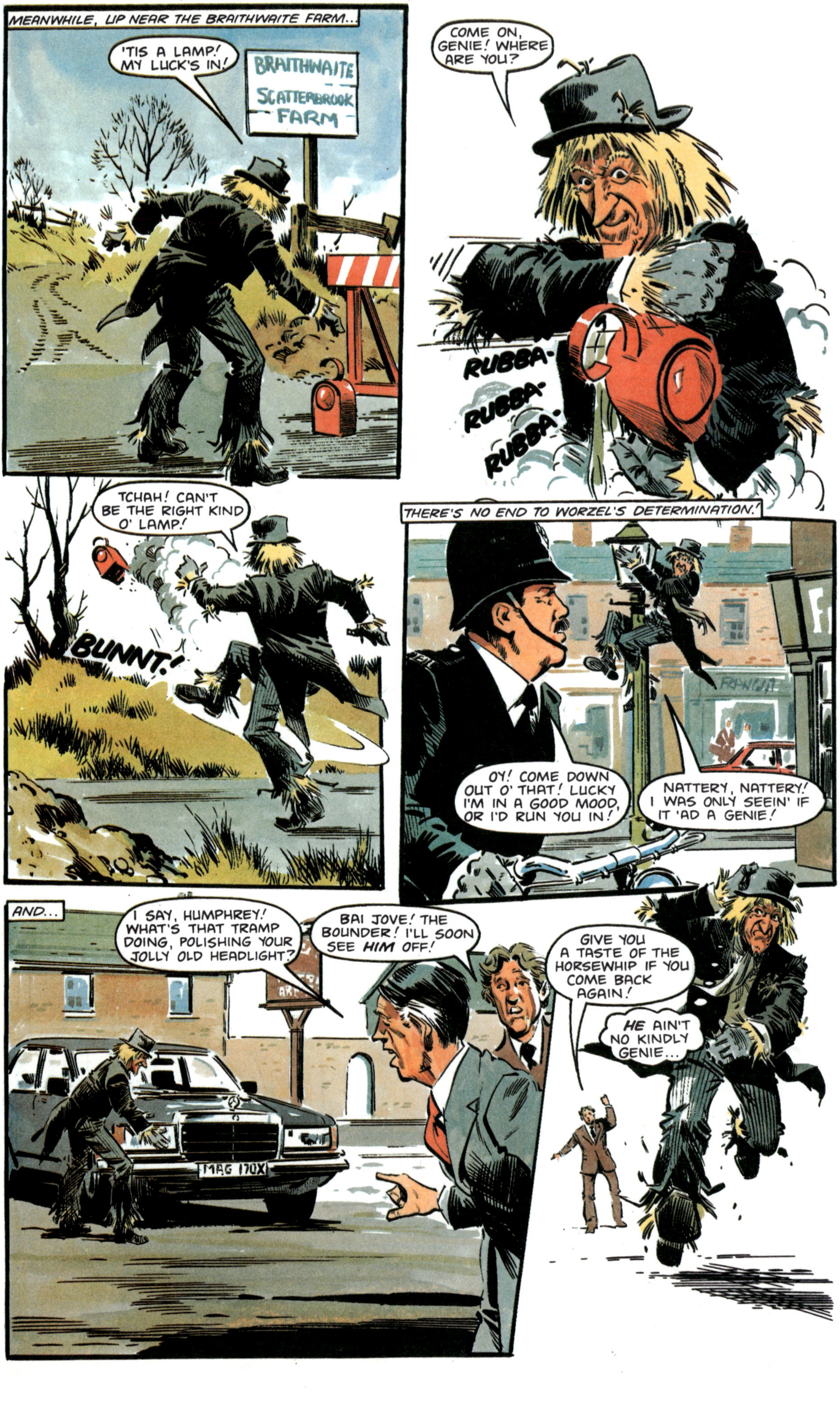
MEANWHILE, UP NEAR THE BRAITHWAITE FARM...
'TIS A LAMP! MY LUCK'S IN!
BRAITHWAITE SCATTERBROOK FARM
COME ON, GENIE! WHERE ARE YOU?
RUBBA-RUBBA-RUBBA-
TCHAH! CAN'T BE THE RIGHT KIND O' LAMP!
BUNNT!
THERE'S NO END TO WORZEL'S DETERMINATION!
OY! COME DOWN OUT O' THAT! LUCKY I'M IN A GOOD MOOD, OR I'D RUN YOU IN!
NATTERY, NATTERY! I WAS ONLY SEEIN' IF IT 'AD A GENIE!
AND...
I SAY, HUMPHREY! WHAT'S THAT TRAMP DOING, POLISHING YOUR JOLLY OLD HEADLIGHT?
BAI JOVE! THE BOUNDER! I'LL SOON SEE HIM OFF!
MAG 170X
GIVE YOU A TASTE OF THE HORSEWHIP IF YOU COME BACK AGAIN!
HE AIN'T NO KINDLY GENIE...

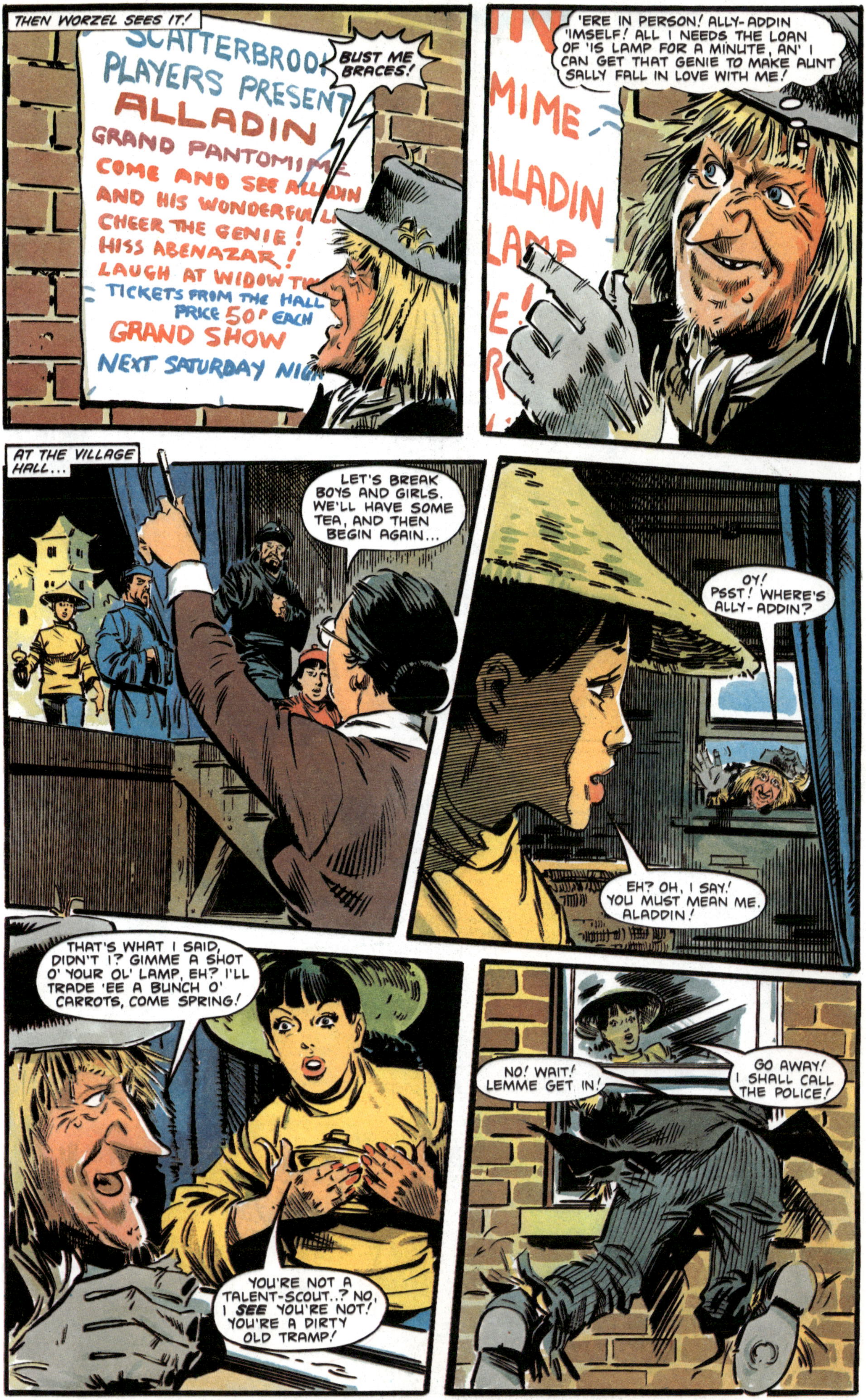
THEN WORZEL SEES IT!
SCATTERBROOK PLAYERS PRESENT
ALLADIN
GRAND PANTOMIME
COME AND SEE ALLADIN AND HIS WONDERFUL
CHEER THE GENIE!
HISS ABENAZAR!
LAUGH AT WIDOW TW
TICKETS FROM THE HALL PRICE 50P EACH
GRAND SHOW
NEXT SATURDAY NIG
BUST ME BRACES!
'ERE IN PERSON! ALLY-ADDIN 'IMSELF! ALL I NEEDS THE LOAN OF 'IS LAMP FOR A MINUTE, AN' I CAN GET THAT GENIE TO MAKE AUNT SALLY FALL IN LOVE WITH ME!
MIME
ALLADIN
LAMP
AT THE VILLAGE HALL...
LET'S BREAK BOYS AND GIRLS. WE'LL HAVE SOME TEA, AND THEN BEGIN AGAIN...
OY! PSST! WHERE'S ALLY-ADDIN?
EH? OH, I SAY! YOU MUST MEAN ME. ALADDIN!
THAT'S WHAT I SAID, DIDN'T I? GIMME A SHOT O' YOUR OL' LAMP, EH? I'LL TRADE 'EE A BUNCH O' CARROTS, COME SPRING!
YOU'RE NOT A TALENT-SCOUT..? NO, I SEE YOU'RE NOT! YOU'RE A DIRTY OLD TRAMP!
NO! WAIT! LEMME GET IN!
GO AWAY! I SHALL CALL THE POLICE!

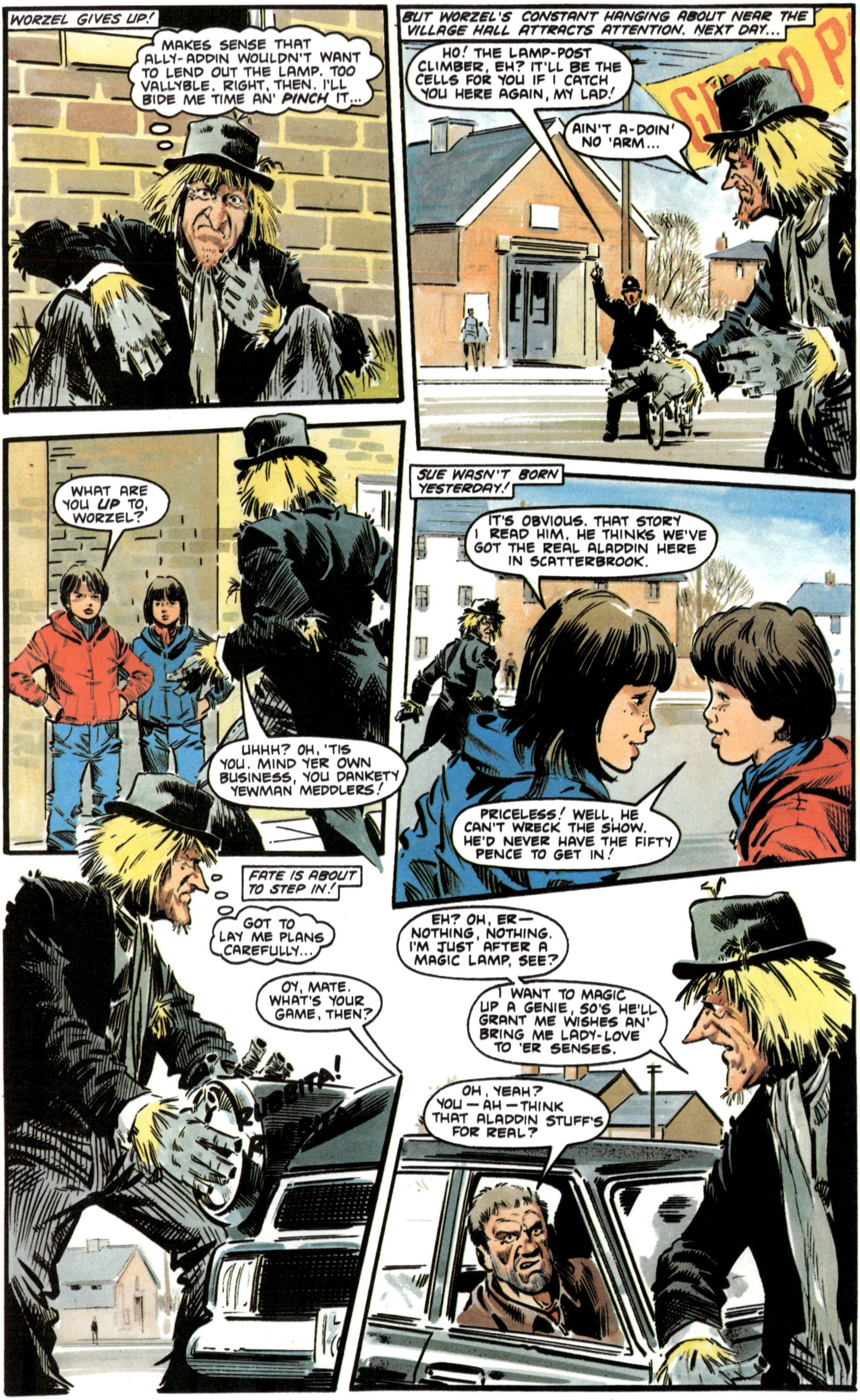

WORZEL GIVES UP!
MAKES SENSE THAT ALLY-ADDIN WOULDN'T WANT TO LEND OUT THE LAMP. TOO VALLYBLE. RIGHT, THEN. I'LL BIDE ME TIME AN' PINCH IT...
BUT WORZEL'S CONSTANT HANGING ABOUT NEAR THE VILLAGE HALL ATTRACTS ATTENTION. NEXT DAY...
HO! THE LAMP-POST CLIMBER, EH? IT'LL BE THE CELLS FOR YOU IF I CATCH YOU HERE AGAIN, MY LAD!
AIN'T A-DOIN' NO 'ARM...
WHAT ARE YOU UP TO, WORZEL?
UHHH? OH, 'TIS YOU. MIND YER OWN BUSINESS, YOU DANKETY YEWMAN MEDDLERS!
SUE WASN'T BORN YESTERDAY!
IT'S OBVIOUS. THAT STORY I READ HIM. HE THINKS WE'VE GOT THE REAL ALADDIN HERE IN SCATTERBROOK.
PRICELESS! WELL, HE CAN'T WRECK THE SHOW. HE'D NEVER HAVE THE FIFTY PENCE TO GET IN!
FATE IS ABOUT TO STEP IN!
GOT TO LAY ME PLANS CAREFULLY...
RUBBITA!
OY, MATE. WHAT'S YOUR GAME, THEN?
EH? OH, ER— NOTHING, NOTHING. I'M JUST AFTER A MAGIC LAMP, SEE?
I WANT TO MAGIC UP A GENIE, SO'S HE'LL GRANT ME WISHES AN' BRING ME LADY-LOVE TO 'ER SENSES.
OH, YEAH? YOU — AH — THINK THAT ALADDIN STUFF'S FOR REAL?

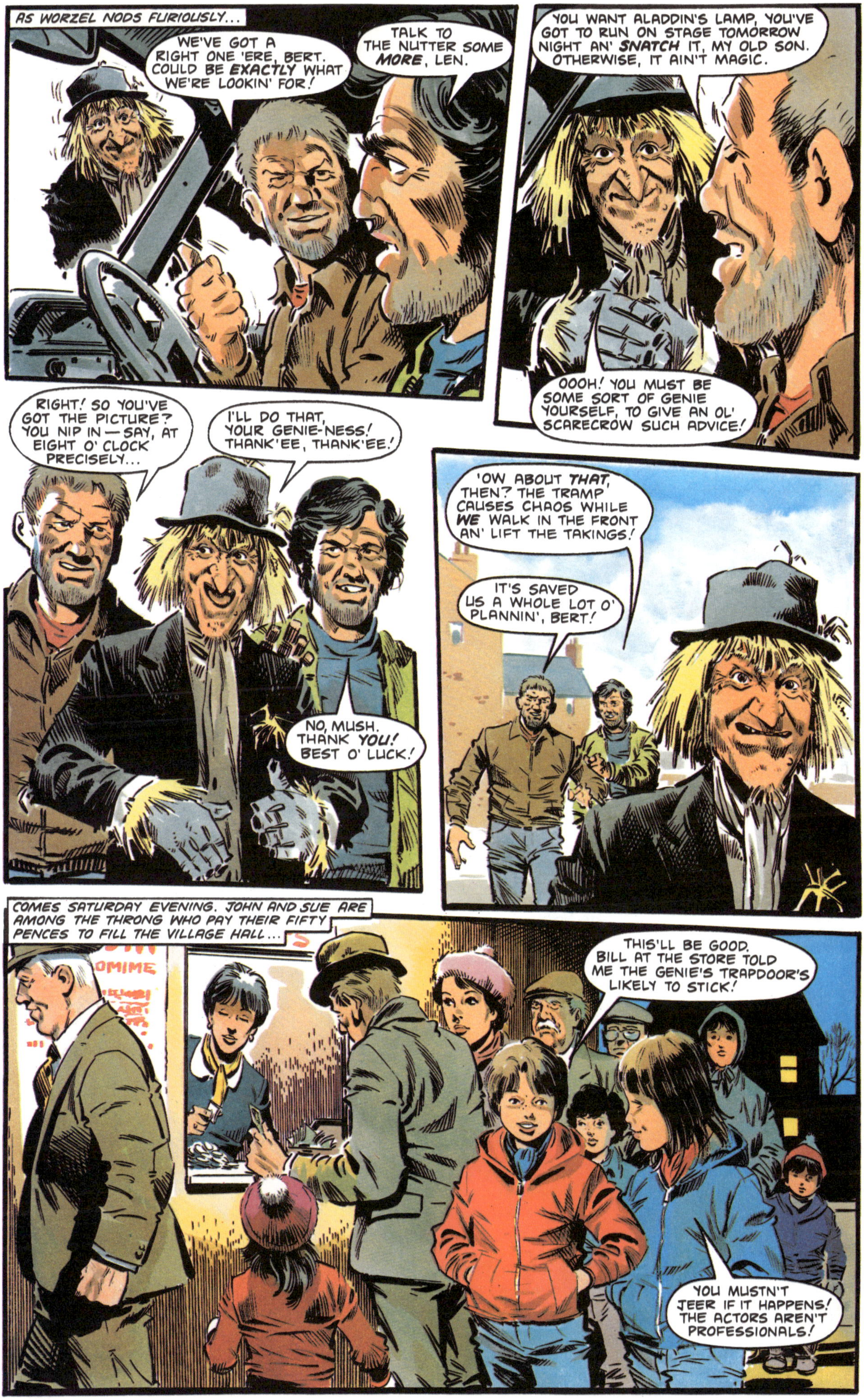
AS WORZEL NODS FURIOUSLY...
WE'VE GOT A RIGHT ONE 'ERE, BERT. COULD BE EXACTLY WHAT WE'RE LOOKIN' FOR!
TALK TO THE NUTTER SOME MORE, LEN.
YOU WANT ALADDIN'S LAMP, YOU'VE GOT TO RUN ON STAGE TOMORROW NIGHT AN' SNATCH IT, MY OLD SON. OTHERWISE, IT AIN'T MAGIC.
OOOH! YOU MUST BE SOME SORT OF GENIE YOURSELF, TO GIVE AN OL' SCARECROW SUCH ADVICE!
RIGHT! SO YOU'VE GOT THE PICTURE? YOU NIP IN—SAY, AT EIGHT O' CLOCK PRECISELY...
I'LL DO THAT, YOUR GENIE-NESS! THANK'EE, THANK'EE!
NO, MUSH. THANK YOU! BEST O' LUCK!
'OW ABOUT THAT, THEN? THE TRAMP CAUSES CHAOS WHILE WE WALK IN THE FRONT AN' LIFT THE TAKINGS!
IT'S SAVED US A WHOLE LOT O' PLANNIN', BERT!
COMES SATURDAY EVENING. JOHN AND SUE ARE AMONG THE THRONG WHO PAY THEIR FIFTY PENCES TO FILL THE VILLAGE HALL...
THIS'LL BE GOOD. BILL AT THE STORE TOLD ME THE GENIE'S TRAPDOOR'S LIKELY TO STICK!
YOU MUSTN'T JEER IF IT HAPPENS! THE ACTORS AREN'T PROFESSIONALS!

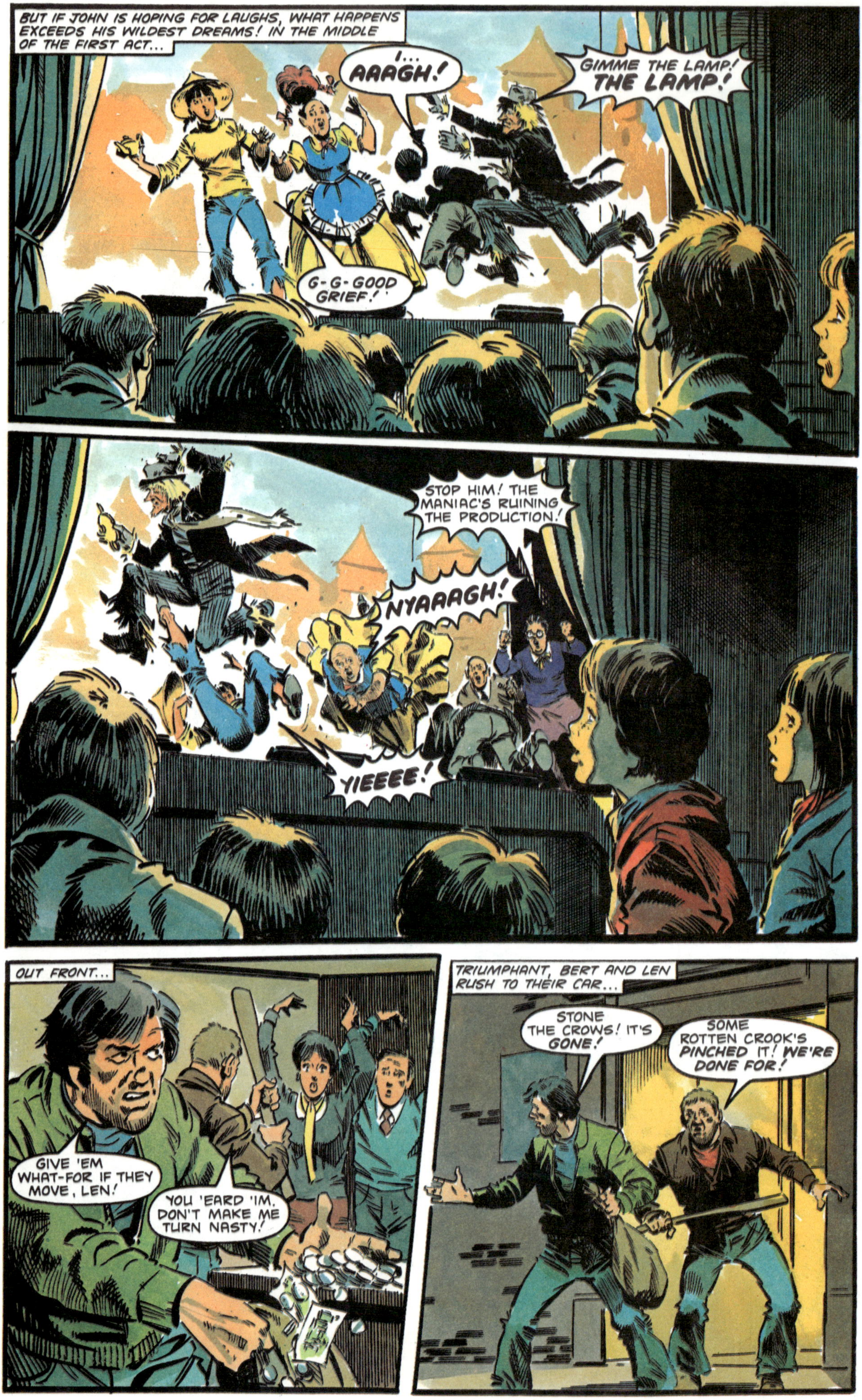

BUT IF JOHN IS HOPING FOR LAUGHS, WHAT HAPPENS EXCEEDS HIS WILDEST DREAMS! IN THE MIDDLE OF THE FIRST ACT...
I... AAAGH!
GIMME THE LAMP! THE LAMP!
G-G-GOOD GRIEF!
STOP HIM! THE MANIAC'S RUINING THE PRODUCTION!
NYAAAGH!
YIEEEE!
OUT FRONT...
GIVE 'EM WHAT-FOR IF THEY MOVE, LEN!
YOU 'EARD 'IM. DON'T MAKE ME TURN NASTY!
TRIUMPHANT, BERT AND LEN RUSH TO THEIR CAR...
STONE THE CROWS! IT'S GONE!
SOME ROTTEN CROOK'S PINCHED IT! WE'RE DONE FOR!

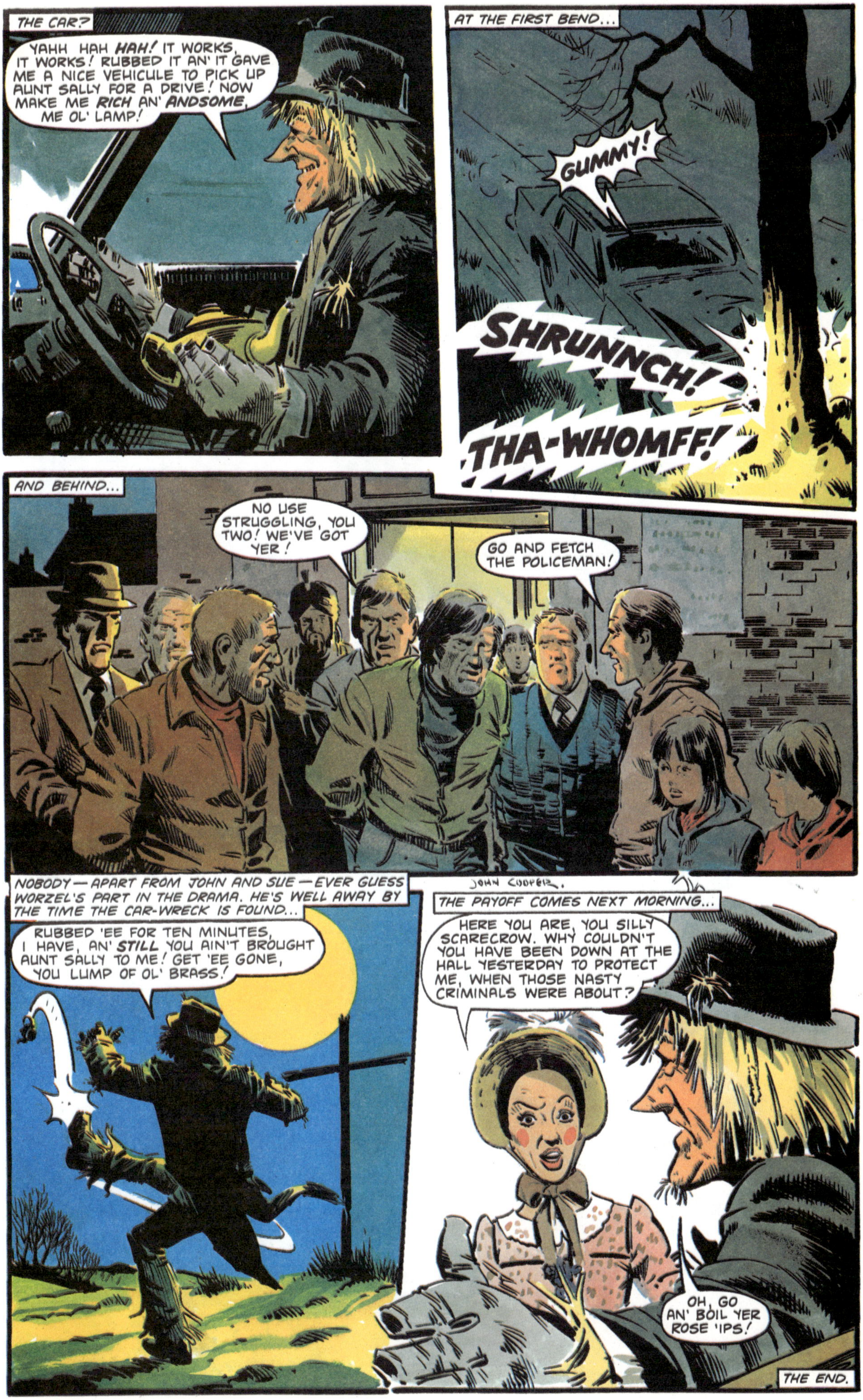
THE CAR?
YAHH HAH HAH! IT WORKS, IT WORKS! RUBBED IT AN' IT GAVE ME A NICE VEHICULE TO PICK UP AUNT SALLY FOR A DRIVE! NOW MAKE ME RICH AN' ANDSOME, ME OL' LAMP!
AT THE FIRST BEND...
GUMMY!
SHRUNNCH!
THA-WHOMFF!
AND BEHIND...
NO USE STRUGGLING, YOU TWO! WE'VE GOT YER!
GO AND FETCH THE POLICEMAN!
NOBODY—APART FROM JOHN AND SUE—EVER GUESS WORZEL'S PART IN THE DRAMA. HE'S WELL AWAY BY THE TIME THE CAR-WRECK IS FOUND...
RUBBED 'EE FOR TEN MINUTES, I HAVE, AN' STILL YOU AIN'T BROUGHT AUNT SALLY TO ME! GET 'EE GONE, YOU LUMP OF OL' BRASS!
JOHN COOPER.
THE PAYOFF COMES NEXT MORNING...
HERE YOU ARE, YOU SILLY SCARECROW. WHY COULDN'T YOU HAVE BEEN DOWN AT THE HALL YESTERDAY TO PROTECT ME, WHEN THOSE NASTY CRIMINALS WERE ABOUT?
OH, GO AN' BOIL YER ROSE 'IPS!
THE END.

Saucy Nancy

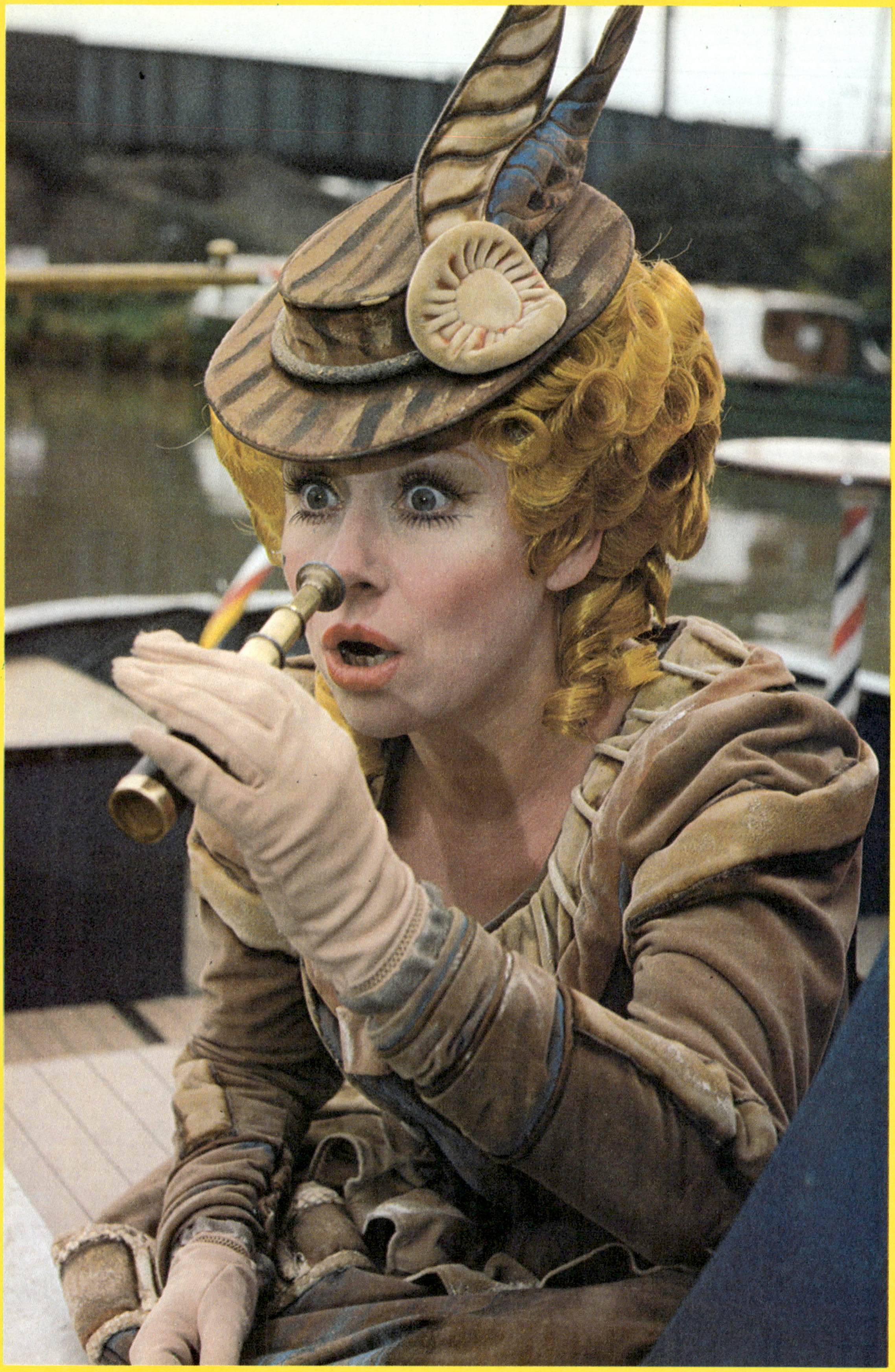

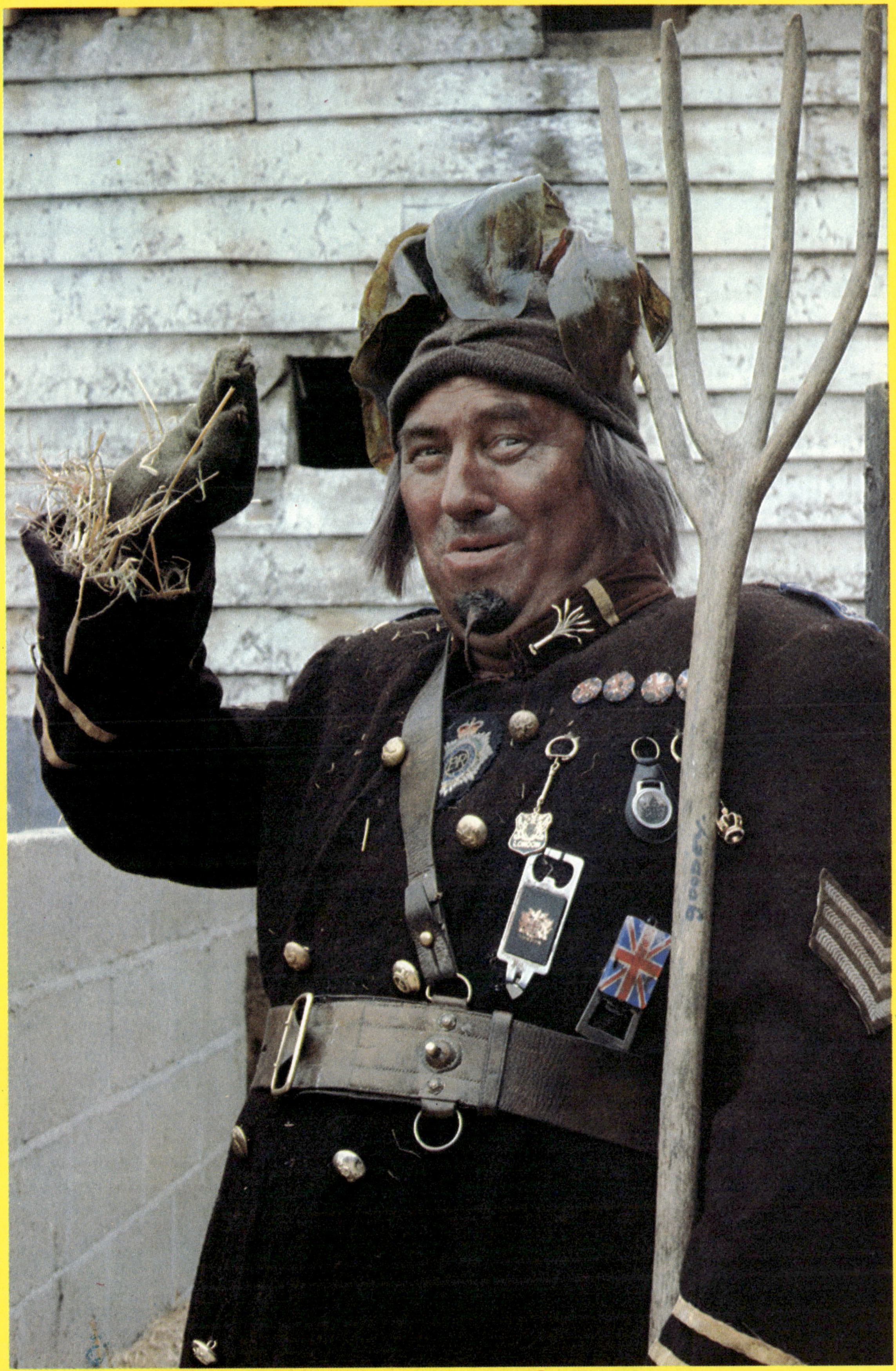

Sergeant Beetroot

AS EASY AS PIE!

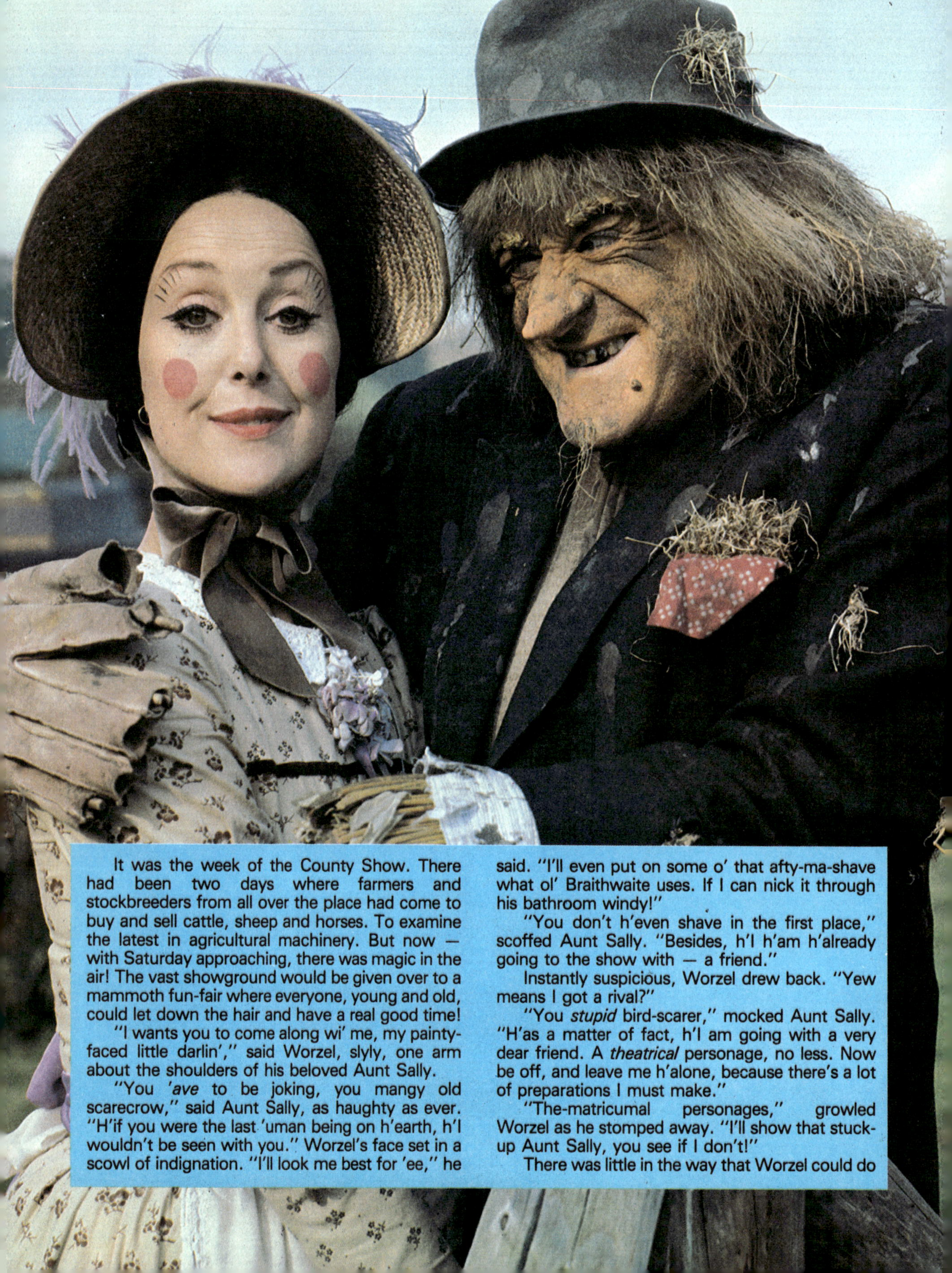

It was the week of the County Show. There had been two days where farmers and stockbreeders from all over the place had come to buy and sell cattle, sheep and horses. To examine the latest in agricultural machinery. But now — with Saturday approaching, there was magic in the air! The vast showground would be given over to a mammoth fun-fair where everyone, young and old, could let down the hair and have a real good time!

"I wants you to come along wi' me, my painty-faced little darlin'," said Worzel, slyly, one arm about the shoulders of his beloved Aunt Sally.

"You *'ave* to be joking, you mangy old scarecrow," said Aunt Sally, as haughty as ever. "H'if you were the last 'uman being on h'earth, h'I wouldn't be seen with you." Worzel's face set in a scowl of indignation. "I'll look me best for 'ee," he said. "I'll even put on some o' that afty-ma-shave what ol' Braithwaite uses. If I can nick it through his bathroom windy!"

"You don't h'even shave in the first place," scoffed Aunt Sally. "Besides, h'I h'am h'already going to the show with — a friend."

Instantly suspicious, Worzel drew back. "Yew means I got a rival?"

"You *stupid* bird-scarer," mocked Aunt Sally. "H'as a matter of fact, h'I am going with a very dear friend. A *theatrical* personage, no less. Now be off, and leave me h'alone, because there's a lot of preparations I must make."

"The-matricumal personages," growled Worzel as he stomped away. "I'll show that stuck-up Aunt Sally, you see if I don't!"

There was little in the way that Worzel could do

of smartening himself up, but at least he went back up to his old barn, brushed the stray seeds from his ragged clothes, and did his best. And meanwhile, down in the meadows that had been given over to the marquees, pounds, and other temporary edifices of the County Show, locals from every village for miles around were gathering . . .

Martin Rivers was what you'd call a unit director. A 'with-it' and blase executive of Commercialeyes Productions, he was in charge of a two-man camera team, their task to make a short advertising film for the owner of the funfair. And Martin Rivers was not entirely happy. "It's all very well, dear boy," he said to Jackson, his senior cameraman. "But what can we *get* here? I mean, apart from people just enjoying themselves?" Jackson shrugged. "Surely that's all that's needed, boss. We're doing this commercial for Barnum O'Shea's funfair, right? So the slogan is — 'Fun all the way with Barnum O'Shea'. Seems straightforward enough to me."

"Tchah!" Rivers tutted irritably. "It's all so — so *predictable*!"

The junior assistant, Walker, tugged at his chief's elbow, and pointed. "If you're looking for good pictures, Mr Rivers, there's a good 'un over there. See? Those two birds . . ."

Rivers followed his minion's direction, and his eye fell upon Aunt Sally and her companion — an extremely attractive young lady in old-fashioned clothes. The pair of them were strolling languidly past a row of 'try-your-luck' stalls, their noses in the air. "Hmmm," said Rivers. "Okay. Follow them, chaps. They *are* rather photogenic. I wonder what prompted them to come here in fancy dress . . .?"

It was Aunt Sally who first caught sight of the two men with the movie camera and their flamboyant boss following them. She said: "H'I say, Martina, we seem to 'ave h'attracted some h'attention."

Martina, her companion, who had started life as a most superior mannequin in one of London's highest stores (she had thought of herself as 'the wonder of the windows') glanced round and fluttered her eyelids. She had done a stint in a museum of fashion, had been used as background in a stage show, and considered herself — as Aunt Sally fully endorsed — theatrical. "Smile dear," she said, and posed graciously. "My experience tells me that these gentlemen are making some kind of film. Perhaps it's the break I've been waiting for — and of course, there may be a part for *you* in this!"

Aunt Sally's already lofty ideas soared to dizzy heights. She preened herself.

And then came the voice of Martin Rivers. Commanding. Hectoring. "I say, ladies! Please! I beg you! Don't just *stand* there!" He gestured to a gaily-painted, traditional roundabout, with its florid horses. "Be my guests! Up on the ride!"

Simpering, Aunt Sally and Martina did as they were bid. Totally unaware that, just behind them, a figure had darted out from the shadows between a 'test your strength' machine and a fortune teller's booth. It was Worzel, and he was chuckling vastly. "'twern't no rival after all," he laughed. "Nobbut one o' your lady-friends, Aunt Sally, Right! I'll show 'ee now! By the time the afternoon's out, I'll 'ave *her* eatin' out of me hand. 'Tis time I made you jealous!"

Camera whirred as Aunt Sally and Martina went sedately round on the carnival horses. Neither was conscious of the leering face that appeared between and behind them . . .

"Confound it to blazes," raved Martin Rivers.

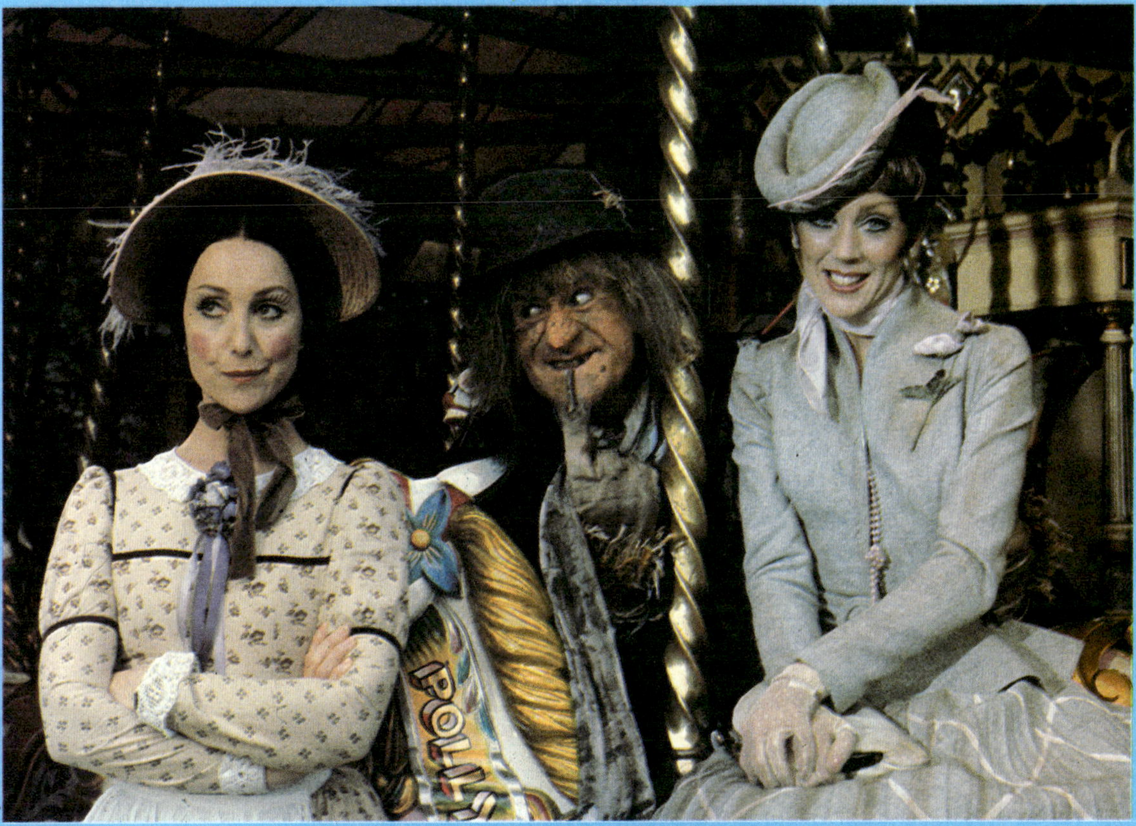

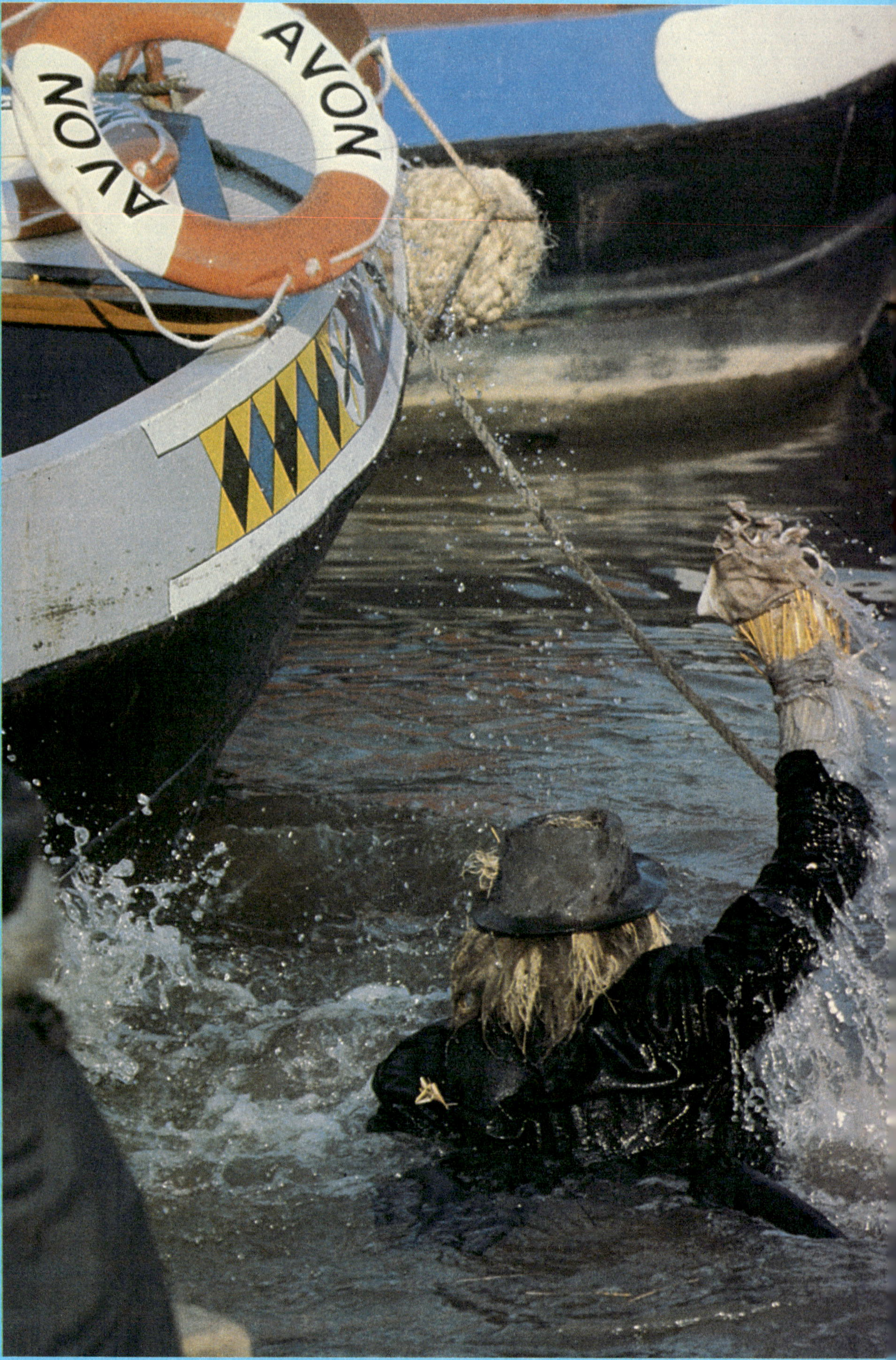
AVON
AVON

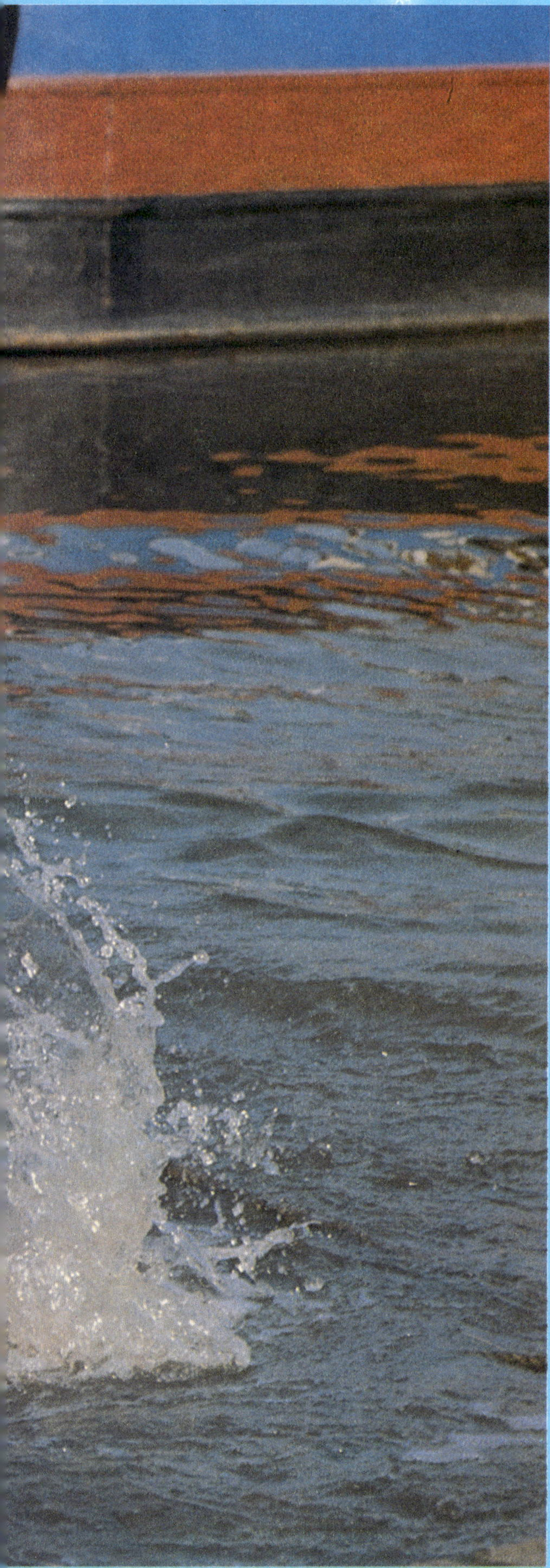

"A superb shot — ruined by that whiskery old tramp! Where the deuce did *he* spring from?"

Aunt Sally and Martina looked somewhat bewildered, but glances over their shoulders reveal nothing, for Worzel — unbalanced by the whirling of the ride, had fallen off, and had rolled uncontrollably beneath the circling platform, his mouth full of dirt.

"Ladies, permit me," said Rivers as the roundabout stopped. "This way. Perhaps you'd condescend to take a boat on the canal? At my expense, of course!"

"Charmed," said Martina. She looked for confirmation at the starry-eyed Aunt Sally. "H'I 'ave 'eard of you people from 'Ollywood."

"Hardly that," said Rivers. "But I think we can make this little junket — er — worth your while."

"I can see it now," breathed Martina. "You and I, Aunt Sally — the stars of the eighties! Our own television show! World-wide acclaim!"

"Just what h' I'ave h' always felt h'I was cut out for," bubbled her companion.

Worzel, who had spent a good five minutes getting his right boot out of one of the bits of machinery under Barnum O'Shea's roundabout, cast irritably around for a sign of his erstwhile lady friends. It was pure chance that took him down to the canal, which O'Shea's expertise had turned into a temporary marina, with colourful barges and narrow-boats, dinghies and rowing skiffs, and staff in truly nautical dress ready to entertain the visitors. It was also pure chance that made him catch sight of Aunt Sally, in the distance, and put his own feet wrong on one of the short wooden jetties. A wild cry, an almighty splash, and Worzel was in the drink, and floundering, while cackling onlookers jeered and cheered! Someone at least had the wits to throw him a lifebelt . . .

The junior assistant, Walker, had noticed him, and the camera whirred briefly on Worzel, until Martin Rivers himself brought his team back to basics. "Tush, Walker! This way, this way! See — our ladies are paddling their canoe! Catch the gladness in their smiles!" He sighed wearily. "I don't know. It's not good enough. 'Fun all the way with Barnum O'Shea?' I wish I could think of something more — more — *zesty*!"

Soaking wet, Worzel dragged himself out of the canal and huddled himself near an antique traction engine that was part of the fair — a relic of Barnum O'Shea's own forefathers. Worzel was afraid of fire in itself, but as long as he kept away from the coal-fired furnace of the thing, he could at least dry out. By this time, he felt thoroughly irritated, and had forgotten his desire to shine up to Martina and make Aunt Sally jealous. Unreasonably — for in fact they didn't even know he was at the show — he blamed the two females for his misfortune. "Blamedy wummen," he grumbled to himself. "Nothin' ever goes right for a pore ol' scarecrow like me. They'm all airs an' graces, an' all I get is a chance to look more raggedy than ever!"

A small child, who had been staring at him for some time, came up with all the wisdom that such small children often show. "Don't be sad, mister funny," said the infant. "You can have this, if you like." The child offered Worzel a half-sucked lolly, and Worzel graciously accepted it. "Well, thank'ee kindly," he said, with uncharacteristic charm. "Just what I needs to cool me down!"

It was a good lolly. Full of flavour, and decidedly more-ish. As Worzel consumed it, he began to realise just how peckish he felt.

At last, he threw the stick away, and with a final pat on the head for the round-eyed youngster, he shambled across towards a large marquee where the sign clearly read 'TEA TENT'.

At the same time, at another entrance to that marquee — for it had two — Martin Rivers and his team were ushering Aunt Sally and Martina inside. "It won't be much," muttered Rivers to Jackson, "But let's have a shot of them with cakes and lemonade or whatever. Honestly, this is all getting me down."

"Don't worry, Mr Rivers," said Jackson, and Walker nodded agreement beside him. "We'll get 'em on the swings, afterwards. They *are* photogenic ladies."

Aunt Sally and Martina were placed strategically at a table loaded with goodies, and treated to whatever they wanted. With the camera-lens upon them, they were eager — no, *overjoyed* to play their part. And as they scoffed all they could eat, that was when Worzel — at the far end of the tent, caught sight of them again. He had been refused service. After all, one does not get refreshment for nothing, and if Worzel had imagined it was all for free, he'd been disappointed. With the retort of the woman behind the counter ringing in his ears — "No tramps get hand-outs here!" he saw Aunt Sally about to delicately munch a chocolate biscuit. Worzel's cool

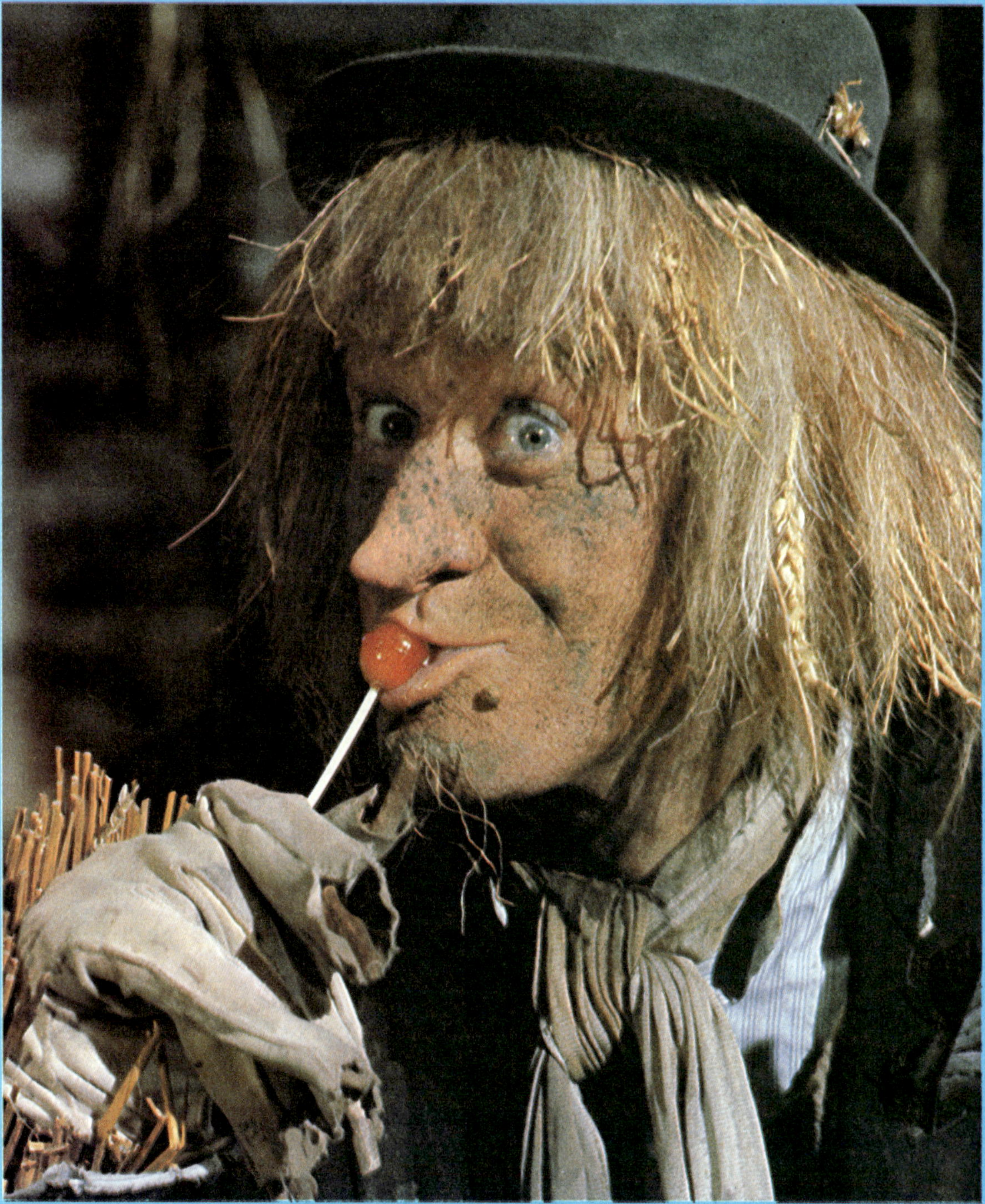

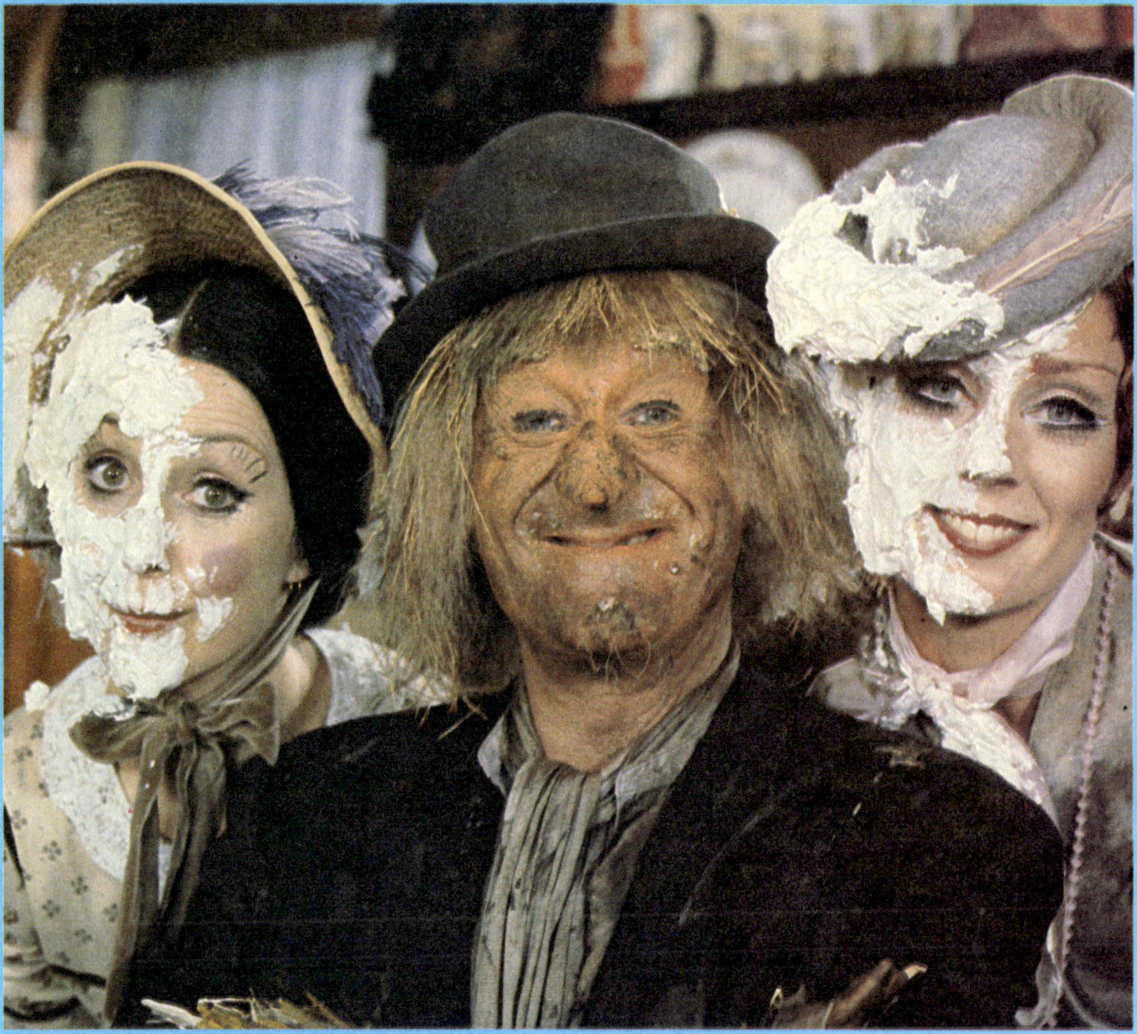

evaporated. A strangled cry of rage burst from his throat, and he reached out to grab a lemon-meringue pie that lay on the table before him. His hand drew back, and he flung it, so that it burst like a bomb on the side of Aunt Sally's head! "Crammy-faced ol' wooden' 'ead," he yelled. "Take that!"

Next second, all bedlam broke loose! Martina it was who saw Worzel, and she snatched up a handy custard flan and returned it — with unerring accuracy, in his direction. He ducked, though — and the flan hit the woman behind the counter. Whooping, Worzel scooped up a handful of trifle and hurled it at Aunt Sally, who received the lot on one painted cheek!

Pies, flans and pastries flew back and forth, exploding spectacularly whether on or off target, and the people in charge of the Tea-Tent screamed, floundered, slipped and fell as chaos became complete. Worzel, in his element, continued to plaster the two females while managing, somehow, to dodge retribution!

A heavy voice — that of the senior woman in charge of the tent, spoke thickly through a face-pack of meringue. "Someone-is-going-to-jail-for this!"

Worzel knew it would be him. He backed off. Aunt Sally and Martina were also advancing on him, thristing, it seemed, for blood!

But now Martin Rivers capered between them, his face wreathed in smiles of delight, his arms waving ecstatically in the air! "Perfect," he blared. "Absolutely perfect! Oh joy, oh *bliss*!"

Drop-jawed, Worzel, Aunt Sally, Martina — even the bespattered attendants, turned to gape at him.

"I'll pay for everything," said Rivers, hardly able to contain his glee. "It's positively, absolutely the *greatest*! Pure slapstick, and I've got it all on film! Can't you see the new slogan . . .? 'Fun and Frolic — the O'Shea Way! It's as *easy as pie* — so don't be lazy, go crazy!"

"What be he a-talkin' about?" said Worzel, nervously, allowing his hand to be wrung by the unit director.

Walker spoke. "I think my boss is offering you a job, mate," he said "Along with these two ladies, if they're willing. Just to publicise O'Shea's funfair."

Martin Rivers, already, was pacing around, hand to forehead muttering about 'altered captions,' and 'new angles' — but Worzel didn't hear him. He was looking at Aunt Sally and Martina, both of whom were basking in the idea that they'd be properly on film.

And sure enough, they were. All three of them. It was only for the once, but it was a long, long time before Worzel, smugly, let Aunt Sally forget that it was thanks to *him* that she'd become an actress . . .

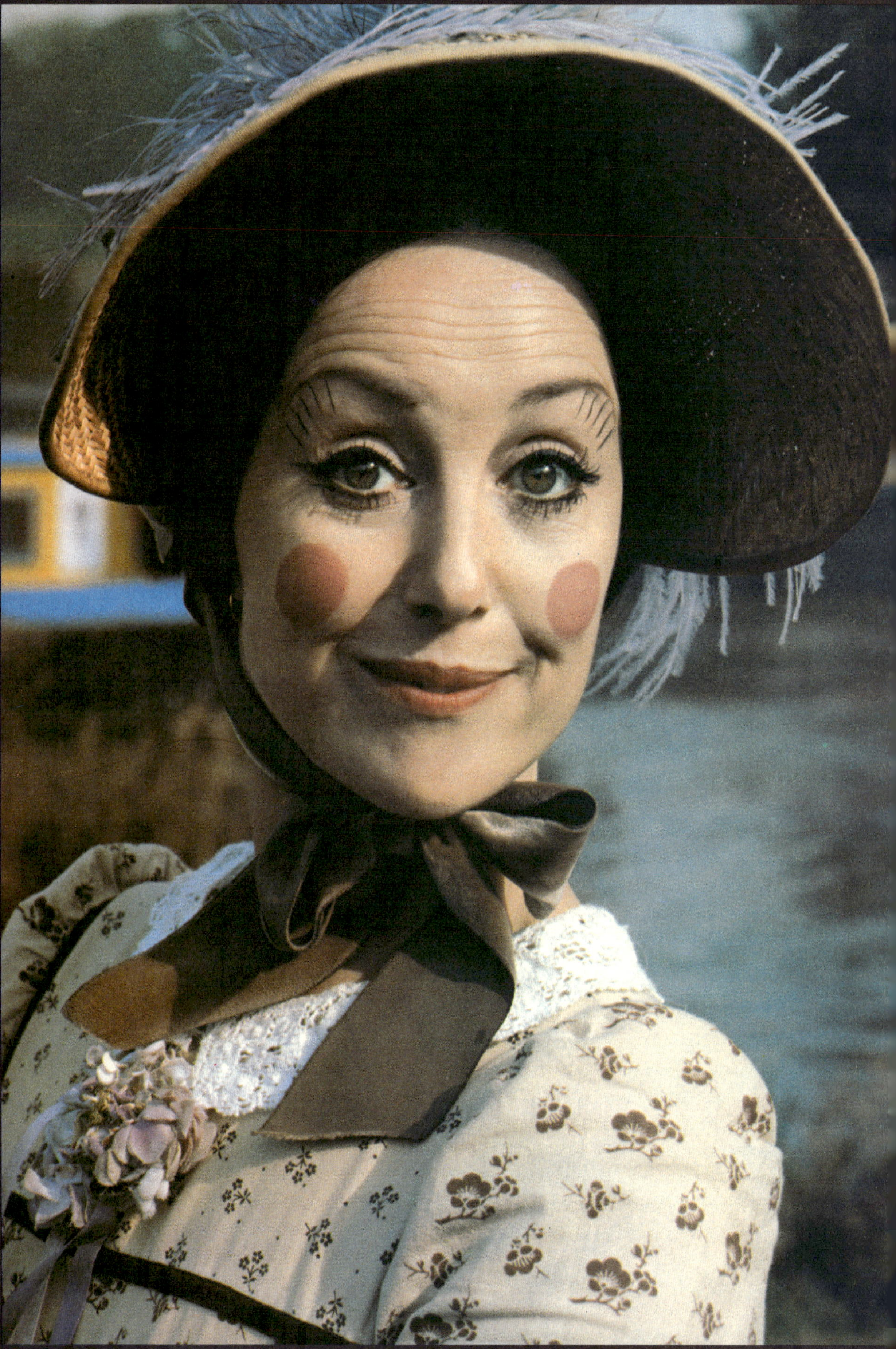

Una Stubbs

bringing Aunt Sally to life

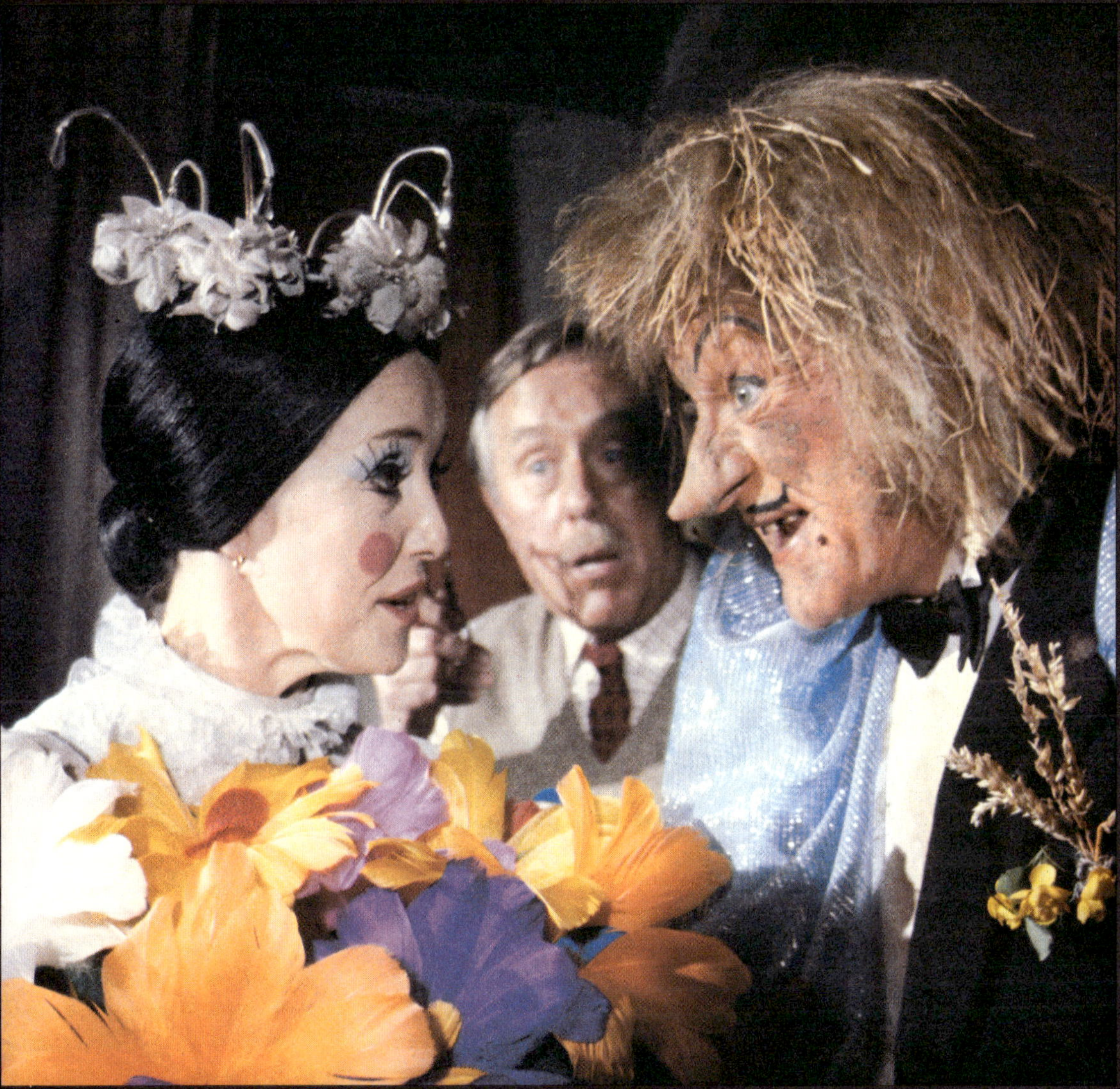

It's a freezing cold day in London's Tottenham Court Road. Through the window we watch black taxis crawl through the slush and passers-by huddle under their coats and hats to protect themselves from the sleet hurling down from the murky skies.

In the Horseshoe Rehearsal Room it is warm and inviting — the cast of the **Worzel Gummidge Christmas Show** are in the middle of a work-out before they go into rehearsals proper for the approaching stage production.

The room is buzzing with activity. Small children practise barre-work in front of a mirror in their tiny point shoes. In one corner a girl practises the words to a song, humming them over and over to herself in a soft voice. In another, two girls chat animatedly, pirouetting as they go.

In this melée walks a tiny figure clad in black leotard and tights. "Hi Una, come and practise with us," calls one girl from the corner. The star of the show smiles in acknowledgement and walks over to join them. In a moment she is totally involved, high-kicking and skipping around like an effervescent teenager.

Una's love of dancing is evident. She began to learn very young because, she says modestly, "I had a brother and sister who were obviously very talented at school and I didn't show an aptitude for anything except dancing, so I was sent off to learn as soon as possible."

From the moment she put on her first pair of ballet shoes, she knew she didn't want to do anything else, and as a young dancer she landed a job high-kicking at the London

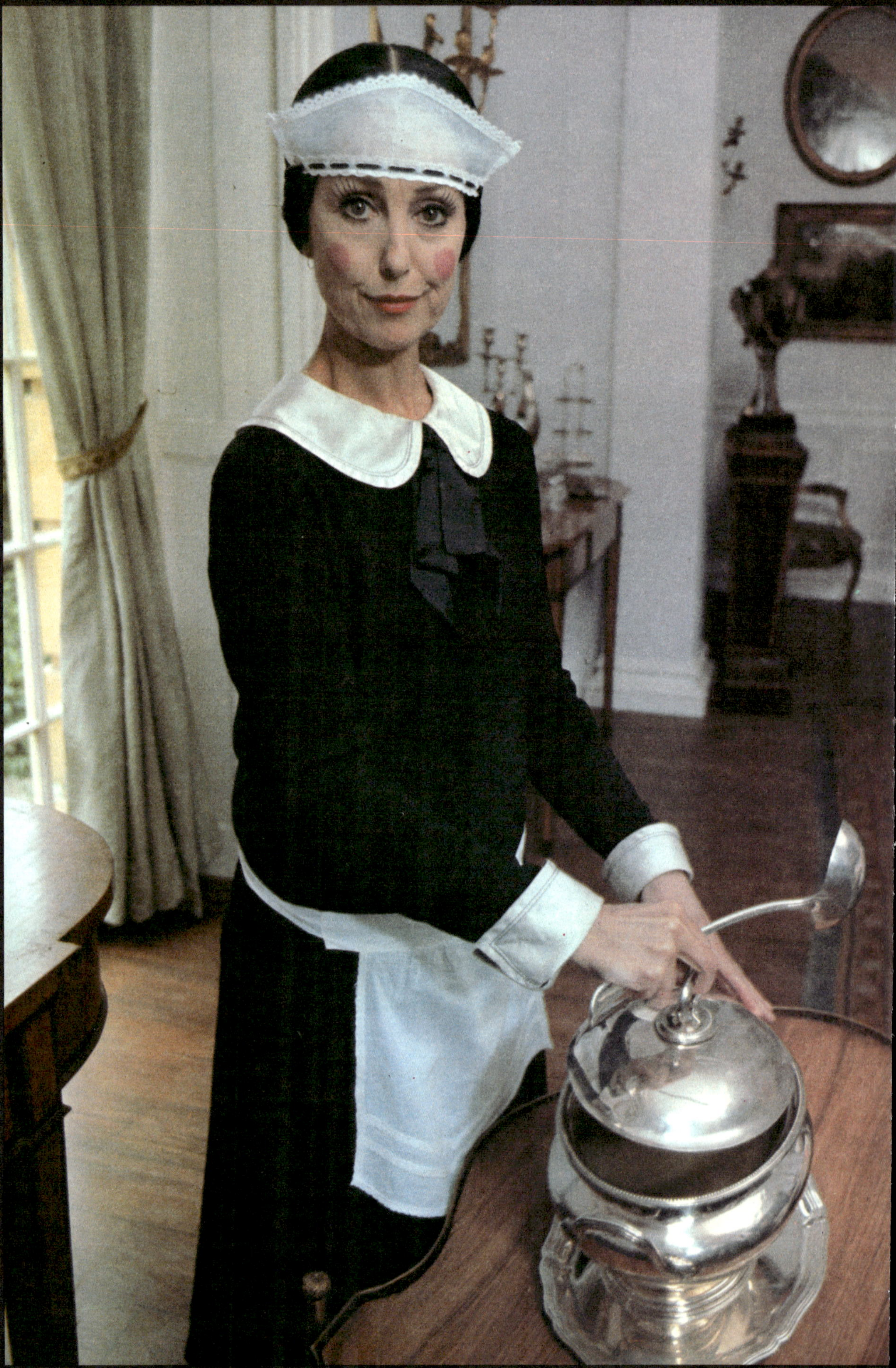

Palladium, where her determination and vivacity earned her the nickname of 'Basher Stubbs'.

Accident-prone then as now, from time to time her dancing shoes went rocketing off in the middle of a routine and landed among the audience. Luckily no one suffered any permanent damage. "At least it got me noticed," she says.

From the Palladium, she danced and sang her way through musicals and pantomimes, forming a strong working partnership with Cliff Richard along the way. They made the film **"Summer Holiday"** together and she was a regular guest on his shows. Una also danced for several years on **"Cool For Cats"**, a sixties version of **"Top Of The Pops"**.

She decided to turn to acting and immediately became a star as 'Rita', the dim daughter of Alf Garnett in the comedy, **"Till Death Do Us Part"**. The show ran for eight years and in the meantime, Una developed her talent for song and dance by appearing in musicals during breaks in filming — only this time she was the star instead of the chorus girl.

After a while, Una tires of rehearsing, skips over and flings herself into a chair to rest before the serious run-through. She is so full of charm and panache that the reasons for her popularity among the rest of the cast become self-evident. With her delightful personality and charming manner she makes you feel at ease straight away, and her delicate features mean she looks as fragile in real life as the china doll she plays in Worzel Gummidge.

Even Aunt Sally is rooted in her dancing days. "I was working in a musical fairytale with Jon Pertwee several years ago when he first had the idea of making Worzel Gummidge," she explains. "I played a princess, but wanted to make her a little different from traditional pantomime characters, I decided to play the part as if she were a doll come to life."

In the story, the princess is woken from her death-bed, so Una would sit up, waggle her feet in wonder, then go off into a stylized dance routine, stiff and doll-like, waggling her fingers and toes. Everything was conveyed by the quality of movement, as in a mime. Jon Pertwee was so impressed that he asked Una there and then if she would play the part of Aunt Sally if he could get the project off the ground.

In real life, 'Aunt Sallys' originated in fairs which were held to celebrate harvest and spring-time. As amusements became popular, the revelries were often too expensive for the poor people to join in, so in the 1820's a travelling gypsy showman called Old Corey Dyne set out to prove that a true showman

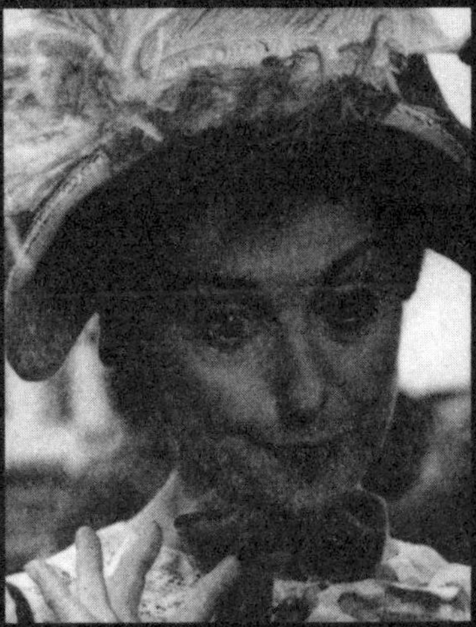

didn't need elaborate and costly exhibitions to attract customers.

His booth was an old hat turned upside-down on the ground with a stake driven through it. On top of the stake rested a half-penny which challengers had to knock off with wooden balls. If the coin dropped outside the hat he awarded a prize. The game became extremely popular and it later developed into a coconut shy and also the game of knocking down skittles in the shape of a bossy old aunt.

Una, thank goodness, is nothing like the snobby, superior character she plays as Aunt Sally, although she admits she does revel in playing a baddie. "It's the first time I've ever played someone really unpleasant and it really can be fun!

"When I got the part, Beryl Reid, who I'd just finished working with, gave me some really good advice. She told me that if you play a baddie, you have to go all the way and be truly awful — never play for sympathy. So that's what I've done and it seems to have worked. My sons were horrified when they first saw the programme, but the shock seems to have died down now."

Una likes nothing better than to be at home with her three sons, Jason, Christian and Joe. They live in a idyllically pretty house in London where every inch of wall-space is covered with framed pictures — drawings the boys have done since play-school days alongside Una's own tapestries and embroideries.

She spends every spare moment looking after the house, but her home 'improvements' haven't always been spectacularly successful. Like the time she got the bright idea of painting her bedroom — in the middle of the night.

Unable to sleep, she worked away the night, then pulled back the curtains next morning to reveal bright yellow paint spattered all over the carpet and the clothes in her louvre-doored wardrobe with yellow stripes across the sleeves.

She still acts on impulse, but it is precisely her bubbly, enthusiastic character that has made her such a popular guest on shows like **"Give Us A Clue"** in which she tends to forget she's on TV because, "It's just like playing a party game at home."

Una springs out of her chair. Resting time is over and she has to get down to work. The children clamour for her attention and she giggles infectiously at their antics.

"These are the kind of shows I enjoy most of all," she says, "where I can just let myself go and sing and dance to my heart's content." And with that she is dragged off into the crowd to lead the first number...

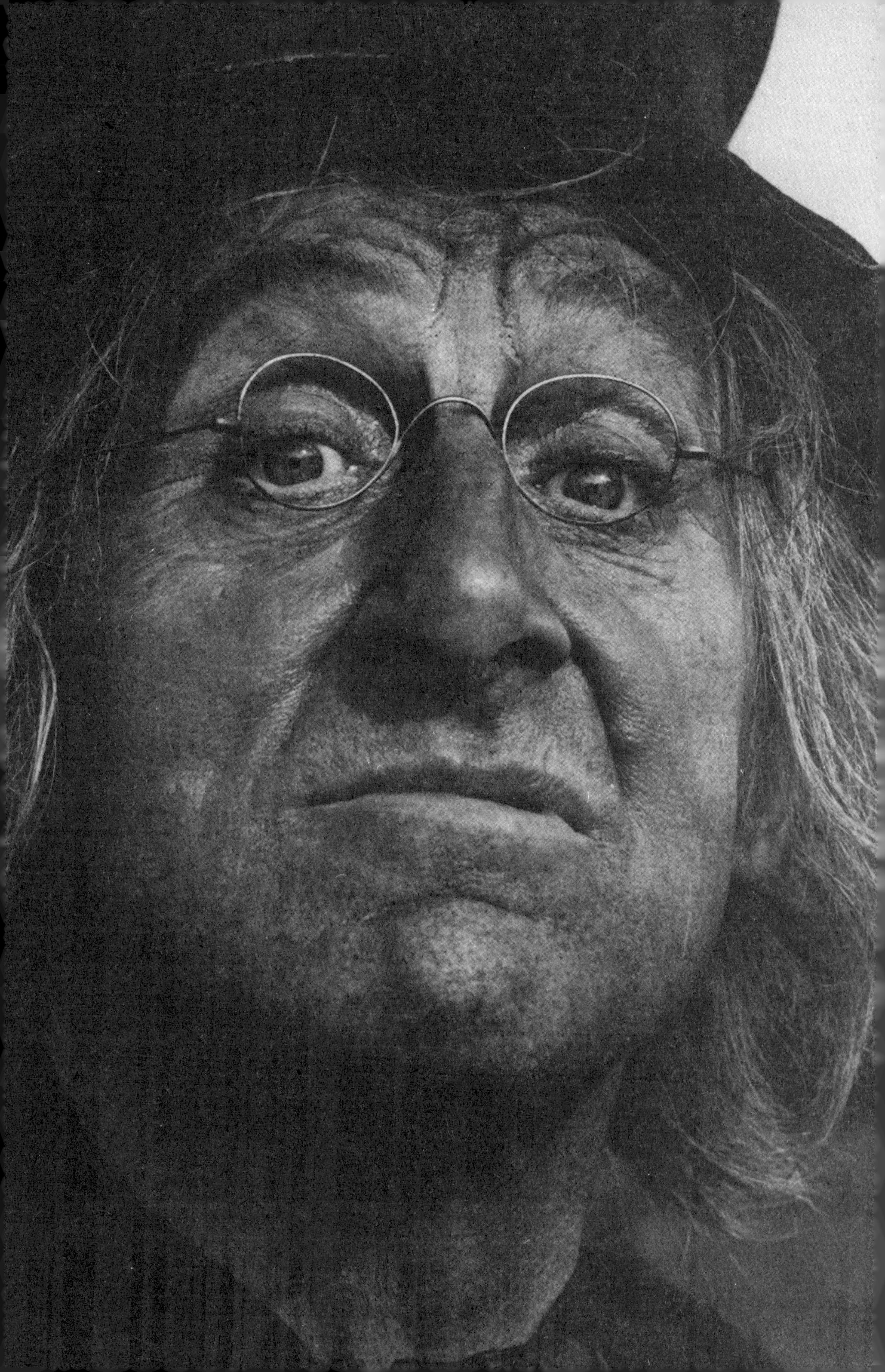

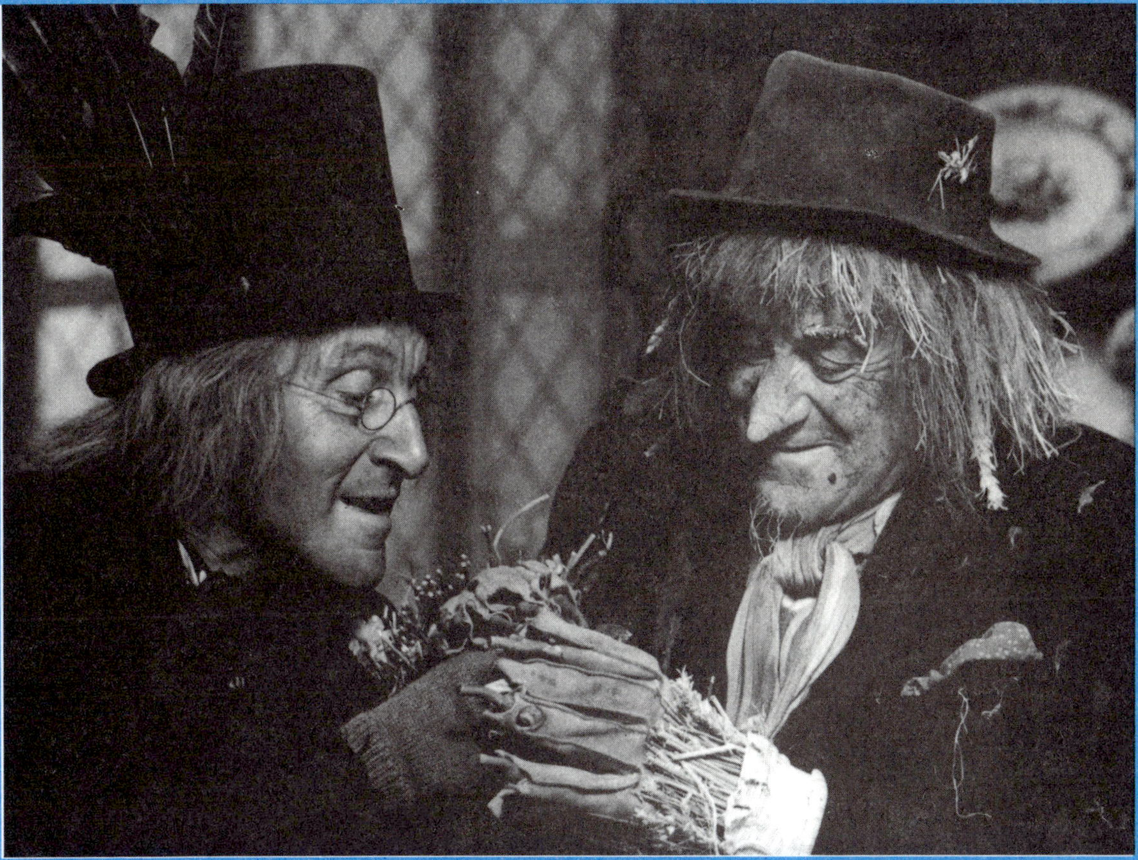

The Crowman

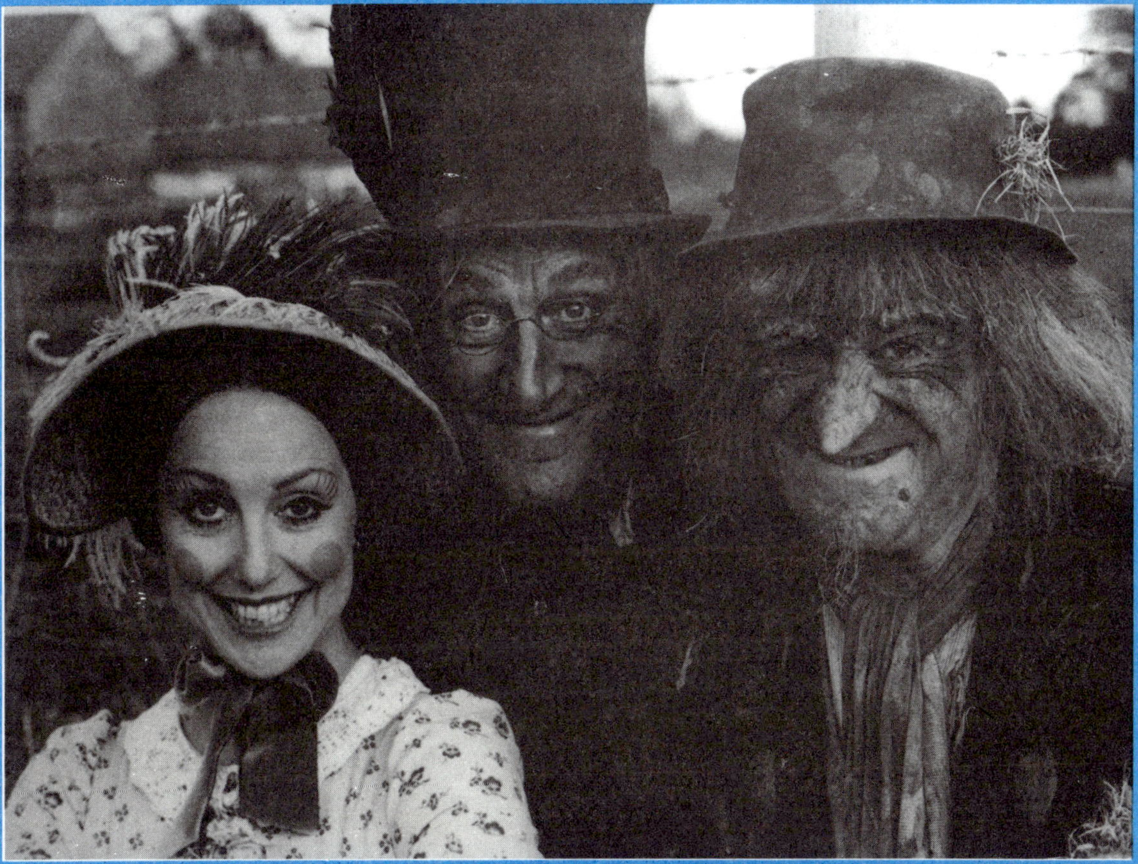

Worzel's River Race!

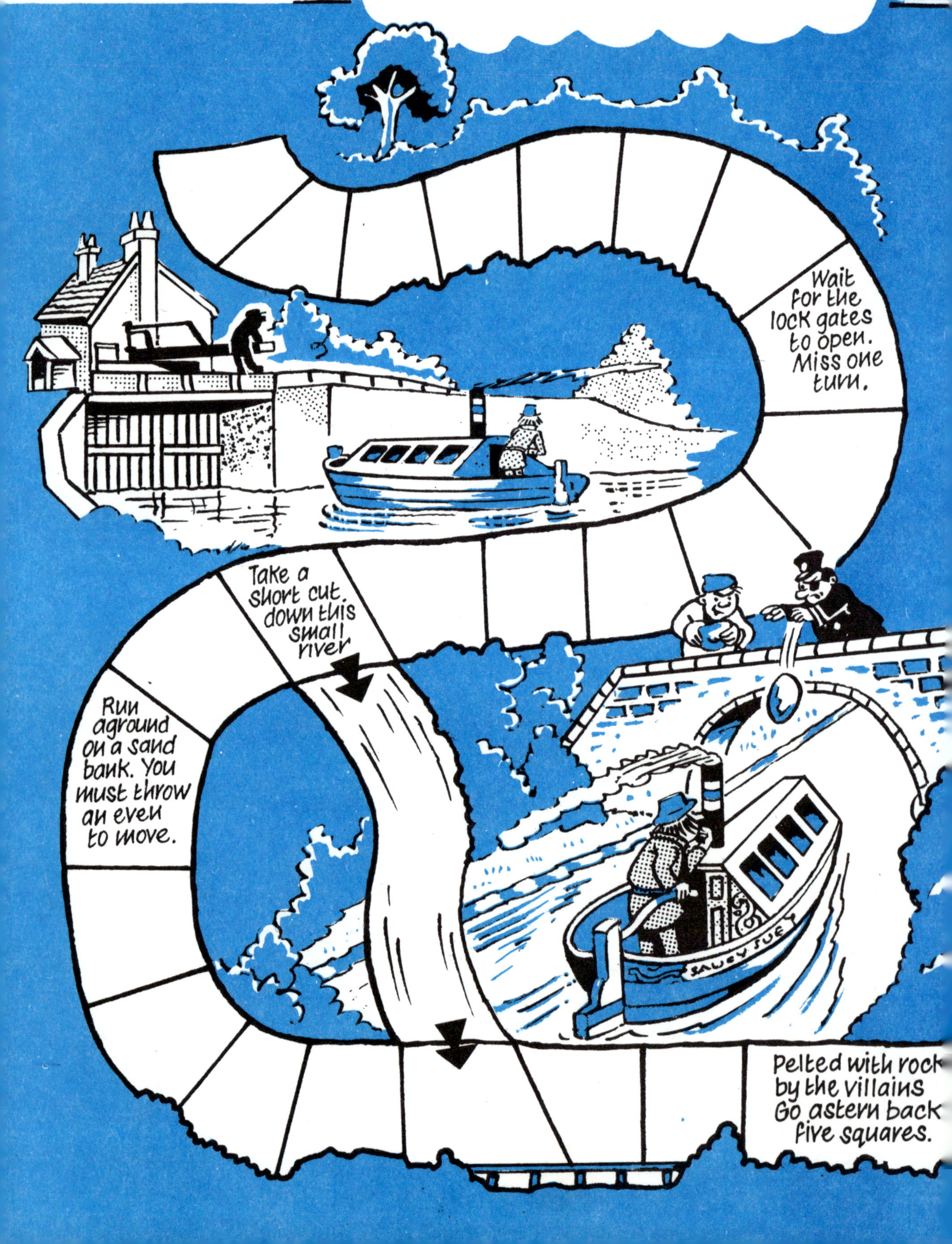

The rascally Captain Scrimshaw has kidnapped Aunt Sally and taken her to the Old Mill. So Worzel Gummidge has borrowed a boat and is chasing down river after them! Join in with dice and counters!

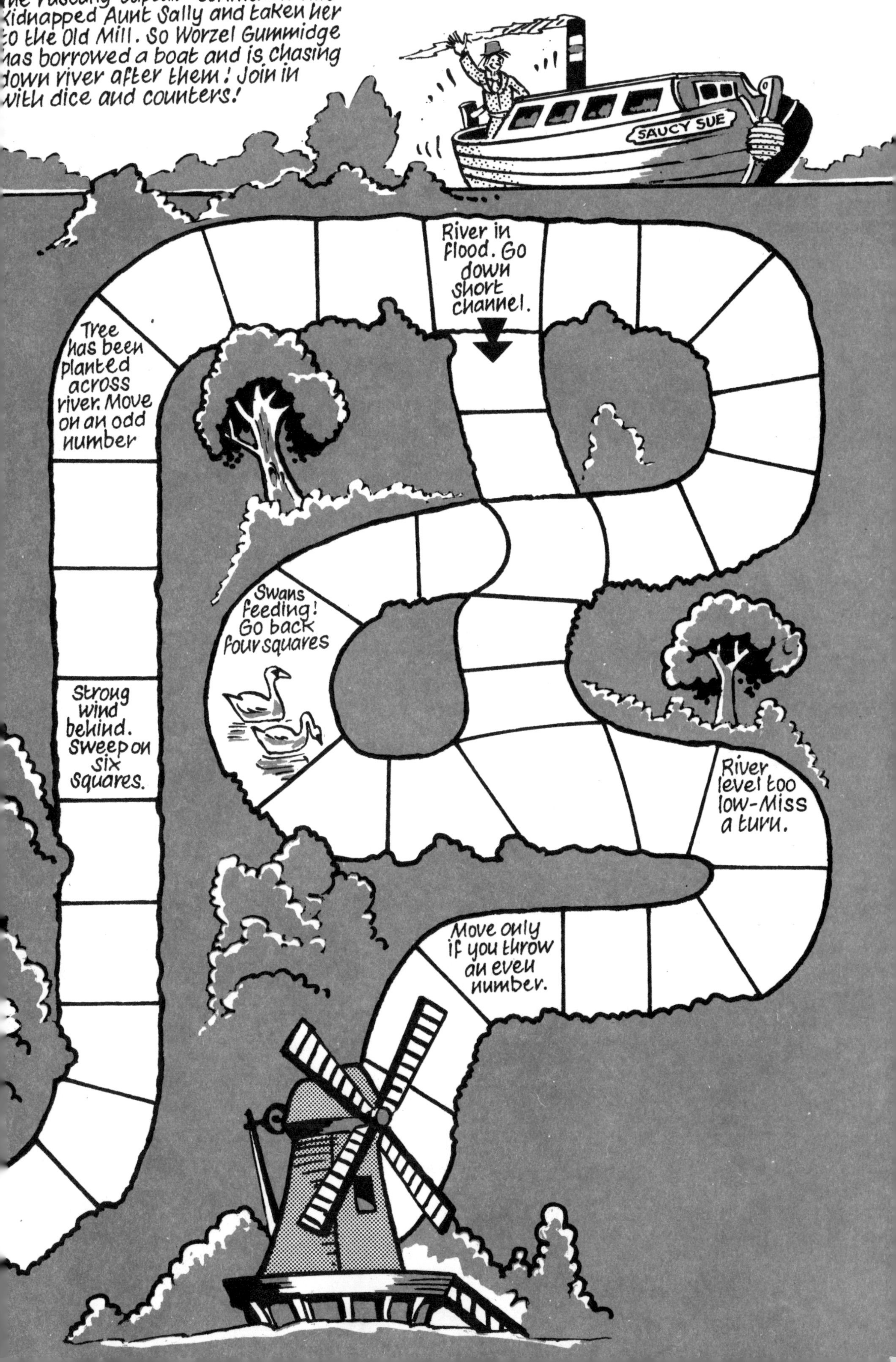

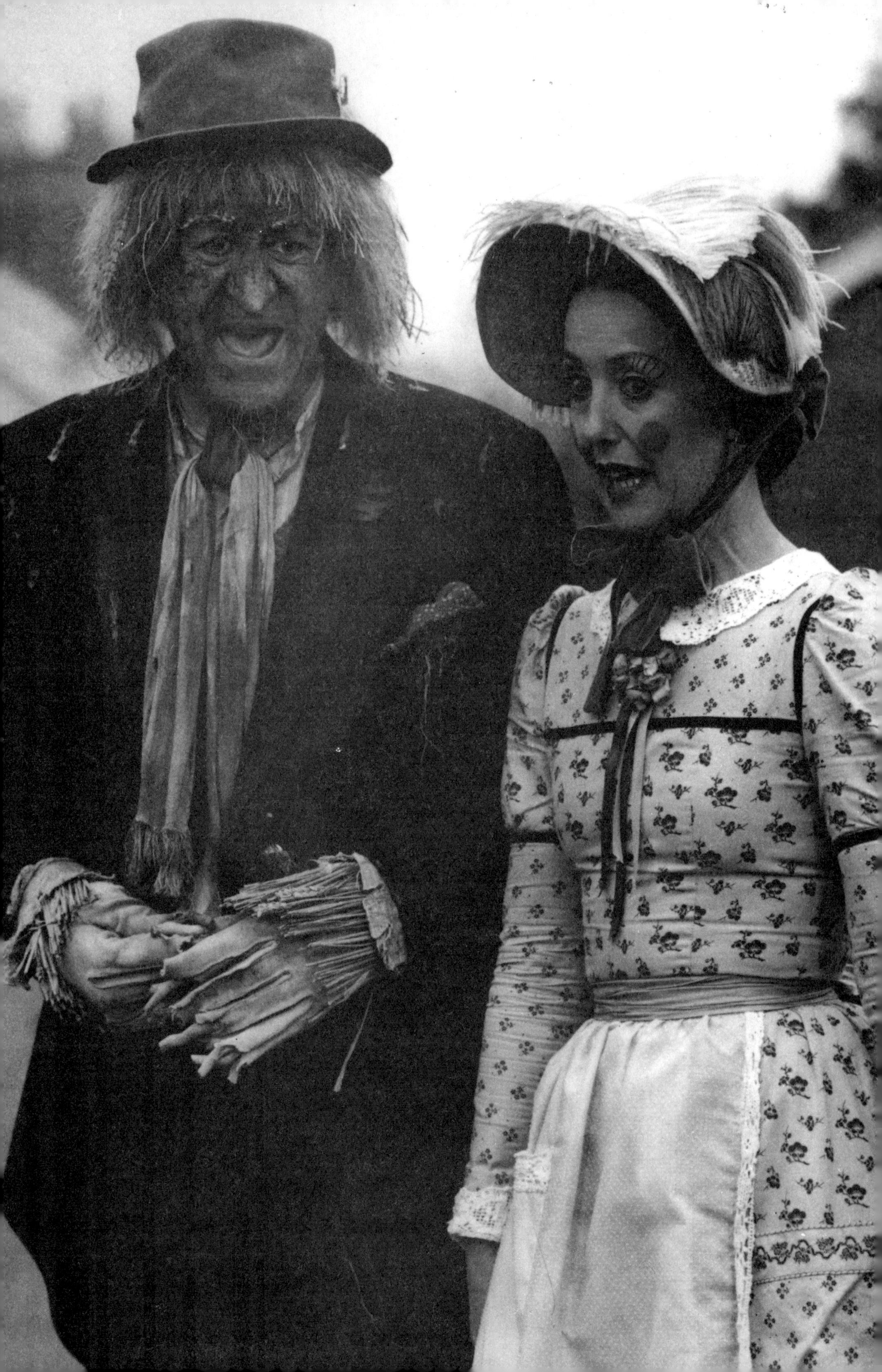

WORZEL PROBLEMWORD

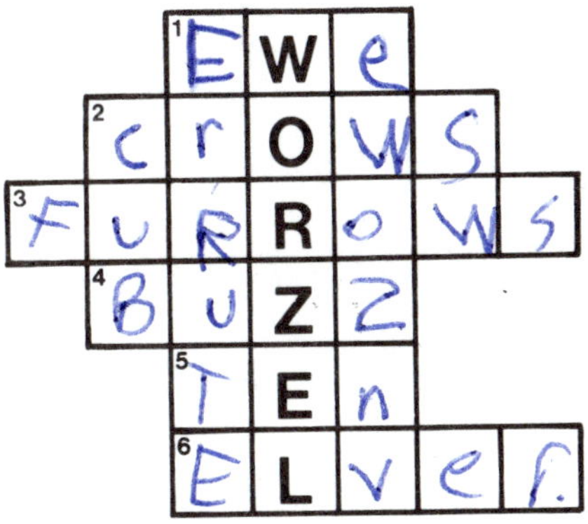

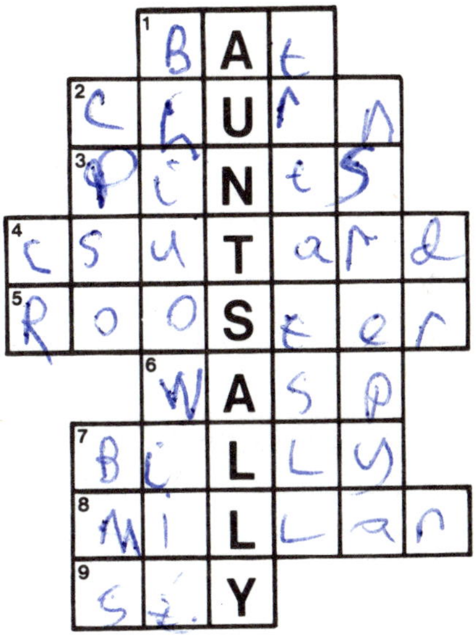

a) 1. Female sheep
2. Worzel frightens them away.
3. Grooves made by a plough in a field.
4. The noise of a bee.
5. ________Acre Field.
6. A baby eel.

b) 1. It flies at night.
2. Keep milk in this on the farm.
3. There are 8 in a gallon.
4. Rhubarb and ________.
5. Another name for a cockerel.
6. Beware! This insect stings.
7. Male goat.
8. He lives in a windmill.
9. Home of a pig.

Answers. a)
1. Ewe.
2. Crows.
3. Furrows.
4. Buzz.
5. Ten.
6. Elver.

b)
1. Bat.
2. Churn.
3. Pints.
4. Custard.
5. Rooster.
6. Wasp.
7. Billy.
8. Millar.
9. Sty.

LUCK OF THE DEVIL

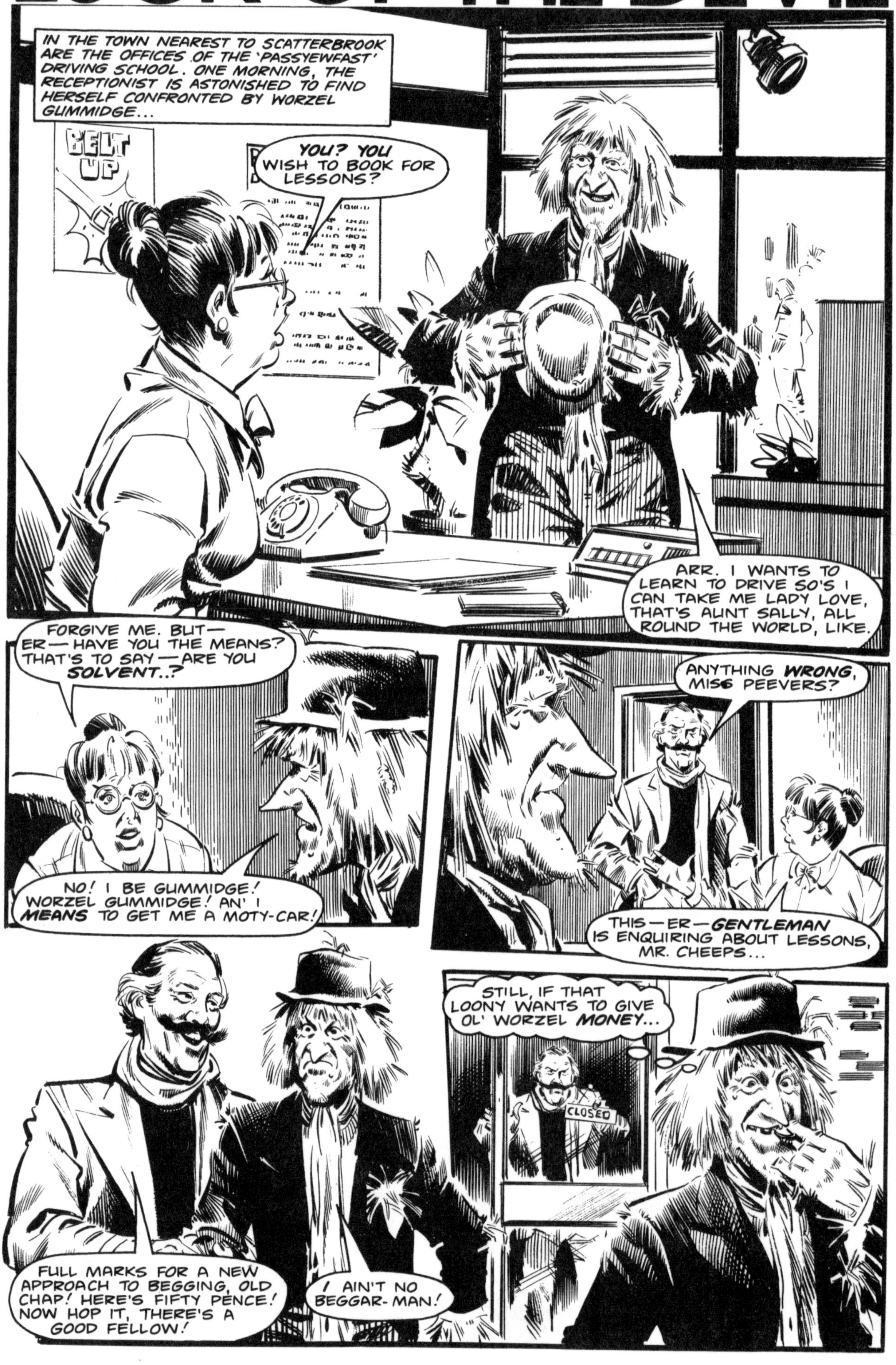

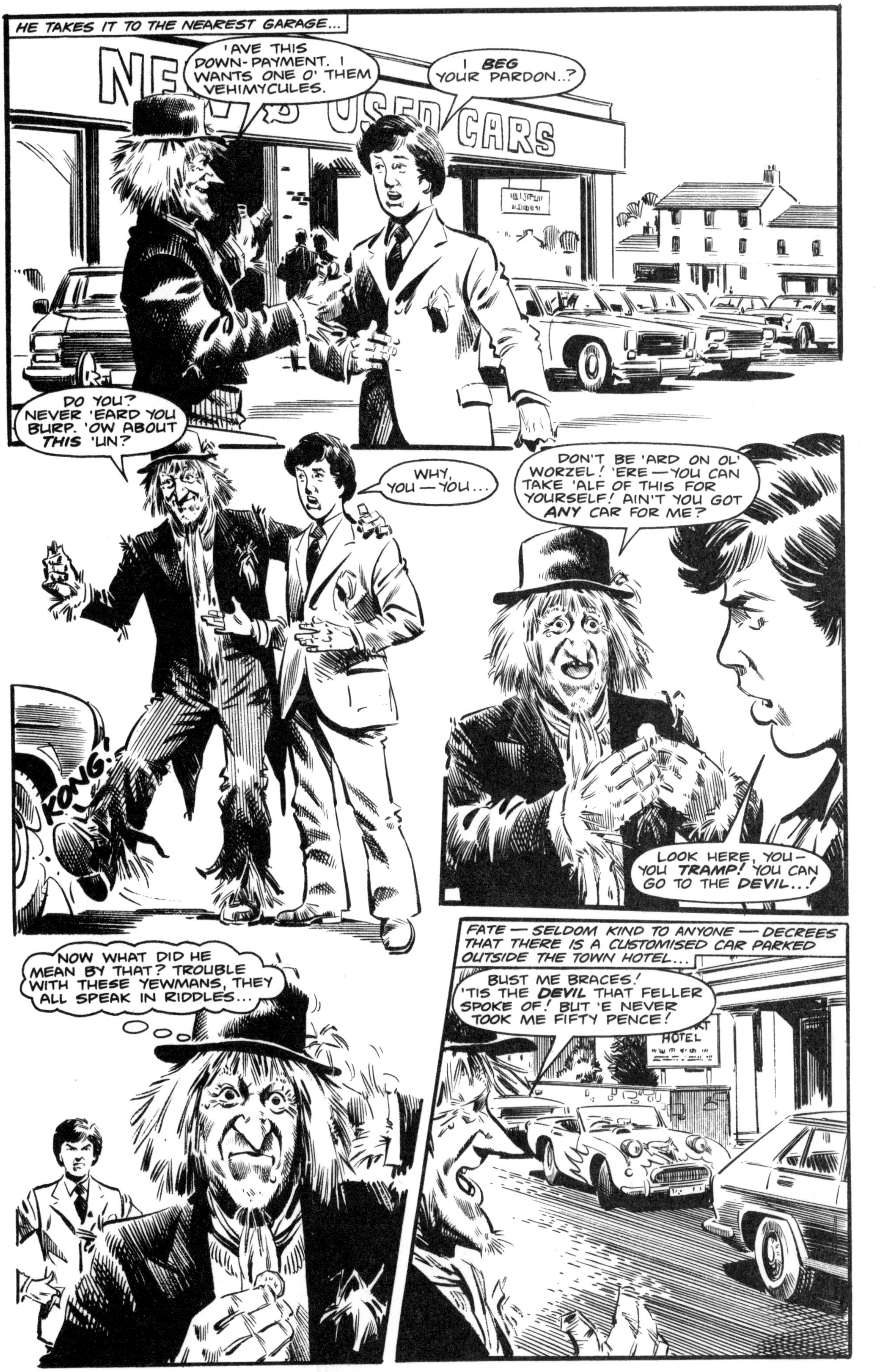
HE TAKES IT TO THE NEAREST GARAGE...
NE... USED CARS
'AVE THIS DOWN-PAYMENT. I WANTS ONE O' THEM VEHIMYCULES.
I BEG YOUR PARDON..?
DO YOU? NEVER 'EARD YOU BURP. 'OW ABOUT THIS 'UN?
WHY, YOU — YOU...
KONG!
DON'T BE 'ARD ON OL' WORZEL! 'ERE — YOU CAN TAKE 'ALF OF THIS FOR YOURSELF! AIN'T YOU GOT ANY CAR FOR ME?
LOOK HERE, YOU — YOU TRAMP! YOU CAN GO TO THE DEVIL...!
NOW WHAT DID HE MEAN BY THAT? TROUBLE WITH THESE YEWMANS, THEY ALL SPEAK IN RIDDLES...
FATE — SELDOM KIND TO ANYONE — DECREES THAT THERE IS A CUSTOMISED CAR PARKED OUTSIDE THE TOWN HOTEL...
BUST ME BRACES! 'TIS THE DEVIL THAT FELLER SPOKE OF! BUT 'E NEVER TOOK ME FIFTY PENCE!
HOTEL

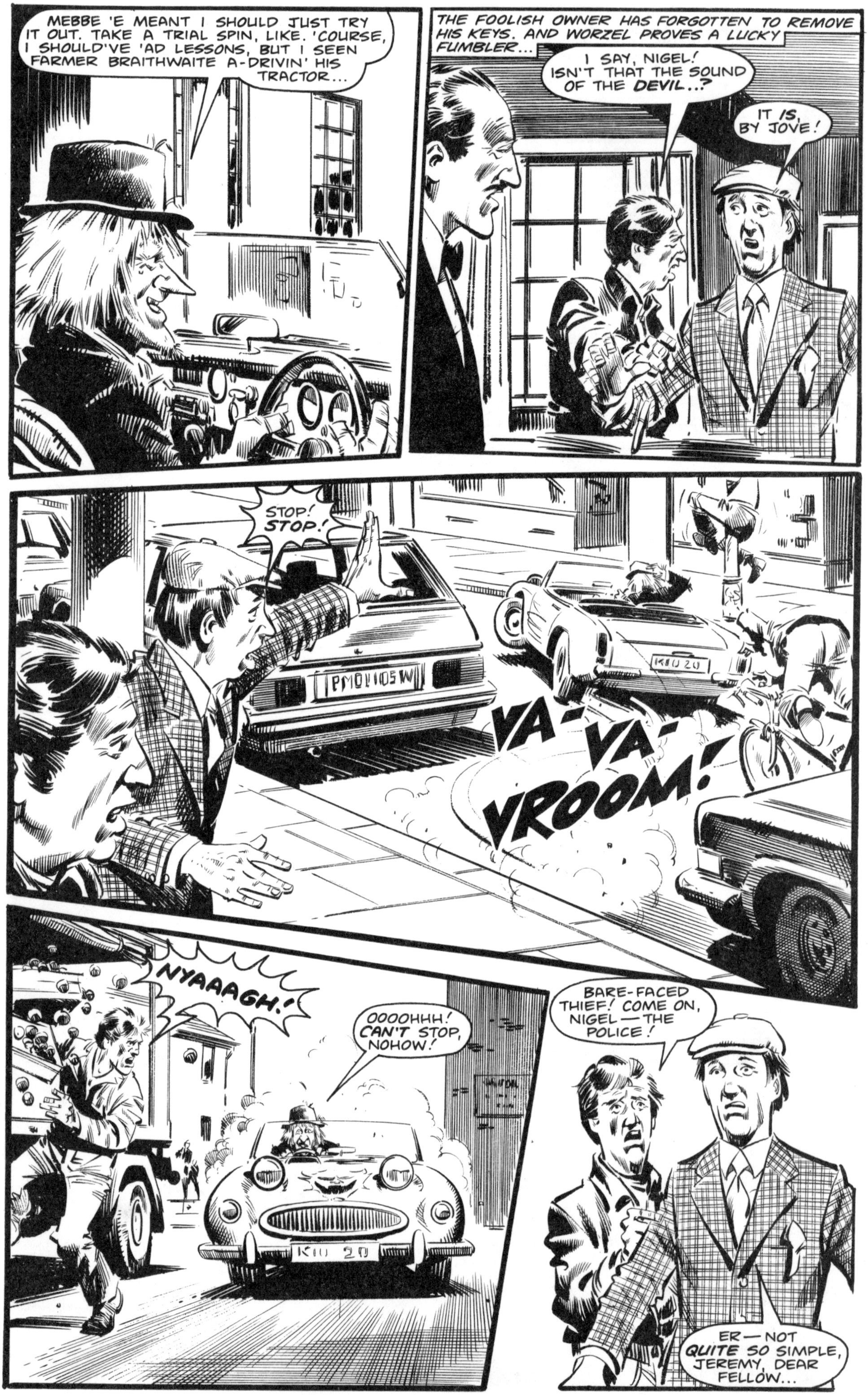
MEBBE 'E MEANT I SHOULD JUST TRY IT OUT. TAKE A TRIAL SPIN, LIKE. 'COURSE, I SHOULD'VE 'AD LESSONS, BUT I SEEN FARMER BRAITHWAITE A-DRIVIN' HIS TRACTOR...
THE FOOLISH OWNER HAS FORGOTTEN TO REMOVE HIS KEYS. AND WORZEL PROVES A LUCKY FUMBLER...
I SAY, NIGEL! ISN'T THAT THE SOUND OF THE DEVIL..?
IT IS, BY JOVE!
STOP! STOP!
PM0 105W
KIU 20
VA-VA-VROOM!
NYAAAAGH!
OOOOHHH! CAN'T STOP, NOHOW!
KIU 20
BARE-FACED THIEF! COME ON, NIGEL — THE POLICE!
ER — NOT QUITE SO SIMPLE, JEREMY, DEAR FELLOW...

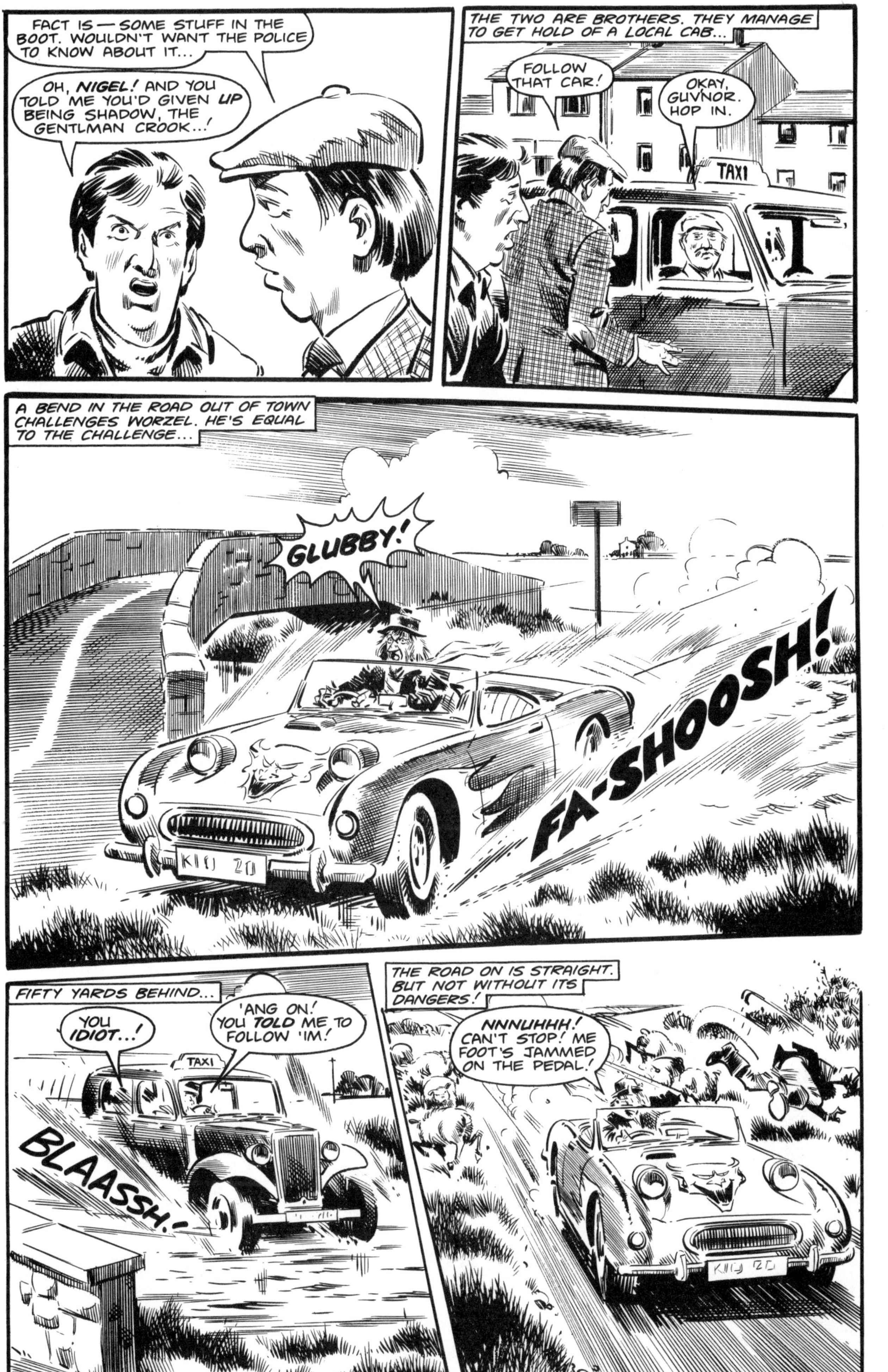

FACT IS — SOME STUFF IN THE BOOT. WOULDN'T WANT THE POLICE TO KNOW ABOUT IT...
OH, NIGEL! AND YOU TOLD ME YOU'D GIVEN UP BEING SHADOW, THE GENTLMAN CROOK...!
THE TWO ARE BROTHERS. THEY MANAGE TO GET HOLD OF A LOCAL CAB...
FOLLOW THAT CAR!
OKAY, GUVNOR. HOP IN.
TAXI
A BEND IN THE ROAD OUT OF TOWN CHALLENGES WORZEL. HE'S EQUAL TO THE CHALLENGE...
GLUBBY!
FA-SHOOSH!
KUJ 20
FIFTY YARDS BEHIND...
YOU IDIOT...!
'ANG ON! YOU TOLD ME TO FOLLOW 'IM!
TAXI
BLAASSH!
THE ROAD ON IS STRAIGHT. BUT NOT WITHOUT ITS DANGERS!
NNNUHHH! CAN'T STOP! ME FOOT'S JAMMED ON THE PEDAL!
KUJ 20

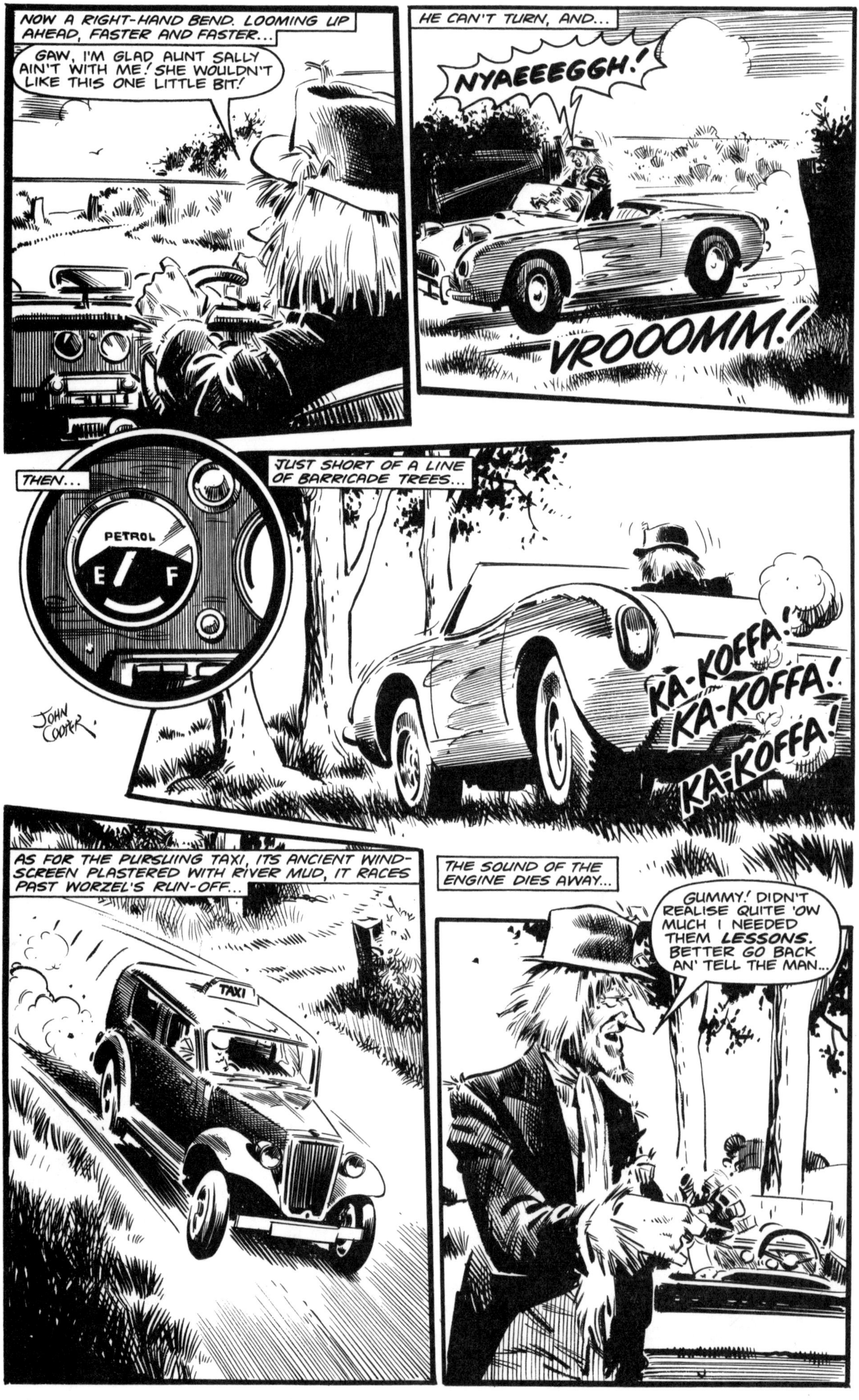
NOW A RIGHT-HAND BEND. LOOMING UP AHEAD, FASTER AND FASTER...
GAW, I'M GLAD AUNT SALLY AIN'T WITH ME! SHE WOULDN'T LIKE THIS ONE LITTLE BIT!
HE CAN'T TURN, AND...
NYAEEEEGGH!
VROOOMM!
THEN...
PETROL
E F
JUST SHORT OF A LINE OF BARRICADE TREES...
KA-KOFFA!
KA-KOFFA!
KA-KOFFA!
JOHN COOPER
AS FOR THE PURSUING TAXI, ITS ANCIENT WIND-SCREEN PLASTERED WITH RIVER MUD, IT RACES PAST WORZEL'S RUN-OFF...
TAXI
THE SOUND OF THE ENGINE DIES AWAY...
GUMMY! DIDN'T REALISE QUITE 'OW MUCH I NEEDED THEM LESSONS. BETTER GO BACK AN' TELL THE MAN...

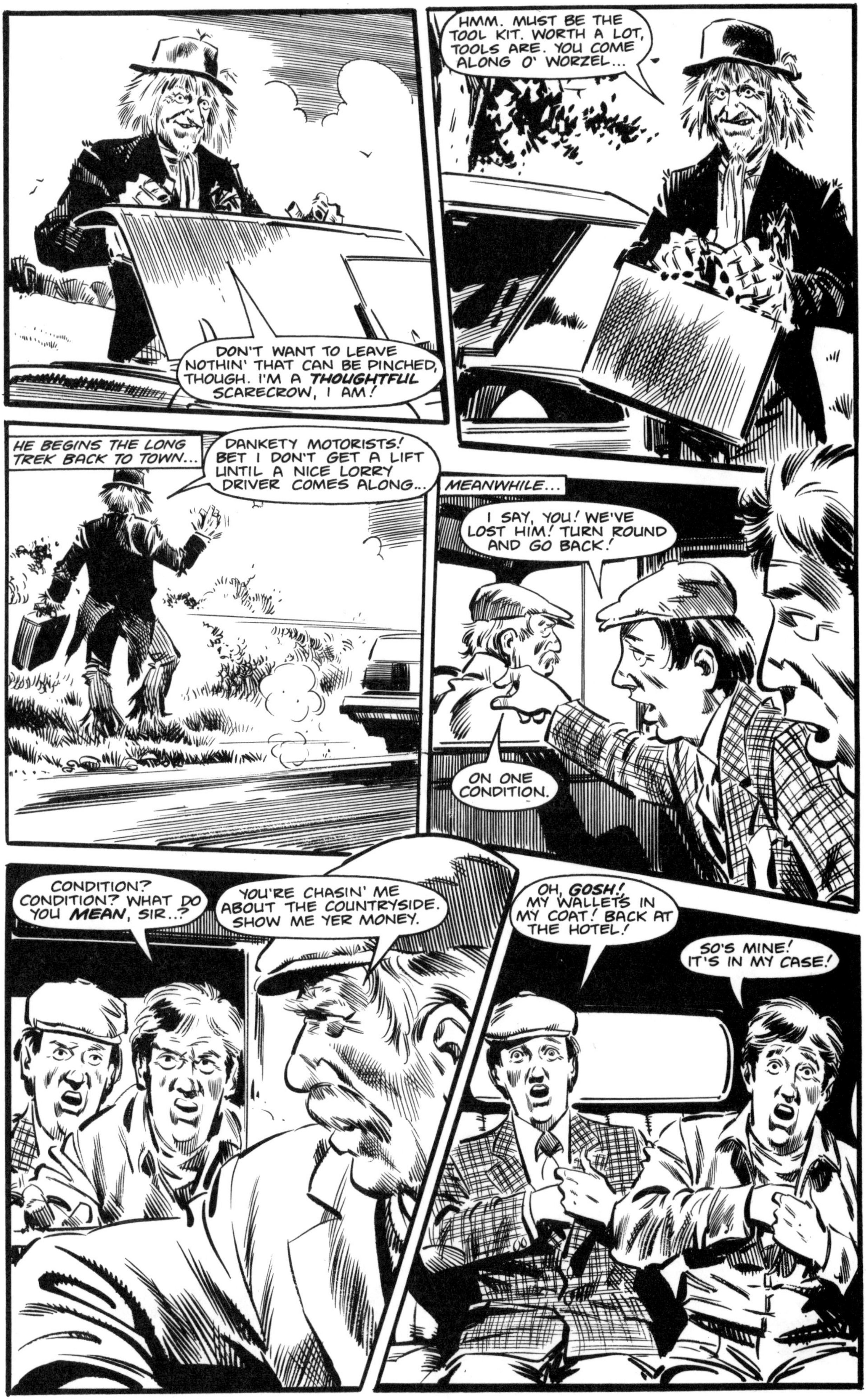

DON'T WANT TO LEAVE NOTHIN' THAT CAN BE PINCHED, THOUGH. I'M A THOUGHTFUL SCARECROW, I AM!
HMM. MUST BE THE TOOL KIT. WORTH A LOT, TOOLS ARE. YOU COME ALONG O' WORZEL...
HE BEGINS THE LONG TREK BACK TO TOWN...
DANKETY MOTORISTS! BET I DON'T GET A LIFT UNTIL A NICE LORRY DRIVER COMES ALONG...
MEANWHILE...
I SAY, YOU! WE'VE LOST HIM! TURN ROUND AND GO BACK!
ON ONE CONDITION.
CONDITION? CONDITION? WHAT DO YOU MEAN, SIR..?
YOU'RE CHASIN' ME ABOUT THE COUNTRYSIDE. SHOW ME YER MONEY.
OH, GOSH! MY WALLET'S IN MY COAT! BACK AT THE HOTEL!
SO'S MINE! IT'S IN MY CASE!

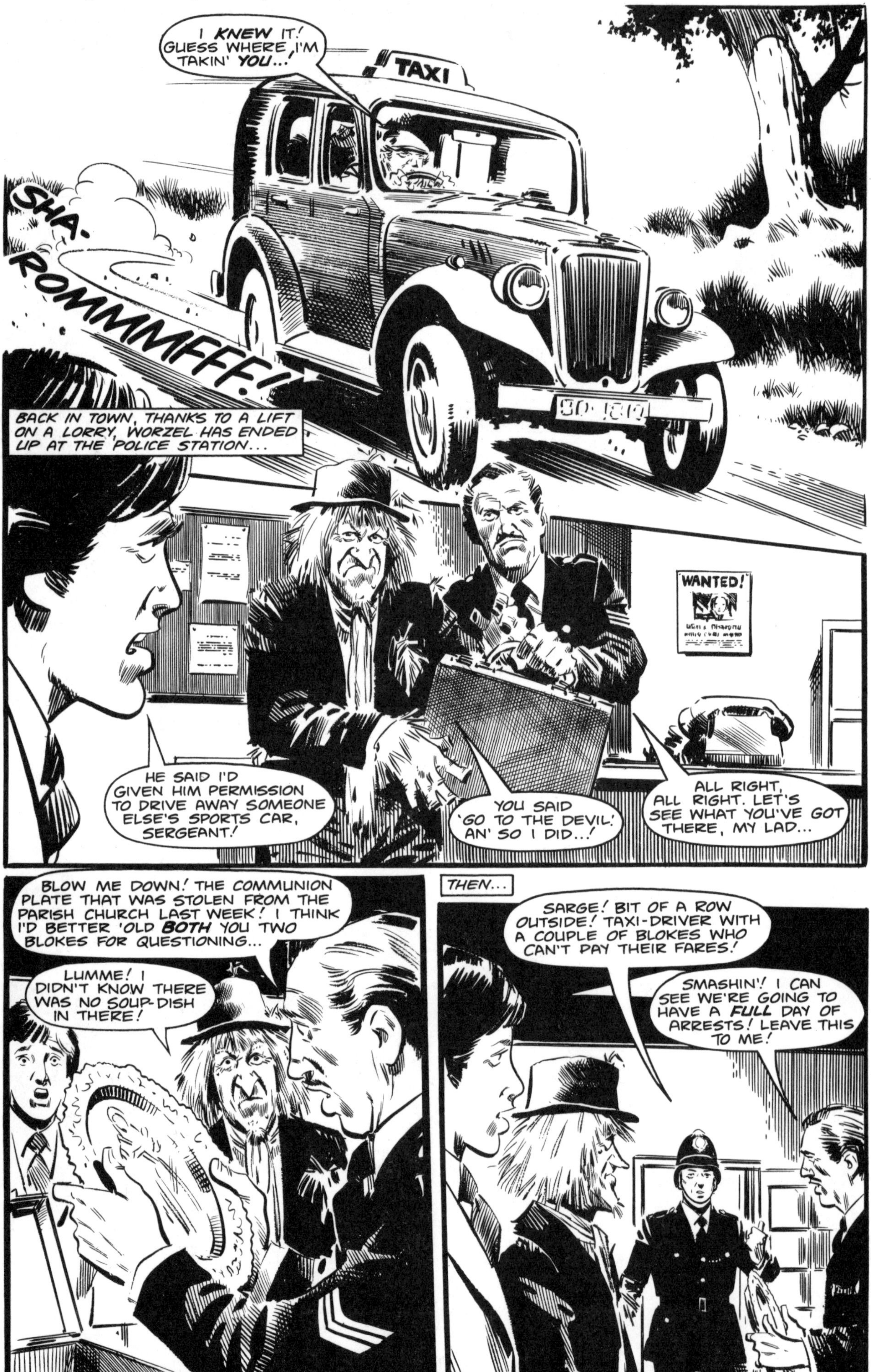
I KNEW IT! GUESS WHERE I'M TAKIN' YOU...!
TAXI
SHA-ROMMMMFFF!!
BACK IN TOWN, THANKS TO A LIFT ON A LORRY, WORZEL HAS ENDED UP AT THE POLICE STATION...
WANTED!
HE SAID I'D GIVEN HIM PERMISSION TO DRIVE AWAY SOMEONE ELSE'S SPORTS CAR, SERGEANT!
YOU SAID 'GO TO THE DEVIL!' AN' SO I DID...!
ALL RIGHT, ALL RIGHT. LET'S SEE WHAT YOU'VE GOT THERE, MY LAD...
BLOW ME DOWN! THE COMMUNION PLATE THAT WAS STOLEN FROM THE PARISH CHURCH LAST WEEK! I THINK I'D BETTER 'OLD BOTH YOU TWO BLOKES FOR QUESTIONING...
LUMME! I DIDN'T KNOW THERE WAS NO SOUP-DISH IN THERE!
THEN...
SARGE! BIT OF A ROW OUTSIDE! TAXI-DRIVER WITH A COUPLE OF BLOKES WHO CAN'T PAY THEIR FARES!
SMASHIN'! I CAN SEE WE'RE GOING TO HAVE A FULL DAY OF ARRESTS! LEAVE THIS TO ME!